ATLANTIC OCEAN
MEXICO
Gulf of Mexico
CUBA
DOMINICAN REPUBLIC
HAITI
BELIZE
GUATEMALA
HONDURAS
Caribbean Sea
EL SALVADOR
NICARAGUA
COSTA RICA
PANAMA
VENEZUELA
PACIFIC OCEAN
Isla Del Coco
COLOMBIA
ECUADOR
PERU
BRAZIL
Nueva Guinea
NICARAGUA
Punta Gorda
Río San Juan
Río San Juan
Barra del Colorado
Río San Carlos
Río Chirripo
ALAJUELA
HEREDIA
Tortuguero
Río Toro
Puerto Viejo de Sarapiquí
CARIBBEAN SEA
La Fortuna
LIMÓN
Ciudad Quesada
Zarcero
Guápiles
Sarchí
Sacramento
Siquirres
Río Reventazón
Alajuela
Heredia
SAN JOSÉ
Puerto Limón
Juan Santamaría
Cartago
Río Grande
Turrialba
Río Banano
Tapantí
Orosi
Tárcoles
SAN JOSÉ
CARTAGO
LIMÓN
Cahuita
Puerto Viejo de Talamanca
Bribri
Jacó
COSTA RICA
San Gerardo de Dota
Quepos
San Isidro de El General
Río Uren
Río Teribe
Dominical
Río General
Buenos Aires
PANAMA
Palmar Norte
Isla Boca Brava
Río Colon
San Vito
Isla Violin
Río Sierpe
PUNTARENAS
Bahía Drake
Isla del Caño
Rincón
Golfito
Ciudad Neily
Coto 47
Puerto Jiménez
Zancudo
David
Golfo Dulce
La Cuesta
Y
nternational airport
omestic airport
rry
-American Highway
or road
ernational border
ovincial border
rry route

A Portrait of Costa Rica

*D*OMINATED BY MOUNTAIN RANGES *and verdant forests, gouged by fertile valleys, and flanked by lovely beaches and the ocean, Costa Rica is undoubtedly one of the most beautiful places on earth. Vivid colors of nature, a virtually unmatched range of outdoor activities, friendly, hospitable people, and the subtle charm of an essentially rustic lifestyle – all combine to make the country one of the world's favorite tropical holiday destinations.*

Costa Rica's official emblem

Straddling the Meso-American isthmus at the juncture of North and South America, this diminutive nation is barely 300 miles (480 km) north to south and 175 miles (280 km) at its widest point, near the Nicaraguan border. Occupying one of the world's most geologically unstable areas, the country is subjected to powerful tectonic forces that trigger earthquakes and punctuate the landscape with smoldering volcanoes. With scores of micro-climates, the emerald landscape is a quiltwork of 12 different life zones, from coastal wetlands to subalpine grassland.

Costa Rica is characterized by a homogeneity of culture unique among Central American nations, with the Spanish influence being all-encompassing and indigenous culture having little impact. However, non-Spanish cultures exist in a few pockets, such as the Jamaican ethos of the Caribbean coast. Another distinctive feature is the nation's conservation ethic, as evidenced by its nationwide network of wildlife parks and refuges, which embraces about 30 percent of its area – more than any other nation on earth.

Conserving Nature's Wonders

The greatest appeal of Costa Rica is its astonishing wealth of flora and fauna, protected within more than 190 biological reserves, national parks,

A farmhouse on the flanks of Volcán Arenal, in the Northern Zone

◁ **A milkman pushing his cart along a street in one of San José's residential districts**

The guanacaste tree, Costa Rica's national tree

wildlife refuges, and similar entities. The Reserva Natural Absoluta Cabo Blanco was created as the first protected reserve in the country in 1963. Since then, new parks and reserves have been set up every year, and refuges established by private foundations are gaining national status.

However, destruction of the natural habitat continues at alarming rates, even in some protected regions. The park service is understaffed and lacks the funds to compensate owners for expropriated land. Thus, the wetlands of Refugio Nacional de Vida Silvestre Caño Negro are imperiled by landowners reclaiming precious marshlands for farming. Animal populations are declining in Parque Nacional Manuel Antonio due to loss of habitat. Illegal hunting menaces the populations of jaguars, tapirs, and wild pigs in Parque Nacional Corcovado. Logging continues to eat away the forests, which have been diminished by two-thirds since Columbus stepped ashore in 1491.

Fortunately, there are several conservation organizations, which are unstinting in their creative efforts to save flora and fauna. Also, the government's focus on integrating protected regions by grouping them into ten distinct regional units within a Sistema Nacional de Areas de Conservación (National System of Regional Conservation Areas) is a giant step in the right direction.

The Government

A democratic republic, Costa Rica has a government headed by an elected president, who is assisted by two vice presidents and a cabinet of 17 members. The Asamblea Legislativa (Legislative Assembly) is a single chamber of 57 popularly elected *diputados* (deputies), limited to two terms. The president appoints regional governors, who preside over the seven provinces of San José, Alajuela, Cartago, Guanacaste, Heredia, Limón, and Puntarenas.

Two parties dominate the political scene and have traditionally alternated in power with each election. The social-democratic Partido de Liberación Nacional (National Liberation Party) champions welfare programs, while the conservative Partido de Unidad Social Cristiana (Social Christian Unity Party) is pro-business. All citizens between 18

The famed Reserva Biológica Bosque Nuboso Monteverde (Monteverde Cloud Forest Biological Reserve)

and 70 years of age are mandated to vote. A Special Electoral Tribunal appointed by the Supreme Court oversees the integrity of elections.

Costa Rica declared neutrality in 1949 and has no official army, navy, or air force, although branches of the police force have a military capability. Citizens proudly proclaim that since the late 19th century, only two brief periods of violence have marred the nation's democratic development, and the country has avoided the bloodshed that has afflicted neighboring countries. However, it has not been aloof from Latin American issues: in 1987, President Oscar Arias won the Nobel Peace Prize for brokering peace on the isthmus.

Papayas being sorted for sale in a town market

The Economy

Costa Rica's thriving economy is today powered mainly by tourism. With its stupendous landscape of mountains, beaches, and forests full of exotic flora and fauna, the country offers opportunities for outdoor life and active adventures matched by few countries. The focus is on ecotourism, promoted by the Instituto Costarricense de Turismo (Costa Rica Tourism Institute) under the advertising slogan of "Costa Rica – No Artificial Ingredients." Another factor aiding tourism is the country's reputation for stability in an area rent by political upheavals. Well-planned specialized lodges, large hotels, and beach resorts serve the spectrum from budget to deluxe markets.

Resident in Costa Rican colors

San José is one of Central America's major financial centers with a burgeoning high-technology industrial sector. Beyond the capital, the country is still largely agricultural. Land ownership is widespread, except in Guanacaste, where large-scale cattle *fincas* (farms) prevail. Coffee and bananas are Costa Rica's two most important crops.

The People

Costa Ricans are known as Ticos because of their habitual use of this term as a diminutive – for instance, "*momentico*" for "just a moment," instead of the usual "*momentito*." The majority are descendants of early Spanish settlers. Indigenous peoples account for a fraction of the population, and live tucked away in remote reserves. Concentrated on the Caribbean coast, Afro-Caribbeans are mainly descended from Jamaicans who came as contract labor in the 19th century, and form a large community. A sizeable Chinese

The bustling capital city, San José

Traditional oxcart used for farming in the Costa Rican countryside

population also exists, mainly in the Caribbean province of Limón. In recent years, tens of thousands of North Americans and people of other nationalities have settled in Costa Rica, drawn partly by its fabulous climate.

About eight out of ten Costa Ricans are nominally Catholic, and a large portion of the population are regular practitioners of the faith. The most venerated figure is La Negrita, the country's patron saint, who is believed to grant miracles. Although proselytizing is illegal, the influence of evangelical Christians has grown in recent years, especially in poorer parts of the country and among the indigenous communities.

Effigies carried along a street as part of Good Friday celebrations

The country has the highest rate of literacy and life expectancy in Latin America. Virtually the entire nation is tapped into the Internet, and mobile telephone use is the highest in Central America. Roads and electricity extend into even the most remote backwaters, and today few communities are entirely isolated from the modern world. In fact, Josefinos (residents of San José) lead a typically modern urban lifestyle, and the capital has a well-developed and entrepreneurial middle-class. However, old traditions survive in the countryside, where a peasant lifestyle still prevails, the horse is the main form of transport, and oxen are used as day-to-day beasts of burden.

Life revolves around the family – usually headed by a matriarch – and an immediate circle of *compadres* (friends and fellow workers). Individuals tend to guard their personal lives closely and are more inclined to invite acquaintances to dine at restaurants than to welcome them into their homes. However, Ticos are a warm-hearted people and always treat strangers with great civility.

Costa Ricans are proud of their country's neutrality and stable democracy. Although a recent influx of immigrants with "Indian" features from neighboring countries has caused much resentment, Ticos are generally a liberal, tolerant people with a concern for societal harmony and welfare.

The Arts and Sports

Crafts dominate the artistic scene, mainly because of the tremendous creativity displayed by artisans. Woodcarvers such as Barry Biesanz produce hardwood bowls of immense delicacy. The indigenous influence lives on in the creation of gold jewelry, which adopts the pre-Columbian motif of animist figurines. Other native crafts include the pottery created by the community of Guaitíl in the style of their Chorotega ancestors.

A traditional dance performance near Cartago

The arts scene was, until recent years, dominated by the nation's *campesino* (peasant) heritage, which found its most influential expression with the Group of New Sensibility in the 1920s. Headed by Teodorico Quirós Alvarado (1897–1977), the movement evolved a stylized art form depicting idyllic rural landscapes, with cobbled streets, adobe dwellings, and peasants with oxcarts against volcanic backgrounds. Their influence remains to this day, notably in miniature paintings that are a staple in many homes and souvenir stores.

An exception to the insipid art of the mid-20th century were the powerful depictions of peasant life by the internationally renowned sculptor Francisco Zúñiga (1912–98). In recent years contemporary artists such as Rodolfo Stanley and Rolando Castellón have invigorated the scene with compelling avante-garde works.

Carlos Luis Fallas's novel, *Mamita Yunai* (1941), narrating the plight of banana workers, is the sole literary work of international note. Costa Ricans are great theatergoers, however, and theater venues are scattered all over San José and some other cities. Josefinos dress up to hear the National Symphony Orchestra perform in the Teatro Nacional and at the less formal annual International Festival of Music, while the young dress down to dance to fast-paced Latin merengue in clubs and bars. Virtually every town has a bandstand where people enjoy folk music featuring the *marimba*, a form of xylophone. The guitar is the main accompaniment to the *punto guanacasteco*, the national folk dance performed by men and women in traditional costume.

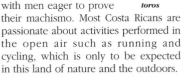

A local soccer match in progress in Heredia

Played on weekends by local teams throughout the country, soccer is the national obsession for men. Rodeos and *topes* (horse parades) are a focus of general festivities, while *corridas de toros* (non-fatal bull-running) are popular with men eager to prove their machismo. Most Costa Ricans are passionate about activities performed in the open air such as running and cycling, which is only to be expected in this land of nature and the outdoors.

Corridas de toros

Landscape and Wildlife

One of Costa Rica's butterflies

FEW COUNTRIES ON earth can rival Costa Rica for diversity of flora and fauna. Despite its tiny size, the nation is home to almost 5 percent of the world's identified living species, including more types of butterflies than the whole of Africa. This astonishing wealth of wildlife is due to the country's great variety in relief and climate, from lowland wetlands to cloud-draped mountaintops. As a result, Costa Rica boasts 12 distinct "life zones," each with a unique combination of climate, terrain, flora, and fauna.

Perfectly conical Arenal, Costa Rica's most active volcano

LOWLAND RAINFOREST

Rainforests *(see pp22–3)* cloak many of the plains and lower mountain slopes of the Caribbean lowlands and Pacific southwest. These complex ecosystems harbor a large proportion of the country's wildlife. Tapirs and jaguars inhabit the understory, while birds and monkeys cavort in the treetops.

***Sloths** hang from branches and live upside-down their entire lives. Both the two-toed and three-toed species eat only leaves. These slow-moving creatures have an extremely slow metabolic rate.*

***Red-eyed tree frogs** are difficult to spot, as they usually cling to the underside of leaves.*

***Leafcutter ants** cut and chew leaves into mulch that is used to fertilize fungi, whose spores the ants then eat.*

MONTANE CLOUD FOREST

More than half of Costa Rica is over 3,300 ft (1,000 m) above sea level. Much of the higher elevation terrain is swathed in cloud forest *(see p129)*, where mists sift through the treetops and branches are festooned with bromeliads and dripping mosses. Bird and animal life is profuse.

***Three-wattled bellbirds** are rarely seen but often heard: their distinct call sounds like metal being struck. The male grows three worm-like wattles.*

***Spider monkeys** have long, spindly limbs and prehensile tails – ideal for life in the upper stories of the forests.*

***Kinkajous**, tree-dwelling relatives of the raccoon, have prehensile tails, and are nocturnal.*

Coasts

The total length of Costa Rica's coastline is over 800 miles (1,290 km). On the Pacific, promontories and scalloped bays are common, while the Caribbean coast is almost ruler-straight. Small patches of coral reef fringe the coast off the Central Pacific and southern Caribbean shores. Many beaches provide nesting grounds for various species of marine turtles *(see p171)*.

***Marine turtles** each lay about 100 eggs in nests above the high-tide mark.*

***Beaches** in Costa Rica come in every color, from white and gold to chocolate and black. Most are backed by forest.*

***Hammerhead sharks** swim in large congregations off Isla del Coco* (see p193).

Dry Forest

Once covering most of Guanacaste and Nicoya, dry forests *(see p133)* today cover only about 200 sq miles (520 sq km) of Costa Rica. The mostly deciduous flora sheds its leaves during the seasonal drought, making wildlife easier to spot. Conservationists are trying to revive dry forest ecosystems.

***Bats** comprise more than half of all mammal species in Costa Rica. The tropical dry forests have over 70 species of bats.*

***Anteaters** rip open termite nests and anthills with their scythe-like claws.* Tamanduas *are a type of tree-dwelling anteater.*

***Iguanas** are camouflaged green for an arboreal life. Males turn orange during the mating season.*

Wetland

Wetlands range from coastal mangroves *(see p185)* such as the Terraba-Sierpe delta in the Pacific southwest, to inland lagoons such as Caño Negro in the north. Many habitats are seasonal, flooding in the wet season from May to November; wildlife gathers by waterholes in the December–April dry season.

***Mangroves**, which thrive in alluvial silts deposited by rivers, form a vital nursery for marine creatures and avian fauna, such as the frigate bird.*

***Roseate spoonbills**, herons, egrets, and many other wading birds and waterfowl inhabit bodies of fresh water.*

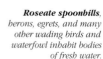

***Crocodiles** and small caimans live in Costa Rica's freshwater lagoons and lowland rivers. The American crocodile can grow to 16 ft (5 m).*

The Rainforest Ecosystem

THE LOWLANDS OF COSTA RICA are enveloped in tropical rainforest, its canopies forming an uninterrupted sea of greenery. Hardwood trees, such as mahogany and kapok, may tower 200 ft (61 m) or more, and rely on wide-spreading roots to support their weight. The forests comprise distinct layers, from ground to treetop canopy. Each layer has its own distinct microclimate as well as flora and fauna, with the vast majority of species concentrated at higher levels. Animals such as kinkajous, sloths, and arboreal snakes are adapted for life in the branches, which are weighed down by vines, epiphytes, and other vascular plants.

MAIN RAINFOREST ENVIRONMENTS

- PN Carara *see p114*
- PN Corcovado *see p191*
- PN Tapantí-Macizo la Muerte *see p101*
- PN Tortuguero *see p167*
- RNVS Gandoca-Manzanillo *see p172*

***Bromeliads** adorn the branches. These epiphytes ("air plants") have nested leaves that meet at the base to form cisterns. Leaf litter falling into these tanks provides nourishment for the plants.*

***Creeping vines** of many varieties grow on the tree trunks, and use grappling hooks and other devices to reach sunlight.*

***Buttress roots** have evolved to hold towering trees steady. These thin flanges radiate out in all directions from the base of the trunk, like the fins of a rocket. The largest can be 10 ft (3 m) high and extend 16 ft (5 m) from the base.*

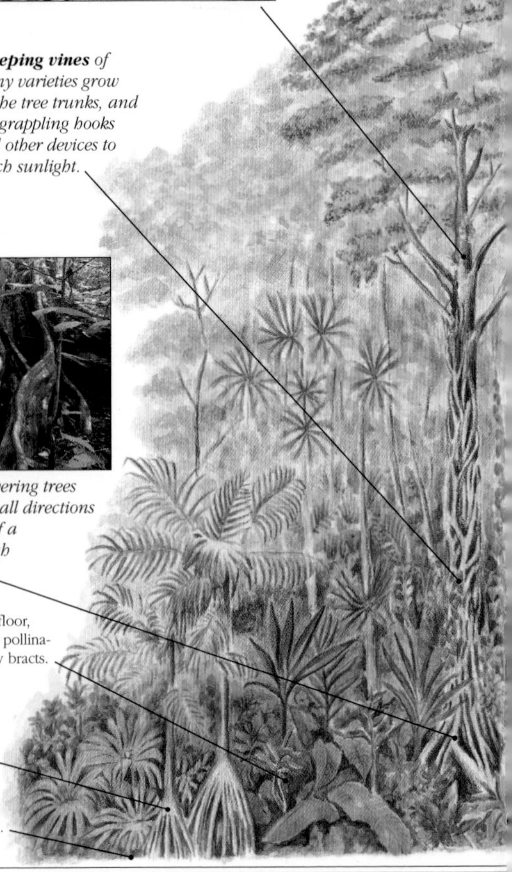

Heliconias grow abundantly on the forest floor, and draw hummingbirds, insects, and other pollinators to their flaming red, orange, and yellow bracts.

Walking palms literally migrate across the forest floor atop stilt roots only loosely attached to the ground.

The soil of rainforests is thin since leaf litter decomposes rapidly and nutrients are swiftly recycled. Heavy rainfall further leaches the soil.

Emergent trees *rise above the forest canopy where their crowns are often buffeted by high winds. Many species bloom flamboyantly in season.*

The upper canopy forms an unbroken stretch of foliage. About 80 percent of rainforest vegetation is concentrated here, as is most wildlife.

Orchids

Understory *species, adapted for varying amounts of sunlight, may grow to 80 ft (24 m) tall. Many are genetically coded to grow rapidly whenever a large tree falls, which opens a space for new growth.*

The forest floor is sparsely vegetated. Rain on the canopy can take up to an hour to reach the ground.

Fauna

Rainforests shelter many of the largest and most endangered mammal species, such as tapirs, peccaries, and jaguars. Most animal and bird species are well camouflaged and difficult to spot in the shadows of the dark, dappled forest.

Squirrel monkeys*, or* titis, *are the smallest as well as most endangered of Costa Rica's monkeys, and are found only in Pacific southwest rainforests. They live in large bands and are omnivorous.*

The jaguar*, known locally as* tigre, *requires a large territory for hunting. It is endangered, mainly because of illicit hunting and loss of rainforest habitat* (see p113).

Pit vipers *are well camouflaged and perfectly adapted for stealthy hunting in the understory, where they feed on small birds and rodents.*

Toucans *are easily recognized by their distinctive calls and colorful beaks. These predominantly fruit-eating birds are found in all of Costa Rica's rainforests.*

The harpy eagle*, the largest member of the eagle family, clings to existence in the rainforests of Corcovado and Gandoca-Manzanillo.*

Canopy Tours

COSTA RICA IS THE WORLD LEADER in "canopy tours," which allow active travelers to explore the forest canopy more than 100 ft (30 m) above the jungle floor. Facilities such as suspended walkways and rappels by horizontal zipline cable, which usually link a series of treetop platforms, offer a monkey's-eye view. "Aerial trams" (modified ski lifts) are a more sedentary option. Such experiences can be a fascinating way to learn about treetop ecology and compare various forest environments, from rainforest to montane cloud forest. Zipline tours are more for the thrill – it is unlikely that wildlife will be spotted while whizzing between trees at high speed. The one drawback of canopy tours is that they often disturb the local ecology, scaring away many creatures.

Treetop platforms *are usually built around the trunks below the treetop canopy, and are supported by branches. Some tours offer the option of overnighting on the platform.*

Aerial trams *operate like ski lifts, using similar technology. Naturalist guides accompany visitors on the Rainforest Aerial Trams (near Jacó and Parque Nacional Braulio Carrillo) and Arenal Rainforest Tram to educate visitors about forest ecology.*

All forest types in Costa Rica, from dry forest to montane cloud forest, host canopy tours. By going on several tours, visitors can experience diverse habitats.

Trails *with interpretive signs, found at most canopy tour sites, provide insights into life at ground level. Combined with the tours, they provide a broad understanding of the interrelationships between ecology at different levels. Most trails are slippery – sturdy footwear with good grip is recommended.*

***Zipline tours** follow "trails," comprising a series of steel cables that run between trees or span canyons, and can exceed 1 mile (2 km). Sped by gravity, the visitor "flies" between the spans, securely attached in a harness.*

Towers and cables made of reinforced concrete and steel are built to the highest standards according to government regulations.

Visitors' centers are located at some sites, and often feature restaurants, exhibits, and gift stores.

***Suspended walkways** held aloft by steel cables permit the best wildlife viewing. Visitors can follow their own pace and stop at will to watch a creature. Many sites have "trails" formed from a series of walkways.*

Locations of the Best Canopy Tours

- Bahía Culebra *see p136*
- Bahía Drake *see p190*
- Genesis II *see p96*
- Jacó *see p114*
- Laguna de Arenal *see p149*
- Monteverde *see pp124–8*
- Montezuma *see p112*
- PN Rincón de la Vieja *see p132*
- Rainforest Aerial Tram *see p159*
- Rainmaker Conservation Project *see p115*
- Rara Avis *see p159*
- Tabacón *see p148*
- Termales del Bosque *see pp154*

***Bridges**, built for utilitarian purposes before the canopy tour concept took hold, have been incorporated into some tours. Some of the more ramshackle ones can be slightly unnerving.*

The Beginnings

The American scientist Dr. Donald Perry pioneered the concept of the "canopy biologist" in the 1970s, when he developed a system of ropes, pulleys, and a radio-controlled cage to move through the treetops at his research site near Rara Avis. Perry's successful "automated web" led him to eventually build an aerial tram that would permit the public the same privileged access for educational purposes.

Dr. Donald Perry exploring the forest canopy at Rara Avis

Birds of Costa Rica

Mealy parrot

NIRVANA FOR BIRDERS, Costa Rica has more than 850 bird species – about 10 percent of the world's known total, and twice as many as the USA and Canada combined. Although the national bird is the clay-brown *yiquirro* (robin), many others are more exotically plumed. Tanagers, manakins, and trogons, inhabit the thick forests, where they are hard to spot despite their bright plumage. Waders such as egrets, ibis, and spoonbills are easily seen amid the wetlands, while vultures and raptors are commonly sighted soaring overhead or squatting atop poles.

Bird-watching *with experienced naturalist guides is richly rewarding. Carry binoculars and a tripod.*

Trogons *are pigeon-sized forest birds identified by their black and white striped tails. Most come in two-color combinations, such as blue and yellow, or green and red. The most beautiful member of the trogon family is the resplendent quetzal* (see p179)*, an iridescent emerald-green bird, which was considered sacred in Mayan culture.*

The green macaw or Buffon's macaw *(lapa verde)* is an endangered species restricted to the northern lowlands.

Toucans*, easily recognized by their oversized bills, are found from elevations of 2,000 ft (610 m) to sea level. The keel-billed toucan has a banana-yellow chest, a black body, and a startling rainbow-striped beak* (left). *The smaller aracaris and toucanets are more varied in color.*

Parrots and Macaws

Garrulous creatures of the forest, the parrot family ranges from small, swift, short-tailed parrakeets to the giants of the parrot kingdom, the long-tailed macaws *(above)*. Most parrots are green with varying patches of red, white, and/or yellow. They have hooked bills and powerful claws for grasping fruits and nuts. Costa Rica is home to 16 species of parrots and two species of macaws.

Seabirds

Costa Rica's shores are crowded with seabirds. Oystercatchers, spotted sandpipers, and whimbrels scurry around at the water's edge. Coastal mangroves are home to blue heron, ibis, and neotropic cormorants, while several offshore islands are important nesting sites for boobies, laughing gulls, and storm petrels.

Brown pelicans *are present year-round on the Pacific coast and can be spotted easily as they dive for fish.*

Frigate birds *nest in colonies on top of coastal shrubs. During the mating season, males inflate bright red chest pouches to woo the females that fly overhead.*

Migratory birds *flock to Costa Rica's wetlands, especially toward the end of the December–April dry season. Blue-winged teal, Muscovy ducks, black-bellied whistling ducks, and other winter migrants arrive in their tens of thousands.*

Hummingbirds*, named for the bee-like "hum" of their wings beating at a blurry 100 times per second, are able to hover as they sip nectar from flowers through hollow, needle-like beaks. They are very territorial despite their tiny size: males can often be seen in spectacular aerial battles.*

Macaws are usually found in pairs. These colorful birds are an extraordinary sight as they fly overhead, screeching loudly.

The scarlet macaw *(lapa roja)* is blood red, with wings of yellow and blue. It is commonly seen in Santa Rosa, Carara, Manuel Antonio, and Corcovado National Parks.

Tanagers *are small, vibrant birds that live in the forests. The summer tanager* (left) *is a flame-red bird. The blue-gray tanager is variegated in peacock hues. Short wings permit fast flight through the forest. About 50 species of tanagers live in Costa Rica.*

Vultures *are found across Costa Rica; the country has four species of this bird of prey, and about 50 other types of raptors, including owls, the osprey, the laughing falcon, and the endangered harpy eagle, the world's largest eagle.*

WETLAND BIRDS

Costa Rica is on the migratory path of numerous waterfowl, such as black-bellied whistling ducks, which stop seasonally at Palo Verde *(see p130)* and similar flooded regions. Jabiru, roseate spoonbills, and cormorants are among the permanent wetland species.

Northern jacana *have elongated toes for walking across floating lilypads. Male jacana rear the young.*

Bare-throated tiger-herons *are graceful waterbirds. Costa Rica hosts about 20 species of herons.*

Sunbitterns *spread their wings to reveal distinctive patterns that are designed for defense.*

Beaches of Costa Rica

Most of Costa Rica's shoreline, which extends for 800 miles (1,290 km), is lined with beaches in a range of colors, from sugar white to varying shades of gray and brown. On the straight Caribbean coast, beaches stretch for miles, while the ones on the serrated Pacific coast are separated by rocky headlands. In most places, thick forest edges right up to the shore, lending a dramatic beauty to even the dullest brown sands. The coastal waters are relatively murky due to silt washed down by numerous rivers and there are few coral reefs. Beaches run the gamut from developed areas, with resorts and various amenities, to isolated, virtually undiscovered stretches of sand. Dozens of beaches offer great swimming and surfing *(see p137).*

***Playa Naranjo**, hemmed by tropical dry forest, is difficult to access, but offers tremendous wildlife viewing, including sightings of leatherback turtles. Mangroves nearby harbor caimans and crocodiles* (see p137).

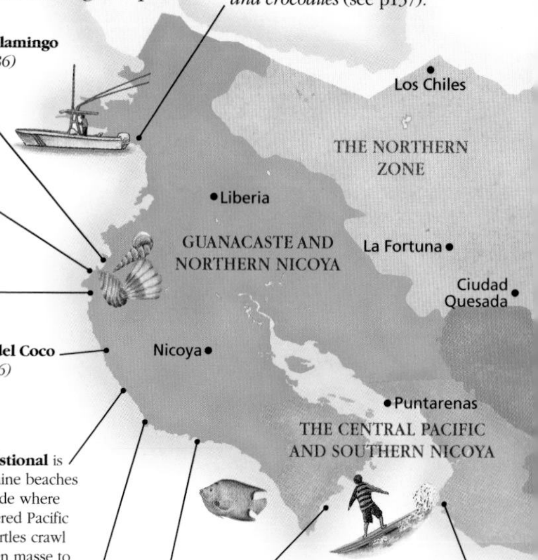

Playa Conchal, or "Shell Beach," is acclaimed for its snow-white beach, comprised of billions of minute seashells. The turquoise waters are unusually clear *(see p136).*

Playa Flamingo *(see p136)*

Playas del Coco *(see p136)*

Playa Ostional is one of nine beaches worldwide where endangered Pacific ridley turtles crawl ashore en masse to nest *(see p140).*

***Playa Grande** is Costa Rica's most important nesting site for leatherback turtles. This long, scalloped beach of coral-gray sands is also a famed surfing destination, attracting hundreds of surfers every year* (see p136).

Playa Jacó, popular with surfers and lined with hotels, is Costa Rica's most developed resort *(see p114).*

Playa Montezuma is a beautiful, coconut-fringed, cream-colored beach. Its rough waters are unsafe for swimming *(see p112).*

***Playa Guiones** is several miles long and extremely deep at low tide* (see p140). *It has tidepools, and in recent years it has been the site of* arribadas (see p141) *of Pacific ridley turtles.*

***Playa Carrillo** is virtually undeveloped, despite the hotels dotting the nearby hills. Fishing boats gather in a cove at the southern end of this palm-shaded beach, which is backed by an airstrip.*

***Tortuguero's beach** is a prime nesting site for green turtles, which emerge glistening from the surf to lay eggs. Jaguars are sometimes glimpsed on this unbroken, 23-mile (37-km) long gray beach, feasting on turtles* (see p167).

***Cahuita's beaches** – Playa Negra with its black sands and the golden Playa Blanca – are edged by rainforest. The forest and the coral reef bordering Playa Blanca are protected within Parque Nacional Cahuita* (see p170).

***Playa Cocles** is a popular surfing center. Splendidly scenic, it is perfect for sunbathing, although swimmers should beware the riptides.*

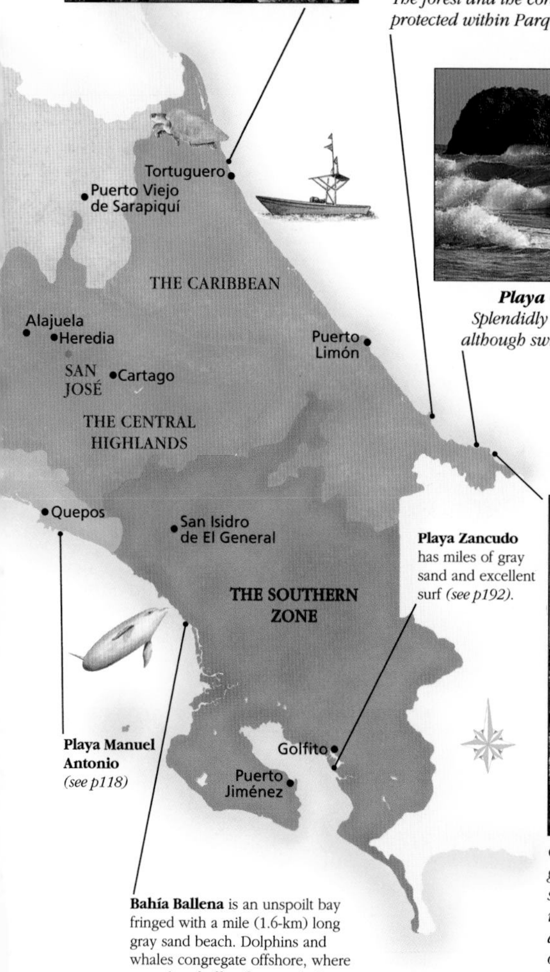

Playa Zancudo has miles of gray sand and excellent surf *(see p192).*

Playa Manuel Antonio *(see p118)*

Bahía Ballena is an unspoilt bay fringed with a mile (1.6-km) long gray sand beach. Dolphins and whales congregate offshore, where a coral reef offers fine snorkeling.

***Gandoca-Manzanillo**, a remote gray-black beach, is backed by swamps and mangroves, which are inhabited by crocodiles, manatees, and varieties of birds. Four species of marine turtles nest in the sands* (see p172).

The Story of Costa Rican Coffee

A cup of Costa Rican coffee

COSTA RICA IS famed for its flavorful coffee. *Coffea arabica* – a bush native to Ethiopia – was introduced to the country in 1779. For more than a century, beginning in the 1830s, the *grano de oro* (golden grain) was Costa Rica's foremost export, funding the construction of fine buildings. The nation's mountains provide ideal conditions for the coffee plant, which prefers consistently warm temperatures, distinct wet and dry seasons, and fertile, well-drained slopes. More than 425 sq miles (1,100 sq km), concentrated in the Central Highlands, are dedicated to coffee production.

***Guided tours** of plantations and* beneficios *(processing factories) give visitors a chance to see beans being processed, as well as offering demonstrations of "cupping" (tasting).*

Coffee Plantations

After being raised in nurseries, 8 to 12 month-old coffee seedlings are planted beneath shade trees in long rows perpendicular to the slope to help avoid soil erosion. They require precise amounts of sunlight, water, and fertilizer.

Coffee seedlings ready to be planted

Worker weeding in a coffee plantation

Shade trees allow the proper amount of sunlight to filter through.

Elevations between 2,650 and 4,900 ft (800–1,500 m) are ideal for coffee estates.

The volcanic soil contains the nutrients that coffee bushes require.

The Early Days

Before the construction of the railroads in the late 19th century, coffee beans were packed in gunny sacks and transported to the port of Puntarenas in *carretas* (oxcarts). Trains of oxcarts loaded with coffee traveled down the mountains of Costa Rica in convoys. From Puntarenas, the beans were shipped to Europe, a journey that took three months.

***Carreta* (oxcart) transporting sacks of coffee**

Berries to Beans

Typically it takes four years for the shiny-leafed coffee bush to mature and fruit. With the arrival of the rains in early May, small white blossoms appear, giving off a jasmine-like scent. The fleshy green berries containing the beans gradually turn red as they ripen. Each berry contains two hemispherical seeds, or beans. Well-tended bushes produce *cerrezas* (cherries) for about 40 years.

White coffee blossoms

Green and red berries

The harvest *normally begins in November. Traditionally, entire families would head into the fields to help with harvesting. Although children can still be seen picking coffee, today Nicaraguans and indigenous peoples form the majority of the labor pool.*

The red berries are hand-picked by workers.

Handwoven wicker baskets are usually used to hold the berries.

Coffee workers *wait in line to measure baskets of freshly harvested coffee. The berries are shipped to a* beneficio *for processing.*

***At the* beneficio**, *the berries are cleaned. The fleshy outer pulp is then stripped off and returned to the slopes as fertilizer.*

The moist beans *are dried, either in the traditional manner by being laid out in the sun, or in hot-air ovens.*

The dried beans *have their leathery skins removed before being roasted.*

Packaging

The roasted beans are sorted by quality, size, and shape. Export-quality beans are vacuum-sealed in foil bags and typically come in light roast, dark roast, espresso, decaffeinated, and organic varieties. Lower grade beans for the domestic market are sold loose at local markets as *café puro* (unadulterated) or *café traditional* (containing 10 percent sugar).

Coffee packed for export

Roasted coffee beans

Different varieties of coffee

Ground coffee

Coffee bags

Coffee liqueur

The Indigenous Groups

Sparsely inhabited at the time of Columbus's arrival, the country today has 40,000 indigenous inhabitants, who account for less than 1 percent of the total population. They belong to seven main tribes – Chorotega, Boruca, Bribri, Cabécar, Guaymí, Guatuso/Maleku, and Huetar. Living relatively marginalized from mainstream society in 22 remote reserves, the tribes sustain themselves by hunting and farming; and some continue to create traditional handicrafts. The aboriginal way of life is under constant threat by missionary activity and by the government's habitual espousal of logging and mining interests over those of indigenous peoples. Few tribes speak their native language, and even fewer have been able to keep their religious traditions free from outside influences.

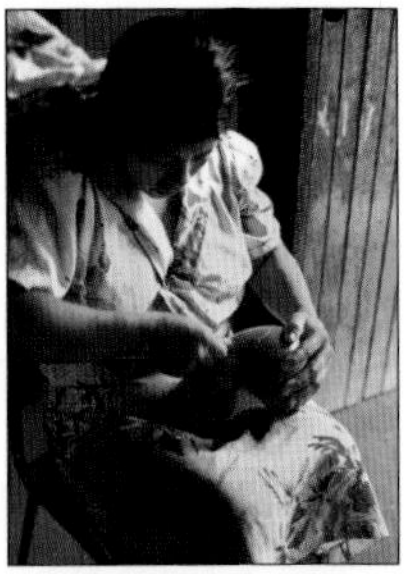

***The Guatuso/Maleku** retain their language and customs. They are known for bark cloth* (mastate) *painted with the fingertips.*

***The Bribri** today comprise 10,000 individuals, who cling to their collective faith in Sibú, the creator of the universe. They welcome visits to the Reserva Indígena KeköLdi* (see p173), *where some Bribri continue to live in traditional huts.*

Carved and painted gourds, called *jícara* by the Bribri, are used as vessels and objects of decoration by most indigenous groups. Pictured here is a Bribri *jícara*.

Motifs depict natural elements. To preserve tribal identity, names of the elements are carved in traditional languages as well as in Spanish.

Huts are thatched to the ground.

A traditional Bribri hut – a windowless, conical structure

Indigenous Artifacts

Many of the traditional crafts of Costa Rica's indigenous peoples emphasize their relationship with the rainforest. Age-old techniques continue to be used in contemporary works. Crafts, clothing, and musical instruments of several tribes, as well as shamanic totems, are displayed in the Museo de Cultura Indígena *(see p155).*

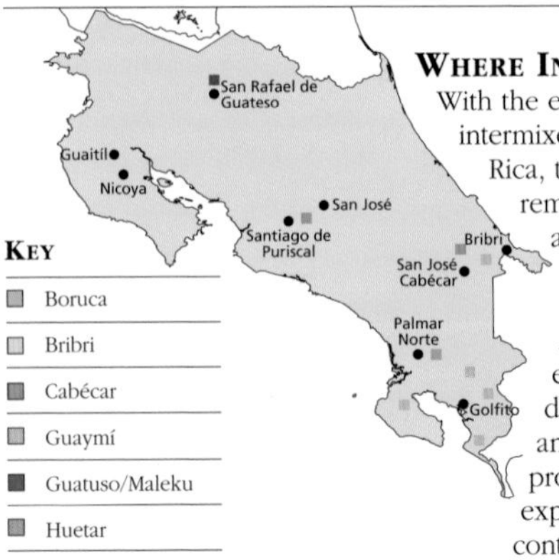

Where Indigenous Peoples Live

With the exception of the Chorotega, who have intermixed with other peoples in northwest Costa Rica, the indigenous population is relegated to remote regions in the Talamanca Mountains and the Pacific southwest. The tribes live in reserves administered by the National Commission for Indigenous Affairs (CONAI), which works to promote education, health services, and community development. However, it is underfunded, and has met only modest success in protecting the indigenous cultures from exploitation by commercial interests, which continue to encroach on tribal land.

The Chorotega *of Guanacaste and Northern Nicoya were the largest tribe in the pre-Columbian era. Today, about 1,000 true-blood Chorotegas live in matriarchal families, and take pride in their distinctive pottery.*

The Boruca *cling precariously to ancestral lands in the hills west of the Terraba valley. They are famed for their balsa-wood masks* (mascaras) *of animals representing supernatural beings, used in the Fiesta de los Diablitos* (see p184).

Chorotega pottery*, with its characteristic earth-tones, continues to be produced in Guaitíl* (see p143).

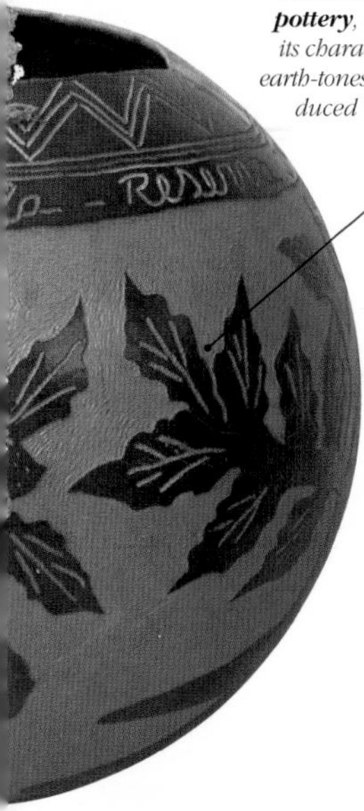

Designs are created by pecking tender green gourds with a needle. The residual skin surrounding the design is then scraped away. As the gourd dries, the skin turns dark brown.

The Huetar *of the Puriscal region still practice the ancient Festival of the Corn but in many other aspects have been integrated into mainstream society.*

ULú (healing cane) used by shamans

The Cabécar *live in the Talamanca-Cabécar Reserve* (see p173) *and today consist of about 5,000 individuals. Shamanic rituals remain an integral part of Cabécar culture.*

The Guaymí *retain a strong cultural identity, including the Guaymí language. Uniquely, women still wear the traditional garment with decorative triangular patterns, as well as* collares *(necklaces) of colorful beads.*

Guaymí painters *experiment freely with scenes of daily life, images of natural forms, and spiritual symbols.*

Traditional Guaymí dress

COSTA RICA THROUGH THE YEAR

A MAJOR FACTOR in planning a visit to Costa Rica is the weather. The dry season (December–April) offers the best climate and draws the most visitors. Christmas and New Year, as well as Easter, when Costa Rica celebrates its most colorful festivals, are the peak periods: schools and offices close, and the nation goes on holiday. Late April and May are relatively less crowded. Promoted by the tourism department as the "green" season, the wet months (May–November) see fewer visitors and lower prices: for those willing to brave the rains, this is a good time to visit. Religious ceremonies and folk festivities are held year-round, though the celebrations usually lack the color and vitality of Mexico and Guatemala. *Topes* (horse shows) and rodeos are the staples of provincial events. Note that while many rodeos include bull-baiting, visitors can choose not to view the events. The Caribbean moves to its own beat, and a strong Afro-Caribbean heritage influences its festivities.

Ticos in traditional dress

Floats depicting Costa Rican fauna, Fiesta de la Luz, San José

DRY SEASON

THE COOLER, drier months are ideal for beach holidays, especially in Guanacaste and Northern Nicoya, where it hardly rains. Town squares are ablaze with jacaranda and flame-of-the-forest. With coastal waters in the south at their clearest, scuba diving is excellent. Wildlife viewing is also at its best, with deciduous trees dropping their leaves. Dirt roads with river fordings are more easily passed, although off-road driving can kick up billowing clouds of dust. However, this is peak season throughout the nation, with high prices and fully booked hotels and car rentals.

DECEMBER

Fiesta de los Negritos *(Dec 8)*, Boruca. The indigenous Boruca peoples celebrate their traditions with costumed dancing and drum and flute music.

Fiesta de la Yegüita *(Dec 12)*, Nicoya. The Festival of the Little Mare recalls a Chorotega legend and blends Indian and Catholic rituals. Villagers carry an image of La Virgen de Guadalupe in procession, and there are *corridas de toros* (bull runs), as well as fireworks and concerts *(see p142)*.

Los Posadas *(Dec 15)*. Before Christmas, carolers go house to house by night and are rewarded with food and refreshments.

Tope Nacional de Caballos *(Dec 26)*, San José. During the nation's most famous *tope*, the country's finest horsemen show off their skills in a parade of more than 3,000 horses along Paseo Colón.

Fiesta de la Luz *(Dec 26)*, San José. The nocturnal Festival of Light features floats decorated with colorful Christmas lights. The "Parade of Lights" passes from Parque Sabana to downtown via Paseo Colón. Fireworks light up the night sky.

Carnaval Nacional *(Dec 27)*, San José. Locals don costumes and dance in the streets to live music. A competition of brightly decorated floats is the highlight of the procession.

People dressed as devils at the Fiesta de los Diablitos

***Carretas* (oxcarts) gather for the Día del Boyero celebrations, Escazú**

Fiesta de Zapote *(late Dec)*, Zapote. Citizens flock to this suburb of San José for the fairground, fireworks, *topes* and rodeos.
Fiesta de los Diablitos *(Dec 31–Jan 2)*, Buenos Aires and Boruca. Men dressed as devils rush through the two villages in the Boruca Indian community's reenactment of battles between their forebears and the Spanish *(see p184)*.

January

Fiesta de Palmares *(first two weeks of Jan)*, Palmares (near Alajuela). Concerts, rodeos, fireworks, and music highlight this festival, which also features fairgrounds and sporting events.
Fiesta Patronal de Santo Cristo *(mid-Jan)*, Santa Cruz. Rodeos, folk dancing, street festivities, and a parade of *carretas* (oxcarts) mark this 2-day celebration honoring Santo Cristo de Esquipulas.
Festival de las Mulas *(late Jan)*, Playas Esterillos (near Jacó). Popular festival with mule races on the beach, as well as a crafts fair, *corridas de toros*, and music and dance.

February

Expo Perez Zeledón *(early Feb)*, San Isidro de El General. Cattle fair and orchid show, also featuring *topes*, rodeo, beauty contests, carousels, and displays of agricultural machinery.
Good Neighbors Jazz Festival *(mid-Feb)*, Manuel Antonio. Jazz ensembles perform at hotels and other venues through the area.
Carnaval de Puntarenas *(last week of Feb)*. Parade floats, street fairs, music, and dancing enliven this coastal city for a week.

March

Día del Boyero *(2nd Sun)*, San Antonio de Escazú. A parade of colorfully decorated traditional oxcarts honors the *boyero* (oxcart driver). The streets come alive with music and dance.
International Festival of the Arts *(2nd week)*, San José. Theaters and other venues bustle with live theater, dance performances, music concerts, visual art exhibits, and conferences.
Southern Caribbean Music Festival *(Mar–Apr)*, Puerto Viejo de Talamanca and Cahuita. Performers spanning the spectrum from classical to calypso and reggae enliven these towns.
Semana Santa *(Mar or Apr)*. Easter Week is the most important holiday celebration of the year, with processions nationwide, notably in Cartago and San Joaquín de Flores near Heredia. Costumed citizens reenact Christ's crucifixion in passion plays.

April

Día de Juan Santamaría *(Apr 11)*, Alajuela. Marching bands, a beauty pageant, and *topes* are part of the celebrations honoring the young national hero who was killed fighting against William Walker in the War of 1856 *(see p45)*.
Feria del Ganado *(mid-Apr)*, Ciudad Quesada. The nation's largest cattle fair also features a horse parade and *corridas de toros*.
Romería Virgen de la Candelaria *(3rd Sun)*, Ujarrás. A pilgrimage from Paraiso to Ujarrás terminates with games and celebrations to honor the supposed miracle attributed to the Holy Virgin that saved the town of Ujarrás from pirate invasion in 1666 *(see p100)*.
Semana Universidad *(last week)*, San José. The campus of the University of Costa Rica is the setting for week-long free activities, including open-air art shows, concerts, and the crowning of the university queen.

The San José Symphony performing at a music festival

Wet Season

The onset of the rains marks the beginning of the off-season. Mountainous parts are prone to landslides, and many roads are washed out. Nonetheless, mornings are typically sunny, while afternoon rains help cool off sometimes stifling days. This is the best time for surfing in the Pacific, and olive ridley turtles begin their *arribadas* *(see p141)*. Sportfishing is also at a premium, especially in northern Pacific waters. Toward the end of the wet season, Costa Rica is at its lushest, and swollen rivers provide plenty of whitewater thrills. The Pacific southwest is subject to severe thunderstorms in October and November.

May

Día de los Trabajadores *(May 1)*. Trade unions organize marches in major cities to honor workers on Labor Day.
Fiesta Cívica *(early May)*, Cañas. Cowboy traditions are displayed at *corridas de toros* and *topes*. Street fairs feature folkloric music, dance, and traditional food.
Corpus Christi *(May 29)*, Pacayas and Cartago. The two towns hold religious parades and church services.

Pilgrims at Cartago's Basilica de Nuestra Señora de los Ángeles

June

Monteverde Ecotouristic Fair *(mid-Jun)*. Educational and cultural activities are the highlights of this themed event. A stage hosts live theater, music, and other events. Costa Rican cuisine is also served.
Día de San Pedro y San Pablo *(Jun 29)*, San José. St. Peter and St. Paul are honored in religious celebrations around the city.
Compañía de Lírica Nacional *(mid-Jun–mid-Aug)*, San José. The National Lyric Opera Company presents a 2-month long opera festival in San José's sumptuously decorated Teatro Mélico Salazar *(see p58)*.

July

Festival de la Virgen del Mar *(mid-Jul)*, Puntarenas. The "Sea Festival" honors Carmen, Virgin of the Sea, with religious processions, a carnival, fireworks, and a boating regatta.
Día de la Anexión de Guanacaste *(Jul 25)*. The annexation of Guanacaste by Costa Rica in 1824 is celebrated nationwide with music and folkloric dancing. Rodeos and bullfights are held at Liberia and Santa Cruz.
Chorotega Tourist Fair *(late Jul)*, Nicoya. This celebration of traditional Chorotega culture features artisan displays, indigenous foods, and several educational activities.
International Festival of Music *(Jul–Aug)*. International musicians perform predominantly classical music at venues around the nation.

August

Día de Nuestra Señora de la Virgen de los Ángeles *(Aug 2)*, Cartago. Costa Rica's most important religious procession to honor its patron saint, La Negrita, draws the faithful from around the nation. The devout carry crosses or crawl on their knees to Cartago's famous basilica *(see p94)*.

Recorrido de toros **(bullfight) at a fiesta in Parque Nacional Santa Rosa**

A San José parade celebrating Día de la Independencia

Liberia Blanca Culture Week *(early Aug)*, Liberia. Cowboys come to town, and citizens don traditional attire to honor local traditions with music, dancing, and food.
Día de las Madres *(Aug 15)*. On Mother's Day, everyone honors their mother, who is usually taken out to lunch or dinner and serenaded by hired mariachis.
National Adventure Tourism Festival *(late Aug)*, Turrialba. Mountain biking, whitewater rafting, and kayaking are among the activities highlighted.
Día de San Ramón *(Aug 31)*, San Ramón (near Alajuela). The local patron saint is carried in procession. Tico culture is celebrated with marimba music, *topes*, processions, and regional dishes.
Semana Afro-Costarricense *(Aug or Sep)*, Puerto Limón and San José. This week-long festival celebrates Afro-Costa Rican culture. Activities range from art shows and lectures to musical performances and beauty pageants.

September

Correo de la Candela de Independencia *(Sep 14)*. Runners carrying a Freedom Torch from Guatemala travel from town to town, arriving in Cartago at 6pm, when the entire nation sings the national anthem. At night, children carry home-made lanterns in procession throughout the country.
Día de la Independencia *(Sep 15)*. Costa Rica's independence from Spain in 1821 is celebrated nationwide with street festivities, *topes*, and school marching bands.
Orosi Colonial Tourist Fair *(mid-Sep)*. Cultural events and exhibits celebrate the region's colonial heritage.

October

Carnaval *(2nd week)* Puerto Limón. Ticos flock to the coast for a vibrant, no-holds-barred, Caribbean-style Mardi Gras with parade floats, street fairs, live reggae and calypso music, and beauty pageants *(see p165)*.
Día de las Culturas *(Oct 12)*. Columbus's discovery of America is celebrated with cultural events throughout the nation, notably in Puerto Limón; the city's Carnaval culminates on this day.

A band at Puerto Limón's famous Caribbean-style Carnaval

Public Holidays

Año Nuevo (New Year's Day; Jan 1)
Jueves Santo (Easter Thursday)
Viernes Santo (Good Friday)
Día de Juan Santamaría (Apr 11)
Día de los Trabajadores (Labor Day; May 1)
Día de la Anexión de Guanacaste (Jul 25)
Día de Nuestra Señora de la Virgen de los Ángeles (Aug 2)
Día de las Madres (Mother's Day; Aug 15)
Día de la Independencia (Sep 15)
Día de las Culturas (Columbus Day; Oct 12)
Navidad (Christmas Day)

Fiesta del Maíz *(mid-Oct)*, Upala (near Caño Negro). Locals craft clothes out of corn husks and make corn-based foods in a traditional celebration of *maíz* (corn).
Día del Sabanero *(Oct 18)*. *Topes* and celebrations mark Cowboy's Day. Liberia and Parque Nacional Santa Rosa have the most lively festivities.

November

Días de Todos Santos *(Nov 2)*. All Souls' Day is celebrated nationwide with church processions. Families visit cemeteries to remember loved ones and lay marigolds and other flowers on graves.
La Ruta de los Conquistadores *(mid-Nov)*. This week-long, coast-to-coast mountain bike championship, which aims to retrace the route of the Spanish conquerors across Costa Rica, is considered one of the world's most challenging.
Feria Agroecoturística *(mid-Nov)*, Atenas (near Alajuela). Log-felling contests, tractor tours, horseback rides, and an orchid show at the Escuela de Ganadería reserve.
Fiesta de las Carretas *(late Nov)*, San José. Oxcarts are paraded from Parque Sabana and along Paseo Colón.

The Climate of Costa Rica

Most of Costa Rica experiences distinct dry (December–April) and wet (May–November) seasons, which Ticos call *verano* (summer) and *invierno* (winter). There are dozens of regional micro-climates: San José and the *meseta central* (central plateau) are delightfully warm year-round; the eastern lowlands are swept by rain-laden Caribbean breezes; the southern Pacific coast has high precipitation; and in the dry season temperatures regularly rise above 35° C (94° F) in the parched northwest. Temperatures are affected by the varying altitudes, and can drop to below 0° C (32° F) on mountain summits. However, the sun is strong at all times of the year across Costa Rica, with sunrise at about 6am and sunset at 6pm.

La Fortuna

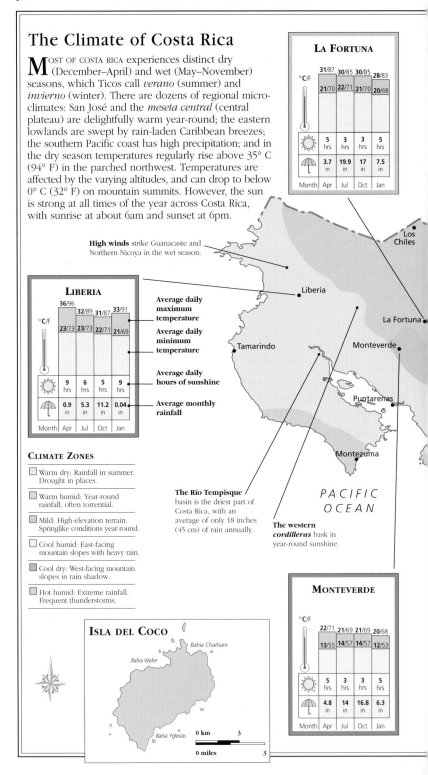

Month	Apr	Jul	Oct	Jan
°C/F max	31/87	30/85	30/85	28/83
°C/F min	21/70	22/71	21/70	20/68
Sunshine	5 hrs	3 hrs	3 hrs	5 hrs
Rainfall	3.7 in	19.9 in	17 in	7.5 in

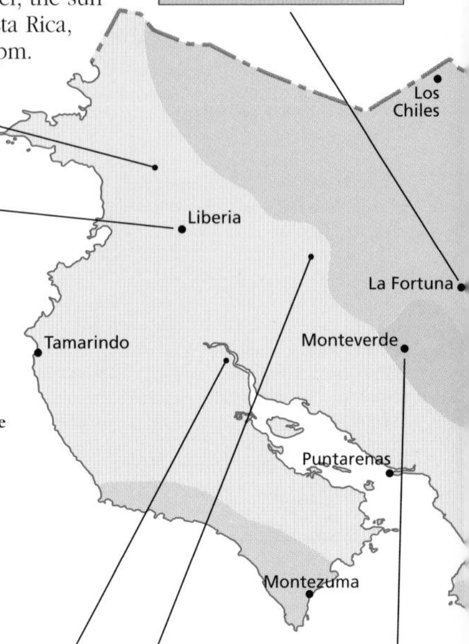

High winds strike Guanacaste and Northern Nicoya in the wet season.

Liberia

Month	Apr	Jul	Oct	Jan
°C/F max	36/96	32/89	31/87	33/91
°C/F min	23/73	23/73	22/71	21/69
Sunshine	9 hrs	6 hrs	5 hrs	9 hrs
Rainfall	0.9 in	5.3 in	11.2 in	0.04 in

Average daily maximum temperature

Average daily minimum temperature

Average daily hours of sunshine

Average monthly rainfall

The Río Tempisque basin is the driest part of Costa Rica, with an average of only 18 inches (45 cm) of rain annually.

The western *cordilleras* bask in year-round sunshine.

Climate Zones

- Warm dry: Rainfall in summer. Drought in places.
- Warm humid: Year-round rainfall, often torrential.
- Mild: High-elevation terrain. Springlike conditions year-round.
- Cool humid: East-facing mountain slopes with heavy rain.
- Cool dry: West-facing mountain slopes in rain shadow.
- Hot humid: Extreme rainfall. Frequent thunderstorms.

Monteverde

Month	Apr	Jul	Oct	Jan
°C/F max	22/71	21/69	21/69	20/68
°C/F min	13/55	14/57	14/57	12/53
Sunshine	5 hrs	3 hrs	3 hrs	5 hrs
Rainfall	4.8 in	14 in	16.8 in	6.3 in

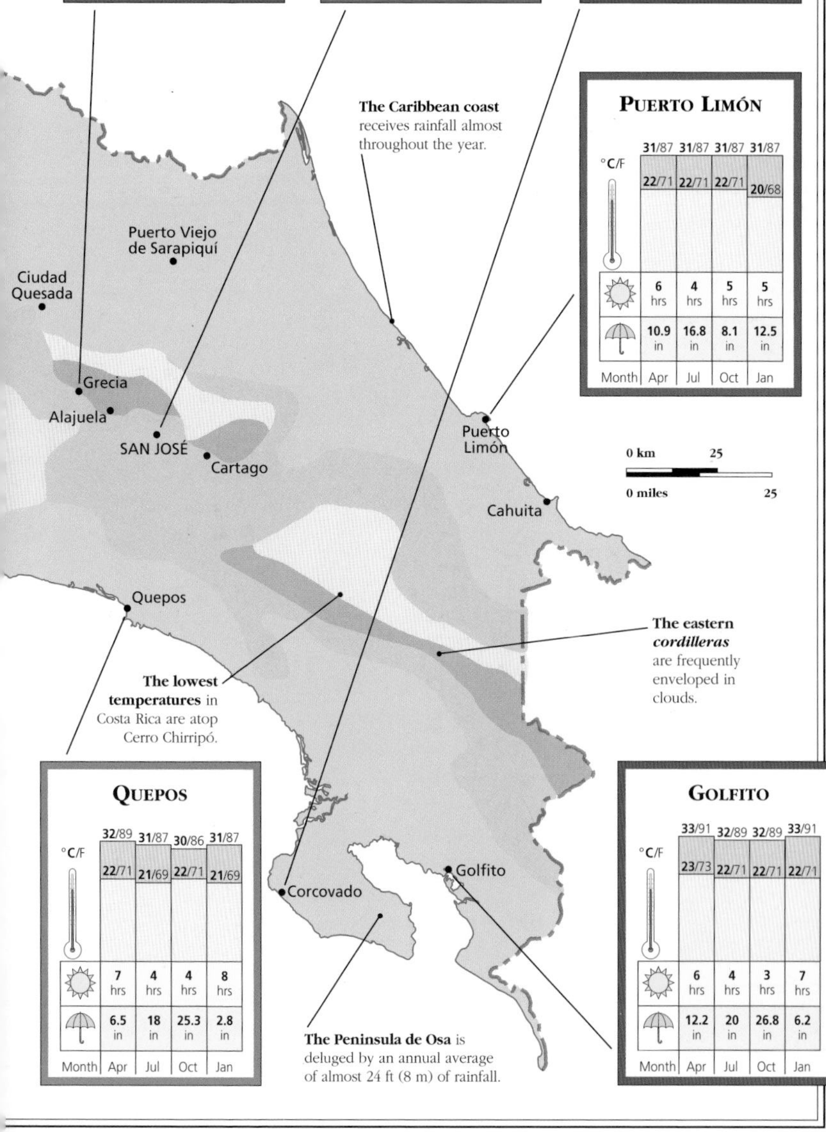
Puerto Viejo de Sarapiquí
Ciudad Quesada
Grecia
Alajuela
SAN JOSÉ
Cartago
Puerto Limón
Cahuita
Quepos
Corcovado
Golfito
0 km 25
0 miles 25
The Caribbean coast receives rainfall almost throughout the year.
The eastern *cordilleras* are frequently enveloped in clouds.
The lowest temperatures in Costa Rica are atop Cerro Chirripó.
The Peninsula de Osa is deluged by an annual average of almost 24 ft (8 m) of rainfall.

Grecia

Month	Apr	Jul	Oct	Jan
°C/F (max)	31/87	28/82	27/80	29/84
°C/F (min)	18/64	18/64	18/64	17/62
Sunshine	7 hrs	5 hrs	4 hrs	8 hrs
Rainfall	2.7 in	7.6 in	12.8 in	0.3 in

San José

Month	Apr	Jul	Oct	Jan
°C/F (max)	26/78	25/77	25/77	23/73
°C/F (min)	16/60	17/62	16/60	15/59
Sunshine	5 hrs	4 hrs	5 hrs	8 hrs
Rainfall	1.7 in	8.5 in	13 in	0.4 in

PN Corcovado

Month	Apr	Jul	Oct	Jan
°C/F (max)	33/91	32/89	32/89	33/91
°C/F (min)	23/73	22/71	22/71	22/71
Sunshine	6 hrs	3 hrs	3 hrs	7 hrs
Rainfall	11 in	19 in	27.6 in	6.2 in

Puerto Limón

Month	Apr	Jul	Oct	Jan
°C/F (max)	31/87	31/87	31/87	31/87
°C/F (min)	22/71	22/71	22/71	20/68
Sunshine	6 hrs	4 hrs	5 hrs	5 hrs
Rainfall	10.9 in	16.8 in	8.1 in	12.5 in

Quepos

Month	Apr	Jul	Oct	Jan
°C/F (max)	32/89	31/87	30/86	31/87
°C/F (min)	22/71	21/69	22/71	21/69
Sunshine	7 hrs	4 hrs	4 hrs	8 hrs
Rainfall	6.5 in	18 in	25.3 in	2.8 in

Golfito

Month	Apr	Jul	Oct	Jan
°C/F (max)	33/91	32/89	32/89	33/91
°C/F (min)	23/73	22/71	22/71	22/71
Sunshine	6 hrs	4 hrs	3 hrs	7 hrs
Rainfall	12.2 in	20 in	26.8 in	6.2 in

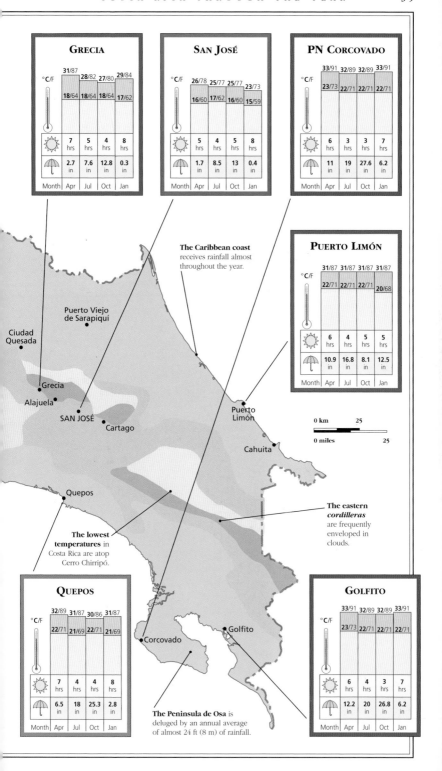

THE HISTORY OF COSTA RICA

CONTEMPORARY COSTA RICA *has been shaped by a relatively benign history devoid of the great clash between pre-Columbian and Spanish cultures that characterized the formative period of neighboring nations. Following the colonial era, Costa Rica evolved stable democratic institutions that permitted sustained economic development. The nation's declaration of neutrality in 1948 continues to help forge its identity today.*

When Christopher Columbus landed off the coast of Central America in 1502, the region had a history that went back 10 millennia. The indigenous peoples who inhabited the thickly forested and rugged terrain were relatively isolated from the more advanced and densely populated imperial cultures of Meso-America to the north and the Andes to the south. They were divided into several distinct ethnic groups and further subdivided into competing tribes ruled by *caciques* (chiefs). These peoples left no written record.

Pre-Columbian hunter

The semi-nomadic Chibchas and Diquis, who occupied the southern Pacific shores, were hunters and fishermen. They were expert goldsmiths as well, and also produced granite spheres of varying sizes for ceremonial purposes. The highland valleys were the domain of the Coribicí, subsistence agriculturalists skilled at using the "lost wax" technique to create gold ornaments. These groups had affinities with the Andean cultures, with whom they traded. The Votos of the northern lowlands were matriarchal and, like most other groups, used shamans to assist in the fertility rites that dominated religious belief. The agriculturalist Chorotega of the northwest lowlands were the most advanced. They traded with Meso-America, were famed for their elaborate jade ornamentation, and created a written language and calendar of Mayan origin. Most tribal names were ascribed by the Spanish and often indicated individual *caciques.*

Inter-clan warfare was common. Slaves from neighboring tribes were captured for labor and ceremonial sacrifice, while women were taken as concubines. Gold ornamentation indicated status. High-ranking individuals were interred with their wealth; their slaves were often killed and buried alongside to serve them in the afterlife. Each tribe lived communally in large thatched huts, and although modest urban settlements have been discovered, principally at Guayabo on the southern slopes of Volcán Turrialba, nowhere did elaborate temple structures result.

TIMELINE

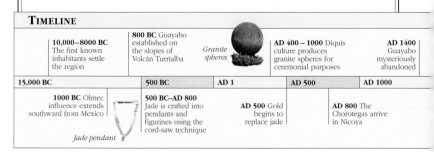

10,000–8000 BC The first known inhabitants settle the region

800 BC Guayabo established on the slopes of Volcán Turrialba

Granite spheres

AD 400 – 1000 Diquis culture produces granite spheres for ceremonial purposes

AD 1400 Guayabo mysteriously abandoned

15,000 BC | 500 BC | AD 1 | AD 500 | AD 1000

1000 BC Olmec influence extends southward from Mexico

Jade pendant

500 BC–AD 800 Jade is crafted into pendants and figurines using the cord-saw technique

AD 500 Gold begins to replace jade

AD 800 The Chorotegas arrive in Nicoya

◁ **A detail of a fresco by Diego Rivera (1886–1957) depicting the Spanish conquest in Central America**

The Spanish Conquest

Columbus arrived in Bahía de Cariari, on the Caribbean coast, while on his fourth voyage to the New World. He spent 17 days in the land he called *veragua* (mildew), and his descriptions of the gold worn by the chiefs spelled doom for the indigenous population. Spanish conquistadors soon followed in his wake, driven by the quest for silver and gold. However, they failed to find any local source of the precious metals.

Bust of Columbus and his son, Puerto Limón

Colonization was initiated in 1506 when Ferdinand of Spain dispatched Diego de Nicuesa to settle and govern the region. Nicuesa's expedition north from Panama proved a disaster, as his troops were decimated by tropical diseases and guerrilla attacks. In 1522, a second expedition led by Gil González Davila explored the Pacific coast, converting the natives and seizing vast quantities of gold. Davila named the region *la costa rica* (rich coast). Many natives were enslaved under the *encomienda* system that granted Spaniards rights to native labor. Villa Bruselas, inland from today's Puntarenas, was Spain's first permanent settlement in Costa Rica, founded by Francisco Fernández de Córdoba in 1524. Davila's group and Córdoba's township, however, succumbed to tropical hardships and violent resistance by the natives. Despite this, by 1543, when the region was incorporated into the Captaincy-General of Guatemala, which extended from Yucatán to Panama, most lowland areas had been charted and Spain's conquest was assured. Many natives were shipped to work the gold and silver mines of Peru and Mexico, while thousands died of smallpox, measles, influenza, and other European diseases that culminated in a 17th-century pandemic.

In 1559, Juan de Cavallón founded the settlement of Castillo de Garcimuñoz, with Spaniards, black slaves, and Indians brought from Guatemala and Nicaragua. Appointed governor in 1562, Juan Vásquez de Coronado penetrated the fertile Central Highlands and established El Guarco (today's Cartago) as capital of the region. For the next 250 years Costa Rica was a neglected colony of Spain, virtually forgotten by the governors of New Spain, based in Mexico.

The Subsistence Era

By the 17th century, the relatively small supply of gold had been shipped to Spain, and the country had nothing to trade. Settlement was

Theodor de Bry's (1528–98) copperplate print depicting gold being seized by Spanish conquistadors

Timeline

1502 Columbus lands on September 18

1506 Diego de Nicuesa named governor. Attempts colonization

1522 Davila successfully explores the Pacific coast

1542 *Encomienda* law repealed to little effect; indigenous peoples remain in servitude

1559 Philip II issues royal edict ordering the conversion of the native population

1563 Governor Coronado founds Cartago and explores much of Costa Rica

Juan Vásquez de Coronado

1611–60 A great pandemic kills thousands

1641 Survivors of a slave-ship establish a free community of Miskitos

1655 Spain closes port of Puerto Limón following pirate raids

1500 | 1525 | 1550 | 1575 | 1600 | 1625 | 1650

concentrated in the central valley of the interior highlands, where the absence of a large indigenous population and near total neglect by colonial authorities forced the Spanish settlers to work their own land. As a result, most of the land remained sparsely developed and agriculture existed at barely more than subsistence level. Moreover, the *mestizo* population (of mixed Spanish and Indian parentage) was small and the majority of inhabitants were predominantly Spanish. Thus, unlike the rigid feudal societies of its neighbors, Costa Rica evolved a fairly egalitarian social structure dominated by the independent farmer of meager means.

A 19th-century etching of Hacienda Santa Rosa, Guanacaste

The northwestern regions of Nicoya and Guanacaste on the Pacific coast were exceptions. Spanish landowners established large cattle estates here, and exacted harsh tribute and labor from Indians and *mestizos* through the *encomienda* and *repartimiento* systems. The densely forested Caribbean coast, meanwhile, was part of the "Spanish Main," the domain of pirates and smugglers, who traded precious hardwoods, such as cocoa and mahogany, through the small port of Puerto Limón (it was closed by the Spanish in 1665 to combat smuggling). All through the 17th century, English buccaneers such as Henry Morgan and autonomous bands of Miskitos (a community of mixed-blood Indian and African slaves) regularly marauded inland settlements.

Buccaneer, 17th century

By the 18th century, exports of tobacco and hides to Europe began to boost national fortunes. Simple townships of adobe structures developed: Heredia (1706); San José (1737); and Alajuela (1782). Immigration from Europe gathered pace, and in the 1740s the increased demand for labor led to the forced resettlement of natives who had fled enslavement in the initial years of colonization and established communities in the Talamanca Mountains. On the whole, far-flung Costa Rica's parochial citizenry was spared the harsh taste of monopolistic, bureaucratic colonial rule; lacked an elite social class; and remained divorced from the bitter fight for independence from Spain that engulfed Central America at the end of the 18th century.

1723 Volcán Irazú erupts, destroying Cartago

1747 Talamanca Indians are forcibly resettled in the highlands

1808 Coffee introduced from Jamaica

1675 | 1700 | 1725 | 1750 | 1775 | 1800

1706 Heredia founded

1737 Villanueva de la Boca del Monte founded. Later renamed San José

1782 Alajuela founded

Coffee beans

The Formative Years of the Republic

The news that Spain had granted independence to the Central American nations on September 15, 1821, reached Costa Rica a month later. The country was torn between the four leading townships: the progressive citizens of San José and Alajuela favored total independence, while the conservative leaders of Cartago and Heredia preferred to join the newly formed Mexican empire. Although the four city councils met and drafted a constitution, the Pacto de Concordia, the discord erupted into a brief civil war in which the progressives triumphed. Costa Rica became a soverign state of the short-lived Federation of Central America, formed by Guatemalan General Francisco Morazán. Under a law called the Ley de Ambulancia, the capital was to rotate between the four cities every four years.

General Francisco Morazán

Costa Rica's independence from Spain coincided with a boom in coffee production and the evolution of a monied middle-class dedicated to public education and a liberal democracy unique on the isthmus. Juan Mora Fernández was elected the first head of state in 1824. In 1835, Braulio Carrillo came to power. A liberal autocrat, he set up legal codes, as well as promoting a centralized administration in San José and large-scale coffee production. San José's growing prominence under Carrillo led to great resentment, which culminated in the War of Leagues (La Guerra de la Liga) in September 1837, when the other three townships attacked San José, although without much success. In 1838, Carrillo declared Costa Rica's independence from the Federation, but was ousted by Morazán, on behalf of the emergent coffee oligarchy. Morazán was briefly named head of state in 1842, before being executed for attempting to conscript Costa Ricans to revive the Federation.

The Coffee Era

Costa Rica's smallholding farmers benefitted immensely from Europe's taste for coffee. Thousands of acres were planted, while income from the exports of *grano de oro* (golden grain) funded the construction of fine edifices in San José. This economic prosperity went hand in hand with a rare period of aggression, starting in 1856 when William Walker, a Tennessean adventurer, invaded Guanacaste. President Juan Rafael

Costa Rican workers picking ripe coffee berries, woodcut, 1880

Timeline

1821 The Central American nations gain independence

1823 Federation of Central America proclaimed. Civil war

1824 Guanacaste secedes from Nicaragua to join Costa Rica

1830s Coffee boom

1835–7 Ley de Ambulancia establishes rotating capitals

1837 San José becomes permanent capital

1838 Costa Rica withdraws from the Federation, declares independence

1849 *Cafetaleros* elevate Juan Rafael Mora to power, initiating political dominance of coffee barons

1856 William Walker invades Costa Rica

1869 General Tomás Guardia establishes compulsory, free education for all

1820 | 1830 | 1840 | 1850 | 1860 | 1870

President Juan Rafael Mora (1814–60)

Bas-relief in San José's Museo de Arte Costarricense

Mora raised a makeshift army that repulsed Walker but also created a group of ambitious, self-styled generals who from then on meddled in politics at the behest of their *cafetalero* (coffee baron) patrons. The most significant was General Tomás Guardia, who seized power in 1870. Guardia proved a progressive reformer, who promoted the construction of the Atlantic Railroad, which linked the highlands with Puerto Limón. The prodigious feat of hewing a railroad through the forested, rain-sodden, mountainous terrain was achieved by New York-born entrepreneur Minor Cooper Keith (1848–1929). Part of his terms for the project was a 3,100-sq-mile (8,050-sq-km) land lease in the Caribbean lowlands, on which he set up a banana plantation, and eventually established the influential United Fruit Company.

By the end of the 19th century, Costa Rica had evolved into a modern nation-state in which its citizens were active participants. When Bernardo Soto lost the presidential election in 1889 and refused to step down, street demonstrations forced his resignation. Similarly, students and women toppled war minister Federico Tinoco Granados, who staged a coup in 1917. However, the inter-war years were beset with labor unrest and social problems, which were exacerbated by a widening rift between the wealthy elite and impoverished underclass. Although the 1940–44 administration of President Rafael Angel Calderón established several bold social reforms, including a social security system, tensions rose as the country became increasingly polarized. The Calderón administration formed an anti-Nazi alliance with the Catholic Church and the Communist Party. This pitted itself against an equally unlikely anti-Calderonista alliance of intellectuals, labor activists, and the rural elite.

William Walker

In 1860, when he was executed, Walker was only 36. He was born in Nashville, and graduated as a doctor before starting to pursue a dream of extending slavery all over the Americas. In 1855, he rallied mercenaries and, with the blessing of President James Buchanan, invaded Nicaragua to establish a pro-US government. He went further, though, and proclaimed himself president. A year later he unsuccessfully attacked Costa Rica. Walker fled to New York, but returned to Central America in 1857, still filled with ambition. After a brief time in jail, he met his fate in front of a Honduran firing squad.

William Walker (1824–60)

1880 **1890** **1900** **1910** **1920** **1930** **1940**

1889 Liberal constitution drafted

1890 Atlantic Railroad completed

Atlantic Railroad

1897 A coffee tax finances construction of the Teatro Nacional in San José

1917 Federico Tinoco Granados seizes power

1925 Sigatoka disease devastates banana fields

1930s United Fruit Company expands its political and economic influence

1934 Workers win the right to unionize

1940–44 Calderón sponsors social reforms and founds the University of Costa Rica

1942 A German U-boat sinks a Costa Rican cargo vessel on July 2, leading to anti-German riots

The 1948 Civil War

In 1944, Teodoro Picando succeeded fellow party member Calderón after a violent and fraudulent election. Calderón ran for office four years later, but was defeated by a journalist, Otilio Ulate Blanco. Calderón objected, and the building housing the ballots was set ablaze by unknown arsonists. The Calderonista-dominated Congress annulled the election, and Ulate was arrested. This explosive situation paved the way for José "Don Pepe" Figueres, a radical utopian socialist. On March 11, 1948, Figueres declared the War of National Liberation to purify national politics. The badly trained and poorly equipped government forces were no match for Figueres' highly motivated guerrillas and, after 44 days of fierce fighting that claimed about 2,000 lives, Picando surrendered.

Figueres entered San José in triumph on March 29, and established the "Second Republic." He outlined the fundamental principles that have more or less shaped Costa Rica's political philosophy – social progress, ethical government, and solidarity with neighboring nations. Figueres nationalized the banking system, and enacted enlightened social reforms. In 1949, he forced congressional passage of a new constitution that disbanded the army, declared Costa Rica neutral, and extended universal suffrage to the Afro-Caribbean population. Still, key opponents and communists were executed in a bid to further consolidate his power. After 18 months as provisional president, Figueres handed the reins of government to Ulate.

Revolutionary soldier

President José Figueres leading the parade of victorious civilian troops, San José, 1949

Years of Prosperity and Terror

The 1950s, 60s, and 70s witnessed accelerating prosperity along with the rapid expansion of the welfare state. Costa Rica's stability was severely threatened, however, by developments in Nicaragua, where on July 19, 1979, the Somoza regime was toppled by left-wing Sandinistas. Somoza's right-wing supporters, the Contras, set up clandestine bases in Costa Rica and were supported by the CIA in their attempts to overthrow the Sandinistas. These activities turned the northern border into a war zone. Meanwhile, Costa Rica's banana and coffee crops failed, while a transfer of capital out of the country led to an economic freefall. The Reagan administration pressured President Luis Alberto Monge to show support for the Nicaraguan right-wing paramilitary operations on Costa Rican soil in exchange for

Timeline

1948 The "Second Republic" established

1949 New constitution adopted; Figueres later hands power to the winner of the 1948 election

1963 Volcán Irazú erupts during President John F. Kennedy's visit

1945 | 1950 | 1955 | 1960 | 1965 | 1970

1948 Figueres launches War of National Liberation

1950s Pan-American Highway (Carretera Interamericana) connects Nicaragua and Panama

1955 Nicaragua invades Costa Rica but is repulsed at Santa Rosa

Social security symbol

1970s Expansion of social security system

economic aid. Costa Rica's neutrality was dangerously compromised.

In 1986, Figueres' protegé Oscar Arias Sánchez became president. The youthful leader protested against the activities of the US-backed Contras, and negotiated a peaceful resolution of regional conflicts. As a result, in August 1987, leaders of five Central American nations signed a treaty committing to free elections and a cessation of violence. Arias was awarded the Nobel Peace Prize for his role as mediator. He was succeeded in 1990 by Rafael Angel Calderón, son of the great reformer. The conservative Calderón administration introduced reforms to alleviate the country's international debt – at the time the world's largest per capita. Austerity measures helped, to some extent, to regenerate Costa Rica's economy. However, sustained economic growth in recent decades has not alleviated the country's numerous social problems.

Pedestrians crossing Avenida 2, San José

The Environmental Era

In a curious twist of fate, Calderón was replaced in 1994 by José María Figueres, son of Don Pepe, the elder Calderón's political nemesis. The 1980s had seen the beginnings of a huge tourism boom, which was fueled by Costa Rica's stewardship of its natural resources. Figueres committed himself to environmental protection, but several economic scandals, anti-government demonstrations, escalating poverty, and a series of natural disasters bedeviled his administration. The troubles continued with the subsequent administrations of Miguel Angel Rodríguez (1998–2002) and Abel Pacheco de la Espriella (2002–). Their attempts to privatize the electricity and telecommunications industries provoked nationwide strikes and civil unrest. This in no way put a stop to the phenomenal development of ecotourism, however, as the country became an increasingly popular destination for intrepid outdoor travelers. Recent years have witnessed the creation of more and more protected areas and new restrictions on logging.

José "Don Pepe" Figueres

"Don Pepe" (1906–90)

Figueres, born on September 25, 1906, to Catalan immigrants, was largely self-educated. He studied in the USA in the 1920s, and returned to Costa Rica inspired by utopian ideals. After the 1942 anti-German riots, Don Pepe denounced the Calderón government in a radio address, during which he was arrested and exiled to Mexico. On his return in 1944, he set up a guerrilla training camp at La Lucha Sin Fin (The Endless Struggle), a farm high in the mountains south of San José, before launching the War of National Liberation. He founded the Partido de Liberación Nacional and was elected to two terms as president (1953–7 and 1970–74). He died on June 8, 1990.

Oscar Arias

1980s Costa Rica-based Contras destabilize the country

1987 Arias wins Nobel Peace Prize

1991 Earthquake causes damage on April 22

1997 President Clinton in Costa Rica for summit of American leaders

2003 Supreme Court rules that former presidents may be re-elected

1975 | 1980 | 1985 | 1990 | 1995 | 2000

1981 Costa Rica defaults on international loans

1990s Large-scale immigration strains the social system. Drug trafficking accelerates. Costa Rica established as a world-leader in ecotourism

1994 Banco Anglo Costarricense declares bankruptcy

2000 Attempts to privatize electricity and telecommunications generate civil unrest

Costa Rica Area by Area

Costa Rica at a Glance

Brimming with natural wonders, Costa Rica's incredibly diverse terrain offers lush rain- and cloud forests that host an array of colorful fauna, craggy mountains, smoke-spewing volcanoes, and stunning beaches in every shade from gold to taupe to black. Wildlife and adventure activities abound, ranging from canopy tours and turtle-watching to scuba diving and whitewater rafting. It is best to concentrate on the national parks and other natural attractions; very few towns are of interest. This guide divides the country into seven regions; each area is color-coded as shown here.

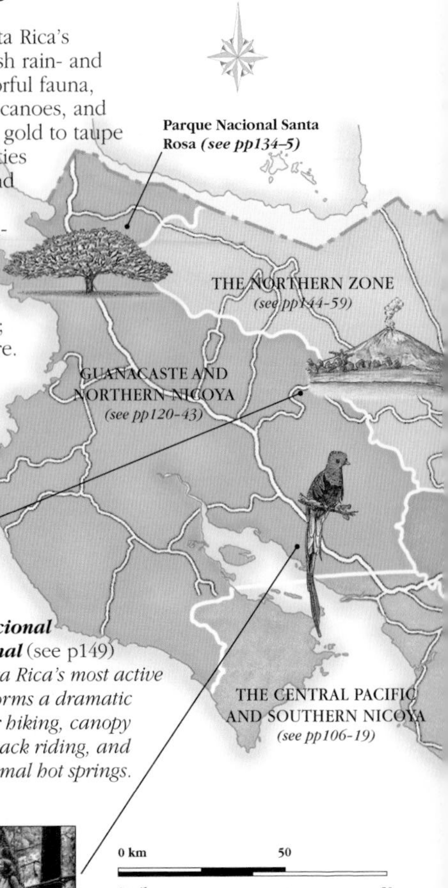

Parque Nacional Volcán Arenal (see p149) *features Costa Rica's most active volcano. It forms a dramatic backdrop for hiking, canopy tours, horseback riding, and soaks in thermal hot springs.*

Monteverde (see pp124–8) *is famous for its cloud forest reserves, which draw birders eager for a sighting of resplendent quetzals.*

Isla del Coco

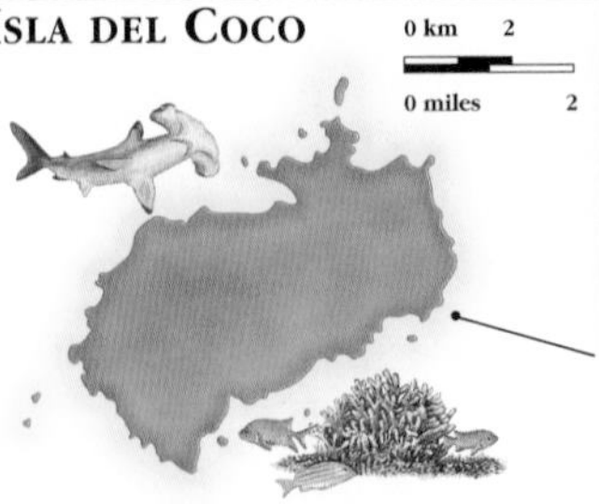

Isla del Coco (see p193), *off the southwest coast, is remote and rugged. Hammerhead and whale sharks draw scuba divers.*

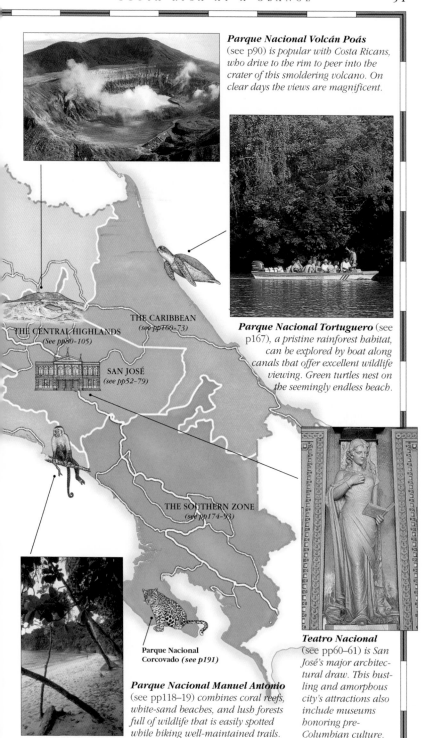

Parque Nacional Volcán Poás (see p90) *is popular with Costa Ricans, who drive to the rim to peer into the crater of this smoldering volcano. On clear days the views are magnificent.*

Parque Nacional Tortuguero (see p167), *a pristine rainforest habitat, can be explored by boat along canals that offer excellent wildlife viewing. Green turtles nest on the seemingly endless beach.*

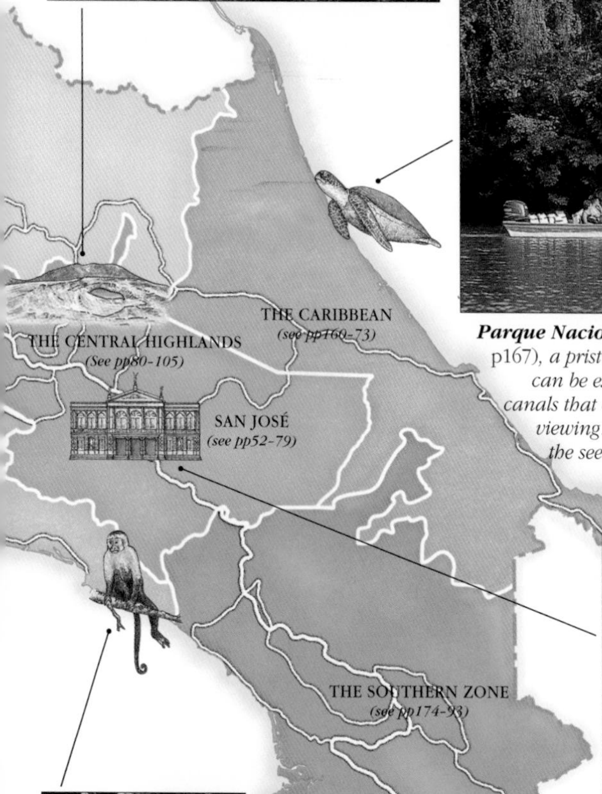

Teatro Nacional (see pp60–61) *is San José's major architectural draw. This bustling and amorphous city's attractions also include museums honoring pre-Columbian culture.*

Parque Nacional Manuel Antonio (see pp118–19) *combines coral reefs, white-sand beaches, and lush forests full of wildlife that is easily spotted while hiking well-maintained trails.*

San José

Nestled amid craggy peaks, *the capital city enjoys a splendid setting and idyllic weather. Its magnificent Teatro Nacional and world-class museums add to San José's attractions. The city's strongest draw, however, is its location in the heart of Costa Rica, which is ideal for hub-and-spoke touring. For many visitors, San José is their first experience of the country, providing an intriguing introduction to the pleasures that await farther afield.*

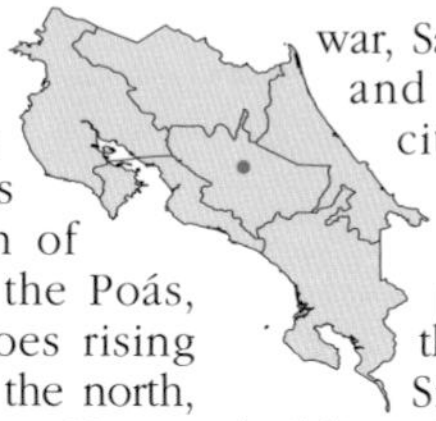

Affectionately called *chepe* (the local nickname for anyone named José) by its inhabitants, San José is perched at an elevation of 3,800 ft (1,150 m), with the Poás, Barva, and Irazú Volcanoes rising gracefully over the city to the north, and the rugged Talamanca Mountains to the south. Temperatures are a springlike 25°C (76°F) year-round, and the air is crisp and clear thanks to near-constant breezes.

Founded in 1737, San José grew very slowly through its first 100 years. Its creation on the eve of the coffee boom in the heart of coffee country, however, was advantageous. By 1823, the town had grown to challenge Cartago – the then capital – for supremacy. Following a brief civil war, San José was named capital and quickly eclipsed other cities as prominent *cafetaleros* (coffee barons) imported skilled European artisans to beautify the city with fine structures. Since the 1960s, high-rise buildings and sprawling slum *barrios* (neighborhoods) have changed the profile of this city of one-third of a million people. Still, San José has its own charm. The main tourist sights, including the Teatro Nacional (National Theater), the gold and jade museums, and numerous plazas, are centered around the city core, within walking distance of one another. Everywhere, traffic squeezes tight at rush hour, when Costa Rican civility gives way to dog-eat-dog driving.

Varieties of fruit arranged temptingly in stalls at the Mercado Central

◁ **Statue in the lavishly decorated foyer of San José's Teatro Nacional**

Exploring San José

Downtown San José features the city's top places of interest. The dazzling Teatro Nacional on Avenida 2, graced by Baroque and Neoclassical architecture, is San José's most remarkable building. The nearby Museo del Oro Precolombino, as well as the Museo de Jade Fidel Tristán Castro and the Museo Nacional in the east – all of which display pre-Columbian artifacts – are also major attractions. Another must-see is the Centro Costarricense de Ciencias y Cultura, to the northwest, with its superb rotating art exhibitions. Busts of prominent historical figures dot Parque España and Parque Nacional. The main historic quarter, Barrio Amón, boasts fine colonial structures along Avenida 9, while the suburb of Escazú offers excellent dining and a lively nightlife.

A quiet, tree-lined street in a residential locality of San José

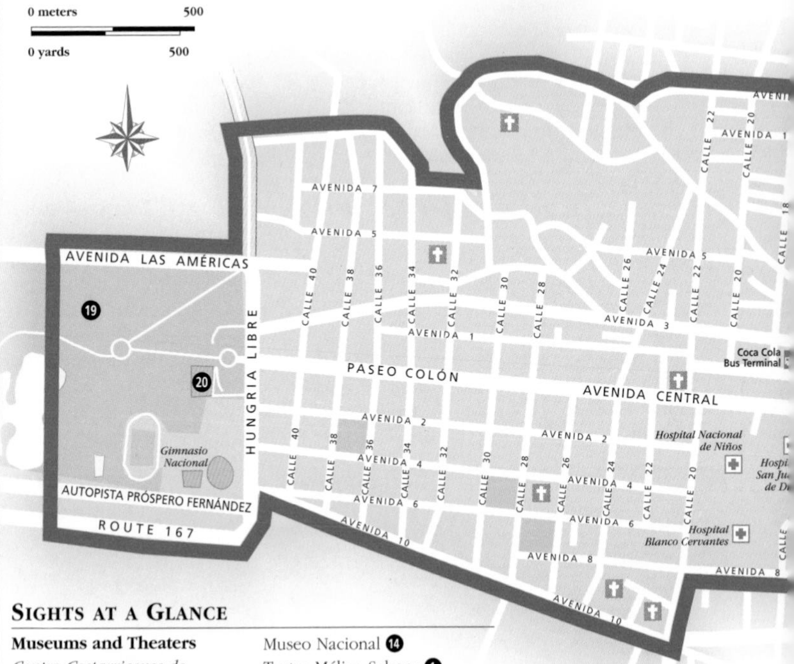

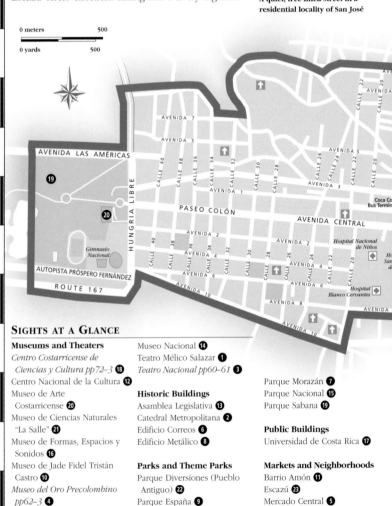

Sights at a Glance

Museums and Theaters
Centro Costarricense de Ciencias y Cultura pp72–3 ⓲
Centro Nacional de la Cultura ⓬
Museo de Arte Costarricense ⓴
Museo de Ciencias Naturales "La Salle" ㉑
Museo de Formas, Espacios y Sonidos ⓰
Museo de Jade Fidel Tristán Castro ⓾
Museo del Oro Precolombino pp62–3 ❹
Museo Nacional ⓮
Teatro Mélico Salazar ❶
Teatro Nacional pp60–61 ❸

Historic Buildings
Asamblea Legislativa ⓭
Catedral Metropolitana ❷
Edificio Correos ❻
Edificio Metálico ❽

Parks and Theme Parks
Parque Diversiones (Pueblo Antiguo) ㉒
Parque España ❾
Parque Morazán ❼
Parque Nacional ⓯
Parque Sabana ⓳

Public Buildings
Universidad de Costa Rica ⓱

Markets and Neighborhoods
Barrio Amón ⓫
Escazú ㉓
Mercado Central ❺

Getting ready for some angling at the man-made lake in Parque Sabana

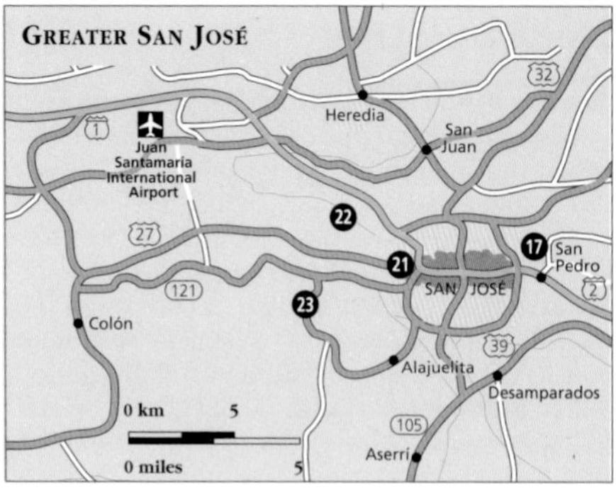

KEY

Area of the main map

SEE ALSO

- ***Where to Stay*** pp200–203
- ***Where to Eat*** pp224–6

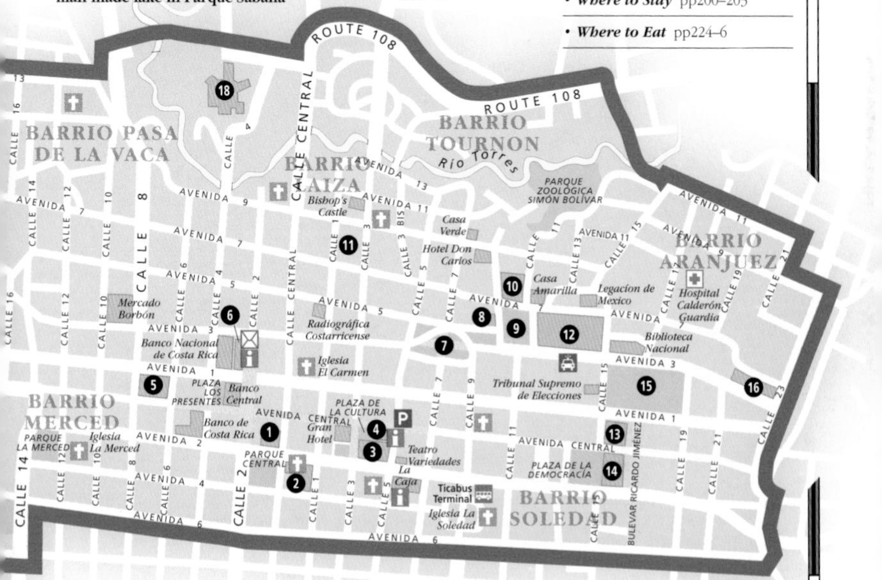

KEY

- Sight/place of interest
- International airport
- Bus station
- Tourist information
- Parking
- Post office
- Hospital
- Church
- Expressway
- Pedestrian street

GETTING AROUND

The main sights, concentrated in downtown San José, are best explored on foot. To explore farther afield, take a taxi – this is a good way of getting around the warren of narrow, congested, one-way streets. Inner-city buses should be avoided, as also self-drive cars for those not used to the aggressive driving style of Costa Ricans. Jose Santamaría International Airport and Tobias Bolaños domestic airport are located 10 miles (17 km) northwest and 4 miles (6 km) west of downtown respectively. The international airport is well-connected by airport taxis and buses to the city center; the domestic airport is served by taxis. For more details, see pages 270–71.

Street-by-Street: San José Center

Laid out in a grid of narrow, heavily trafficked one-way streets, San José's tightly condensed core contains the city's most significant sights. The main artery is the broad Avenida 2, which is thronged with honking taxis and buses threading past tree-shaded Parque Central. Running parallel to it and to the north is the Avenida Central, a pedestrian precinct lined with department stores, specialist shops, and places to eat. At the heart of this stroll-and-shop area lies the small concrete Plaza de la Cultura, which hums with activity all day – it is a popular meeting place for young people and is packed with hawkers as well as musicians and other entertainers.

Teatro Mélico Salazar
Dating from the 1920s, this theater has a Neoclassical façade and a simple interior ❶

Avenida 2
This bustling avenue is lined with important buildings, including banks, between Calles 1 and 3. Traffic flows eastward on this four lane-wide avenue, which slopes downhill east of Calle 3.

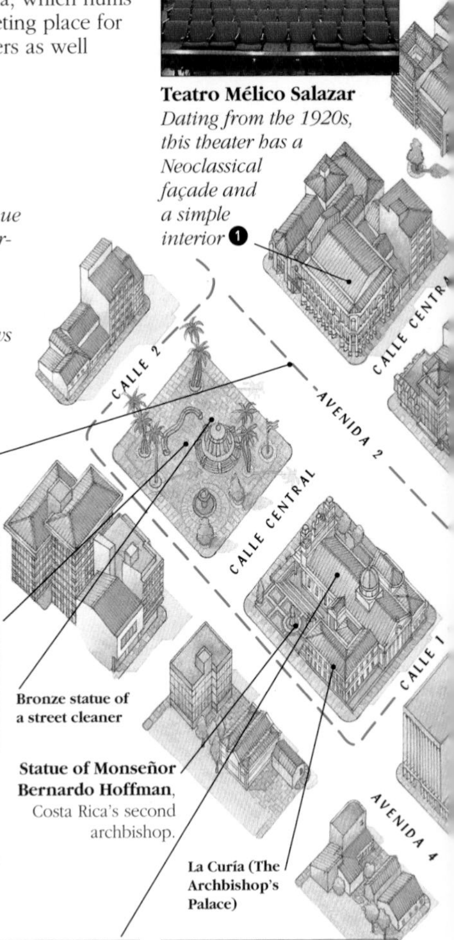

Parque Central
Laid out in 1885 and shaded by palms and guanacaste trees, the compact central plaza has an unusual bandstand, which is supported by arches. Beneath it is the children's library, Biblioteca Carmen Lyra.

Bronze statue of a street cleaner

Statue of Monseñor Bernardo Hoffman, Costa Rica's second archbishop.

La Curía (The Archbishop's Palace)

★ Catedral Metropolitana
The blue-domed Metropolitan Cathedral, built in 1871 in a simple Greek Orthodox style, features an elaborate altar ❷

Star Sights

- ★ Catedral Metropolitana
- ★ Museo del Oro Precolombino
- ★ Teatro Nacional

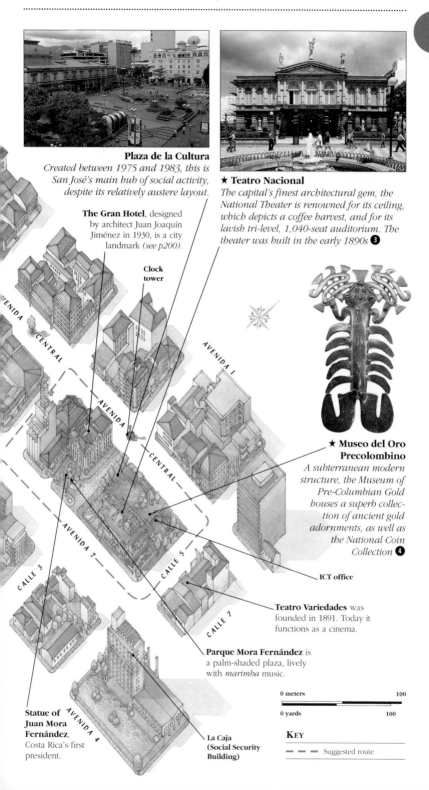

Plaza de la Cultura
Created between 1975 and 1983, this is San José's main hub of social activity, despite its relatively austere layout.

★ Teatro Nacional
The capital's finest architectural gem, the National Theater is renowned for its ceiling, which depicts a coffee harvest, and for its lavish tri-level, 1,040-seat auditorium. The theater was built in the early 1890s ❸

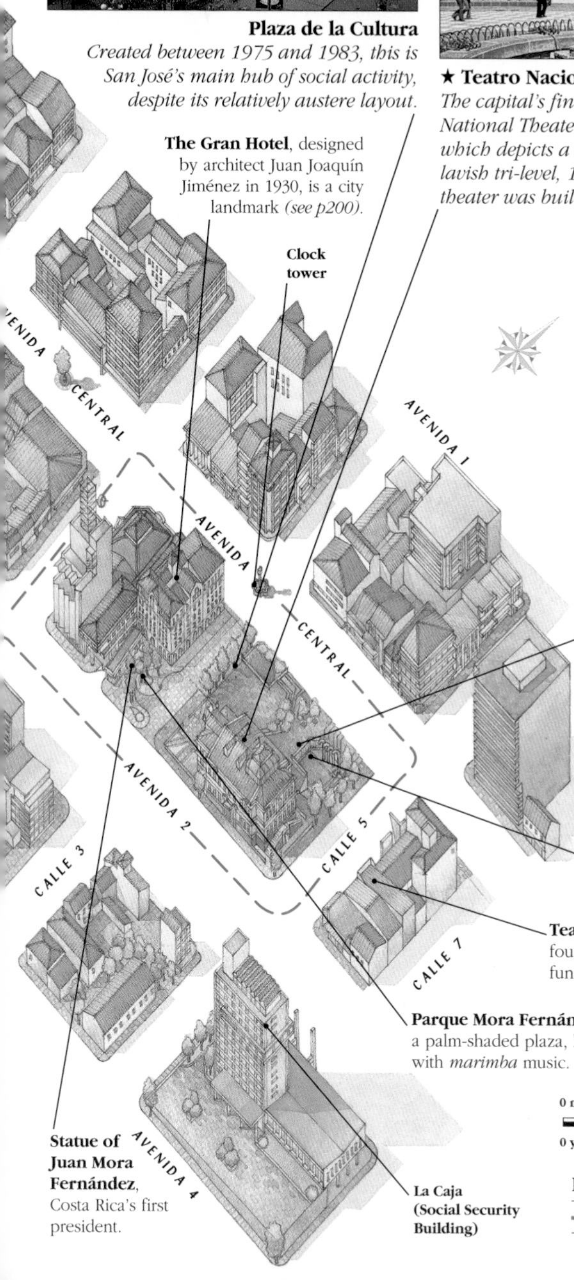

The Gran Hotel, designed by architect Juan Joaquín Jiménez in 1930, is a city landmark *(see p200).*

Clock tower

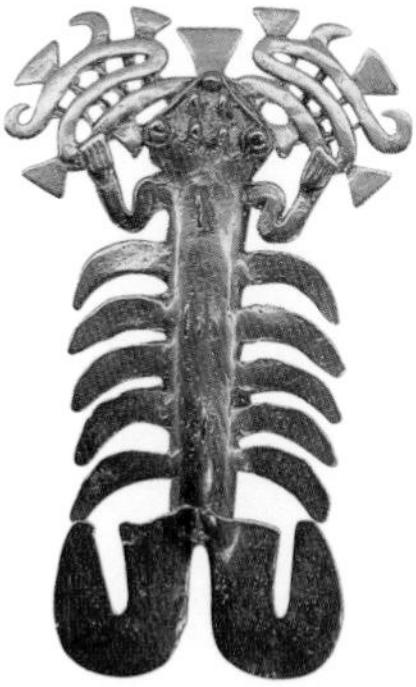

★ Museo del Oro Precolombino
A subterranean modern structure, the Museum of Pre-Columbian Gold houses a superb collection of ancient gold adornments, as well as the National Coin Collection ❹

ICT office

Teatro Variedades was founded in 1891. Today it functions as a cinema.

Parque Mora Fernández is a palm-shaded plaza, lively with *marimba* music.

Statue of Juan Mora Fernández, Costa Rica's first president.

La Caja (Social Security Building)

0 meters 100

0 yards 100

KEY

— — — Suggested route

The horseshoe-shaped auditorium of Teatro Mélico Salazar

Teatro Mélico Salazar ❶

Map 1 C4. Calle Central and Ave 2. *233-5424.* *8am–4pm Mon–Fri.* *by appointment.*

ONE OF THE city's landmarks, this theater was built in 1928 as the Teatro Raventós, and was renamed in 1986 after Manuel "Mélico" Salazar Zúñiga (1887–1950), a celebrated Costa Rican tenor. Designed by architect José Fabio Garnier, it has a Neoclassical façade adorned with fluted Corinthian pilasters. To the left of the entrance is a larger-than-life bronze bust of Zúñiga. To the right is a bas-relief plaque honoring José Raventós Gual, who had the theater built.

The handsome lobby, in checkered green-and-black tile, leads into a triple-tiered, horseshoe-shaped auditorium, which hosts theatrical and musical events, as well as folk shows. The auditorium boasts a striking parquet wooden floor beneath a wood-paneled ceiling, which is decorated with a simple mural and a wrought-iron chandelier.

Catedral Metropolitana ❷

Map 1 C4. Calle Central and Aves 2/4. *221-3820.* *6am–6pm Mon–Sat, 6am–9pm Sun.*

SAN JOSÉ'S pre-eminent church, the Metropolitan Cathedral was built in 1871 to replace the original cathedral, which had been destroyed by an earthquake in 1820. Designed by Eusebio Rodríguez, the austere-looking structure combines Greek Orthodox, Neoclassical, and Baroque styles. Its linear façade is supported by an arcade of Doric columns and topped by a Neoclassical pediment with steeples on each side. Inside, a vaulted ceiling runs the length of the nave, supported by two rows of fluted columns. In a glass case to the left of the entrance is a life-size statue of Christ.

Although entirely lacking the ornate Baroque gilt of many other Latin American churches, the cathedral has many fine features, notably an exquisite Colonial-style tiled floor and beautiful stained-glass windows depicting biblical scenes. The main altar, beneath a cupola, comprises a simple wooden base atop a marble plinth and supports a wooden figure of Christ and cherubs. Behind it, a half-cupola scalloped into the wall contains a mural showing Christ and the Holy Father side by side.

Pillared façade of the austere Catedral Metropolitana

To the left of the main altar is the Capilla del Santísimo (Chapel of the Holy Sacrament), which has walls and ceilings decorated with wooden quadrants painted with floral motifs. The short gallery that leads to the chapel contains a glass-and-gilt coffin with a naked statue of Christ draped with a sash in the colors of the Costa Rican flag.

To the south of the cathedral is **La Curía** (The Palace of the Archbishop), built in 1887. The two-story structure was remodeled in 2002, and is closed to the public. A small garden in front features a life-size bronze statue of Monseñor Bernardo Augusto Thiel Hoffman (1850–1901), the German-born second archbishop of Costa Rica. Hoffman lies buried in the crypt of the cathedral, alongside former president Tomás Guardia *(see p45)*.

Fountain on Avenida Central

Teatro Nacional ❸

See pp60–61.

Museo del Oro Precolombino ❹

See pp62–3.

Mercado Central ❺

Map 1 B3. Calles 6/8 and Aves Central/1. *295-6104.* *8am–4pm Mon–Sat.*

AN INTRIGUING curiosity, San José's Central Market was built in 1881. The building, which takes up an entire block northwest of the Catedral Metropolitana, is itself rather uninspiring, but its warren of narrow alleyways, hemmed in by more than 200 stalls, immerse visitors in a slice of Costa Rican life. This quintessential Latin American market thrives as a chaotic emporium of the exotic, with every conceivable item for sale, from herbal remedies and fresh-cut flowers to snakeskin boots and saddles for *sabaneros* (cowboys).

Toward the center, *sodas* (food stalls) offer inexpensive cooked meals sold at the counter. The market extends one block north to **Mercado Borbón**, which has stalls of butchers, fishmongers, and fruit sellers, and buyers crowded in as thick as sardines. Next to the market's entrance on the southeast corner, there are plaques honoring important political figures.

Pickpockets operate within the tightly packed alleys of the market. Remember to leave your valuables in the hotel safe when you venture out. It is best to tuck your camera well out of sight when it is not in use.

The Edificio Correos, featuring a blend of architectural styles

Edificio Correos ❻

Map 1 B3. Calle 2 and Aves 1/3.
223-9766. *7:30am–6pm Mon–Fri, 7:30am–noon Sat.*
Museo Filatélico de Costa Rica
223-6918. *8am–4:30pm Mon–Fri.* *public hols.*

The building housing the main post office, or Correo Central, was completed in 1917. Designed by Luis Llach in eclectic style, it has a pea-green reinforced concrete façade, which is embellished with Corinthian pilasters. The arched centerpiece is topped by a shield and supported by angels bearing the national coat of arms. There is a tourist information office on the ground floor. The post office is abuzz with the comings and goings of locals picking up their mail at *apartados* (post office boxes) that fill the ground floor of the two-storey atrium.

Philatelists may find a thrill, as well as rare stamps, in the small **Museo Filatélico de Costa Rica** (Philatelic Museum of Costa Rica), which opened in 1985 and takes up three rooms on the second floor. The first room has a fine collection of old telephones and telegraphic equipment that goes back more than a 100 years.

The collection of stamps occupies the other two rooms, which also have exhibits on the history of philately in Costa Rica. The nation's first stamp, from 1863, is displayed here. Other exhibits include important and rare stamps from abroad, including the English Penny Black. The museum hosts a stamp exchange on the first Saturday of every month.

Statue of Juan Mora Fernández opposite Edificio Correos

The Edificio Correos is fronted by a pedestrian plaza shaded by fig trees. Towering over the plaza is a statue of the first president of Costa Rica, Juan Mora Fernández, who was in power from 1824 to 1828.

Nearby, to the southwest of the Edificio Correos is another square, **Plaza Los Presentes**, which is dominated by *Los Presentes*, a contemporary monument in bronze. Created in 1979 by well-known sculptor Fernando Calvo, the monument consists of statues of a dozen Costa Rican *campesinos* (peasant farmers).

Los Presentes **by Fernando Calvo, in Plaza Los Presentes, near Edificio Correos**

Teatro Nacional ❸

Statue of Music

CONSIDERED THE finest historic building in San José, the National Theater was conceived in 1890, when Spanish-born prima donna Adelina Patti sidestepped Costa Rica while on a Central American tour due to the lack of a suitable venue. This spurred the ruling coffee barons to levy a tax on coffee exports to fund the building of a grand theater. Locals claim, disputably, that the structure was modeled on the Paris Opera House. Completed in 1897, it was inaugurated with a performance of *El Fausto de Gournod* by the Paris Opera. Declared a National Monument in 1965, the theater has a lavish Neo-Baroque interior, replete with statues, paintings, marble staircases, and parquet floors made of 10 species of hardwood.

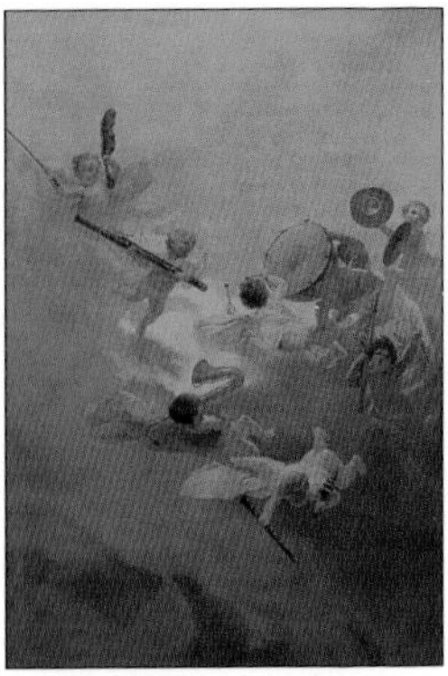

***La Danza de Vignami*, painted on the ceiling of the auditorium**

Teatro Café
The coffee shop adjoining the lobby is decorated in black and white tile, and has marble-topped tables. The ceiling is painted with a triptych.

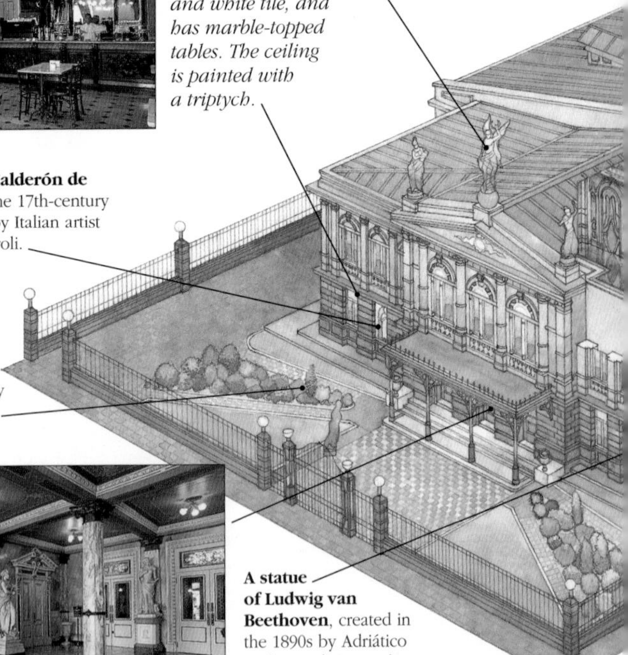

Allegorical statues of the Muses of Music, Dance, and Fame top the Neoclassical façade.

Statue of Calderón de la Barca, the 17th-century dramatist, by Italian artist Adriático Froli.

The small garden is formally patterned and features a life-size marble statue of a female flautist (1997) by Jorge Jiménez Deredia.

A statue of Ludwig van Beethoven, created in the 1890s by Adriático Froli, stands in an alcove.

Entrance Lobby
With its pink marble floor and bronze-tipped Corinthian marble columns, the lobby hints at the splendors to come. The doors are topped by gilt pediments adorned with lions' faces. The wooden ceiling has a simple floral motif.

STAR FEATURES

- ★ Auditorium
- ★ Coffee Mural
- ★ Foyer

★ Coffee Mural
Depicting a coffee harvest, the huge mural on the ceiling of the intermezzo, between the lobby and the auditorium, was painted in 1897 by Milanese artist Aleardo Villa. The scene is full of errors, with coffee being shown as a coastal crop instead of a highland one.

Visitors' Checklist

Map 1 C4. Calles 3/5 and Ave 2. *221-9417.* *Cemeterio-Estadio.* *9am–4pm Mon–Fri; 9am–noon and 1–5pm Sat.* ***Shows*** *Orquestra Sinfónia Nacional (National Symphony Orchestra) performances Mar–Dec: 8pm Thu and Fri; 10:30am Sun.* *9am–5pm Mon–Sat.*

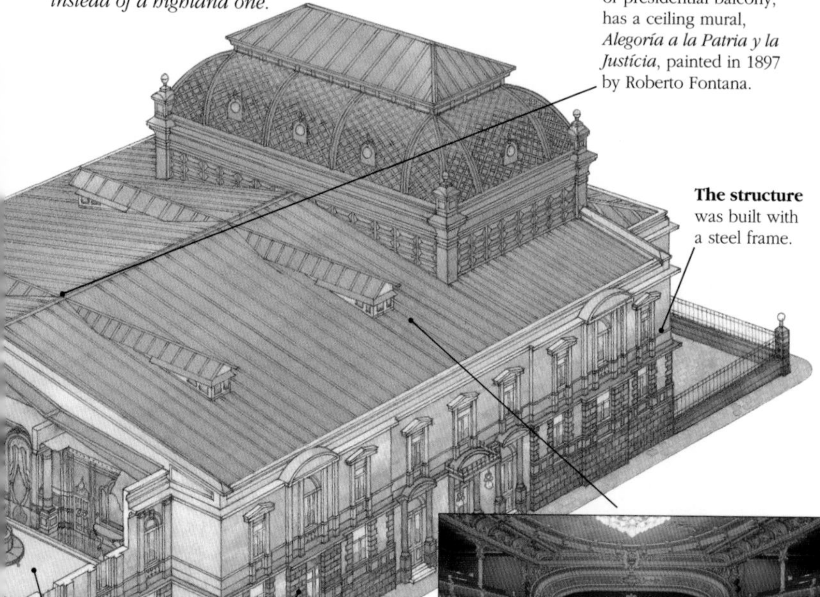

The Palco Presidencial, or presidential balcony, has a ceiling mural, *Alegoría a la Patria y la Justícia*, painted in 1897 by Roberto Fontana.

The structure was built with a steel frame.

The exterior of the building is of sandstone.

★ Auditorium
Dominated by a rotunda ceiling with a mural of cherubs and deities, the red-and-gold auditorium has three floors, a horseshoe shape, and wrought-iron seats. The stage can be lowered and raised.

★ Foyer
A double staircase with gold-gilt banisters leads to the magnificent foyer, which features pink marble and a surfeit of crystals, gilt mirrors, and gold-leaf embellishments. Splendid murals show scenes of Costa Rican life.

Museo del Oro Precolombino ❹

Frog figurine in gold

OCCUPYING THE starkly modern subterranean space beneath the Plaza de la Cultura and managed by the Banco Central de Costa Rica, the Museum of Pre-Columbian Gold boasts a dazzling display of ancient gold items. The collection consists of more than 1,600 pieces of pre-Columbian gold dating back to AD 500. Most of the amulets, earrings, shamanic animal figures, and erotic statuettes exhibited here originated in southwest Costa Rica, attesting to the sophisticated art of the Diquis culture. The uses and crafting of these items are demonstrated with the help of models and other displays, which also depict the social and cultural evolution of pre-Columbian cultures.

★ Museo Numismático
The National Coin Museum exhibits date back to 1516. The displays include coins, bank notes, and unofficial currency such as coffee tokens.

The First Coin
Costa Rica's first coin, called the Medio Escudo, was minted in 1825, when the country was part of the Federation of Central America (see p44).

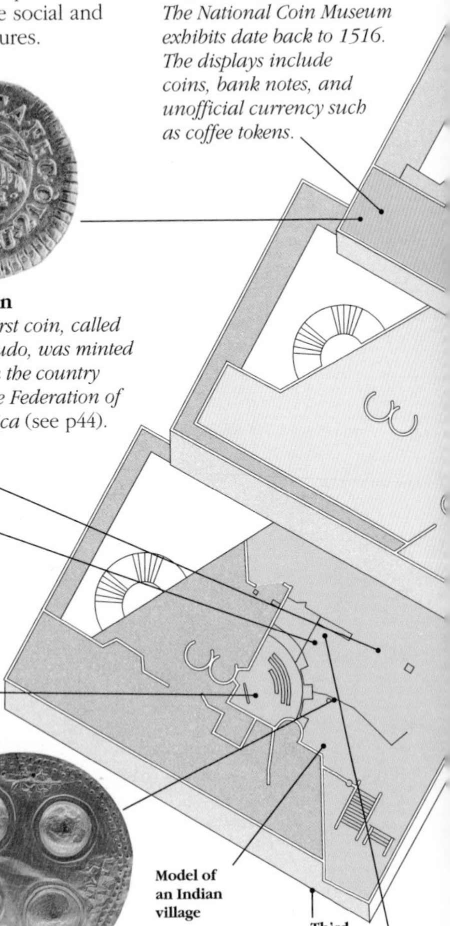

Frog figurines, a traditional symbol of life for indigenous tribes, are among the gold displays.

Auditorium

Model of an Indian village

Third level

★ El Guerrero
The most stunning piece is the life-size warrior adorned with gold ornaments, including a gold headband, chest disc (paten)*, amulets, and ankle rings. Gold objects were a symbol of authority.*

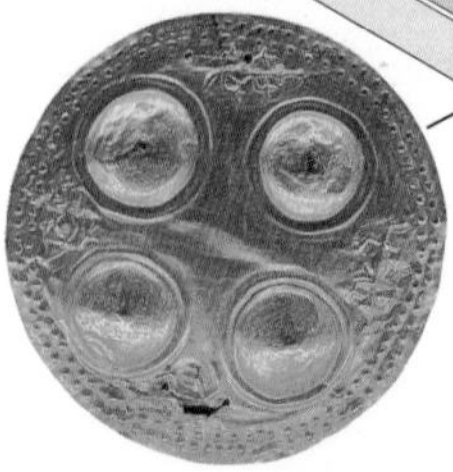

Gold Craftsmanship
This section explains how pre-Columbian cultures utilized repoussé, the technique of decorating metal surfaces by hammering from the back.

El Curandero (The Healer) is a life-size model of a "medicine man" performing a ritual healing using medicinal plants.

STAR FEATURES

- ★ **El Guerrero**
- ★ **Museo Numismático**

Casa de Moneda
Displaying the history of minting in Costa Rica, this section also has antiquarian coin stamps. Costa Rica's coins are today made in Chile.

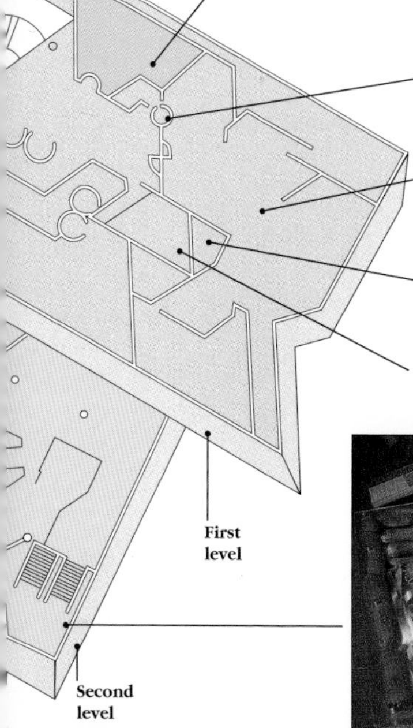

Visitors' Checklist

Map 1 C4. Plaza de la Cultura, Calle 5 and Aves Central/2.
243-4202. all downtown buses. 9:30am– 4:30pm daily. by appt. www.museosdelbanco central.org

Key

- ☐ Casa de Moneda
- ☐ Museo Numismático
- ☐ Temporary exhibition gallery
- ☐ Pre-Columbian culture and metallurgy
- ☐ Gold objects
- ☐ Non-exhibition space

Gallery Guide

The museum occupies three floors below the plaza. Beyond the entrance, a broad foyer leads past the Casa de Moneda to the Museo Numismático. Adjacent, a spiral staircase descends to the second level, which depicts the evolution of pre-Columbian culture and metallurgy. The third level features an auditorium as well as the main gallery, which displays a permanent exhibition of ancient gold items.

Finca 4 Site
This is a replica of a pre-Columbian grave unearthed in the 1950s. Discovered on a banana plantation in southeastern Costa Rica, the grave contained 88 gold objects.

Subterranean Vault
Accessed from Calle 5 by a broad staircase, the Gold Museum is housed in an underground space protected by steel doors.

Lost Wax Technique

Pre-Columbian groups, notably the Chibchas and Diquis of the Pacific southwest, were masterful goldsmiths, skilled in the use of the "lost wax" technique. Here, the desired form is carved in wax, then molded with clay and baked. The wax melts, leaving a negative into which molten metal is poured to attain the required result. Most pre-Columbian pieces were alloys of gold and copper, with the alloy called *tumbaga* being the most commonly used.

Gold shaman figurine

CORREOS TELEGRAFOS

The intriguing Edificio Metálico, constructed entirely of metal

Parque Morazán 7

Map 2 D3 Calles 5/9 and Aves 3/5.

LAID OUT AS Plaza González Víquez on the site of an open-air reservoir in 1930, this small park was later renamed after Francisco Morazán *(see p44)*. The Honduran-born Central American federalist served briefly as president of Costa Rica before being executed in 1842. Shaded by tabebuia (also called trumpet trees) that bloom in the dry season, the park is popular with office workers, schoolchildren, and lovers, although it is to be avoided at night when transvestites gather.

The park's four ornate iron gateways are topped by Roman urns. At its center is the domed Neoclassical **Templo de Música**, built in 1920. Busts honor Morazán and other luminaries such as South American liberator Simón Bolívar (1783–1830). To the park's southwest is a bronze statue of former president Julio García, seated in a chair. Facing the park on the northeast, is an 11-ft (3.5-m) tall statue of another former president, Daniel Quiros, by Costa Rican artist Olger Villegas.

Edificio Metálico 8

Map 2 D3. Calle 9 and Aves 5/7. *222-0026.*

CONSTRUCTED entirely of prefabricated pieces of metal, this intriguing San José edifice, standing between Parque Morazán and Parque España, was designed by French architect Charles Thirio. The metal pieces were cast in Belgium in 1892 and shipped to Costa Rica for welding and assembly in situ. Since then, it has functioned as an elementary school, the Escuela Buenaventura Corrales y Julia Lang. A small bust of Minerva, the Roman goddess of wisdom, sits on top of its imposing Neoclassical façade. Take in a bird's-eye view of its exterior from the lobby of the Museo de Jade Fidel Tristán Castro across the street.

Carved pillars at Casa Amarilla

Parque España 9

Map 2 D3. Calles 9/11 and Aves 3/7. **Casa Amarilla** *223-7555.* *8am–4pm Mon–Fri.* *by appointment.*

SHADED BY densely packed trees and bamboo groves, this leafy plaza is pleasantly full of birdsong. It was here, in 1903, that the Costa Rican national anthem, written by José María Zeledón Brenes (1877–1949) and Manual María Gutiérrez (1829–87), was first performed.

The Colonial-style pavilion in Parque España

On the northeast corner, a quaint Colonial-style *pabellón* (pavilion), erected in 1947, is inlaid with sepia-toned ceramic murals of the apparition of the Lady of Los Angeles, the church of Orosi, and the cathedral of Heredia. A patinated life-size statue of conquistador Juan Vásquez de Coronado *(see p42)* stands at the southwest corner of the park. Brick pathways wind past busts of important figures, including Queen Isabel II of Spain (1830–1904) and philanthropist Andrew Carnegie (1835–1919). Facing the northwest side of the park is the ocher-colored, stuccoed **Casa Amarilla** (Yellow House). Designed by architect Henry Wiffield in an ornate Spanish Baroque style, it was completed in 1916 to house the Pan-American Court of Justice. In later years it served as the Presidential Residence and the Asamblea Legislativa. Today, the Foreign Relations Ministry has its offices here.

The most striking element of Casa Amarilla is the grand ornamental lintel above the front door. The huge ceiba tree outside was planted in 1963 by US President John F. Kennedy when he attended the Summit of Central America Presidents.

The towering building west of the Casa Amarilla is the **Instituto Nacional de Seguro** (INS or the National Institute of Insurance). In its front courtyard, paying homage to the institution of the family, is *La Familia*, a huge sculpture by Francisco Zúñiga *(see p19)*.

The **Legación de Mexico**, 55 yd (50 m) east along Avenida 7, was built in 1924 and is a splendid example of Colonial-style architecture. The armistice of the 1948 War of Liberation was signed here.

◁ The pedestrian plaza in front of the Edificio Correos

Museo de Jade Fidel Tristán Castro ⑩

Map 2 D3. Calle 9 and Ave 7. *287-6034. 8:30am–3:30pm Mon–Fri. public hols.*

LOCATED ON THE top floor of the National Institute of Insurance (INS) building, the Fidel Tristán Castro Jade Museum contains the largest collection of pre-Columbian jade in the Americas. It was founded in 1977 by Fidel Tristán Castro, the first president of the INS. The collection consists of adzes, ceremonial heads, and decorative pieces from 500 BC to AD 800. There are also *metates* (grinding tables made of volcanic stone), ceramics, and gold ornamentation. The Sala de Jade displays jade pendants in kaleidoscopic hues of green and blue, exquisitely backlit to demonstrate their translucent quality. The 11th-floor museum lobby, which contains José Sancho's white marble sculpture *Plenitude*, offers splendid panoramic views of the city through plate-glass windows.

Barrio Amón ⑪

Map 1 C2. Calles Central/9 and Aves 7/13.

THE RICHEST architectural collection in San José is the complex of historic homes in this residential *barrio* (neighborhood), founded in the 1890s by French immigrant Amón Fasileau Duplantier. On the verge of decay until recently, the area is now undergoing restoration.

The most interesting homes are along Avenida 9; the stretch between Calles 3 and 7 is lined with beautiful ceramic wall murals by local artist Fernando Matamoros showing traditional Costa Rican scenes.

Begin at Calle 11, where No. 980 is a two-story colonial mansion boasting a life-size *campesino* (peasant) in precast concrete gazing over the wrought-iron railing. At Calle 7, the **Hotel Don Carlos** *(see p200)* was formerly the residence of President Tomás Guardia *(see p45)* and is a curious blend of Art Deco and Neoclassical styles. One block west, at the corner of Calle 5, is the **Casa Verde**, a clapboard building of New Orleans pine, dating to 1910 and notable for its soaring lounge spectacularly lit by a stained-glass atrium.

Detail of a ceramic mural showing a traditional scene, Barrio Amón

The most audacious building in this *barrio* is the **Bishop's Castle** at Avenida 11 and Calle 3. It was built in 1930 in ornate Moorish style with turrets, crenellations, keyhole windows, a central dome, and a façade decorated with glazed tiles showing scenes from *Don Quixote*.

Centro Nacional de la Cultura ⑫

Map 2 D3. Calles 11/15 and Aves 3/7. *255-3638; Museo de Arte y Diseño Contemporáneo: 257-9370. 10am– 5pm Tue–Sat. public hols. 10am–3pm Tue–Fri by appt.*

IMMEDIATELY EAST of Parque España, the rambling structure of the National Center of Culture takes up a block on the site of the former Fábrica National de Licores (State Liquor Factory). In 1994, the defunct factory was converted into the multi-faceted Centro Nacional de la Cultura (CENAC), although traces of the old distillery can still be seen. The Ministry of Culture is located here, as are venues hosting the National Theater Company and the National Dance Company *(see p245)*. Most of the extant buildings date to 1856, as does the perimeter wall, whose stone west gate is topped by a triangular pediment. Note the *reloj de sol* (sun clock), carved into the perimeter wall to the right of the southeast *portalón* (gate) by architect Teodorico Quirós *(see p19)*.

The **Museo de Arte y Diseño Contemporáneo** (Museum of Contemporary Art and Design) occupies the southeast part of the complex and features permanent and rotating exhibitions of art, architecture, and ceramics in six rooms. *Evelia con baton*, a sculpture by Francisco Zúñiga, stands in the west courtyard.

Detail on the façade of the Centro Nacional de la Cultura

JADE CARVING

Jade carving was introduced to the region by cultures from the north around 500 BC and died out around AD 800, when it was replaced by gold. The indigenous people used saws made of fiber string, as well as drills and crude quartz-tipped chisels, to carve the semi-precious stone into necklaces, pendants, and religious figurines bearing replicas of animal motifs. No local source is known to have existed: jade was traded from Guatemala and neighboring regions.

Jade anthropomorphic figure

Street-by-Street: Around Parque Nacional

Commanding a bluff on the east side of downtown, Parque Nacional, one of the city's largest parks, is a bucolic tree-shaded retreat in the heart of San José. Surrounding the park on three sides are the country's most important government buildings, including the Legislative Assembly complex. Also in the vicinity are many of Costa Rica's significant cultural sights, such as the National Museum. The area makes for pleasant strolling, especially with the recent addition of a pedestrian precinct sloping south from Parque Nacional, which is a lovely place to sit and relax.

Biblioteca Nacional
This modern-looking structure was erected in 1969–71 to house the national library.

Centro Nacional de la Cultura
Occupying the site of the former State Liquor Factory, the National Center of Culture's attractions include the state-of-the-art Museum of Contemporary Art and Design ⓬

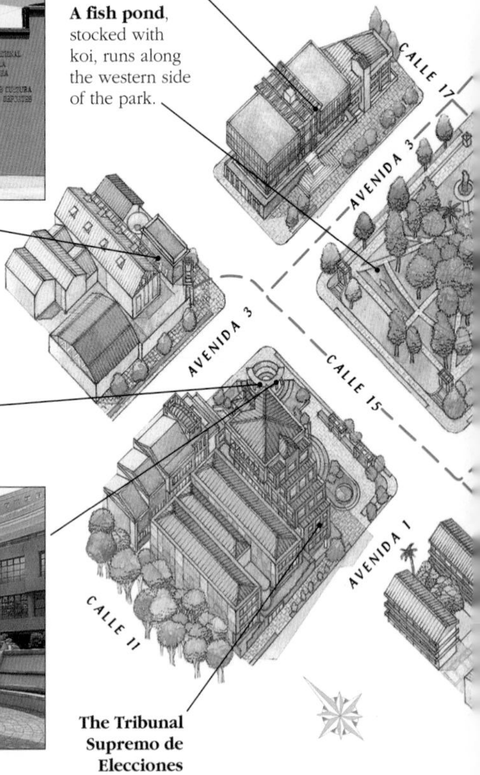

A fish pond, stocked with koi, runs along the western side of the park.

***Epítome del Vuelo* statue**

The Tribunal Supremo de Elecciones building houses the government body that ensures the integrity of elections.

Plaza de la Libertad Electoral
This small, semi-circular plaza honors the nation's democracy. Neoclassical columns enclose a pink granite statue, Epítome del Vuelo *(1996), created by sculptor José Sancho Benito.*

0 meters 100
0 yards 100

Key

– – – Suggested route

Star Sights

★ **Asamblea Legislativa**

★ **Museo Nacional**

★ **Parque Nacional**

★ Parque Nacional
Centered on the impressive granite-and-bronze Monumento Nacional *(1892), this fine park is thick with trees and dotted with busts of several Latin American heroes* ⓯

Bulevar Ricardo Jiménez
This stretch of Calle 17 running south of Parque Nacional is a handsome palm-lined, pedestrian-only causeway. It is also known as the Camino de la Corte.

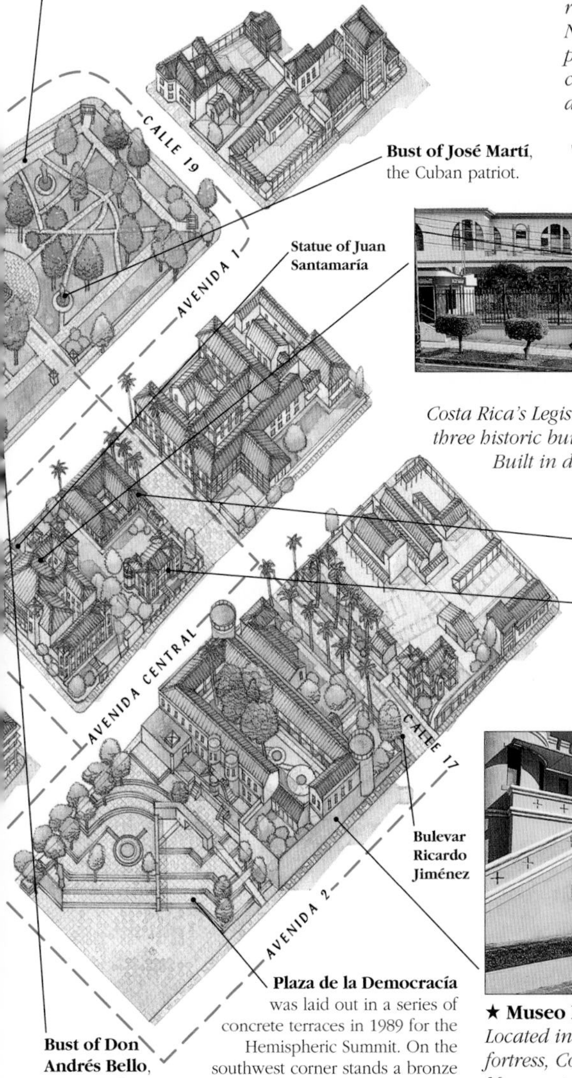

Bust of José Martí, the Cuban patriot.

Statue of Juan Santamaría

★ Asamblea Legislativa
Costa Rica's Legislative Assembly is housed in three historic buildings dating back to 1914. Built in different styles, the structures contain several galleries ⓭

Casa Rosada is occupied by congressional offices.

Castillo Azul, the oldest of the Asamblea Legislativa buildings, earlier served as the presidential palace.

★ Museo Nacional
Located in an early 19th-century fortress, Costa Rica's National Museum traces the history of the nation from pre-Columbian to contemporary times ⓮

Bulevar Ricardo Jiménez

Plaza de la Democracía was laid out in a series of concrete terraces in 1989 for the Hemispheric Summit. On the southwest corner stands a bronze statue of former president José "Don Pepe" Figueres (see p47).

Bust of Don Andrés Bello, a Venezuelan intellectual.

Asamblea Legislativa ⓭

Map 2 E3. Calles 15/17 & Ave Central. *243-2000.* *compulsory: 9am; 243-2622.* ***Legislative debates*** *3pm Mon–Thu; by appointment.* www.racsa.co.cr/asamblea

THE COUNTRY'S seat of government is in an enclave of four buildings, covering an entire block. The main structure, **Edificio del Plenario**, built in 1958, serves as the congress building along with an adjoining edifice. A bronze statue of national hero Juan Santamaría *(see p84)*, torch in hand, stands in the north courtyard. The pink **Casa Rosada**, to the northeast, houses the offices of various political parties.

The Mediterranean-style **Castillo Azul** to the southeast was built in 1911 for Máximo Fernández, then a presidential aspirant. It served as the Presidential Residence until 1927, after which it was briefly the US mission. Since 1989, it has been used for official functions and contains government offices. Its six salons, boasting beautiful hardwood floors and Italian marble, include the Sala Alfredo González Flores, which is used for cabinet meetings, and the Sala Próceres de la Libertad, with its gilt-framed portraits of Latin American liberators such as Simón Bolívar.

Visitors are admitted to the Edificio del Plenario to witness legislative debates. Note that sandals are not permitted for men, nor bare legs for either sex.

Part of the Asamblea Legislativa complex in San José

Pre-Columbian stone spheres in the Museo Nacional

Museo Nacional ⓮

Map 2 E4. Calle 17 & Aves Central/2. *257-1433.* *8:30am–4pm Tue–Sun.* *public hols.* www.museocostarica.com

DRAMATIC and imposing, the crenellated, ocher-colored Bellavista Fortress – opposite the Legislative Assembly – was built in 1917 and served as an army barracks. Its exterior walls, with towers at each corner, are pocked with bullet holes from the 1948 civil war. Following his victory, José "Don Pepe" Figueres *(see pp46–7)* disbanded the army and the fortress became the venue for the National Museum, which had been founded in 1887.

The entrance, on the east side, opens on to a landscaped courtyard displaying pre-Columbian *carretas* (oxcarts), stone *bolas* (spheres), and colonial-era cannons. The museum, to the right of the entrance, is arranged thematically in counterclockwise direction. Rooms are dedicated to geological, colonial, archeological, contemporary, and religious history. The displays start from the first arrival of humans in Costa Rica and go up to the formation of the nation and recent events: a key exhibit is the 1987 Nobel Peace Prize awarded to president Oscar Arias Sánchez *(see p47)*. The museum has a particularly impressive pre-Columbian collection, notably of *metates* (stone tables) and ceramics, as well as spectacular gold ornaments displayed in the Sala de Oro, in the northeast tower. The Sala Colonial is laid out with rustic colonial furniture, and looks as a room would have looked in the 18th century.

Steps lead down from the courtyard to a large netted butterfly garden in the southwest corner. Beyond the butterfly garden lies **Plaza de la Democracía**, which was laid out in 1989. It is an ungainly and unkempt stepped plaza; its saving grace is a 1994 bronze statue of José Figueres.

Parque Nacional ⓯

Map 2 E3. Calles 15/19 and Aves 1/3.

THE LARGEST of San José's inner-city parks, laid out in 1895, this is also its most appealing, although it is to be avoided at night. The peaceful park is set on a gentle hill that rises eastward. Stone benches fringe the irregular paths that snake beneath flowering trees, swaying palms, and bamboo groves.

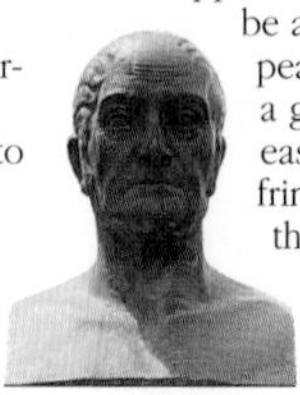

Bust of Don Andrés Bello in Parque Nacional

The massive *Monumento Nacional* is under towering trees at the center. Cast in the Rodin studios in Paris and unveiled on September 15, 1892, it is dedicated to the heroic deeds of the War of 1856. Its granite pedestal has five bronze Amazons representing the Central American nations

Children playing by a fish pond in Parque Nacional

repelling the adventurer William Walker *(see p45)*. Costa Rica stands in the middle holding a flag in one hand and supporting a wounded Nicaragua with the other; El Salvador holds a sword, Guatemala an axe, and Honduras an arch and shield. Bronze bas-reliefs to each side depict scenes from the battles.

Busts dotted around the park honor such Latin American nationalists as the Mexican revolutionary and priest Miguel Hidalgo (1753–1811), the Venezuelan poet and intellectual Don Andrés Bello (1781–1865), and the Cuban patriot and poet José Martí (1853–95).

The park is surrounded by important buildings. The **Biblioteca Nacional** (National Library) is to the north, and to the south, the pedestrianized **Bulevar Ricardo Jiménez**, named for the three-time president, slopes downhill three blocks to the building of the Tribunal of Justice.

Museo de Formas, Espacios y Sonidos ⓰

Map 2 F3. Calles 21/23 and Ave 3. *222-9462.* *9:30am–3pm Mon–Fri.* *public hols.*

THIS SMALL interactive museum, an exploration of form, space, and sound, is housed in the former Estación Ferrocarril al Atlántico (Atlantic Railway Station). Built in 1908, this ornate building, which resembles a pagoda, was later the terminus for the famous "Jungle Train," discontinued in 1991 following a devastating earthquake that destroyed much of the railway line.

The Sala de Formas features sculptures in wood, stone, and metal. The Sala de Espacios displays *maquetas* (scale models) of famous buildings, including the station and the ruins of Ujarrás *(see p100)*. The Sala de Sonidos exhibits a large variety of musical instruments.

Rail buffs will appreciate the vintage rolling stock at the rear of the museum. This includes Locomotora 59, a 1939 steam locomotive imported from Philadelphia for the Northern Railway Company. A bust of Tomás Guardia *(see p45)*, under whom the railroad was established, stands in front of the museum, next to an obelisk commemorating the abolition of capital punishment in 1877.

Display of butterflies at San José's Museo de Insectos

Universidad de Costa Rica ⓱

Calle Central, San Pedro. *207-5508.* **Museo de Insectos**. *207-5318.* *1–4:45pm Mon–Fri.*

SPRAWLED ACROSS the eastern suburb of San Pedro, the 77-acre (32-ha) campus of the University of Costa Rica, founded in 1940, imbues the area with bohemian life. The campus entrance is on Calle Central (off Avenida Central), which throbs with lively student bars and cafés. The campus itself is not particularly appealing, although numerous busts and statues are sprinkled about the tree-shaded grounds. A botanical garden is located in the southwest corner.

The **Museo de Insectos**, in the basement of the Music Department in the northeast corner of the campus, is accessed by a narrow staircase. The museum boasts a large and excellent exhibition of butterflies, beetles, spiders, wasps, and other insects.

The ornate, pagoda-style exterior of Museo de Formas, Espacios y Sonidos

Centro Costarricense de Ciencias y Cultura ⓲

Housed in a fortress-like building that served as the *penitenciario central* (central penitentiary) from 1910 to 1979, the Costa Rican Science and Cultural Center was inaugurated in 1994. The ocher façade, topped by salmon-colored crenellations, presents a dramatic sight at night, when it is illuminated. The center contains the Galería Nacional, whose airy exhibition halls feature paintings, sculptures, and other art forms by Costa Rica's leading exponents of avant-garde art. Also here is the Museo de los Niños, with dozens of thematic hands-on exhibits that provide children with an understanding of nature, science, technology, and culture. The center includes a youth center and auditorium. Scattered around the complex are models of various modes of transport.

Stained-Glass Ceiling
A skylit vidriera *(stained-glass window) by Italian Claudio Dueñas lights the staircase to the Galería Nacional.*

Museo Histórico Penitenciario
The old jail cells are preserved in their original condition in this area. Historic photographs show the jail in former years.

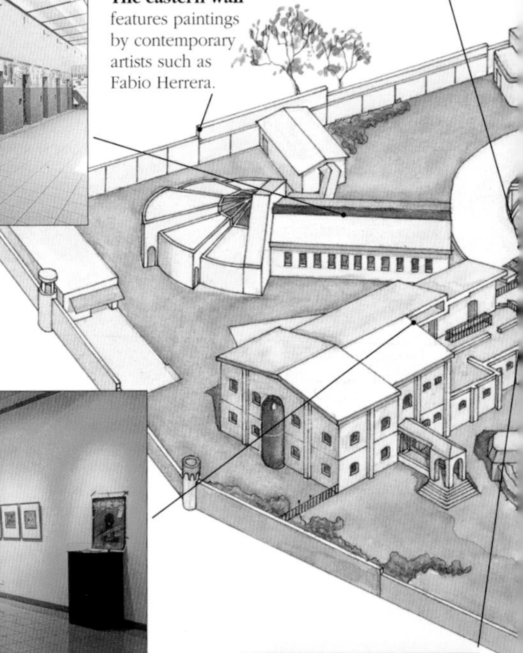

The eastern wall features paintings by contemporary artists such as Fabio Herrera.

★ Galería Nacional
Occupying 14 large rooms upstairs, the National Gallery showcases rotating exhibits of contemporary works by local artists in spotlit rooms converted from former jail cells.

Star Features

- **★ Galería Nacional**
- **★ Museo de los Niños**

Sala Kaopakome
Named for an indigenous Bribri word meaning "Hall of Meetings," this space is used for artistic performances and other events.

Genesis
This granite sculpture (1998) by Jorge Jiménez Deredia shows a woman evolving from an egg.

VISITORS' CHECKLIST

Map 1 B1. Calle 4 and 110 yd (100 m) N of Ave 9. *258-4929.* *Sabana-Cemeterio along Ave 3. Best to take a taxi.* *8am–4:30pm Tue–Fri, 9:30am–5pm Sat–Sun.* www.museocr.com
Auditorio Nacional *222-7647.*

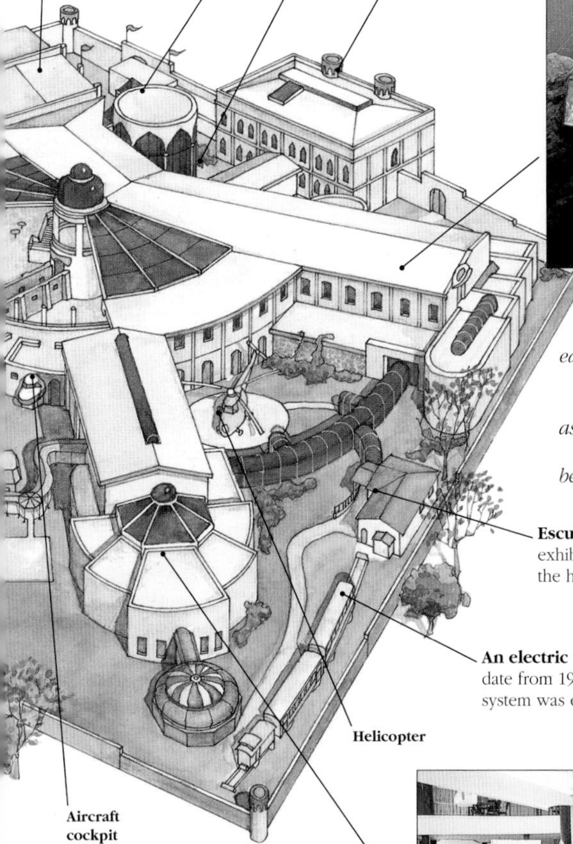

The Auditorio Nacional, the nation's premier auditorium, hosts performances of music and dance.

Imagen Cósmica (1998) by Jorge Jiménez Deredia is a bronze and marble sculpture.

The entrance is in the form of a medieval castle, with twin turrets.

★ Museo de los Niños
The Children's Museum, dedicated to interactive education, is spread throughout 39 separate rooms, with exhibits on the themes of astronomy, Earth, Costa Rica, ecology, science, human beings, and communications.

Escuela "El Grano de Oro" has exhibits on the coffee culture and the history of coffee in Costa Rica.

An electric train and carriages date from 1928–30, when the rail system was electrified.

Helicopter

Aircraft cockpit

Complejo Juvenil
Designed as a learning center for youth, the twin-level complex features a library, with books, audio cassettes, music CDs, interactive games, and an Internet café.

Parque Sabana ⓳

Calle 42/Sabana Oeste and Ave las Américas/Sabana Sur.

OFFICIALLY named Parque Metropolitano La Sabana Padre Antonio Chapui, after the first priest of San José (1710–83), this park was the city's main airfield until 1955, when it was converted into a bucolic retreat and sports venue. The former airport buildings are now the Museo de Arte Costarricense. Looming over the park are the curving **ICE** (Costa Rican Institute of Electricity) tower to the north, and the strangely sloping **Controlaría de la República**, the government's administrative headquarters, to the south.

The somewhat unkempt park, which is accessed from downtown via the wide Paseo Colón, is popular with Costa Rican families, who picnic on weekends beneath the eucalyptus and pine groves. The park's facilities include the National Stadium, jogging and cycling tracks, basketball, volleyball, and tennis courts, riding trails, a swimming pool, a gymnasium, and soccer fields. On the south side, a man-made lake is surrounded by modern sculptures. To the park's west, a cross honors Pope John Paul's visit to Costa Rica in 1983. It is best to stick to the east side of the park, and to avoid it altogether at night.

Flags for sale in downtown San José

Museo de Arte Costarricense ⓴

Calle 42 and Paseo Colón. *222-7155.* *10am–4pm Tue–Sat, 10am–2pm Sun.* *public hols.* *free on Sun.*

COSTA RICA'S leading museum of fine art, on the east side of Parque Sabana, is situated in the Colonial-style former airport terminal that closed in the 1950s. The Costa Rican Art Museum displays more than 3,200 important 20th-century works of art by Costa Rican sculptors and painters, as well as works by a smattering of foreign artists, including Mexican Diego Rivera (1886–1957). Only a fraction of the museum's collection is on display, in rotating exhibitions that change yearly. Many of the works, most of which are privately owned, celebrate an archaic, pastoral way of life, best exemplified by *El Portón Rojo* (1945) by Teodorico Quirós Alvarado *(see p19)*.

Not to be missed are Francisco Amighetti's wooden sculptures and woodcuts. On the second floor, the Salón Dorado has a bas-relief mural in bronze and stucco by French sculptor Louis Ferrón. Sweeping around all four walls, the panorama depicts an idealized version of Costa Rican history from pre-Columbian times to the

View of the Museo de Arte Costarricense, San José

1940s. On the north wall is a representation of Christopher Columbus with Indians kneeling before him.

The **Jardín de Esculturas** (Sculpture Garden) at the back of the museum, exhibits works by prominent sculptors, and also displays pre-Columbian *esferas* (spheres) and petroglyphs. Most intriguing are the *Tres Mujeres Caminando*, Francisco Zúñiga's sculpture of three women, and the granite *Danaide*, a female curled in the fetal position, by Max Jiménez Huete.

Museo de Ciencias Naturales "La Salle" ㉑

Sabana Sur. *232-1306.* *7:30am–4pm daily.* *public hols.*

LOCATED IN THE former premises of the Colegio La Salle school, the La Salle Museum of Natural Sciences was founded in 1960.

A spectacular bird diorama at Museo de Ciencias Naturales "La Salle"

Housing one of the most comprehensive collections of native and exotic flora and fauna in the world, it boasts more than 70,000 items, from molluscs to moths to manatees. A dinosaur exhibit in the central courtyard includes a replica skeleton of a Tyrannosaurus Rex made of resin. The fossil, shell, and butterfly displays are particularly noteworthy. Most exhibits are in dioramas that try to recreate natural environments. Snakes are poised to strike their prey. Fish swim suspended on invisible wire. The stuffed species are a bit moth-eaten, and their contrived contortions often comic. Despite this, the museum provides an interesting introduction to Costa Rica's natural world.

A traditional dance performance at Parque Diversiones

Parque Diversiones (Pueblo Antiguo) ㉒

1 mile (1.6 km) W of Hospital México, La Uruca. 242-9200. 9am–7pm Fri–Sun.

This splendid park, in Barrio La Uruca, 2 miles (3 km) west of downtown, draws local families not only for the roller coasters, water slides, and other pay-as-you-go rides, but also for the marvellous re-creations of typical early-20th-century Costa Rican settings in the adjoining Pueblo Antiguo (Old Village).

Pueblo Antiguo has three sections: the coast, the capital city, and the countryside. Buildings in traditional architectural style include a church, a market, a fire station, a bank, and a railway station. There are several original adobe structures, such as a coffee mill, a sugar mill, and a milking barn, which have been moved here from the countryside. A farmstead is stocked with live animals.

Horse-drawn carriages, oxcarts, and an electric train offer rides, and actors in period costume dramatize the past. Folkloric shows with music and dance bring the place alive on Friday and Saturday evenings. Parque Diversiones has several craft shops as well as a restaurant that serves traditional Costa Rican cuisine.

Victorian-style Casa de Las Tías hotel in San Rafael de Escazú

Escazú ㉓

2 miles (3 km) W of Parque Sabana. *Día del Boyero (Mar).* **Barry Biesanz Woodworks** Barrio Bello Horizonte. *289-4337.* *8am–5pm Mon–Fri, Sat by appt.* www.biesanz.com

This upscale district lies west of Parque Sabana and is accessed by the Carretera Prospero Fernández. It exudes an appeal that it owes partly to its blend of antiquity and modernity, and partly to its salubrious position at the foot of Cerro Escazú mountain. The suburb, which derives its name from the indigenous word *itzkatzu* (resting place), sprawls uphill for several miles. It is divided into three main *barrios* – San Rafael de Escazú, San Miguel de Escazú, and San Antonio de Escazú.

Modernity is concentrated in congested San Rafael de Escazú, where an exquisite Colonial-style church, designed in the 1930s by architect Teodorico Quirós Alvarado, is encircled by high-rise condominiums and US-style malls. Half a mile (1 km) uphill, in San Miguel de Escazú, admire the colonial-era adobe houses, each painted with a strip of blue – many local residents still firmly believe that this will ward off witches.

San Antonio de Escazú, farther uphill, is a farming community. Time your visit here for the second Sunday of March, when flower-bedecked *carretas* (oxcarts) parade during Día del Boyero (Oxcart Drivers' Day), a festival honoring the men who drive the oxcarts. **Barry Biesanz Woodworks** is in the barrio of Bello Horizonte, in east Escazú. This is the workshop of Costa Rica's leading woodcarver and craftsman, who creates elegantly beautiful furniture, bowls, and boxes from Costa Rica's hardwoods. His works are available at the studio and at upscale San José stores.

Detail of church dome in San Miguel de Escazú

San José Street Finder

The map below shows the area covered by the map on pages 54–5, as well as the city center area shown on the Street Finder maps on pages 78–9. It also shows the main highways used for getting around the potentially confusing area that is greater San José.

All map references for places of interest, hotels, and restaurants in San José city center refer to the Street Finder maps in this section. An index of street names and all the places of interest marked on the maps can be found on the facing page. Attractions located to the west of downtown are shown on the map on pages 54–5, while more distant places of interest are plotted on the inset Greater San José map on page 55.

Tourists geared up to explore San José

The busy Calle Central, which runs north–south through the center of downtown San José

Scale of Maps 1–2

0 meters 500

0 yards 500

Key to Street Finder

- Major sight
- Place of interest
- Other building
- Bus station
- Visitor information office
- Hospital
- Police station
- Church
- Post office
- Pedestrian street

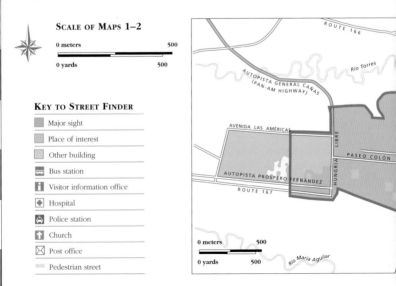

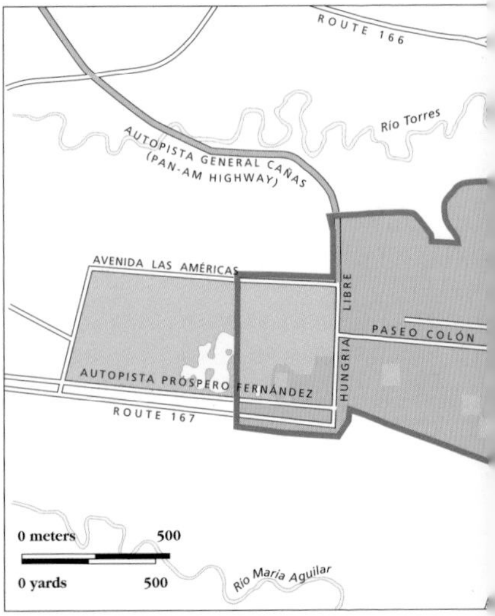

Street Finder Index

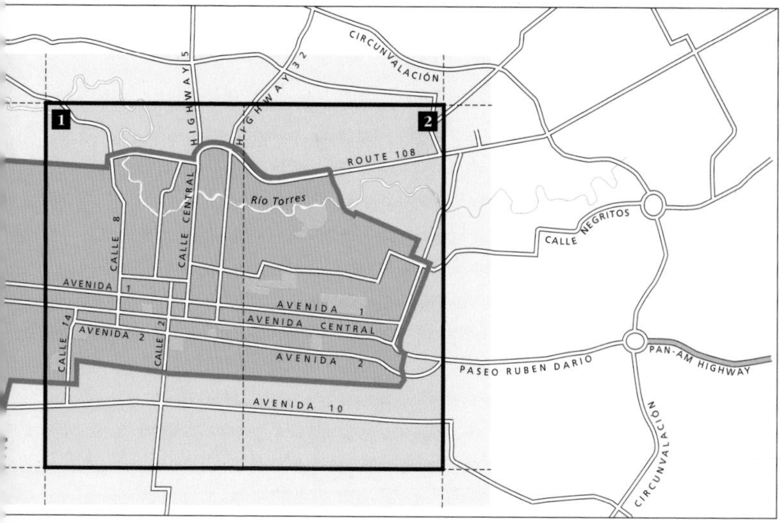

1
A
B
C
1
2
3
4
5
ROUTE 166
AVENIDA 17
AVENIDA 15
AVENIDA 13
AVENIDA 11
CALLE 18
CALLE 16
CALLE 10
CALLE 8
HIGHWAY 5
CARRETERA GUÁPILES
Centro Costarricense de Ciencias y Cultura
CALLE CENTRAL
BARRIO PASA DE LA VACA
Río Torres
CALLE 4
BARRIO LAIZA
AVENIDA 9
AVENIDA 7
Bishop's Castle
AVENIDA 9
CALLE 14
CALLE 12
CALLE 6
CALLE 2
BARRIO AMÓN
AVENIDA 5
AVENIDA 7
CALLE 1
CALLE 3
Mercado Borbón
Radiográfica Costarricense
AVENIDA 3
Edificio Correos
Banco Nacional de Costa Rica
Coca Cola Bus Terminal
AVENIDA 1
Iglesia El Carmen
Parque Sabana
AVENIDA CENTRAL
Mercado Central
PLAZA LOS PRESENTES
Banco Central
Museo del Oro Precolombino
Hospital San Juan de Dios
BARRIO MERCED
PLAZA DE LA CULTURA
Banco de Costa Rica
Gran Hotel
Teatro Mélico Salazar
Teatro Nacional
AVENIDA 2
PARQUE LA MERCED
Iglesia La Merced
PARQUE CENTRAL
Catedral Metropolitana
Teatro Variedades
AVENIDA 4
La Curia
PARQUE SOLÓN NÚÑEZ
AVENIDA 6
Roja Cruz
AVENIDA 8
Sirca Terminal
BARRIO SANTA LUCIA
BARRIO DOLOROSA
AVENIDA 10
Iglesia La Dolorosa
AVENIDA 12
CALLE 5
BARRIO ANGELES
AVENIDA 14
Clínica Bíblica
AVENIDA 16

2
D
E
F
1
2
3
4
5
Centro Comercial El Pueblo
ROUTE 108
ROUTE 108
BARRIO TOURNON
Río Torres
PARQUE ZOOLÓGICA SIMÓN BOLÍVAR
BARRIO OTOYA
BARRIO ARANJUEZ
AVENIDA 15
AVENIDA 13
AVENIDA 11
AVENIDA 11
AVENIDA 11
AVENIDA 9
CALLE 23
CALLE 19
CALLE 21
Casa Verde
Hotel Don Carlos
CALLE 5
CALLE 7
CALLE 11
CALLE 13
CALLE 15
CALLE 17
Museo de Jade Fidel Tristán Castro
Casa Amarilla
Legacíon de Mexico
Hospital Calderón Guardia
AVENIDA 7
AVENIDA 7
Edificio Metálico
PARQUE ESPAÑA
Centro Nacional de la Cultura
Biblioteca Nacional
PARQUE MORAZÁN
AVENIDA 3
PLAZA DE LA LIBERTAD ELECTORAL
PARQUE NACIONAL
Museo de Formas, Espacios y Sonidos
CALLE 23
CALLE 25
Tribunal Supremo de Elecciones
AVENIDA 1
CALLE 7
CALLE 9
CALLE 15
Asamblea Legislativa
AVENIDA CENTRAL
AVENIDA 1
CALLE 29
PLAZA DE LA DEMOCRACÍA
Museo Nacional
CALLE 19
CALLE 21
AVENIDA 2
Ticabus Terminal
Universidad de Costa Rica
BARRIO SOLEDAD
Archivos Nacionales
Iglesia La Soledad
CALLE 27
BULEVAR RICARDO JIMÉNEZ
AVENIDA 6
AVENIDA 6
CALLE 11
CALLE 13
CALLE 15
Tribunales de Justicia
Museo de Criminología & Corte Suprema de Justicia
AVENIDA 8
AVENIDA 8
Clínica Santa Rita
PASEO DE LOS ESTUDIANTES
AVENIDA 10
AVENIDA 10
BARRIO MILFLOR
Servicio de Parques Nacionales
AVENIDA 12
AVENIDA 10 BIS
CALLE 11
CALLE 13
CALLE 15
CALLE 21
AVENIDA 14
AVENIDA 12 BIS
AVENIDA 14
CALLE 17

THE CENTRAL HIGHLANDS

SIMMERING VOLCANOES *dominate the landscape of the Central Highlands as they tower over the country's central plateau – a broad valley at an altitude of around 3,300 ft (1,000 m). With steep slopes lushly covered by verdant forests and coffee bushes, the region offers glorious scenery. The climate is invigorating – one reason why two-thirds of the country's population live here today.*

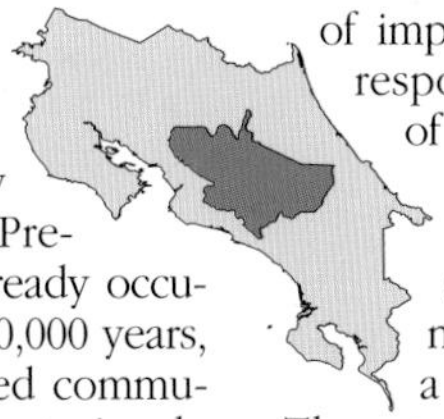

The mild climate and fertile soils of the *meseta central* (central plateau) attracted early Spanish colonial settlers. Pre-Columbian peoples had already occupied the region for about 10,000 years, although their most evolved community – Guayabo – was mysteriously abandoned before the Spanish arrival and overgrown by tropical jungle until discovered 500 years later. Today, the indigenous communities are relegated to the remote margins of the Talamanca Mountains.

Agricultural communities evolved throughout the valley and, eventually, farther up the mountain slopes. During the period of Spanish rule, these humble adobe villages were relatively isolated, and even larger urban centers, such as Alajuela and Heredia, garnered few structures of importance. Earthquakes were responsible for the destruction of much colonial-era architecture, including some fine churches, and most of the surviving historically significant buildings are barely a century old.

The region has some stunning drives along roads that wind up the mountainsides through green coffee plantations, dairy pastures, and, higher up, cool forests of cedar and pine. Most of the mountain forests are now protected, and national parks and wildlife refuges provide excellent opportunities for hiking and wildlife viewing. Sights and activities ranging from butterfly farms and coffee *fincas* to canopy tours and world-class whitewater rafting make the area a thrilling microcosm of the country's tourist attractions.

The striking Iglesia de Sarchí, standing in Sarchí's main square

◁ **Rafting on Río Pacuare, one of the world's finest whitewater rafting destinations**

Exploring the Central Highlands

MOUNTAINS SURROUND THIS temperate region. Bustling Alajuela is a good base for exploring Volcán Poás, where it is possible to drive to the summit. Nearby is Heredia, a center of coffee production. To the north-west, the road to Sarchí and Zarcero makes a superb drive. Two other lovely drives are the Route of the Saints and the Orosi Valley. Costa Rica's main pre-Columbian site, the Monumento Nacional Guayabo, lies to the east of San José. For the more adventurous, Reventazón and Pacuare Rivers are ideal for rafting, while the cloud-forested upper slopes of the Poás, Barva, and Turrialba Volcanoes offer great hiking opportunities. Other options include coffee tours at plantations such as Café Britt and the Doka Estate.

The decorated interior of Iglesia de San José de Orosi

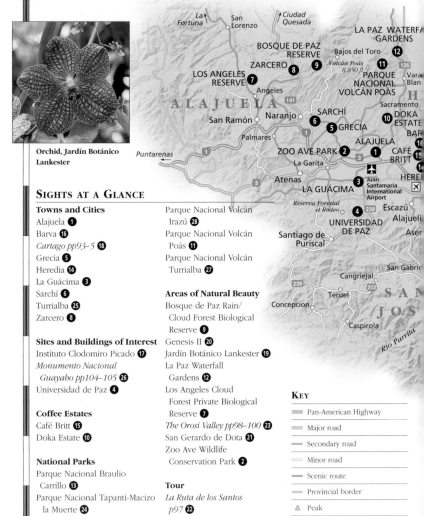

Orchid, Jardín Botánico Lankester

Sights at a Glance

Towns and Cities
Alajuela ❶
Barva ⓰
Cartago pp93–5 ⓲
Grecia ❺
Heredia ⓮
La Guácima ❸
Sarchí ❻
Turrialba ㉕
Zarcero ❽

Sites and Buildings of Interest
Instituto Clodomiro Picado ⓱
Monumento Nacional Guayabo pp104–105 ㉖
Universidad de Paz ❹

Coffee Estates
Café Britt ⓯
Doka Estate ❿

National Parks
Parque Nacional Braulio Carrillo ⓭
Parque Nacional Tapantí-Macizo la Muerte ㉔
Parque Nacional Volcán Irazú ㉘
Parque Nacional Volcán Poás ⓫
Parque Nacional Volcán Turrialba ㉗

Areas of Natural Beauty
Bosque de Paz Rain/Cloud Forest Biological Reserve ❾
Genesis II ⓴
Jardín Botánico Lankester ⓳
La Paz Waterfall Gardens ⓬
Los Angeles Cloud Forest Private Biological Reserve ❼
The Orosi Valley pp98–100 ㉓
San Gerardo de Dota ㉑
Zoo Ave Wildlife Conservation Park ❷

Tour
La Ruta de los Santos p97 ㉒

Key
Pan-American Highway
Major road
Secondary road
Minor road
Scenic route
Provincial border
△ Peak

Panoramic view from the slopes of Volcán Irazú

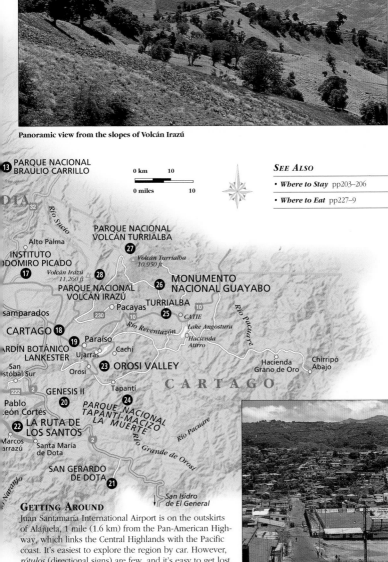

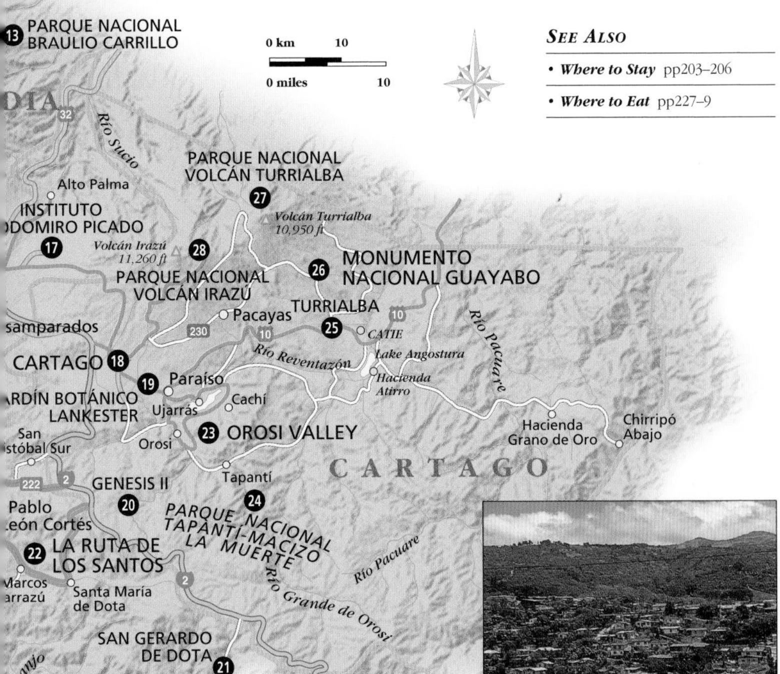

SEE ALSO

- ***Where to Stay*** pp203–206
- ***Where to Eat*** pp227–9

GETTING AROUND

Juan Santamaría International Airport is on the outskirts of Alajuela, 1 mile (1.6 km) from the Pan-American Highway, which links the Central Highlands with the Pacific coast. It's easiest to explore the region by car. However, *rótulos* (directional signs) are few, and it's easy to get lost. Avoid nighttime driving and beware of potholes, sharp bends, and fog at higher elevations. Public buses run between most towns and to places of interest, but service can be erratic. Organized tours are available, and private guides and transfers can be arranged from San José.

View of a small town near Grecia

Alajuela ❶

Road Map D3. 12 miles (19 km) NW of San José. *43,000.* *Sat.* *Día de Juan Santamaría (Apr 11); Festival de Mangos (Jul).*

SITTING AT THE base of Volcán Poás, this busy market town is Costa Rica's third largest city. The mango trees that shade the main square, Plaza del General Tomás Guardia, are the source of Alajuela's nickname, "City of Mangoes." Centered on a triple-tiered fountain with cherubs at its base, the plaza has a bandstand, and benches with built-in chess sets. It is dominated by the simple, domed **Catedral de Alajuela**, with a Classical façade. More interesting is the Baroque **Iglesia Santo Cristo de la Agonía**, five blocks east, which dates only from 1935. The interior boasts intriguing murals. The former jail, one block north of the main plaza, houses the **Museo Cultural y Histórico Juan Santamaría**, honoring the local drummer-boy who gave up his life torching William Walker's hideout in the War of 1856 *(see pp44–5)*. Call ahead to arrange a screening of a video about the event. A bronze statue of Santamaría, rushing forward with rifle and flaming torch, stands in tiny Parque Juan Santamaría, which is two blocks south of the main plaza.

Iglesia Santo Cristo de la Agonía

ENVIRONS: Southeast of Alajuela, **Flor de Mayo** is a breeding center for green and scarlet macaws. These endangered birds are raised for release into the wild.

Museo Cultural y Histórico Juan Santamaría
Calles Central/2 and Ave 3. *441-4775.* *10am–6pm Tue–Sun.* *Tue–Fri.*
www.museojuansantamaria.go.cr

Flor de Mayo
Río Segundo de Alajuela, 2 miles (3 km) SE of Alajuela. *441-2658.* *by appointment.* *by donation.*
www.hatchedtoflyfree.org

Interior of Alajuela's Museo Cultural y Histórico Juan Santamaría

Zoo Ave Wildlife Conservation Park ❷

Road Map D3. Hwy 3, La Garita, 2 miles (3 km) E of Pan-Am Hwy. *433-8989.* *from San José (Sat–Sun at 8am) & Alajuela.* *9am–5pm daily.* www.zooave.org

WITH THE largest collection of tropical birds in Central America, Costa Rica's foremost zoo covers 145 acres (59 ha). The privately owned zoo is one of only two in the world to display resplendent quetzals. More than 60 other native bird species, including five of the nation's six toucan species, can be seen in large flight cages. Mammals are represented by deer, peccaries, pumas, tapirs, and the four native monkey species. Crocodiles, caimans, and snakes are among the dozens of reptile species found here.

Many of the animals and birds were confiscated from poachers, or otherwise rescued by the National Wildlife Service. Zoo Ave is also a breeding center and has successfully raised endangered species such as green and scarlet macaws. The breeding center and wildlife rehabilitation are off-limits.

An enclosure at Zoo Ave Wildlife Conservation Park

La Guácima ❸

Road Map D3. 7.5 miles (12 km) S of Alajuela. *15,500.*

THIS SPRAWLING community is known for the ritzy Los Reyes Country Club, the setting for polo matches from November to April. Nearby, **The Butterfly Farm** supplies live pupae to international zoos. Some 60 native butterflies species flit around a netted tropical garden. Learn about lepidopteran ecology on an educational two-hour tour. Sunny mornings, when butterflies are most active, are the best times to visit.

Horse-lovers will find a visit to **Rancho San Miguel**, on the outskirts of La Guácima, worthwhile. This stable and stud farm raises Andalusian horses and offers horseback-riding lessons, as well as a dressage and horsemanship show in the manner of the Lipizzaners of the Spanish Riding School at Vienna.

The Butterfly Farm
Guácima Abajo, 330 yd (300 m) SE of Los Reyes Country Club. *438-0400.* *8:30am–5pm daily.* *8:45am, 11am, 1pm, and 3pm.*
www.butterflyfarm.co.cr

Rancho San Miguel
2 miles (3 km) N of La Guácima. *438-0849.* *9am–5pm daily; by reservation.* ***Shows*** *7:30pm on Tue, Thu, Sat.*

Costa Rica's Colorful Butterflies

A LEPIDOPTERIST'S DREAM, Costa Rica has more than 1,250 butterfly species. The butterfly population increases with the onset of the rain from May to July, when breeding activity peaks. Most species of butterfly feed on nectar, although some prefer rotting fruit, bird droppings, and even carrion. Butterflies discourage predators through a variety of means. Many, such as the Heliconiinae, which eat plants containing cyanide, taste acrid; they advertise this to potential predators through distinct coloration – typically black striped with white, red, and/ or yellow – that other species mimic. Some are colored mottled brown and green to blend in with the background. Several butterfly species move seasonally between upland and lowland, while others migrate thousands of miles: the black-and-green Uranidae flits between Honduras and Colombia every year.

A moth species of Costa Rica

BUTTERFLY "FARMS"
These let visitors stroll through netted enclosures where dozens of species fly, forage, and reproduce. Some farms breed butterflies for export.

***Caterpillars**, the larvae of moths and butterflies, start feeding the instant they emerge from the eggs. These voracious eaters sport impressive camouflage and defenses. Many have poisonous spikes; one species even resembles a snake.*

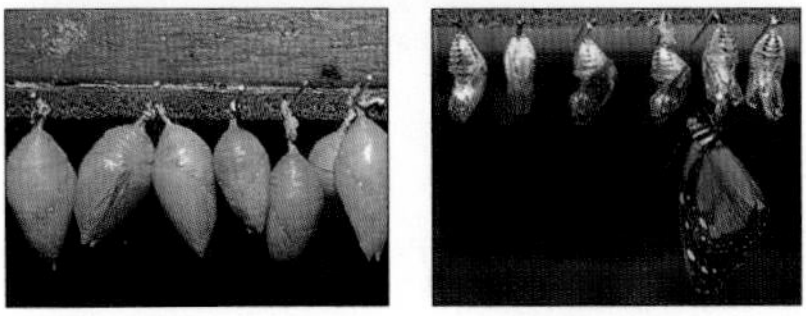

***A chrysalid** is created when a caterpillar attaches itself to a leaf or twig and its body hardens to form an encasement. Some caterpillars spin cocoons of silk; others roll leaves into cylinders, tying them with silken threads. They then pupate and emerge as butterflies.*

***Morphos** are dazzling, neon-bright butterflies whose iridescent upper wings flash with a fiery electric-blue sheen in flight. The wings are actually brown, not blue. The illusion is caused by the tiny, layered, glass-like scales on the upper wing. There are more than 50 species of this neotropical butterfly.*

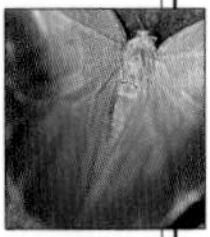

Morpho's wing

TYPES OF BUTTERFLIES
With 10 percent of all known butterfly species in the world, Costa Rica has lepidopteria ranging from tiny glasswings with transparent wings, to the giants of the insect kingdom, such as teal-blue morphos.

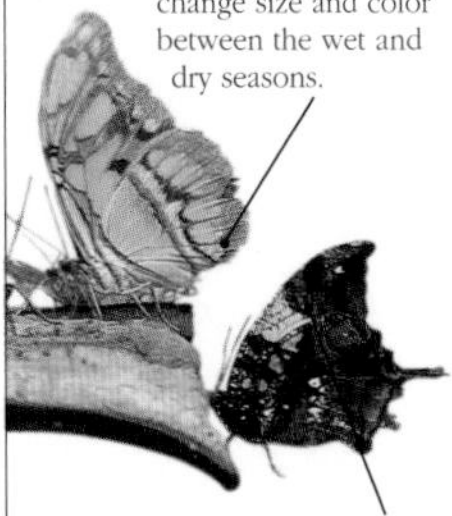

Malachite butterflies change size and color between the wet and dry seasons.

Swallowtails, found in open habitats and rainforest, have trailing hindwings.

***Owl-eyes'** hindwings resemble the startling face of an owl, including two huge black, yellow-ringed "eyes."*

***The postman** feeds on poisonous passion flower leaves as a caterpillar, making the butterfly bad-tasting to predators.*

Grecia's striking red-colored church, Iglesia de Grecia

Universidad de Paz ❹

Road Map D3. 8 miles (13 km) W of Escazú. *to Ciudad Colón, then by taxi. 205-9000. 6am–3pm Mon–Fri. by appointment. Thu, Fri, Sat.* www.upeace.org

A UNITED NATIONS institution, the University of Peace (UPAZ) enjoys an idyllic setting on 750 acres (300 ha) donated by the owners of Hacienda Rodeo, a cattle estate and forest reserve on which the campus is located. Founded in 1980, the university is dedicated to research and education for the promotion of peace.

The botanical gardens within the campus contain busts of famed pacifists such as Mahatma Gandhi, Russian novelist Alexey Tolstoy, and Henry Dunant, founder of the Red Cross. Particularly moving is the life-size statue *Peace Pilgrim* by Fernando Calvo, dedicated to Mildred N. Ryder (1908–81), who, from age 44 until her death, walked for the cause of world peace.

Trails lead into the **Reserva Forestal el Rodeo**, a 4.6-sq-mile (12-sq-km) primary forest reserve sheltering deer, monkeys, wild cats, and more than 300 species of birds.

Grecia ❺

Road Map C3. 11 miles (18 km) NW of Alajuela. *14,000.*

A PEACEFUL market town founded in 1864 and recently voted the nation's cleanest town, Grecia's claim to fame is the **Iglesia de Grecia**, made of rust-red prefabricated steel plates. Trimmed in white filigree, the church has twin spires and a wooden interior with an elaborate marble altar.

Close to Grecia, the open-air **World of Snakes** displays 300 snakes. Visitors are allowed to handle the non-venomous species.

World of Snakes
0.5 mile (1 km) SE of Grecia. *494-3700. 8am–4pm daily.* www.snakes-costarica.com

Sarchí ❻

Road Map C3. 18 miles (29 km) NW of Alajuela. *11,000. Plaza de la Artesanía, Sarchí Sur. Festival de las Carretas (Feb).*

THE COUNTRY'S foremost crafts center is set in the midst of coffee fields on the southern flank of Volcán Poás. The town is famous for its wooden furniture, leather rocking chairs, and hand-painted oxcarts, decorated with signature floral motifs and geometric designs. The whitewashed buildings of Sarchí Norte, the town center, are graced by similar motifs. Don't miss the pink-and-turquoise **Iglesia de Sarchí** in the town plaza. One of its twin spires is topped by a trademark oxcart wheel.

Iglesia de Sarchí, which contains fine statuary by local artisans

Craft stores and *mueblerías* (furniture workshops) are concentrated in Sarchí Sur, 0.5 mile (1 km) east. A good place to buy souvenirs is **Fábrica de Carretas Joaquín Chaverrí** *(see p239)*. Decorative oxcarts of various sizes are handmade in *tallers* (workshops) at the rear. More fascinating is **Taller Eloy Alfaro**, the only remaining *taller* in the country that makes oxcarts for the fields. Sarchí is popular with tour groups – avoid visiting the town on weekends.

Handmade stool, Fábrica de Carretas Joaquín Chaverrí

Fábrica de Carretas Joaquín Chaverrí
Sarchí Sur. *454-4411. 8am–6pm daily.*
oxcarts@racsa.co.cr

Taller Eloy Alfaro
164 yd (150 m) N of Sarchí Norte. *454-4131. 6am–5pm Mon–Thu, 6am–3pm Fri.*

Los Angeles Cloud Forest Private Biological Reserve ❼

Road Map C3. 20 miles (32 km) NW of Sarchí. *461-0301. to San Ramón, then by taxi. 8am–5pm daily.*
www.villablanca-costarica.com

PROVIDING EASY access to a cloud forest environment, this 3-sq-mile (9-sq-km) reserve reverberates with the calls of aricaris, bellbirds, and three species of monkeys. Wild cats prowl the mist-shrouded forests, which range from 2,300 ft to 5,900 ft (700–1,800 m) in elevation and are

The impressive topiary archway on the central path of Parque Francisco Alvardoa, Zarcero

accessed by a comprehensive network of trails classified by length and degree of difficulty. The reserve has horseback rides, guided hikes, and a canopy tour *(see pp24–5)*. Rain ponchos and umbrellas are provided free to visitors.

The reserve adjoins a dairy farm once owned by Rodrigo Carazo Odio, who was Costa Rica's president between 1978 and 1982. Clouds swirl around the colonial farmhouse that sits atop the Continental Divide and today serves as the Villablanca Cloud Forest Hotel *(see p205)*. Nearby, the tiny **La Mariana** chapel has a high ceiling covered with handpainted tiles, each devoted to a different female saint. Outside, an effigy of the black saint San Martín de Porres welcomes visitors.

Zarcero ❽

Road Map C3. 14 miles (22 km) NW of Sarchí. *3,800.* *Feria Cívica (Feb).*

THIS QUIET mountain town, at an elevation of 5,600 ft (1,700 m), has a spectacular setting, with lush pastures and forested mountains all around. It is renowned for its cheese, called *palmito*.

At the heart of the town, the main attraction is **Parque Francisco Alvardo**, a spacious park with well-tended gardens and topiary features. Since 1960, gardener Don Evangelisto Blanco has been transforming the park's cypress bushes into various fanciful forms: an ox and cart, an elephant with lightbulbs for eyes, a helicopter and airplane, a bullfight with matador and charging bull, and even a monkey riding a motorcycle. An Art Noveau-style topiary archway frames the central pathway, which leads to a simple whitewashed church with a painted interior.

Bosque de Paz Rain/Cloud Forest Biological Reserve ❾

Road Map C2. 9 miles (14 km) E of Zarcero. *234-6676.* *to Zarcero, then by taxi.* *9am–4pm daily; only by appointment.* www.bosquedepaz.com

SET DEEP IN THE valley of the Río Toro on the northern slopes of Volcán Platanar, this 4-sq-mile (10-sq-km) reserve connects Parque Nacional Volcán Poás *(see p90)* with remote Parque Nacional Juan Castro Blanco. Some 14 miles (22 km) of trails lead through primary and secondary forest, which span rain-sodden montane growth to cloud forest at higher elevations. The prodigious rainfall feeds the reserve's many waterfalls, as well as the streams that rush past a hummingbird and butterfly garden.

On clear days, *miradores* (viewpoints) offer fabulous vistas, as well as a chance to spot sloths, wild cats, and howler, capuchin, and spider monkeys. A favorite of bird-watchers, the reserve has more than 330 species of birds, including resplendent quetzals and three-wattled bellbirds.

Meals and accommodation are offered in a rustic log-and-riverstone lodge *(see p204)*.

TRADITIONAL OXCARTS

The quintessential symbol of Costa Rica, the traditional *carreta* (oxcart) was once a regular feature on farmsteads and for transporting coffee beans. The wheels, about 4 ft to 5 ft (1.2–1.5 m) in diameter and bound with a metal belt, are spokeless. In the mid-19th century, the carts began to be painted in bright colors enlivened with stylized floral and geometric starburst designs. Metal rings were added to strike the hubcab and create a chime unique to the cart when in motion. Though still made in the traditional manner, almost all of today's *carretas* are purely decorative; miniature versions serve as liquor cabinets. Full-size oxcarts can cost up to $5,000.

A hand-painted oxcart, Sarchí

A vast expanse of coffee plants on the Doka Estate

Doka Estate ⑩

Road Map D3. Sabanilla de Alajuela, 7 miles (11 km) N of Alajuela. *from Alajuela.* 449-5152. *8am–5pm Mon–Fri, 8am–4pm Sat–Sun.* *9am, 10am, 11am, 1:30pm,and 2:30pm daily; reservation recommended.* www.dokaestate.com

Located on the lower slopes of Volcán Poás, this coffee *finca* was founded in 1929 by merchant Don Clorindo Vargas. Still owned by the Vargas family, the estate has some 6 sq miles (15 sq km) planted in coffee bushes and employs about 200 permanent employees; an additional 3,000 temporary workers are hired during the harvest season, which lasts October through January.

The Doka Estate, which still follows the time-honored tradition of drying coffee beans by laying them out in the sun, welcomes visitors eager to learn about coffee production and processing *(see pp30–31)*. A guided tour of the *beneficio* , which dates from 1893 and was named a National Historic Landmark in 2003, starts on a delicious note with a coffee-tasting session. The tour demonstrates the various stages involved in coffee production and ends in the roasting room. The estate offers great views down the slopes and across the valley. There is a small hotel nearby *(see p205)*.

Parque Nacional Volcán Poás ⑪

Road Map D1. 23 miles (37 km) N of Alajuela. *from Alajuela and San José.* 482-2165. *May–Nov: 8am–3:30pm daily; Dec–Apr: 8am–4:30pm daily.* *during phases of volcanic activity.*

The nation's most visited national park was inaugurated on January 25, 1971. Covering 25 sq miles (65 sq km), the park encircles Volcán Poás (8,850 ft/2,700 m), a restless giant that formed more than one million years ago and is ephemerally volatile, with peak activity occurring in an approximately 40-year cycle.

The gateway to the park is the mountain hamlet of **Poasito**. The summit of the volcano is reached by an immensely scenic drive, which winds along coffee fields, horticultural gardens, and dairy pastures, with spectacular views back down the valley. From the parking lot, a 5-minute walk along a paved path leads to the rim of one of the world's largest active craters. A viewing terrace grants visitors an awe-inspiring view down into the heart of the hissing and steaming caldera (collapsed crater, *see p153*), which is 895 ft (300 m) deep and a mile (1.6 km) wide. It contains an acidic turquoise lake, sulfurous fumaroles, and a 245-ft (75-m) tall cone that began to form in the 1950s. On clear days, it is possible to get magnificent views of both the Caribbean Sea and the Pacific Ocean.

The park has two smaller, dormant craters. The **von Frantzius Cone**, north of the active crater, is the original eruptive summit. The **Botos Cone**, to the southwest, is filled by the jade-colored **Botos Lake**, accessed by a trail that leads through forests of stunted myrtle, magnolia, and laurel draped with bromeliads and mosses. Over 80 species of birds, such as fiery-throated hummingbirds, emerald toucanets and resplendent quetzals, have been identified in the forests. Mammal species include margays and the Poás squirrel, a species endemic to the volcano.

Facilities at the national park include an exhibition hall where audiovisual presentations are given on Sundays. Clouds typically form by midmorning, so it is best to arrive early. Bring warm clothing: the average temperature at the summit is 12°C (54°F), but cloudy days can be bitterly cold. If possible, visit midweek – locals wielding blaring radios crowd the park on weekends. Tour operators offer guided excursions to the park.

Toucans at Parque Nacional Volcán Poás

Botos Lake in a dormant volcano, Parque Nacional Volcán Poás

◁ A view of the magnificent crater of Volcán Poás

La Paz Waterfall Gardens ⓬

Road Map D2. Montaña Azul, 15 miles (24 km) N of Alajuela. *482-2720.* *from San José.* *8:30am–5pm; last admission: 4pm.* www.waterfallgardens.com

THIS MULTIFACETED attraction's main draw is five thunderous waterfalls plummeting through deeply forested ravines on the northeast slopes of Volcán Poás. Paved pathways lead downhill through pristine forest to the cascades, where spray blasts visitors standing on platforms above, below, and in front of the falls. Access to some falls involves negotiating metal staircases, and the climb back uphill requires stamina.

The landscaped grounds feature the **Hummingbird Garden**, which draws 26 species of hummers – about 40 percent of the nation's 57 species. A self-guided tour is aided by educational posters. As many as 4,000 butterflies flit about the **Butterfly Garden**, which is enclosed by a massive netted dome the length of a football field. Adjoining is a laboratory where the beautiful insects can be seen as they emerge from pupae. Other attractions include birding tours led by renowned ornithologists.

The park's restaurant has a veranda with marvelous views over the valley and forest. Deluxe accommodations are available at the Peace Lodge *(see p206)*.

The Butterfly Garden in La Paz Waterfall Gardens

Water merging with sulfuric flow, Parque Nacional Braulio Carillo

Parque Nacional Braulio Carrillo ⓭

Road Map D2. Guápiles Hwy, 12 miles (20 km) N of San José. *San José–Guápiles.* *Zurquí ranger station, Hwy 32, 268-1038.* *8am–4pm Tue–Sun.*

NAMED FOR Costa Rica's third chief of state, this sprawling 185-sq-mile (480-sq-km) park ranges in elevation from 120 ft (36 m) at La Selva in the northern lowlands to 9,500 ft (2,900 m) at the top of Volcán Barva. It is bisected by the Guápiles Highway, which links San José with Puerto Limón; it was the construction of this highway that prompted the creation of the park in 1978 to protect the capital's major watershed. Despite its proximity to San José, the park is one of the nation's most rugged, with dense rainforest cover, and subject to torrential rains. It protects five life zones, including cloud forest at higher elevations. Wildlife is diverse, with 135 mammal species, 500 species of birds, and several species of snakes.

The main entrance is the **Zurquí** ranger station, from where a short trail leads to a *mirador* (viewpoint). The easiest hiking is from the **Quebrada González** ranger station, located 8 miles (13 km) farther north, near the Rainforest Aerial Tram *(see p159)*. The most rewarding hiking is around the summit of Volcán Barva, on the west side of the park and accessed by 4WD via the **Puesto Barva** ranger station above the village of Sacramento. From here, a trail leads through cloud forest to the crater.

The dormant Barva has a trio of volcanic promontories; these feature at least 13 eruptive cones, several of which are filled with lakes. Tapirs are frequently seen around Danta and Barva Lakes.

Experienced hikers can tackle longer trails, taking several days, which descend the northern slopes via deep canyons. There are no facilities, and proper equipment is essential.

Margay at Parque Nacional Braulio Carrillo

There have been instances of armed robberies and theft from cars parked near trailheads. Hikers must report to the ranger stations when setting out and returning. Tour operators in San José can arrange half-day or full-day tours. On the southern slope, adjoining the park, the Cerro Dantas Wildlife Refuge has the **Cerro Dantas Ecological Center**, which offers environmental study programs and guided hikes.

Cerro Dantas Ecological Center
22 miles (35 km) N of Heredia. *274-1997.* *6am–4pm daily.* *by reservation.* www.cerrodantas.co.cr

Stained glass at La Parroquia de la Imaculada Concepción, Heredia

Heredia ⓮

Road Map D3. 7 miles (11 km) NW of San José. *42,500.* *by appointment.* *Sat.* *Easter Parade in San Joaquín de Flores (Mar/Apr).*

A PEACEFUL and orderly town founded in 1706, Heredia has a smattering of important colonial buildings at its heart and a bustling student life, owing to the presence of a branch of the University of Costa Rica *(see p71)*. It is centered on Parque Nicolas Ulloa, popularly called Parque Central. Shaded by large mango trees, the park contains numerous busts and monuments. Dominating the park is the squat, weathered cathedral **La Parroquia de la Imaculada Concepción**. Built in 1797, the cathedral has a triangular pediment, lovely stained-glass windows, and a two-tone checkerboard floor of marble.

On the north side of Parque Central, the forecourt of the municipality office features the *Monumento Nacional a la Madre*, an endearing bronze sculpture of a mother and child by Miguela Brenes. Adjoining the Municipalidad, to the west, the colonial-era **Casa de la Cultura** occupies the home of former president Alfredo González Flores (1877–1962). It is now an art gallery and a tiny museum. Nearby is **El Fortín**, an interesting circular fortress tower built in 1876.

ENVIRONS: A major attraction in the lively town of Santa Barbara de Heredia, northwest of Heredia, is the **Ark Herb Farm**. Its orchards and gardens spread over 20 acres (8 ha). The farm exports medicinal herbs. North of Heredia, the steep upper slopes of Volcán Barva are popular getaway spots for Josefinos for their crisp air and solitude. Tyrolean-style houses set amid cypress and pine forests can be rented at **Monte de la Cruz**, a reserve with trails. In July–August, **Hotel Chalet Tirol** *(see p205)* hosts the International Festival of Music. To the southeast of Heredia is the environmental park **INBioparque**, with exhibits relating to conservation and biodiversity.

Casa de la Cultura
Calle and Ave Central.
260-1619.
9am–9pm daily.

Ark Herb Farm
Santa Barbara de Heredia, 3 miles (5 km) NW of Heredia. *846-2694.*
9am–4pm daily, by appointment.
9:30am, by appointment.
www.arkherbfarm.com

INBioparque
3 miles (5 km) SE of Heredia. *507-8107.* *8am–6pm daily; last admission: 4pm.*
www.inbio.ac.cr

Visitors admiring tropical flowers at Ark Herb Farm, near Heredia

Café Britt ⓯

Road Map D3. Santa Lucía, 0.5 mile (1 km) N of Heredia. *260-2748.*
organized transfers from San José.
mandatory; Dec 15–Apr: 9am, 11am, and 3pm; May–Dec 15: 11am.
Concerts, lectures, films.
www.coffeetour.com

A MECCA FOR coffee lovers and one of the country's most visited tourist attractions, this *beneficio* (processing mill) roasts and packs gourmet coffees. Entertaining guided tours are led by *campesinos*, played by professional actors in period costume. The guides' homespun repartee unfolds a spellbinding love story along with a fascinating educational narrative on the history and production cycle of coffee, from the plantation to the cup. Visitors are led through the 6-acre (2.5-ha) coffee estates before taking a hard-hat tour of the packing facility, where they breathe in the tantalizing aroma of roasting beans. The tour ends in the coffee bar and dining room, after a multimedia presentation that highlights coffee's role in cultivating Costa Rican democracy and molding a national identity.

Label of a Café Britt product

Barva ⓰

Road Map D3. 2 miles (3 km) N of Heredia. *4,900.* *from Heredia.* *Festival de San Bartolomé (Aug 24).*

ONE OF THE country's oldest settlements, this quaint town was founded in 1613, with the official name San Bartolomé de Barva. Located at the base of Volcán Barva, the town contains many simple 18th-century adobe houses with traditional red-tile roofs.

The flower-filled and palm-shaded town square, laid out in 1913, is graced by the pretty **Iglesia de San Bartolomé de Barva**, erected in 1867 on the site of an Indian burial ground. It replaced two earlier churches felled by earthquakes. On one side is a grotto dedicated to the Virgin of Lourdes.

The **Museo de Cultura Popular**, on the outskirts of Barva, provides a portrait of late-19th-century life, with period pieces laid out in the fashion of the times. The building is a former home of ex-president Alfredo González Flores. A part of the dung-and-straw adobe masonry is exposed to view. The kitchen serves traditional meals.

Museo de Cultura Popular
Santa Lucía de Barva, just S of Barva. 260-1619. *9am–4pm Mon–Fri, 10am–5pm Sat–Sun.*

Instituto Clodomiro Picado 17

Road Map D3. Dulce Nombre de Coronado, 5 miles (8 km) NE of San José. *229-0344. from San José. 8am–4pm Mon–Fri; only for groups by appointment.* www.icp.ucr.ac.cr

Locally known as the "Snake Farm," this institute welcomes visitors eager to learn about ophidian ecology and to satisfy a primeval fascination with reptiles. Founded in 1970, it is named after Nicaraguan-born Dr. Clodomiro Picado Twight (1887–1944), who pioneered research into serums, immunizations, and vaccinations. Now a part of the University of Costa Rica, the institute is one of the world's foremost research centers for snake venom. It also investigates toxic frogs, wasps, and other venomous insects. Visitors can witness the *terciopelo* (fer-de-lance) being "milked" for venom. A planned serpentarium, to be open to the general public, will exhibit wasps, scorpions, and all 18 local venomous snake species.

Sign of the Instituto Clodomiro Picado, the "Snake Farm"

Cartago 18

Road Map D3. 13 miles (21 km) E of San José. *60,000. Corpus Christi (May/Jun); Día de Nuestra Señora de la Virgen de los Ángeles (Aug 2).*

Costa Rica's first city and original colonial capital was founded in 1563 by conquistador and Spanish governor Juan Vásquez de Coronado *(see p42)*. Named for the Spanish word for Carthage, it lost its capital status to San José at the Battle of Ochomogo in 1823. The city was destroyed when Volcán Irazú erupted in 1723. Most of the subsequent colonial structures were felled by violent earthquakes in 1841 and 1910. Despite its size, the city today has limited appeal, and is an agro-industrial center.

However, Cartago remains the nation's religious capital, centered on the Byzantine-style **Basilica de Nuestra Señora de los Ángeles** *(see pp94–5)*, dedicated to Costa Rica's patron saint, La Negrita.

Memories of the earthquake of April 13, 1910, remain in the ruins of the **Iglesia de la Parroquia**, originally built in 1575 and destroyed five times by earthquakes before its final demise. The mossy ruins now form the centerpiece of a small garden adjoining the stark central plaza.

Jardín Botánico Lankester 19

Road Map D3. 4 miles (6 km) E of Cartago. *552-3247. from Cartago. 8:30am–4:30pm daily.*

Operated by the University of Costa Rica as a research center since 1973, these luxuriant botanical gardens were founded in 1917 by English horticulturalist and coffee-planter, Charles Lankester West. Covering 27 acres (11 ha), they display almost 3,000 neotropical species in separate sections dedicated to specific plant families. The highlight is the showy orchid collection, spread throughout the garden. The 1,100 species are best seen in the dry season, especially from February to April. Pathways snake through a bamboo tunnel, a swathe of premontane forest, a medicinal plant garden, a butterfly garden, and a cactus garden. Visitors are given an orientation talk before setting out on a self-guided tour.

An orchid in Jardín Botánico Lankester

The weather-beaten ruins of Iglesia de la Parroquia, Cartago

Cartago: Basilica de Nuestra Señora de los Ángeles

Detail on pillar

Named in honor of the country's patron saint, the Virgin of Los Ángeles (also called La Negrita), Cartago's Cathedral of Our Lady of the Angels is Costa Rica's most important church. Legend has it that on August 2, 1635, a mulatto peasant girl called Juana Pereira found a small figurine of a dark-skinned Virgin Mary on a rock. The statue was put away in safe custody twice and mysteriously returned to the rock both times. The basilica was built to mark the spot. Destroyed in 1926 by a massive earthquake, it was rebuilt in 1929. The impressive Byzantine-style edifice features a stone exterior with a decorated façade and is topped by an octagonal cupola. A spring flowing beneath the basilica is considered to have curative powers.

Side Altars
The side altars contain a series of shrines to saints such as San Antonio de Padua, San Cayetano, San Vicente de Paul, and the black saint, San Benito de Palermo. There are also life-size statues of Jesus, Mary, and Joseph.

★ La Negrita Statue
The 8-inch (20-cm) high statue of Mary, the discovery of which supposedly led to the construction of the church, is installed in a shrine above the main altar. The shrine is encrusted with gold and precious stones.

Façade
The façade has Moorish-style arches and fluted pilasters capped by angels.

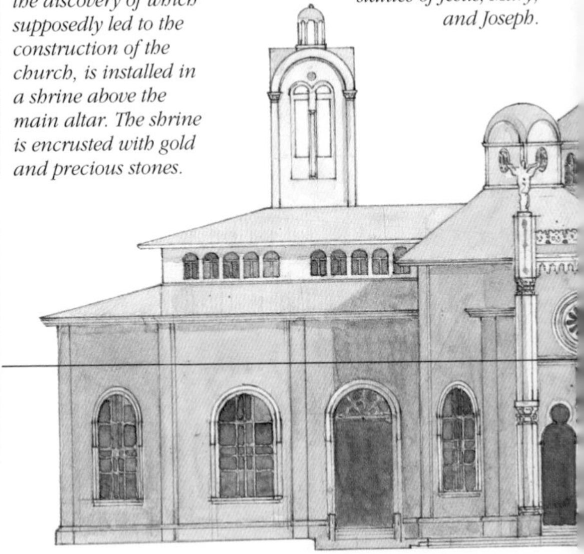

The La Negrita Pilgrimage

Every August 2, devout Costa Ricans join in the Día de Nuestra Señora de la Virgen de los Ángeles procession. Thousands walk the 15 miles (24 km) from San José to Cartago – many crawl much of the way on their knees; others carry crosses. Devotees descend to the subterranean Cripta de la Piedra to touch the rock and collect holy water from the underground spring. The statue of La Negrita is paraded through the city before being replaced in its shrine.

Pilgrims and tourists outside the church

The Ceiling
The wooden ceiling is centered on an octagonal, wood-paneled dome ringed by windows through which sunlight pours in, illuminating the nave and producing a sense of religious exaltation.

VISITORS' CHECKLIST

Calle 14/16 and Aves 2/4, Cartago. [tel] 551-0465. [bus] *from San José (Calle 5 and Aves 18/20).* [open] *6am–7pm daily.* [services] *regular services throughout the day.* [wheelchair access]

★ The Nave
The elaborate interior in the shape of a double cross is made entirely of hardwoods, painted with decorative floral patterns of white alabaster. Parabolic arches are supported atop cloverleaf-shaped wooden pillars.

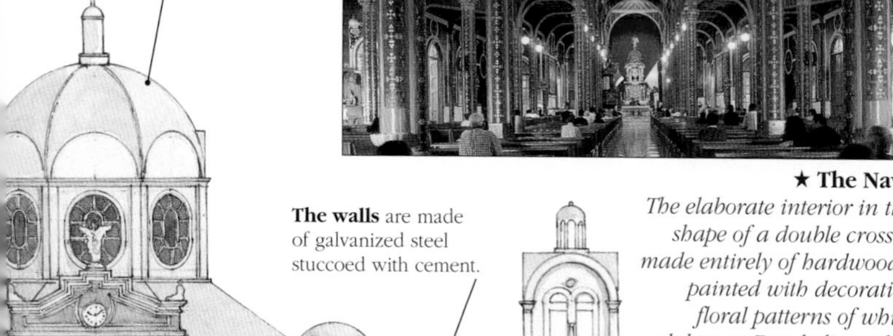

The walls are made of galvanized steel stuccoed with cement.

The Cripta de la Piedra (Crypt of the Rock) is the subterranean shrine containing the rock where the La Negrita statue was supposedly found. Entered via a ramp to the rear of the basilica, it is filled with votive offerings.

STAR FEATURES

- ★ The Nave
- ★ La Negrita Statue

Stained-Glass Window
The basilica boasts several fine vitrales *(stained-glass panes) depicting biblical scenes. The finest are in the Sacristy, in the southeast corner, and depict Jesus with various saints.*

Thick cloud forests protected in the private reserve, Genesis II

Genesis II ⓴

Road Map D3. La Damita, 22 miles (35 km) S of Cartago. ☎ *381-0739.* 🚌 *to Km 58, then hike or by 4WD.* 🕐 *24 hrs.* *by reservation.* www.genesis-two.com

BORDERING Parque Nacional Tapantí-Macizo la Muerte *(see p101)*, this private reserve protects 94 acres (38 ha) of dense tropical cloud forest at an elevation of 7,700 ft (2,350 m). Clouds swirl amid the towering oaks, blanketing abundant bromeliads, tree ferns, and delicate orchids. More than 12 miles (19 km) of loop trails lace the forests, providing fine opportunities for hikers to spot kinkajous, sloths, and monkeys. With luck, ocelots and other wild cats, as well as several species of snakes, lizards, and frogs, can also be seen here.

Quetzals dart between the trees, flashing scintillating green and blood-red plumage. With more than 200 other species of avifauna, birding is fabulous. The **Talamanca Treescape** offers an exhilarating zipline tour of the forest canopy.

A warm jacket and raingear are essential. It is best to stay overnight at the rustic lodge *(see p204)*, but day visitors are also welcome.

ENVIRONS: Hanging on a slope with magnificent views, **Finca Eddie Serrano** *(see p205)* is a dairy farm famous for its large population of quetzals. It offers accommodation in charming log cabins.

San Gerardo de Dota ㉑

Road Map D4. 5.5 miles (9 km) W of Pan-Am Hwy at Km 80. *1,000.* 🚌 *to Km 80, then hike or arrange a transfer with a San Gerardo hotel.*

ONE OF THE best sites in Costa Rica for quetzal-watching, this small community is tucked into the bottom of a steep valley furrowed by Río Savegre. Go down a switchback from the Pan-Am Highway to reach the town, which was first settled in 1954 by Don Efraín Chacón and his family. Today, the Chacóns' **Savegre Mountain Hotel Biological Reserve** protects around 1,000 acres (400 ha) of cloud forest and houses the Quetzal Education Research Complex (QERC). This study center for quetzal ecology is the tropical campus of the Southern Nazarene University of Oklahoma. April to May is nesting season, when quetzals are most abundant. More than 170 other bird species are present seasonally.

Dramatic scenery, crisp air, and blissful solitude reward the few travelers who take the time to make the sharp descent into San Gerardo de Dota. Fruits grow in profusion in orchards surrounded by meadows and centenary oaks.

About 22 miles (35 km) of trails crisscross the forest. Activities include guided treks from the frigid heights of Cerro Frío (Cold Mountain) at 11,400 ft (3,450 m) to San Gerardo de Dota at 7,200 ft (2,200 m). Other trails lead along the banks of the gurgling river, which is stocked with rainbow trout.

Savegre Mountain Hotel Biological Reserve, San Gerardo de Dota

Savegre Mountain Hotel Biological Reserve
☎ *740-1028.* www.savegre.co.cr

La Ruta de los Santos ㉒

SOUTH OF SAN JOSÉ, the Cerro de Escazú rise steeply from Desamparados to the town of Aserrí. Twisting roads then pass through San Gabriel, San Pablo de León Cortés, San Marcos de Tarrazú, Santa María de Dota, and San Cristóbal Sur in the steep-sided coffee country known as Tarrazú. These off-the-beaten-track communities – named for saints Gabriel, Paul, Mark, Mary, and Christopher – give this fabulously scenic drive through verdant highlands and valleys its apt name, "Route of the Saints."

TIPS FOR DRIVERS

Tour length: *95 miles (153 km) round-trip.*
Stopping-off points: *A great place to stop for a bite en route is the charming Bar Restaurante Vaca Flaca, while the homey La Casona de Sara in Santa María serves filling meals* (see p228).
Information: *Beneficio Coopedota ☎ 541-2828. Beneficio Coopetarrazú ☎ 546-6098.*

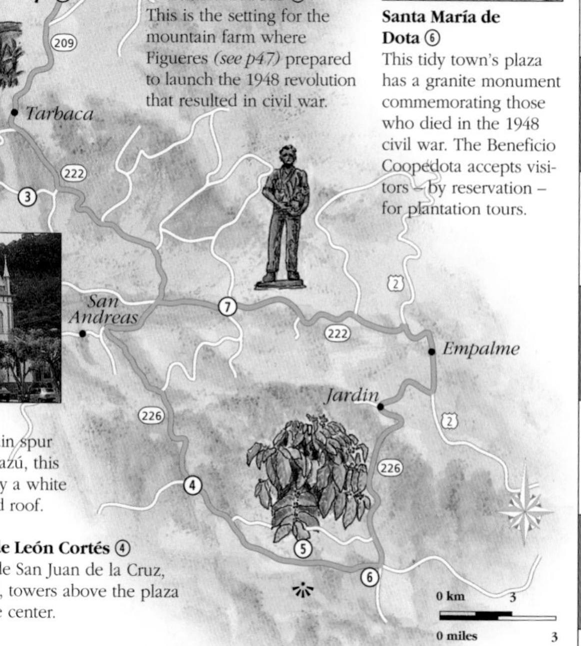

Desamparados ①
This town is dominated by its handsome church in Neoclassical style.

Aserrí ②
The mountainside above Aserrí offers superb vistas across the valley toward Barva, Irazú, and Turrialba Volcanoes.

Santa María de Dota ⑥
This tidy town's plaza has a granite monument commemorating those who died in the 1948 civil war. The Beneficio Coopedota accepts visitors – by reservation – for plantation tours.

San Cristóbal Sur ⑦
This is the setting for the mountain farm where Figueres *(see p47)* prepared to launch the 1948 revolution that resulted in civil war.

San Gabriel ③
Occupying a mountain spur overlooking Río Tarrazú, this town is dominated by a white church with a domed roof.

San Pablo de León Cortés ④
The Iglesia de San Juan de la Cruz, built in 1997, towers above the plaza in this coffee center.

San Marcos de Tarrazú ⑤
Surrounded by coffee-covered slopes, the region's most important town boasts a fine church. Arrange a visit to Beneficio Coopetarrazú coffee mill in advance.

KEY

- Tour route
- Highway
- Other road
- Viewpoint

The Orosi Valley ㉓

SOUTH OF CARTAGO, the land falls away steeply into the Orosi Valley, a large gorge hemmed to the south by the Talamanca Mountains. Río Reventazón drains the valley and joins Lago de Cachí, also fed by other streams and raging rivers tumbling out of hills enveloped by cloud forest. Shiny-leafed coffee bushes cover the valley, which was an important colonial center and has two of Costa Rica's oldest religious sites. The ruins of the 17th-century church in the village of Ujarrás, set at the edge of Lago de Cachí, are the highlight of a visit to the valley. Orosi village is home to the country's oldest extant church. The valley's social life centers on this tranquil hamlet. Looping around the Orosi Valley is Route 224, which passes the main points of interest and makes for a perfect half- or full-day tour.

View of the spillways of Cachí Dam on Lago de Cachí

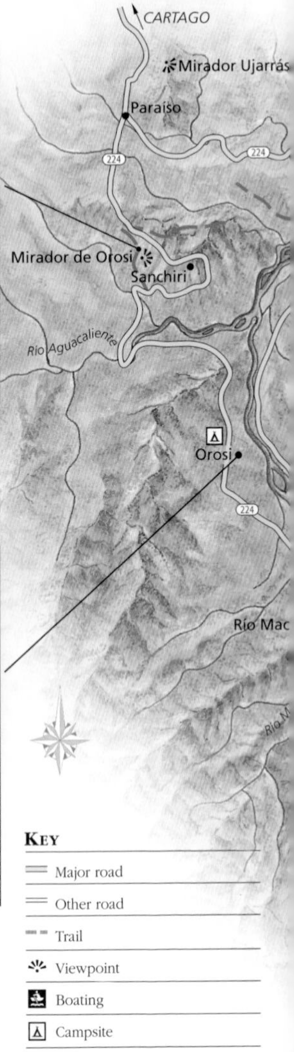

Mirador de Orosi

Operated by ICT (Instituto Costarricense de Turismo), this mirador *(viewpoint) offers stunning views over the valley and has picnic tables on lawns abuzz with hummingbirds.*

Orosi

Surrounded by coffee plantations and peppered with waterfalls, the picturesque village of Orosi is known for the colonial-era Iglesia de San José de Orosi, which contains a small museum of religious art. Orosi has several thermal mineral springs called balnearios (see p100).

Ujarrás
This village has all but vanished after being flooded in 1833. It is known for the ruins of the Iglesia de Nuestra Señora de la Límpia Concepción, built in 1693 (see p100).

Visitors' Checklist

Road Map D3. Cartago. *14,000. hourly from Cartago to Orosi. Buses also run to Cachí via Ujarrás.* *533-3333 (Orosi Tourism); 533-3082 (MINAE). Romería Virgen de la Candelaria (3rd Sun of Apr), Orosi Colonial Tourist Fair (Sep).* **La Casona de Cafetal** *11am–6pm daily.* **Parque de Purisíl** *8am–5pm daily.*

Paradero Lacustre Charrarra offers picnic areas, a swimming pool, and recreational and sport facilities *(see p100).*

La Casona de Cafetal, a lakeside coffee *finca*, offers hiking trails and horseback rides.

Casa el Soñador
This is the home of the Quesada family – famous woodcarvers whose naive bas-relief art forms adorn their property (see p100).

Lago de Cachí
Trout-fishing is popular in this lake, created to generate hydroelectric power by damming Río Reventazón (see p100).

Parque de Purisíl, a recreational park high above the Río Grande Valley, is exquisitely landscaped with cascades and alpine flowers. There are hiking trails in the nearby cloud forest, and trout-fishing is on offer in small man-made lakes.

Exploring the Orosi Valley

Wood carving, Iglesia de San José de Orosi

THE FIRST COLONISTS arrived in the valley of Río Reventazón in 1564 to convert the indigenous Cabécar people who were led by a *cacique* (chief) named Orosi. The valley soon became an important religious center. It is the colonial relics that draw visitors to the region, but the scenery is no less appealing. Route 224, which encircles the valley, brings in an ever-increasing number of tourists.

Iglesia de San José de Orosi's interior, dominated by wood and terra-cotta

Ujarrás

8 miles (13 km) SE of Cartago.

Located at the edge of Lake Cachí and surrounded by coffee bushes, the hamlet of Ujarrás features the ruins of the **Iglesia de Nuestra Señora de la Límpia Concepción**, completed in 1693. The ruins stand in a charming garden awash with tropical flowers.

The site previously housed the shrine La Parroquia de Ujarrás. According to legend, a converted Indian found a wooden box containing a statue of the Virgin Mary. He carried it to Ujarrás, where it suddenly became too heavy for even a team of men to lift. The local priest considered this a sign from God that a shrine should be built here. When pirates led by Henry Morgan attacked the region in 1666, local inhabitants prayed at the shrine for salvation. A defensive force led by Spanish governor, Juan Lopez de la Flor, routed the pirates and in gratitude built a church in honor of the Virgen del Rescate de Ujarrás (Virgin of Rescue). Damaged in a flood in 1833, the church was thereafter abandoned. Every third Sunday in April, pilgrims walk to the shrine from Paraíso, which is 4 miles (6 km) to the west, in honor of the Virgin.

Orosi

5 miles (8 km) S of Paraíso. *8,862.*
Balnearios Termales Orosi *533-2156. 7:30am–4pm Wed–Mon.*
Museo de Arte Religioso *533-3051. 9am–noon and 1–5pm Tue–Sun.*

Nestling neatly on the banks of Río Grande de Orosi, this small village is a coffee growing center. Mineral hot springs gush from the hillsides and can be enjoyed in orderly and well-maintained pools at **Balnearios Termales Orosi**.

Ruins of Nuestra Señora de la Límpia Concepción, Ujarrás

Orosi's pride is the beautifully preserved **Iglesia de San José de Orosi**, the oldest functioning church in Costa Rica. Built by Franciscans in 1743–66 and dominated by a solid bell tower, the whitewashed church has withstood several earthquakes, despite its plain adobe construction. The interior features a beamed ceiling, terra-cotta floor, and simple gilt-adorned wooden altar. The Franciscan monastery adjoining the church is now the **Museo de Arte Religioso**, displaying period furniture and religious icons dating back three centuries. Most of the items – such as paintings, statuary, and altar pieces – come from Mexico and Guatemala.

Lago de Cachí

Paradero Lacustre Charrarra
1.6 mile (2 km) E of Ujarrás. *574-7557. 8am–5pm daily.*
charrarralfacom@racsa.co.cr
Casa el Soñador 5 miles (8 km) E of Orosi. *577-1186. 9am–6pm daily.*

This massive lake was created between 1959 and 1963, when the ICE (Costa Rican Institute of Electricity) dammed Río Reventazón. The Presa de Cachí (Cachí Dam) funnels water down spillways to feed massive hydroelectricity turbines. Visitors can enjoy kayaking, canoeing, and boating on the lake, arranged by local tour operators. The national tourist board operates **Paradero Lacustre Charrarra**, a recreational complex offering boating from the north shore. Horseback riding is also on offer.

On the southern shore is **Casa el Soñador** (Dreamer's House), the pretty bamboo-and-wood home of sculptor Macedonio Quesada Valerín (1932–94). Carved figures representing the town gossips lean out of the upper-story windows and a bas-relief of Leonardo da Vinci's *The Last Supper* adorns the exterior. Macedonio's sons carry on their father's tradition of carving walking sticks, religious figures, and ornaments from coffee plant roots. The house serves as an art gallery for the works of other local artists.

A waterfall at Parque Nacional Tapantí-Macizo la Muerte

Parque Nacional Tapantí-Macizo la Muerte ㉔

Road Map D3. 5.5 miles (9 km) S of Orosi. ☎ *771-3297.* 🚌 *to Orosi, then by jeep-taxi.* ◯ *7am–5pm daily.* 🎫

South of the Orosi Valley, the vibrantly green Tapantí-Macizo National Park, created in 1982, protects 225 sq miles (583 sq km) of the Talamanca Mountains. Ranging in elevation from 3,950 ft to 8,350 ft (1,200–2,550 m). It features diverse flora, from lower montane rainforest to montane dwarf forest on the upper slopes. The national park is deluged with rains almost throughout the year, which feed the fast-flowing rivers rushing through it; February to April are the least rainy months, and the best time to visit.

Spectacularly rich in wildlife, the park has animals such as anteaters, jaguars, monkeys, tapirs, and even otters in streams. Tapantí is a birder's heaven – more than 260 bird species inhabit its thick forests. Resplendent quetzals frequent the thickets near the ranger station, which has a small nature display.

Well-marked trails lace the rugged terrain. A particularly pleasant and easy hike is **Sendero La Catarata**, which leads to a waterfall. Fishing in the park is permitted from April to October.

Turrialba ㉕

Road Map E3. 27 miles (44 km) E of Cartago. 👥 *32,000.* 🚌

This pleasant regional center squats in a broad valley on the banks of Río Turrialba at 2,130 ft (650 m) above sea level, against the base of Volcán Turrialba *(see p103)*. Once an important transportation hub midway between San José and the Caribbean, Turrialba had to forego that position with the opening of the Guápiles Highway in 1987, and cessation of rail service in 1991. Rusting railroad tracks serve as reminders of the days when the Atlantic Railroad thrived.

There is little of interest in the town; its importance lies in being a center for kayaking and rafting trips on Río Reventazón and Río Pacuare, and serving as a good base for exploring nearby attractions.

Wooden tortoise, Turrialba

Environs: The valley bottom southeast of Turrialba is filled by the 630-acre (255-ha) **Lake Angostura**, created by the building of a dam in 2000 to generate hydroelectricty. It lures several species of waterfowl and is a watersports center, although it is gradually being choked by water hyacinths. Río Reventazón (Exploding River) below the dam has class III–IV rapids and is fabulously scenic, as is the nearby Río Pacuare, also favored by rafters *(see p102)*.

Hotel Casa Turire, on the south shore of Lake Angostura, is a charming deluxe hotel offering biking, hiking, horseback riding, and many other activities *(see p205)*.

East of Turrialba, the **Centro Agronómico Tropical de Investigación y Enseñanza (CATIE)**, or Center for Tropical Agriculture Investigation and Learning, has trails through 3 sq miles (9 sq km) of landscaped grounds, forests, and orchards, which grow exotic fruits. A lake attracts waterfowl and other colorful birds. Guided tours provide fascinating insights into ecology and animal husbandry. Farther east is **Parque Viborana**, a serpentarium that exhibits several species of snakes, including boas, in a large walk-in cage. The guided tour includes a lecture on snake ecology.

Women in traditional dress can be seen at **Reserva Indígena Chirripó**, an incredibly scenic indigenous reserve in the Talamanca Mountains beyond Moravia del Chirripó, southeast of Turrialba.

Centro Agronómico Tropical de Investigación y Enseñanza (CATIE)
2.5 miles (4 km) E of Turrialba.
☎ *558-2000.* *by appointment.*
W www.catie.ac.cr

Parque Viborana
Pavones, 5.5 miles (9 km) E of Turrialba. ☎ *538-1510.*
◯ *9am–5pm daily.* *by appointment.*

Casa Turire, a delightful hotel near Turrialba

Whitewater Rafting

COSTA RICA BOASTS rivers that are perfect for whitewater rafting. The best of the runnable rivers flow down from the mountainous Central Highlands to the Caribbean, cascading through narrow canyons churned by rapids, and interspersed with calm sections. Small groups paddle downstream in large purpose-built rubber dinghies, led by experienced guides. Trips can be anything from half a day to a week-long, catering to every level of experience: rivers are ranked from Class I (easy) to Class VI (extremely difficult). May, June, September, and October are the best months, when heavy rainfall gives rivers an extra boost. Rafting is organized by professional operators who provide gear, meals, and accommodations *(see p251)*.

Rafter in a life-jacket

***Costa Rica's whitewater rivers** offer an extraordinary combination of scenic beauty, wildlife sightings, and thrills. One of the finest rafting destinations, Río Reventazón* (left) *caters to enthusiasts of differing skill levels, with separate sections that have difficulty ratings ranging from Class II to V.*

Rafters should wear T-shirts, shorts, and sneakers or sandals, and carry spare clothes.

Guides steer and give commands from the rear.

Safety gear such as life-jackets and helmets are mandatory.

RAFTING DOWN RÍO PACUARE

Torrential Río Pacuare is ranked among the world's top five whitewater rivers. Rafting trips of varying duration take thrill-seekers on adrenaline-packed rides along thickly forested, wildlife-rich gorges, rushing currents, and amazing rapids.

***Calm stretches** provide ample scope for wildlife viewing – kingfishers, parrots, toucans, caimans, iguanas, and varieties of monkeys are among the easily seen fauna.*

***Numerous waterfalls** pour down the sides of the river's gorges. Some fall hundreds of feet, showering rafters with cool water on hot days.*

***Pounding rapids** are found all along Rio Pacuare's course, and offer rides ranked Class III and IV in difficulty. A proposed dam may flood the rapids.*

***Riverside stops** are arranged for hearty breakfasts and lunches. Overnight halts in wilderness lodges or tents on longer trips also offer opportunities for hiking and soaking in the scenery.*

Monumento Nacional Guayabo 26

See pp104–105.

Parque Nacional Volcán Turrialba 27

Road Map D3. 15 miles (24 km) NW of Turrialba. *to Santa Cruz, then by jeep-taxi.* *232-5324 (MINAE).*

THE EASTERNMOST volcano in Costa Rica, the 10,950-ft (3,340-m) high Turrialba has been dormant for more than a century following a period of violent activity in the 1860s.

The volcano's name comes from the Huetar Indian words *turiri* and *abá*, which together mean "river of fire." Local legend says that a girl named Cira, lost while exploring, was found by a young man from a rival tribe, and they fell in love. When the girl's enraged father eventually found the two lovers and prepared to kill the young suitor, Turrialba spewed a tall column of smoke, signifying divine assent.

Established in 1955, the Turrialba Volcano National Park protects 5 sq miles (13 sq km) of land, much of which is covered in cloud forest. The upper forests contain gnarled and twisted oak and myrtle trees.

Dirt roads go to within a few miles of the summit, which is then accessible by trails. Stamina is required for the switchback hike to the top. From there, it is possible to see the Cordillera Central and the Caribbean coast in clear weather. A trail also descends to the floor of the largest crater, where sulfurous gases hissing out of active fumaroles and heat radiating from the ground betray the tremendous energy of the dormant giant.

There are no public facilities or transport within the park, but the privately run **Volcán Turrialba Lodge** *(see p206)*, on the western flank of the volcano at 9,200 ft (2,800 m), provides a base from which to explore the area.

Deep green lake in the largest crater of Parque Nacional Volcán Irazú

Parque Nacional Volcán Irazú 28

Road Map D3. 19 miles (30 km) N of Cartago. *551-9398.* *from San José, Sat–Sun.* *8am–3:30pm daily.*

ENCIRCLING THE upper slopes of Volcán Irazú, this 7-sq-mile (18-sq-km) park was established in 1955. At 11,260 ft (3,430 m), the cloud-covered Irazú is Costa Rica's highest volcano, and historically its most active – the first written reference to an eruption was in 1723. Several devastating explosions occurred between 1917 and 1921, and it famously erupted on March 13, 1963, when US President John F. Kennedy was in the country to attend the Summit of Central America Presidents.

Signage at Parque Nacional Volcán Irazú

The name Irazú is derived from the Indian word *istarú*, which means "mountain of thunder." Legend has it that Aquitaba, a local chief, sacrificed his daughter to the volcano gods. Later, in a battle with an enemy tribe, Aquitaba called on the gods for their aid. The volcano erupted, spewing fire on the enemy, while a boiling river of mud swept away their village.

The road to the summit winds uphill past vegetable fields. A viewing platform lets visitors peer down into a 985-ft (300-m) deep, 0.5-mile (1-km) wide crater, containing a pea-green lake. Four other craters can be accessed, but there are active fumaroles, and the marked trails should be followed. Although the volcano is often covered by fog, the cloud line is frequently below the summit, which basks in bright sunshine. Arriving early increases the chances of clear weather and good views. The lunar landscape of the summit includes a great ash plain called **Playa Hermosa**. Hardy vegetation, such as myrtle and the large-leaved "poor man's umbrella," maintains a tenuous foothold against acidic emissions in the bitter cold. Wildlife is scarce, although it is possible to spot birds such as the sooty robin and endemic volcano junco.

Monumento Nacional Guayabo 26

PROCLAIMED A NATIONAL MONUMENT in 1973, Guayabo, on the southern slope of Volcán Turrialba, is the nation's most important pre-Columbian site. Although minor in scale compared to the Mayan remains of Mexico, the 540-acre (218-ha) site, which is still shrouded in mystery, is considered to be of great cultural and religious significance. Believed to have been inhabited between 1500 BC and AD 1400, Guayabo is said to have supported a population as high as 10,000, before being abandoned for reasons unknown. The jungle quickly reclaimed the town, which was discovered in the late 18th century by naturalist Don Anastasio Alfaro. The peaceful site, most of which is yet to be excavated, has mounds, petroglyphs, walled aqueducts, and paved roads. Pottery, gold ornaments, flint tools, and other finds are displayed in San José's Museo Nacional *(see p70)*.

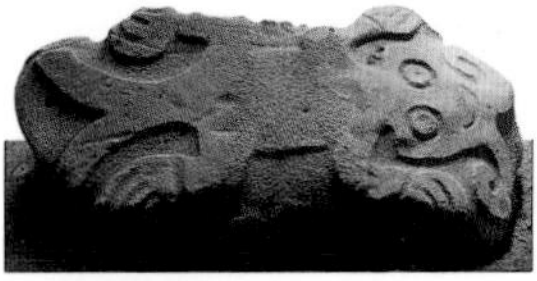

Petroglyphs
The most noteworthy of the petroglyphs scattered around the site are along the Sendero de los Montículos. The Monolitho Jaguar y Lagarto *has a lizard on one side and, on the other, a spindly bodied jaguar with a round head.*

Cisterns
Rectangular water tanks are situated in the western side of the town, and are spanned by a three-slab bridge.

Premontane rainforest surrounding the site hosts several bird species, such as aracaris and oropendolas.

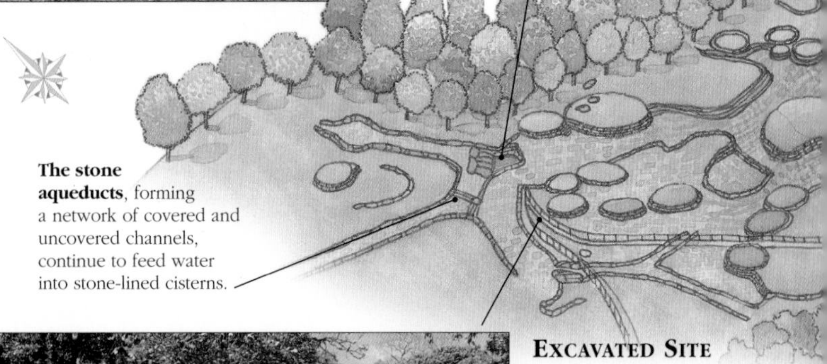

The stone aqueducts, forming a network of covered and uncovered channels, continue to feed water into stone-lined cisterns.

EXCAVATED SITE
Initiated in 1968, excavation of the site was led by archeologists from the University of Costa Rica. To date, only about 12 acres (5 ha) have been retrieved. Parts of the causeway and key structures have been rebuilt, and restoration work is ongoing.

Sendero de los Montículos
A 1-mile (1.6-km) self-guided trail leads from the entrance to a lookout, El Mirador Encuentro con Nuestro Origenes (The Encounter with Our Origins Lookout), before dropping down to the main archeological site. Along the way, visitors can stop at 15 interpretive points that explain the social organization of the Guayabo tribe.

STAR SIGHTS

★ **Calzada (Causeway)**

★ **Montículos (Stone Foundations)**

★ Montículos (Stone Foundations)
Believed to date from AD 300–700, the circular and rectangular mounds of stone on the site were the foundations of conical wooden structures.

Visitors' Checklist

Road Map E3. 12 miles (19 km) N of Turrialba. *559-0099.* *from Turrialba.* *8am–3:30pm daily.* www.sinac.go.cr

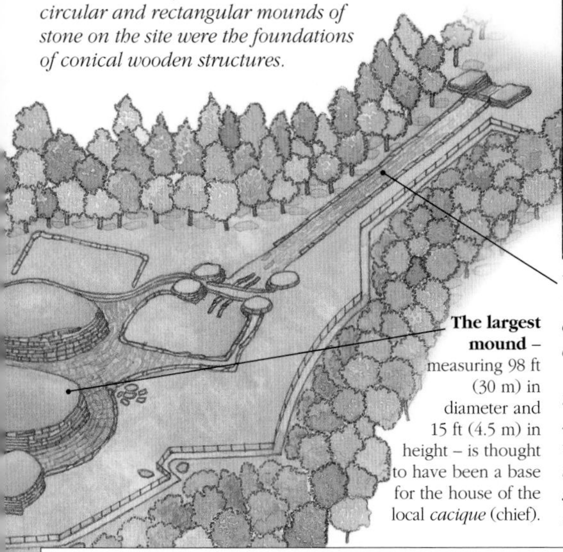

The largest mound – measuring 98 ft (30 m) in diameter and 15 ft (4.5 m) in height – is thought to have been a base for the house of the local *cacique* (chief).

★ Calzada (Causeway)
The 21-ft (6.5-m) wide causeway is believed to have extended between 2.5 and 7.5 miles (4–12 km) from the main town. About 246 yd (225 m) have been reconstructed, including two rectangular stone structures thought to have been used as sentry posts.

Plan of Site

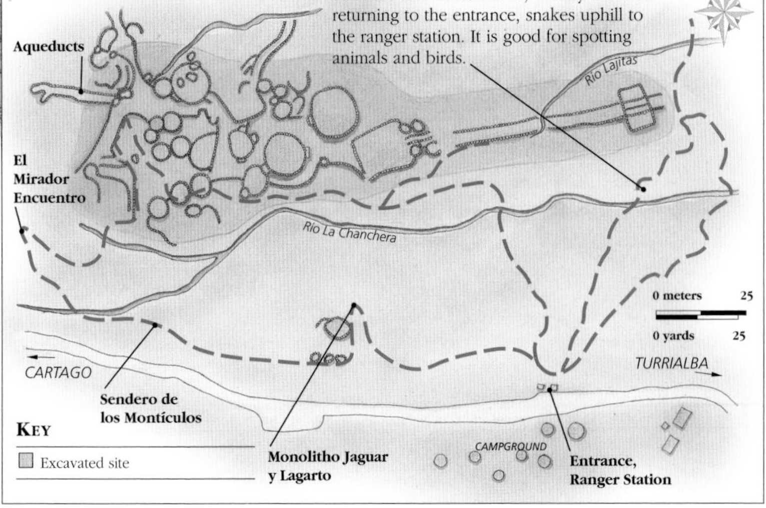

THE CENTRAL PACIFIC AND SOUTHERN NICOYA

FINE WHITE BEACHES ARE *scattered along the shores of Southern Nicoya, while the sun-drenched Central Pacific coastline is pummeled by non-stop surf and fringed with forest. The region acts as a transition between two ecosystems – the drier Meso-American to the north and the humid Andean to the south – with flora and fauna of both ecosystems. As a result, its wildlife reserves, such as Parque Nacional Manuel Antonio, are among the nation's best.*

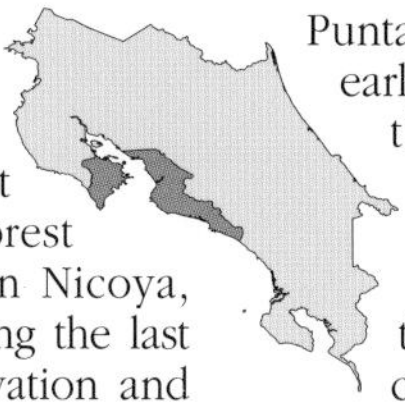

Mangroves line the shores of the Gulf of Nicoya, which is studded with islands that are important nesting sites for birds. Forest areas, notably in Southern Nicoya, were heavily denuded during the last century, but major conservation and reforestation efforts are now extending the protected areas.

Spanish conquistadors explored the region in the early 16th century and established short-lived settlements, which fell victim to tropical diseases and the ferocious resistance of indigenous tribes. However, the Indians were swiftly defeated. The principal city of the region, Puntarenas, was founded in the early 1800s. It flourished due to the 19th-century coffee trade, and developed into the nation's main port for coffee exports to Europe. In the early decades of the 20th century, bananas were planted along the narrow coastal plain farther south. They were replaced in the 1970s by African oil palms, which today dominate the economy and extend for miles between the shore and forested mountains. In recent decades, Jacó has blossomed as a beach resort for surfers, while the town of Quepos retains its stature as a major sportfishing base.

Locals waiting for the bus in a small town in Southern Nicoya

◁ Yacht on the serene blue waters off Playa Blanca, on Costa Rica's Pacific coast

Exploring the Central Pacific and Southern Nicoya

BEACHES AND NATIONAL PARKS, teeming with wildlife, are the highlights of this region. The main town is the fishing port of Puntarenas, from where it is possible to take a day-trip by ferry to Isla Tortuga with its fabulous beach. Other fine beaches in Southern Nicoya await at off-the-beaten-track Montezuma and Malpaís, which are popular with surfers and budget travelers. Nearby Cabo Blanco is the site of the nation's oldest wildlife refuge. Inland from the Central Pacific coast, nature lovers can enjoy a crocodile safari on Río Tárcoles and hikes in Parque Nacional Carara, where scarlet macaws, monkeys, and other wildlife can be easily spotted. Major attractions along this coast are the lively surfing town of Jacó and the sportfishing center of Quepos, which gives access to Parque Nacional Manuel Antonio, one of the country's most popular wildlife parks.

Reserva Natural Absoluta Cabo Blanco

SIGHTS AT A GLANCE

Towns and Cities
Jacó 9
Malpaís 7
Montezuma 5
Puntarenas 1
Quepos 12
Tambor 4

National Parks and Reserves
Parque Nacional Carara 8
Parque Nacional Manuel Antonio pp118–19 13
Refugio Nacional de Vida Silvestre Curú 2
Reserva Natural Absoluta Cabo Blanco 6

Areas of Natural Beauty
Boca Damas 11
Isla Tortuga 3
Rainmaker Conservation Project 10
Valle del Río Savegre 14

A riot of colors at the Tango Mar Resort in the fishing village of Tambor

Gleaming sportfishing boats lined up at Los Sueños Marina, near Jacó

An eye-catching sportfishing sign at Quepos docks

SEE ALSO

- ***Where to Stay*** pp206–208
- ***Where to Eat*** pp229–31

GETTING AROUND

Jacó and Quepos, in the Central Pacific region, and Southern Nicoya's Tambor are linked by daily scheduled flights to Juan Santamaría International Airport and San José's Tobias Bolaños domestic airport. Puntarenas, Jacó, and Quepos are served by bus from San José; several companies cater solely to tourists.

Puntarenas is the gateway for ferries to Southern Nicoya. A regular car and passenger ferry service links it with Paquera; from here, a bus service operates to Montezuma along badly deteriorated Highway 160. In the Central Pacific region, well-paved Highway 34 runs along the shore, linking all the major tourist sights. Away from the coastal highways, most roads are dirt tracks that can be treacherous during the wet season. A 4WD vehicle is essential if you plan to drive around.

KEY

- Pan-American Highway
- Major road
- Secondary road
- Minor road
- Provincial border

Puntarenas 1

Road Map B3. 75 miles (120 km) W of San José. *100,000.* *Carnaval (last week of Feb); Festival de la Virgen del Mar (mid-Jul).*

Often seen as a provincial backwater, the city of Puntarenas (Sandy Point) was once an important port. First settled in 1522 by the Spanish, Puntarenas later became the main shipping point for coffee beans, brought from the highlands in *carretas* (oxcarts). City fortunes waned in 1890, once the Atlantic Railroad was built, and many of its wooden structures are dilapidated. Today this slightly down-at-heel town exists on fishing, as attested to by rows of decrepit fishing boats moored at the wharves. It remains the main gateway for excursions to Isla Tortuga and for ferries to Paquera and Naranjo, on the Peninsula de Nicoya.

Brown pelican, Puntarenas

The town occupies a 3-mile (5-km) long, thin peninsula fringed on the south by a beach offering good views across the Gulf of Nicoya. A broad estuary runs along the north shore, where extensive mangrove forests are home to waterfowl such as roseate spoonbills, storks, pelicans, and frigate birds.

Puntarenas is favored as a *balneario* (bathing resort) by Josefinos who flock to the seafront boulevard, Paseo de las Turistas. The main draw in town is the **Museo Histórico Maritimo**, situated in the former 19th-century city jail. The museum has displays on indigenous cultures, maritime history, the coffee era, and the local flora and fauna.

Serene white beaches of Refugio Nacional de Vida Silvestre Curú

Environs: The sweeping sands of **Playa San Isidro**, 5 miles (8 km) east of town, are crowded on weekends with beachgoers from San José.

Museo Histórico Maritimo
Calles 5/7 and Ave Central. *661-5036.* *9:45am–noon and 1– 5:15pm Tue–Sun.*

Refugio Nacional de Vida Silvestre Curú 2

Road Map B3. 2 miles (3 km) S of Paquera. *641-0004.* *Paquera–Cobano.* *7am–4pm daily; advance notice preferred.* *by appt.* www.curutourism.com

Part of a much larger privately owned hacienda, the seldom-visited 210-acre (85-ha) Curú National Wildlife Refuge protects five distinct habitats extending inland from Golfo Curú.

The majority of the hilly reserve is tropical deciduous and semi-deciduous forest populated by capuchin and howler monkeys, anteaters, agoutis, and sloths, as well as several species of wild cats and more than 220 species of birds. Endangered spider monkeys have also been successfully reintroduced. Since the number of visitors is low, it is possible to spot animals more easily than at many other refuges. Marked trails provide access.

Three beautiful beaches – **Playa Colorada**, **Playa Curú**, and **Playa Quesera** – are tucked inside the fold of green headlands and extend along 3 miles (5 km) of coastline. Hawksbill and olive ridley turtles crawl ashore at night to nest in the soft white sand. Whales and dolphins can sometimes be seen swimming in the warm offshore waters, while the mangrove swamps and lagoons that extend inland along Río Curú are good for spotting caimans.

Environs: The **Profelis Wildcat Center**, located on a 13-sq-mile (34-sq-km) private refuge 7 miles (11 km) northwest of Curú National Wildlife Refuge, was established in the hope of reversing the decline in Costa Rica's endangered native feline population *(see p113)*. Profelis (Programa para la Conservación de Felinos, or the Feline Conservation Program) takes in jaguarundis, margays, ocelots, and oncillas that have been confiscated or rescued by the authorities and prepares them for reintroduction to the wild. It promotes environmental awareness, investigates wild cat behavior, and has an active breeding program.

There is a visitor center, with audiovisual presentations, an educational trail, and exhibits.

Profelis Wildcat Center
San Rafael de Paquera, 5 miles (8 km) W of Paquera. *641-0646.* *8am–3pm Mon–Fri, 8am–noon Sat; by reservation.* www.seibermarco.de/profelis

Fishing and excursion boats moored at the Puntarenas docks

Kayaking on offer at Isla Tortuga, along with other beach activities and watersports

Isla Tortuga ❸

Road Map B3. 2 miles (3 km) SE of Curú. *organized excursions.*

THIS BEAUTIFUL sun-bleached island – actually twin islets, Isla Tolinga and unoccupied Isla Alcatraz – offshore of Curú is run as a privately owned 765-acre (310-ha) nature reserve. Isla Tolinga, which has no accommodation, is very popular for day-visits.

Isla Tortuga is rimmed by white beaches that dissolve into waters of turquoise and startling blues. Coconut palms lean over the beach. The hilly interior is covered by deciduous forest, accessed by a short but steep trail that leads to the highest point of the island (570 ft/ 175 m). Signs point out rare hardwoods, such as *indio desnudo* (naked Indian).

Catamaran *Manta Ray* to Isla Tortuga

The preferred activity is to laze in a hammock while sipping the island cocktail – coco loco (rum, coconut milk, and coconut liqueur) – served in a coconut shell. The warm waters are great for snorkeling. There are no jet skis to break the blissful silence, but visitors can choose from an array of other watersports and a short zipline canopy tour.

Trips were pioneered in 1975 by the Calypso cruise company, which operates a 70-ft (21-m) motorized, high-speed catamaran that departs from Puntarenas. Many other companies offer similar excursions, which usually include hotel transfers, round-trip transportation, and buffet lunch. The 90-minute journey is its own reward – dolphins and whales are frequently spotted.

A mid-week visit is best, as weekends can get crowded, and don't forget to carry sunscreen and swimwear.

ENVIRONS: Boobies, pelicans, frigate birds, and other sea birds nest on the scattered islands that comprise the **Reserva Biológica Isla Guayabo y Isla Negritos**, to the north of Isla Tortuga. Visitors are not allowed on shore, and excursion boats pass between the islets that make up the biological reserve.

Tambor ❹

Road Map B3. 11 miles (18 km) SW of Paquera.

A SMALL, LAID-BACK fishing village with a wide silver-gray beach, Tambor lines the aptly named Bahía Ballena (Whale Bay), where whales gather in mid-winter. Palm-fringed sands extend north to mangrove swamps. The village itself is somnolent, but two upscale resorts just outside town draw flocks of foreign beachgoers and Josefinos, most of whom fly in to the airstrip. Visitors can play a round of golf or tennis for a fee at the **Tango Mar Resort** *(see p208)*, which has a 9-hole golf course, or at the **Barceló Los Delfines Golf and Country Club**, which has an 18-hole course. Scuba diving is on offer at the nearby **Playa Tambor Beach Resort and Casino**, which is affiliated to Barceló Los Delfines Club. Other activities popular in Tambor include sportfishing and horseback riding.

ENVIRONS: West of Tambor, the botanical garden and nursery **Vivero Solera** has butterflies and hummingbirds.

Barceló Los Delfines Golf and Country Club
1 mile (1.6 km) E of Tambor. *683-0333.*

Vivero Solera
2 miles (3 km) W of Tambor. *642-0469.* *6am–4pm Mon–Fri, 6am–noon Sat.*

The lush greens of the golf courses of Tambor

Bright signs adorning shop fronts in Montezuma village

Montezuma 5

Road Map B3. 16 miles (26 km) W of Paquera. *from Paquera.* *Montezuma Music Festival (Jul).*

A FAVORITE WITH budget travelers, this offbeat beach community has a laid-back lifestyle, magnificent ocean vistas and beaches, and unpretentious yet hip bars. The compact village is tucked beneath precipitous hills and opens onto a rocky cove with fishing boats bobbing at anchor. Two superb beaches – Playa Montezuma and Playa Grande – unspool eastward, shaded by tall palms and backed by thickly forested mountains. Swimmers should watch out for the riptides. Sliding between treetops on the **Montezuma Canopy Tour** is a safe, fun, and adrenaline-boosting activity, while **Finca Los Caballos** offers invigorating horseback rides in the hills abuting the Reserva Absoluta Nicolas Weissenburg. The reserve, however, currently has no public access. Clambering up the waterfalls to the west of the village is unsafe; instead, cool off in the pools at the base of the waterfalls.

Montezuma Canopy Tour
1 mile (1.6 km) W of Montezuma.
642-0808. *daily.* *9am, 11am, and 3pm.* www.montezumatraveladventures.com

Finca Los Caballos
2 miles (3 km) NW of Montezuma.
642-0124. *9am daily.*
www.naturelodge.net

Reserva Natural Absoluta Cabo Blanco 6

Road Map B4. 6 miles (10 km) W of Montezuma. *642-0093.* *Montezuma–Cabuya. Also taxis from Montezuma.* *8am–4pm Wed–Sun and public hols.*

ESTABLISHED IN 1963 as the nation's first protected area, and elevated to the status of a reserve in 1974, the 4-sq-mile (10-sq-km) Cabo Blanco owes its genesis to the tireless campaign of Olof Wessberg and his wife Karen Morgenson; they also helped set up the Costa Rican National Park Service.

Activities in Montezuma

Cabo Blanco was initially an "absolute" reserve, off-limits to all visitors, but today there is access to the eastern part of the tropical forests that cover the hilly tip of the Nicoya Peninsula. About 85 percent of the reserve is covered by rejuvenated secondary forest and pockets of lowland tropical forest. There are numerous monkeys, as well as anteaters, coatis, and deer. The 3-mile (5-km) long Sendero Sueco trail leads to the beautiful **Playa Cabo Blanco**; other beaches lie along the shore, but exploring should not be attempted when the tide is rising.

Offshore, the sheer walls of Isla Cabo Blanco are stained white by guano deposited by colonies of nesting seabirds, including frigate birds and brown boobies.

Cabo Blanco is accessed from the community of Cabuya, a mile (1.6 km) along a rough dirt road. Tour operators nationwide offer excursions to the reserve; taxis can also be arranged from Montezuma.

Malpaís 7

Road Map B4. 6 miles (10 km) NW of Montezuma. *from Cóbano, 4 miles (6 km) N of Montezuma.*

ITS NAME MAY mean "bad land," but the Malpaís area's Pacific shoreline is unsurpassed for its rugged beauty. Until a few years ago, the region was unknown; today it is a famed surfers' paradise.

Named for their respective gray-sand beaches, three contiguous communities are strung along the dirt road that fringes the shore. Relaxed to a fault, they are characterized by colorful hotels, restaurants, and bars. The main hamlet is **Carmen**, from where the road runs 2 miles (3 km) south, through Santa Teresa, to the fishing hamlet of Malpaís, which gives the area its popular name. Beyond Malpaís, where vultures perch on fishing boats, the beach ends amid tidepools and fantastically sculpted rocks. A 4WD is required for the southern stretch of the road.

The best surf beach is **Playa Santa Teresa**, merging in the north with *playas* that are virtually uninhabited: Los Suecos, Hermosa, and Manzanillo. Santa Teresa boasts the understatedly deluxe Florblanca Resort *(see p206)*, in stunning counterpoint to the budget options.

Surfer and sun-lovers on Playa Santa Teresa's Pacific shoreline

Wild Cats of Costa Rica

Costa Rica has six members of the wild cat family, found in habitats that range from the wetlands to alpine *páramo* (grasslands). All are endangered to a greater or lesser degree, and are difficult to sight. These well-camouflaged, silent predators vary widely in size and coloring. Of the six species found in Costa Rica, four have spotted coats – the jaguar, the ocelot, the margay, and the extremely rare oncilla. Most species are as comfortable in the trees as they are on the ground, using branches as catwalks in their search for arboreal rodents, monkeys, and other edible prey. Cats enjoy superb vision, and are usually active by both night and day.

An oncilla on the lookout for prey

Jaguars (jaguar)*, the largest of neotropical cats, were worshipped by pre-Columbian peoples. They can weigh up to 330 lb (150 kg). These formerly abundant denizens of lowland rainforests and savannas are threatened by deforestation and poachers.*

Jaguarundis (león breñero) *tend to avoid deep rainforest, preferring savanna and lowland forests. These cats have slender, elongated bodies.*

Ocelots (manigordo) *are found throughout the country. These 3-ft (1-m) long cats are ground dwellers and often follow human trails. Uniquely, they have short tails, with black and white rings.*

Margays (caucel) *are tree-dwelling, nocturnal hunters. A special ankle joint rotates 180 degrees, an adaptation for an arboreal lifestyle. The oncilla is a smaller cousin of the margay.*

Pumas (puma)*, although widely found in Costa Rica, are rarely seen. They are large, slender, adaptable, and solitary cats.*

Cat	Identification	Best Places to See	Visibility
Jaguar	Orange or cobalt-gray coat with large black rosettes	PN Corcovado and PN Tortuguero	Elusive
Jaguarundi	Uniform coloring from rust to chocolate brown; long, feline tail	PN Santa Rosa	Most easily spotted
Margay	House-cat sized; distinctively spotted	PN Corcovado	Relatively visible
Ocelot	Gray coat heavily spotted with beige blotches ringed in black	PN Corcovado	Relatively visible
Oncilla	Smaller and darker than the margay; slim tail	PN Tapantí and La Amistad Biosphere Reserve	Rare; unlikely to be seen
Puma	White throat; uniform coat varies from gray-brown to red	PN Santa Rosa and PN Guanacaste	Elusive

Hiking through a lower elevation forest at Parque Nacional Carara

Parque Nacional Carara 8

Road Map C3. 31 miles (50 km) SE of Puntarenas. 200-5023. *from San José and Jacó.* *7am–4pm daily.* www.sinac.go.cr

OCCUPYING A climatological transition zone where dry northerly and humid southerly ecosystems meet, Carara National Park's forests are complex and varied. Despite its relatively small size – 20 sq miles (52 sq km) – the park offers some of the most diverse wildlife viewing in Costa Rica. Species from both the Meso-American and Amazonian environments are abundant, including the endangered spider monkey and the poison-dart frog. The birding is spectacular, with scarlet macaws being a major draw. They can be seen on their twice-daily migration between the forest and nearby coastal mangroves.

Carara's lower elevation forests have easy-to-walk trails that begin at the roadside visitor center; the longest is 5 miles (8 km) around. Guides can be hired to access pre-Columbian sites. Several tour operators in San José arrange day visits.

ENVIRONS: *Carara* is a Huetar Indian word for crocodile. The reptiles are easily seen from the highway as they bask on the banks of Río Tárcoles. Safaris are offered from **Tárcoles**, 2 miles (3 km) southwest of Carara. The spectacular 600-ft (183-m) drop of **Catarata Manantial de Agua Viva** makes the waterfall popular with hikers who cool off in the pools at its base. Nearby, **Jardín Pura Vida** has walking trails through 30 lush acres (12 ha).

Catarata Manantial de Agua Viva
Bijagual, 4 miles (6 km) E of Tárcoles. *661-8263.* *8am–3pm daily.*

Jardín Pura Vida
Bijagual. *200-5040.*
7am–5pm daily. www.puravidagardensandwaterfalls.com

Jacó 9

Road Map C4. 40 miles (65 km) S of Puntarenas. *6,400.* *International Festival of Music (Jul–Aug).*

THRIVING ON THE surfer trade and that of Canadian "snowbirds" escaping the northern winter, Jacó has evolved as the nation's largest and most party-oriented beach resort. Palms shade the 2-mile (3-km) long beach. Despite this, its gray sands are unremarkable, the sea is usually a murky brown from silt washed down by rivers, and riptides make swimming unsafe. There's no shortage of things to do, however – from crocodile safaris to horseback rides – and the nightlife is lively. Many of the nation's top surfers live here, although as a surf center, Jacó is best for beginners.

Lighthouse Point has a butterfly garden as well as tropical gardens where crocodiles and caimans slosh around in lagoons. Outside town, the **Pacific Rainforest Aerial Tram** takes you on a 90-minute guided ride through the treetops on silent open-air gondolas. The modified ski lifts skim the forest floor, soar above giant trees, pass waterfalls, and give fabulous views along the Pacific coast. Guided tours such as the Poison-dart Frog Trail, are also offered along nature trails.

ENVIRONS: Sportfishing and excursion boats set out from Los Sueños Marina at **Playa Herradura**, a gray-sand beach tucked into a broad bay north of Jacó. The marina is part of the **Los Sueños Marriott Ocean & Golf Resort** *(see p207)*, which boasts a championship golf course.

Perched on a headland just north of Playa Herradura, **Hotel Villa Caletas** *(see p207)* is the remarkable

The gray sands of palm-fringed Playa Jacó

creation of French designer Denis Roy. A long ridgetop driveway lined with Roman urns has dramatic vistas out to sea and also provides a striking entry to this deluxe restaurant and hotel. Musicians perform in a Greek-style amphitheater built into the hillside, a setting for the International Festival of Music. The Serenity Spa offers pampering treatments. A winding track leads down to **Playa Caletas**, a rocky beach with a bar and grill. South of Jacó, **Playa Hermosa** is served by dedicated surf hostels. Sand bars provide consistently good breaks swelling in from deep waters offshore.

Lighthouse Point
Bulevar and Costanera Sur (Hwy 34). *643-3083. 24 hrs. by donation.* www.lighthousepointcr.com

Pacific Rainforest Aerial Tram
2 miles (3 km) E of Jacó. *257-5961. 9am–4pm Mon, 6am–4pm Tue–Sun.* www.rainforestram.com

A small lizard at the Rainmaker Conservation Project

Rainmaker Conservation Project ⓾

Road Map D4. Pocares, 4 miles (6 km) E of Hwy 34, 28 miles (45 km) S of Jacó. *777-3565. organized transfers. 8am–2pm Mon–Sat.* www.rainmakercostarica.com

A TRAIL through the rainforest canopy forms the highlight of this private reserve and conservation project, covering 2 sq miles (5 sq km) on the flanks of the Fila Chonta Mountains. The reserve is at an average altitude of 5,600 ft (1,700 m), and protects four distinct ecological habitats, including montane cloud forest at higher elevations.

There are several hiking trails and a river walk, which leads through the Río Seco canyon to a sparkling pool safe for bathing. A steep climb leads uphill to the canopy trail, with suspension bridges slung between treetops forming an aerial walkway. The longest bridge is 170 ft (50 m) long. These are perfect vantage points for spotting sloths, monkeys, iguanas, toucans, and scores of other species, including the extremely rare harlequin toad, recently rediscovered here.

Signs identifying flora at the Rainmaker Conservation Project

Boca Damas ⓫

Road Map D4. 33 miles (53 km) S of Jacó.

CRISSCROSSED BY countless sloughs and channels, this vast *manglare* (mangrove) complex extends along the shoreline between the towns of Parrita and Quepos, at the estuary of Río Damas. Coatis, pumas, white-faced monkeys, and several species of snakes inhabit the dense forests. Crocodiles and caimans lurk in the tannin-stained waters. Stilt-legged shorebirds and boat-billed herons, with their curious keel-shaped beaks, pick among the mudflats in search of molluscs.

Tour operators in Quepos offer kayaking excursions. Guides offer boat trips from the small dock at Damas.

CROCODILE SAFARI

Indiscriminate hunting during the past 400 years has resulted in a decimation of the American *cocodrilo* (crocodile) population. Since gaining protected status in 1981, however, crocodiles have managed to made a comeback. They can be seen in rivers throughout the Pacific lowlands, but are nowhere so numerous as near the mouth of Río Tárcoles, where populations of more than 200 crocodiles per mile have been counted. Boats depart from the village of Tárcoles, near the mouth of the river, for 2-hour crocodile-spotting safaris upriver. The reptiles, which grow up to 16 ft (5 m) in length, often approach to within a few feet. Keep your hands in the boat. You can also expect to see roseate spoonbills, scarlet macaws, and dozens of other Costa Rican bird species.

Crocodiles seen from a bridge over Río Tárcoles, Puntarenas

A relaxed cafeteria and ice cream bar on a downtown Quepos street

Quepos ⓬

Road Map D4. 34 miles (55 km) S of Jacó. 11,000. *Carnaval (Feb–Mar).* www.quepolandia.com

TRADITIONALLY a game fishing base and center for the production of African palm oil, Quepos has blossomed as a tourist center and a gateway to Parque Nacional Manuel Antonio. Relatively quiet by day, the town buzzes at night when its numerous bars and restaurants come alive.

On the north side of town, Boca Vieja village has wooden huts, which are linked by flimsy walkways that overhang the brown sands of **Playa Cocal**. In the hills to the south, quaint clapboard homes recall the 1930s, when the Standard Fruit Company established banana plantations. Panama disease killed them off, and today African oil palms dominate the coastal plains for miles around.

ENVIRONS: South of Quepos, a two-lane road winds over steep headlands down to the hamlet of **Manuel Antonio**, fronted by **Playa Espadilla**, a wide scimitar of gray sand. At the north end of the beach, a lagoon has crocodiles. Dozens of restaurants, bars, and hotels line the route, including **El Avión**, a converted Fairchild C-123 transport plane, which was used by the CIA in the 1970s to run arms to the Nicaraguan Contras *(see p135)*.

Nearby, **Fincas Naturales Wildlife Refuge & Butterfly Garden** offers easy walks through 40 acres (16 ha) teeming with sloths, raccoon-like coatis, leafcutter ants, and phenomenal birdlife.

The **Río Naranjo Valley** extends east of Quepos into the Fila Nara Mountains. The ruins of a Spanish mission, established in 1570, still stand by the roadside. Whitewater rafting trips are a popular excursion from Quepos.

Farther up the valley, **Rancho Los Tucanes** offers guided horseback and 4WD tours of its vanilla and pepper plantations. Trails lead through montane rainforest to the 295-ft (90-m) high Los Tucanos waterfall.

Fincas Naturales Wildlife Refuge & Butterfly Garden
1 mile (1.6 km) S of Quepos. 777-0850. *6am–8pm daily; butterfly garden: 8am–4pm daily.* www.butterflygardens.co.cr

Rancho Los Tucanes
Londres, 7 miles (11 km) NE of Quepos. *779-1001.* *7am–3pm daily.* www.lostucanestours.com

Parque Nacional Manuel Antonio ⓭

See pp118–19.

Valle del Río Savegre ⓮

Road Map D4. 15 miles (25 km) SE of Quepos. *from Quepos.*

CUTTING INLAND into the Fila San Bosco Mountains, the Río Savegre Valley is covered by plantations of African oil palms at its lower levels. Farther up the valley lies the rural community of El Silencio, where the local farmers' cooperative operates an ecotourist center called **Coopesilencio** *(see p208)*. It offers horses for rides down rustic trails into a nature reserve, and has a wildlife rescue center with scarlet macaws, deer, and monkeys.

Modeled on a South African safari camp, **Rafiki Safari Lodge** *(see p208)* is set atop a ridge overlooking the Savegre. It makes a great base for hiking, birding, and horseback riding, as well as for exhilarating whitewater rafting and kayaking trips on Río Savegre. The lodge has a tapir breeding program, which reintroduces these endangered animals in the wild.

Coopesilencio
25 miles (40 km) SE of Quepos. *380-5581.* *9:30am–noon and 1–3:30pm daily.* www.turismoruralcr.com

Plantations of African oil palms in the Valle del Río Savegre

Sportfishing on the Pacific Coast

The ultimate draw for the game-fishing enthusiast, Costa Rica's waters witness the setting of new International Game Fish Association records every year. More anglers have claimed "grand slams" – both species of marlin and one or more sailfish in a single day – on the country's Pacific coast than in any other place on earth. In the wet season (May–November), fishing is best off the Golfo de Papagayo. In the dry season (December–April), when high winds in the Golfo de Papagayo make the waters dangerous, the best fishing is found farther toward the south, out of the year-round marinas of Quepos, Bahía Drake, and Golfito. Angling on the Caribbean coast is different: inshore fishing using light tackle is the norm here *(see p251)*.

Fishing lure

Organized Fishing Trips

Sportfishing vessels often journey 20 miles (32 km) or more from shore to find game fish. Hooking a fish is only the beginning. The real sport lies in the fight that ensues.

***Charter shops** and fishing lodges abound in Costa Rica. Apart from hiring out boats, they can also arrange fishing licenses for visiting anglers.*

***Anglers** strap themselves into the "fighting chair" to bring in larger species. Fights sometimes take hours and can tire the angler almost as much as the fish.*

***A catch-and-release policy** is usually followed by sportfishing operators in Costa Rica. However, maritime laws designed to protect fish stocks from commercial over-exploitation are poorly enforced.*

Deep Sea Fish

A wide variety of game fish await the keen angler on Costa Rica's Pacific coast. Angling is possible year-round, but there are prime areas and peak seasons for each species.

***Yellowfin tuna** are extremely powerful, weighing up to 350 lb (160 kg). They are found in warm currents year-round, but June–October is best.*

***Wahoo** are long, sleek, and explosively fast fish that are found in northern waters between May and August.*

***Dorado** (also called dolphin-fish or mahimahi) have scales that flash a wide range of colors. This dramatic fighter is found from May to October.*

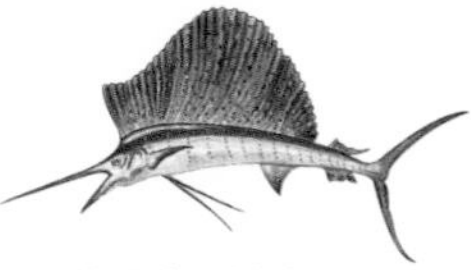

***Sailfish**, hard-fighting giants up to 7 ft (2 m) long, and known for their spectacular leaps when hooked, are plentiful from December to April.*

***Blue marlins** are considered the ultimate prize. The "Bull of the Ocean" puts up a fight like no other. Females weigh up to 1,000 lb (455 kg); males are smaller. August–December are generally the best months.*

Parque Nacional Manuel Antonio ⓭

Signage within PN Manuel Antonio

Named for a Spanish conquistador, and flanked by the ocean and forested hills, this beautiful park was inaugurated in 1972. Although it is the smallest in Costa Rica's park system, covering a land area of 6 sq miles (16 sq km), Manuel Antonio National Park has remarkable biodiversity, with abundant wildlife and magnificent beaches. Sightings of coatis, sloths, toucans, and scarlet macaws along the well-maintained trails are virtually guaranteed. This is one of the most visited parks in the nation: although there is a limit on the daily number of visitors, its wildlife is threatened by overuse, pollution, and unregulated hotel expansion.

Visitors queuing at the park entrance

Playa Espadilla Sur

A long swathe of coral-colored sand curling south from Manuel Antonio village, this beach connects with Playa Espadilla to the north.

Punta Catedral

This former island is now connected to the mainland by a tombolo *(natural land bridge). The rocky promontory has tidal pools at its base and is encircled by a trail that ascends to a* mirador *(viewpoint).*

Playa Manuel Antonio

This scimitar-shaped beach with soft white sands shelves into calm jade waters containing a small coral reef. Snorkeling is splendid, especially in the dry season. Green and Pacific ridley turtles sometimes nest here.

Coral reefs form a refuge for crabs, starfish, shrimp and colorful fish. Dolphins and humpback whales are often seen in this area.

The Manchineel Tree

Manchineel trees

Locally called *manzanillo*, or "beach apple," the manchineel tree is quite common on the beaches, causing problems for unwary visitors seeking its shade. This evergreen species *(Hippomane manicinella)*, identified by its short trunk and bright green elliptical leaves, is very toxic. The sap and bark inflame the skin, while the small yellow apple-like fruit is poisonous. Moreover, if its wood is burnt, the smoke is an irritant to the lungs.

Visitors' Checklist

Road Map D4. 100 miles (160 km) S of San José and 5 miles (8 km) S of Quepos. *777-0644. from San José and Quepos. 8am–4pm Tue–Sun. Limited to 600 visitors a day.*

Sendero Mirador

Ascending a hill and dropping past Playa Escondido, this muddy, 0.8-mile (1.3-km) long trail then rises to a mirador *with great views toward Punta Catedral.*

Monkeys

Capuchin monkeys and tiny squirrel monkeys are easily spotted throughout the park. Do not feed them – the illegal practice is a threat to their health and behavior.

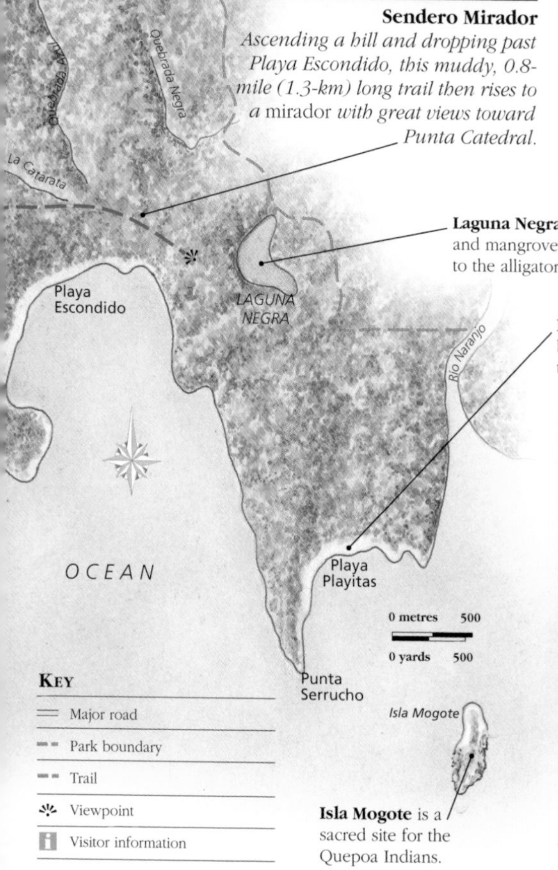

Laguna Negra's brackish waters and mangrove swamps are home to the alligator-like caiman.

Playa Playitas is remote and, being a nesting site for marine turtles, is off-limits to visitors.

Isla Mogote is a sacred site for the Quepoa Indians.

Rocky Islands

An additional 212 sq miles (550 sq km) of the park protects 12 islands that host large colonies of seabirds.

Guanacaste and Northern Nicoya

With its arid plains, *men on horseback, rodeos, and bullfights, the province of Guanacaste is steeped in the hacienda heritage. The region stretches from the cloud-tipped volcanoes of the Cordillera de Guanacaste to the marshes of the Río Tempisque basin and the magnificent surf-washed beaches of Northern Nicoya – paradise for marine turtles and surfers.*

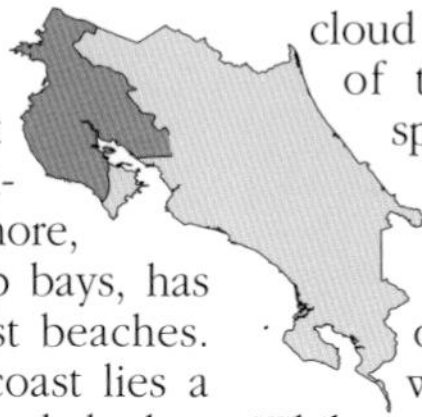

A chain of volcanoes and mountains runs across this vast region, framing it to the east. To the northwest, the rugged Pacific shore, which is serrated by deep bays, has many of the nation's best beaches. Between mountain and coast lies a broad trough whose wetlands harbor crocodiles and waterfowl. To the southwest, the Nicoya Peninsula enfolds the mangrove-fringed Gulf of Nicoya. Although the plains can be searingly hot, the mountains offer cool, beautiful retreats, while refreshing breezes caress the beaches.

In spring, the sparsely foliated deciduous forests of the plains explode in a riot of color while offering the advantage of relatively easy wildlife spotting. Thick evergreen cloud forests on the upper slopes of the mountains provide a splendid study in contrasts.

The Chorotega culture was one of the region's most developed at the time of the Spanish arrival, and was quickly assimilated. While no great pre-Columbian architecture has been discovered, a tradition of superb pottery continues in the Guaitíl area. The predominant culture now is that of the *sabanero* (cowboy), tracing a lineage back to colonial days, when great haciendas were constructed. Raising or tending cattle is still the dominant occupation here, although many inhabitants cling to a way of life established in pre-Columbian times, earning their livelihood from fishing.

Sabaneros **(cowboys) herding cattle at a ranch in Liberia**

◁ **An *espavé* tree *(Anacardium excelsum)* entwined by a strangling fig, Parque Nacional Rincón de la Vieja**

Exploring Guanacaste and Northern Nicoya

The driest of Costa Rica's regions offers possibilities ranging from the spectacular cloud forests of Monteverde to the volcano parks of Rincón de la Vieja, Miravalles, and Guanacaste, and the beach-fringed Parque Nacional Santa Rosa. Birding is superb at Palo Verde, Lomas Barbudal, and near Cañas. To the north is Liberia, with its colonial buildings. Laid-back Playas del Coco to the west is a base for scuba diving, while Playa Flamingo is a sportfishing destination. Farther south is the surf center of Tamarindo, and Playa Grande and Ostional draw marine turtles. Guaitíl is famed for its traditional pottery, while Barra Honda attracts cavers.

Liberia's main plaza, flanked by trees

Sights at a Glance

Towns and Cities

Cañas 3
Guaitíl 22
Islita 19
Liberia 7
Nicoya 20
Nosara 17
Sámara 18
Santa Cruz 21
Tamarindo 15
Tilarán 2

National Parks and Reserves

Parque Nacional Barra Honda 23
Parque Nacional Guanacaste 9
Parque Nacional Palo Verde 4
Parque Nacional Rincón de la Vieja 8
Parque Nacional Santa Rosa pp134–5 11
Refugio Nacional de Vida Silvestre Ostional 16
Reserva Biológica Lomas Barbudal 5

Areas of Natural Beauty

Bahía Culebra 12
Bahía Salinas 10
Monteverde and Santa Elena pp124–8 1
Volcán Miravalles 6

Beaches

Playa Flamingo 14
Playas del Coco 13

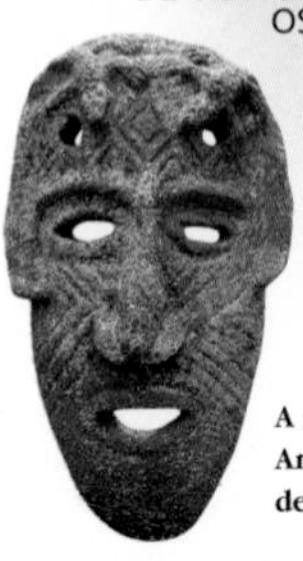

A mask at Rancho Armadillo, Playas del Coco

Cattle crossing a stream near Parque Nacional Palo Verde

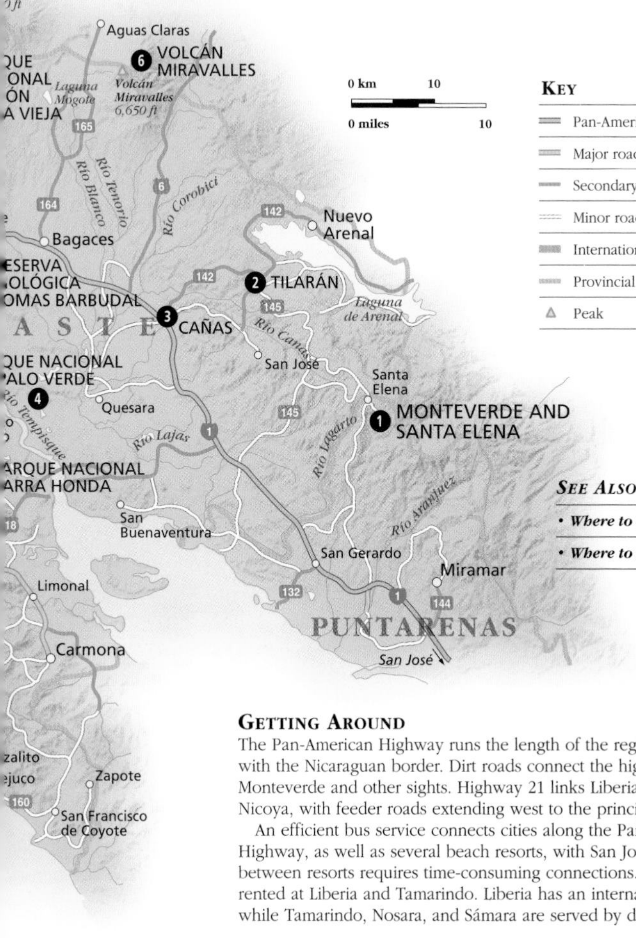

KEY

- Pan-American Highway
- Major road
- Secondary road
- Minor road
- International border
- Provincial border
- Peak

SEE ALSO

• ***Where to Stay*** pp208–12

• ***Where to Eat*** pp231–4

GETTING AROUND

The Pan-American Highway runs the length of the region, connecting with the Nicaraguan border. Dirt roads connect the highway with Monteverde and other sights. Highway 21 links Liberia to Northern Nicoya, with feeder roads extending west to the principal beach resorts.

An efficient bus service connects cities along the Pan-American Highway, as well as several beach resorts, with San José, but bus travel between resorts requires time-consuming connections. Cars can be rented at Liberia and Tamarindo. Liberia has an international airport, while Tamarindo, Nosara, and Sámara are served by domestic airports.

Monteverde and Santa Elena ❶

Monteverde logo

KNOWN WORLDWIDE for its unique cloud forest reserve that helped promote Costa Rica's reputation for ecotourism, Monteverde boasts a pastoral alpine setting at an elevation of 4,600 ft (1,400 m), in the heart of the Cordillera de Tilarán. To the northwest is Santa Elena, which is often considered a part of the Monteverde area. Several other reserves, incorporated within the Zona Protectora Arenal-Monteverde, are found in the area. Monteverde's fame has spawned all manner of attractions, including a variety of tours that permit visitors a monkey's-eye view of the forest canopy. However, even in the face of these ever-increasing services and attractions, Monteverde retains a bucolic charm.

Canopy Tours
Four canopy tours permit visitors to explore the canopy along zipline or by rappeling.

Orquídeas de Monteverde
displays one-third of Costa Rica's orchid species (see p126).

Reserva Bosque Nuboso Santa Elena
Offering similar wildlife species to the Monteverde Cloud Forest Biological Reserve, the Santa Elena reserve is, however, less crowded (see p128).

Finca Ecológico
has four trails through montane tropical forest.

Serpentario
This boasts close-up encounters with snakes that inhabit the local forests, as well as various other amphibians and reptiles (see p126).

Bajo del Tigre Trail
is a self-guided interpretative trail. Three-wattled bellbirds and quetzals are frequently seen.

KEY

- Major road
- Other road
- Trail
- Park boundary
- Visitor information

Monteverde Nature Center and Butterfly Gardens
Dozens of butterfly species flit about inside netted gardens at this educational center, which has displays spanning the insect world (see p126).

Santa Elena
Located downhill of Monteverde, with the locality known as Cerro Plano lying in between, this is the area's main village, with a bank, bus stop, and other services.

Visitors' Checklist

Road Map C2. 42 miles (68 km) N of Puntarenas, 22 miles (35 km) uphill from the Pan-Am Hwy. 4,000. *to Santa Elena and up to Monteverde Cloud Forest Biological Reserve. Monteverde Ecotouristic Fair (mid-Jun).* www.acmonteverde.com
Original Canopy Tour 645-5243. *8am–4:30pm daily.*

La Lechería
Started by immigrant Quakers from the United States, the "Cheese Factory" is the foundation of the local economy. It offers visitors an insider's view of cheese-making (see p126).

Pastures
Monteverde's lush rolling hills are fertile pastures for the cattle that are the source of the area's famous cheeses.

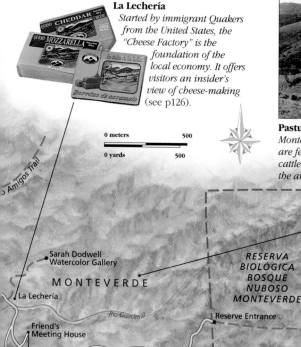

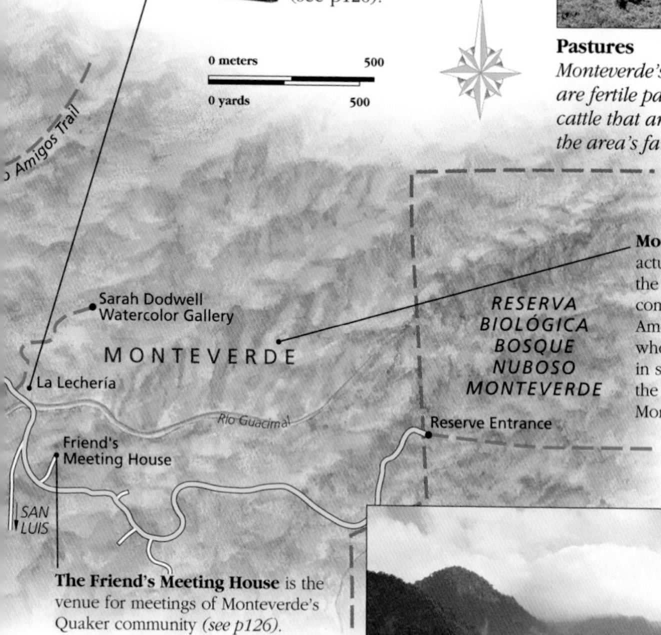

Monteverde is actually the name of the Quaker community of American extract, whose members live in scattered homes in the forests below the Monteverde reserve.

The Friend's Meeting House is the venue for meetings of Monteverde's Quaker community *(see p126).*

Reserva Biológica Bosque Nuboso Monteverde
The world-famous Monteverde Cloud Forest Biological Reserve is the nation's foremost locale for viewing resplendent quetzals – one among more than 400 species of birds found here (see p127).

Exploring Monteverde and Santa Elena

Monteverde Reserve sign

Cool and verdant Monteverde has its fair share of interesting sights, many of which are spread out along the winding dirt road that slopes gently upward from Santa Elena to the Monteverde Cloud Forest Biological Reserve. Other sights are tucked away off side roads, some of which are quite rugged and steep. Walking is a pleasurable option, but the heavily trafficked roads can be muddy or dusty, depending on the weather. It is always a wise idea to take along an umbrella. Dozens of hotels and restaurants line the route. A steeper dirt road leads northeast from Santa Elena to Santa Elena Cloud Forest Reserve, passing several key attractions along the route.

Ranario de Monteverde

330 yd (300 m) SW of Santa Elena.
645-6320. *9am–8:30pm daily.*
www.ranario.com

The Frog Pond of Monteverde displays about 20 species of frogs and amphibians, as well as snakes, salamanders, and lizards in large glass cases that try to replicate their natural environments. Several of Costa Rica's most intriguing *ranas* and *sapos* (frogs and toads) are here, including poison-dart frogs clad in various bright-colored liveries, the endearing red-eyed tree frogs, transparent frogs, and huge marine toads. The best time to visit is evening or night, when the frogs are most active and visitors can hear their distinct calls. The center also has a gift shop.

Serpentario

550 yd (500 m) S of Santa Elena.
645-6002. *9am–8pm daily.*
www.snaketour.com

Among more than 20 species of snakes shown behind glass in this snake house are the fearsome *terciopelo* (fer-de-lance, or *Bothrops asper*) and its nemesis, the *terciopelo-eating musarana (Clelia clelia)*. Most species displayed here can be encountered in local forests. Also exhibited are turtles, iguanas, basilisk lizards, chameleons, and frogs. Although the educational labels are only in Spanish, guides who can speak both English and Spanish are available.

Delicate orchids grown at Orquídeas de Monteverde

Orquídeas de Monteverde

0.8 mile (1.3 km) E of Santa Elena.
645-5509. *8am–5pm daily.*

A great place to learn about orchids *(see p183)*, the Monteverde Orchid Garden has more than 500 local species. They are arranged in 22 groups along a winding self-guided trail labeled with educational signs. Visitors are each handed a magnifying glass to help them appreciate such diminutives as the liverwort orchid *(Platystele jungermannioides)*, the world's smallest flower.

Monteverde Nature Center & Butterfly Gardens

1.2 miles (1.8 km) S of Santa Elena.
645-5512. *9:30am–4pm daily.*

With educational exhibits as well as butterfly arenas representing three distinct habitats, this nature center is an ideal locale for learning about the life cycle of the butterfly. The fascinating displays include dozens of live arachnid and insect species, not the least of which are tarantulas, stick insects, giant rhinoceros beetles, and 5-inch (13-cm) long caterpillars, which can be seen weaving chrysalids.

Educational videos are shown, and a video "bug cam" gives visitors a larger-than-life real-time view of leafcutter ants inside a nest. The highlight of the hour-long guided tour is a large netted flyway where more than 40 species of colorful butterflies flit about amid dense foliage that recreates both lowland rainforest and mid-elevation montane forest environments. Go mid-morning, when the butterflies become active.

La Lechería

2 miles (3 km) SE of Santa Elena. *645-5029.* *7:30am–5pm Mon–Sat, 7:30am–12:30pm Sun.* *9am and 2pm.* www.monteverde.net

Founded by the original Quaker settlers of Monteverde in 1953, the "Cheese Factory" today produces 14 types of

The Quakers

Painting of a Quaker in traditional attire

The original settlers of Monteverde were 44 members of the pacifist Protestant religious group called Quakers. Hailing from Alabama, USA, where they had been jailed for refusing to be drafted, they arrived in Costa Rica in 1951, drawn by the fact that the country had abolished its army following the 1948 Civil War. They settled in the Cordillera de Tilarán, raising dairy cattle to produce the cheese that is now famous throughout the nation. The Quakers have been at the forefront of local conservation efforts in Monteverde.

The Golden Toad

In 1964 scientists discovered a new species of toad *(Bufo periglenes)* in the cloud forest above Monteverde. They named the brilliant orange creature *sapo dorado* (golden toad). In fact, only the male, which is 1-inch (3-cm) long, is bright orange; the female is larger and speckled in patches of black, red, and yellow. Although abundant as recently as 1986, *sapo dorado* has not been seen since 1988 and is now considered extinct.

Golden toads, now extinct

pasteurized cheese, including parmesan, Gouda, and the best-selling Monte Rico, famous throughout Costa Rica. Guided tours show visitors the manufacturing process, resulting in the production of more than 2,200 lb (1,000 kg) of cheese daily. Visitors can buy *cajeta*, a butterscotch spread, and cheeses on-site.

Reserva Biológica Bosque Nuboso Monteverde

4 miles (6 km) SE of Santa Elena.
645-5122. *7am–4pm daily.*
by reservation.
www.cct.or.cr

The dirt road that winds uphill from Santa Elena ends at the 40-sq-mile (105-sq-km) Monteverde Cloud Forest Biological Reserve, the jewel in the crown of the 115-sq-mile (300-sq-km) Arenal-Monteverde Protection Zone. Owned and operated by the Tropical Science Center of Costa Rica, the reserve straddles the Continental Divide and comprises six distinct ecological zones extending down the Pacific and Caribbean slopes. The upper elevation forests of the reserve are smothered by near-constant mists fed by sodden trade winds sweeping in off the Atlantic. On the more exposed ridges, trees are reduced to stunted dwarfs by the battering of the wind.

Wildlife abounds at the Monteverde Cloud Forest Biological Reserve. There are more than 150 species of amphibians and reptiles, and over 500 species of butterflies. More than 100 species of mammals include five wild cats – jaguars, jaguarundis, pumas, margays, and ocelots. The umbrella bird and the endangered three-wattled bellbird are among the 400 species of birds. Quetzals are easily seen, the best viewing time being the April–May mating season, when they are especially active after dawn. Also easily spotted are hummingbirds, which gather at feeders outside the visitor center; the reserve counts more than 30 species. Most wildlife, however, is elusive and difficult to detect.

Iguana at Reserva Biológica Bosque Nuboso Monteverde

The reserve is crossed by 75 miles (120 km) of trails. A self-guided booklet corresponds to educational posts along the most popular trails, which are covered with wooden boardwalks and are linked together to form what is colloquially called "the triangle." Sendero Chomogo is a steep trail leading to a *mirador* (viewpoint) atop the Continental Divide. From here, on rare days when the mists clear, visitors can see both the Pacific and the Caribbean. More challenging trails extend down the Caribbean slopes to the lowlands; these involve a full day's hike, with mud oozing underfoot. Luckily, rubber boots can be rented, along with binoculars to help spot the shyer residents of the reserve. The driest months are between December and April. Hotels organize transport, and both taxis and buses also operate from Santa Elena.

A hike through Reserva Biológica Bosque Nuboso Monteverde

Reserva Bosque Nuboso Santa Elena

4 miles (6 km) NE of Santa Elena. *645-5390. 7am–4pm daily. 7:30am, 11:30am, and 6:30pm, by appt.* www.reservasantaelena.org

Funded and run by the community of Santa Elena, the 2-sq-mile (5-sq-km) Santa Elena Cloud Forest Reserve is dedicated to conservation and education. The students of the local high school play a vital role in its development.

Set at a higher elevation than the more famous and crowded Reserva Biológica Bosque Nuboso Monteverde *(see p127)*, this magical green world is cloudier and wetter, and lush with epiphytes and ferns. Spider and howler monkeys are easily seen, as are resplendent quetzals, orange-bellied trogons, squirrels, and agoutis, which are rodent-like mammals. More elusive are the tapirs, jaguars, ocelots, pumas, and tayras, which belong to the same family as otters and weasels. On clear days, there are fabulous views toward Volcán Arenal in the northeast. A self-guided booklet is available for the 7 miles (11 km) of hiking trails.

Sky Walk/SkyTrek

3 miles (5 km) NE of Santa Elena. *645-5238. 7am–4pm daily. 8am, 10:30am, and 1:30pm.* www.skywalk.co.cr; www.skytrek.com

With high walkways, ziplines, and suspension bridges, this project on the edge of Reserva Bosque Nuboso Santa Elena

A visitor trying the Sky Walk along the cloud forest canopy

offers a variety of ways in which to explore the cloud forest canopy. Thrill-seekers can try the 2-hour SkyTrek. Securely harnessed, visitors slide between treetop platforms along ziplines that total a mile (1.6 km) in length. Two observatory towers offer panoramic views of the Guanacaste and Puntarenas lowlands. The more sedate Sky Walk is just as good for wildlife viewing, with 3,300 ft (1,000 m) of aerial pathways, including five suspension bridges hung between treetop platforms.

Selvatura Park and Jewels of the Rainforest Bio-Art Exhibition

4 miles (6 km) NE of Santa Elena. *645-5929. 7am–5pm daily.* www.selvatura.com

Selvatura has 2 miles (3 km) of treetop walkways with eight suspension bridges that meander through the cloud forest canopy. There is also a 14-platform zipline canopy tour, one of Costa Rica's longest, for a monkey's-eye view of the upper elevation forest. The tour includes an optional "Tarzan Swing," and normally takes about 3 hours.

The highlight is the **Jewels of the Rainforest Bio-Art Exhibition**, which features a superb display of the world's largest private insect collection, put together by entomologist Dr. Richard Whitten. Beautifully laid out in a riot of colors, thousands of stick insects, butterflies, spiders, wasps, beetles, moths, and other insects are exhibited in educational panels arranged according to geographic regions and themes. Other exhibits include giant crustaceans and skulls of prehistoric creatures, such as the saber-toothed tiger. There are also human skulls, ranging from Australopithecus to Homo sapiens. Fascinating videos about insect life are shown in an auditorium. Visitors can also watch Dr. Whitten at work in his Selvatura laboratory via a real-time video link.

Selvatura's other attractions include a hummingbird garden with over 14 species of hummingbirds, a climbing wall, guided nature walks, and a domed, climate-controlled butterfly garden with over 20 species of butterflies, including the shimmering blue morphos. An amphibian and reptile exhibition is planned.

The entrance to Reserva Bosque Nuboso Santa Elena

Cloud Forests of Costa Rica

NAMED FOR THE ephemeral mists that always envelop them, Costa Rica's cloud forests are typically found at elevations above 3,500 ft (1,050 m). More properly called montane tropical rainforests, they show extreme local variations in flora. On wind-swept, exposed ridges, trees and shrubs grow close to the ground as a form of protection, forming elfin forest with a primeval quality. More protected areas have taller vegetation typical of rainforests, with several levels *(see pp22–3)*. However, the lush canopies rarely reach 100 ft (30 m), although massive trees occasionally break through. Epiphytic plants such as orchids and bromeliads cling to branches, which also drip with lichen, fungi, mosses, and liverworts.

Clear-wing butterfly

***Pipers**, found in moist areas, can have large leaves up to 20 inches (50 cm) in size. Costa Rica has 94 species of pipers.*

Swirling mists are created by humid Caribbean trade winds that condense as they sweep up to the Continental Divide.

***Mosses** breathe and draw water directly from the air through roots that hang from branches like an old man's beard.*

FLORA AND FAUNA

The constant interplay of sunshine, clouds, and rainfall in cloud forests produces flora of astounding diversity. Fauna is correspondingly abundant, although the mists and thick foliage hamper sightings.

Trees include guarumo, wild fig, and the huge zapote, with branches often weighed down by epiphytic plants.

***Collared peccaries** forage in large groups and are highly social. They use their long canines to defend themselves.*

***Prong-billed barbets** have a telltale yodel but are reclusive and rarely seen. At night they sleep huddled together.*

***Howler monkeys** are arboreal leaf- and fruit-eaters. Males are known for their intimidating, booming roars.*

Tilarán ❷

Road Map B2. 14 miles (22 km) E of Cañas. *7,700.* *Feria del Día Cívica (Apr–Jun).*

THIS NEAT LITTLE town, at an elevation of 1,800 ft (550 m) on the Continental Divide, has crisp air and a pretty plaza shaded by pines and cypress trees. It makes a delightful stop en route to and from Lake Arenal, although the only sight of note is the 1960s modern-looking, arch-roofed cathedral, decorated with marquetry. An agricultural town surrounded by undulating fields, Tilarán is known for its annual livestock show and rodeo.

Tower, Tilarán cathedral

ENVIRONS: Orchid lovers should visit **Vivero Poporí**, where tropical orchids are raised and more than 20 species of butterflies flutter inside a netted garden.

Vivero Poporí
2 miles (3 km) E of Tilarán. *695-5047.* *7am–5pm daily.*

Cañas ❸

Road Map B2. 48 miles (77 km) N of Puntarenas. *19,000.* *Feria Domingo de Resurrección (Mar/Apr).*

A DUSTY COWBOY town set dramatically in the lee of the Cordillera de Guanacaste, Cañas is also known as Ciudad de la Amistad (City of Friendship). Surrounded by cattle haciendas in the searingly hot Tempisque basin, Cañas is most appealing for its *sabaneros* (cowboys). It sits astride the Pan-Am Highway, and serves as the gateway to Parque Nacional Palo Verde and Lake Arenal.

ENVIRONS: To the north, the **Centro de Rescate Las Pumas** (Puma Rescue Shelter) is a private facility for rescued wild cats. Some of the cats – which include jaguars, pumas, jaguarundis, margays, ocelots, and oncillas – are quite tame, having been raised by the late founder, Lilly Bodmer de Hagnauer. No guard rails prevent visitors from going up to the cages – caution is needed. Nearby, Río Corobicí is popular for rafting trips offered by **Safaris Corobicí**; small rapids add touches of excitement.

Bird-watching from canopied boats at Parque Nacional Palo Verde

Centro de Rescate Las Pumas
Pan-Am Hwy, 3 miles (5 km) N of Cañas. *669-6044.* *8am–4pm daily.* *by donation.*

Safaris Corobicí
Pan-Am Hwy, 3 miles (5 km) N of Cañas. *669-1091.*

Parque Nacional Palo Verde ❹

Road Map B2. 26 miles (42 km) W of Cañas. *200-0125.* *to Puerto Humo, then boat to trailhead leading to park HQ; to Bagaces (14 miles/22 km N of Cañas), then by jeep-taxi.* *8am–4pm daily.*

ONE OF THE country's most diverse national parks, Palo Verde was inaugurated in 1980. Spread over 50 sq miles (130 sq km), it protects a mosaic of habitats including mangrove swamps, marshes, savanna, and tropical dry forest at the mouth of Río Tempisque. Much of the vegetation consists of such drought-tolerant species as ironwood and sandbox, as well as evergreen *paloverde* (green stick) trees, which give the park its name.

Fauna is diverse and abundant. During the dry season from December to April, the trees burst into vibrant bloom. The ripening fruits draw monkeys, raccoon-like coatis, white-tailed deer, peccaries (wild hogs), pumas, and other mammals. In the wet season, much of the area floods and draws flocks of waterfowl to join herons, jabiru storks, ibis, roseate spoonbills and other stilt-legged waders. Palo Verde has more than 300 species of birds, including a large population of scarlet macaws and curassows. **Isla de Pájaros**, in the middle of Río Tempisque, is a major nesting site.

Wildlife viewing is best in the dry season when the deciduous trees lose their leaves and animals collect near waterholes. Lookout points can be accessed by well-maintained trails.

Reserva Biológica Lomas Barbudal ❺

Road Map A2. 4 miles (6 km) SW of Pan-Am Hwy, 12 miles (19 km) NW of Bagaces. *671-1290.* *to Bagaces, then by jeep-taxi.* *8am–4pm daily (subject to change).* *by donation.*

FAMOUS FOR ITS plentiful insect population, not least the 250 species of bees, the seldom-visited Reserva

Rare dry forests of Reserva Biológica Lomas Barbudal

Biológica Lomas Barbudal (Bearded Hills Biological Reserve) protects rare tropical dry forest. Established in 1986, the hilly, densely forested terrain hosts a similar array of wildlife to Parque Nacional Palo Verde. The reserve also has plant species not usually found in dry forests – its waterways are lined with evergreens such as guapinol and fruit-bearing *níspero*.

Trails span the 9-sq-mile (23-sq-km) reserve from the Casa de Patrimonio visitor center on the banks of Río Cabuyo, which has pools that are good for swimming. The best time to visit is during February and March, when the park's trees bloom in spectacular profusion.

Fumaroles near Las Hornillas, Volcán Miravalles

Volcán Miravalles 6

Road Map B2. 16 miles (26 km) N of Bagaces. *from Bagaces.*

This active volcano rises 6,650 ft (2,030 m) above the Guanacaste plains. Few visitors hike the trails that lace the 42-sq-mile (109-sq-km) Miravalles Forest Reserve on the upper slopes. Tapirs are drawn to lakes near the summit, and there are several other species of fauna.

The main draw is **Las Hornillas** (Little Ovens), an area of steam vents and mud pools bubbling and hissing on the western slopes. The Institute of Electricity (ICE) produces power from the super-heated water vapor at **Proyecto Geotérmico Miravalles**. Las Hornillas also feed thermal pools at **Centro Turístico Yökö** and **Centro Turístico Termomanía**, both recreational facilities with accommodation and food. A short trail leads from here to the fumaroles. There are no guard rails and the ground is unstable: keep a safe distance.

Proyecto Geotérmico Miravalles
17 miles (27 km) NE of Bagaces. *673-1111, ext 232.* *by appt.*

Centro Turístico Yökö
2 miles (3 km) E of Guayabo, Hwy 164. *673-0410.* *7am–11pm daily.*

Centro Turístico Termomanía
2 miles (3 km) E of Guayabo, Hwy 164. *673-0233.* *8am–10pm daily.*

Liberia 7

Road Map A2. 16 miles (26 km) N of Bagaces. *39,000.* *665-0135.* *Día de la Anexión de Guanacaste (Jul 25).*

Guanacaste's charming, historic capital, founded in 1769, is known as the White City for its whitewashed adobe houses with terra-cotta tile roofs. The loveliest houses are on Calle Real (Calle Central). A perfect example of Liberia's trademark *puertas del sol* – double doors, one on each side of a corner, to catch both morning and afternoon sun – can be seen at the pretty colonial-era Casa de Cultura. Today, it houses the **Museo de Sabanero**, which focuses on cowboy culture. The main plaza has the modern **Iglesia Imaculada Concepción de María**. Next door, the *ayuntamiento* (town hall) flies Guanacaste's flag, the only provincial flag in the country. Each July, locals celebrate Guanacaste's separation from Nicaragua in 1824. The Iglesia de la Ermita de la Resurección, familiarly known as **Iglesia de la Agonía**, is an engaging 1825 adobe colonial church, which features a small museum of religious art. Liberia is the main gateway to Parque Nacional Rincón de la Vieja *(see p132)* and the beaches of Northern Nicoya.

Interior of a colonial-era house on Calle Real, Liberia

Liberia's Monumento Sabanero

Museo de Sabanero
Calle 1 and Ave 6. *666-1606.* *8am–noon and 1:30–5pm Mon–Sat.*

Iglesia de la Agonía
Calle 9 and Ave Central. *2:30–3:30pm daily.*

Cowboy Culture

A majority of Guanacastecos make their living as *sabaneros* (cowboys), also called *bramaderos* after the hardy Brahma cattle. Proud, folkloric figures, the *sabaneros* ride straight-backed in their elaborately decorated saddles, leading their horses in a high-stepping gait. The most important days of the year in Guanacasteco culture revolve around *topes* (horse shows) and *recorridos de toros* (bullfights). Bulls are ridden and baited, but never killed.

***Sabanero* on a working ranch**

Parque Nacional Rincón de la Vieja ❽

Road Map B1. 19 miles (30 km) NE of Liberia. *661-8139.* *to Liberia, then by jeep-taxi.* *7am–4pm daily; last admission: 3pm.* www.acguanacaste.ac.cr

A MASSIVE VOLCANO, the dramatically beautiful Rincón de la Vieja is studded with nine distinct craters, of which only Rincón de la Vieja crater (5,900 ft/1,800 m) is active. The highest is Santa María (6,250 ft/1,900 m), while Von Seebach crater is filled with an acidic turquoise lake.

The park, established in 1973, protects an area of 55 sq miles (140 sq km). The eastern slopes of the volcano are rain-soaked all year round; the western side has a distinct dry season, and ranges from deciduous forest at lower elevations to cloud forest below the stark moonscape summit.

Visitors can spot capuchin, howler, and spider monkeys, anteaters, sloths, kinkajous, and more than 300 species of birds, including quetzals and three-wattled bellbirds. Pea-green **Lago Los Jilgueros** is visited by tapirs.

The park offers superb hiking. Trails start at the park headquarters, the 19th-century **Hacienda Santa María**, and lead past mud pools, hot sulfur springs, waterfalls, and fumaroles. The challenging 11-mile (18-km) summit trail is a two-day round trip. The summit offers fabulous views as far as Lake Nicaragua.

Hikers must report to the ranger stations when setting out and returning. Santa María ranger station can be reached from Liberia by jeep-taxis, and is linked to Las Pailas ranger station by a trail. The dry season from December to April is the best time to visit.

ENVIRONS: Several nature lodges on the western slopes of the volcano also operate as activity centers. On its south-western flanks, **Hacienda Lodge Guachipelín** *(see p211)*, accessed from Liberia via Curubandé, is a working cattle ranch, specializing in horseback rides. Nearby, **Rincón de la Vieja Lodge** *(see p211)* has a 900-acre (364-ha) private forest reserve. Both lodges offer canopy tours. From Liberia, a road leads via Cañas Dulces to **Buena Vista Mountain Lodge & Adventure Center** *(see p211)* on the north-western slopes. It offers horse-back rides, a canopy tour, and a 1,300-ft (400-m) long water slide. **Hotel Borinquen Mountain Resort Thermae & Spa** nearby has bubbling mud pools and spa treatments.

Hotel Borinquen Mountain Resort Thermae & Spa
19 miles (30 km) NE of Liberia via Cañas Dulces. *666-0363.* www.borinquenresort.com

The impressive Volcán Rincón de la Vieja

Parque Nacional Guanacaste ❾

Road Map A1. 22 miles (35 km) N of Liberia. *666-5051.* *to Liberia, then by jeep-taxi.* *8am–5pm daily.* *by reservation.* www.acguanacaste.ac.cr

THIS REMOTE national park encompasses more than 325 sq miles (840 sq km) of reforested woodland and pasture extending to the top of Volcán Cacao (5,400 ft/1,650 m) and Volcán Orosi (4,900 ft/1,500 m). Facilities are few, but for visitors with a degree of self-reliance, the rewards are immense. The park, an extension of Parque Nacional Santa Rosa, has a variety of habitats, and wild-life viewing is stupendous. Biological stations **Cacao, Pitilla**, and **Maritza** have spartan accommodations.

Pre-Columbian petroglyphs can be seen at **Llano de los Indios**, on the lower western flanks of Volcán Orosi.

Hacienda Los Inocentes ecological center, a former cattle ranch

ENVIRONS: Set on the lower northern slopes of Volcán Orosi, **Hacienda Los Inocentes** specializes in nature tours on horseback.

Hacienda Los Inocentes
Hwy 4, 10 miles (16 km) E of Pan-Am Hwy. *679-9190.* www.losinocenteslodge.com

Bahía Salinas ❿

Road Map A1. 38 miles (62 km) NW of Liberia. *to La Cruz, then by jeep-taxi.*

FRAMED BY CLIFFS to the north, salt pans to the east, and mangrove-fringed beaches to the south, this flask-shaped bay is swept by breezes from December to April. Fishing hamlets line its shores. Hotels at La Coyotera and Playa Copal serve as surfing centers.

Frigate birds use the drafts around **Refugio Nacional de Vida Silvestre Isla Bolaños** to take off. A protected nesting site for pelicans and American oystercatchers, this island is off-limits to visitors.

Costa Rica's Dry Forests

DRY DECIDUOUS forests once swathed the lowlands of the Pacific littoral from Mexico to Panama, covering most of today's Guanacaste and Nicoya. After the arrival of Columbus, the Spanish cleared vast areas of these forests to raise cattle, which still dominate the economy of the Pacific northwest. Today, only about 2 percent of the original cover remains, notably in the Tempisque basin, and Santa Rosa, Rincón de la Vieja, and Guanacaste National Parks. Recent conservation efforts, spearheaded by the US biologist Dr. Daniel Janzen, are returning large areas of savanna and ranchland to their original state. The intent is to link the existing patchwork and regenerate dry forest ecosystems.

The orange bloom of the *poró*

The understory consists of short trees; above are stout-trunked, flat-crowned trees.

Grass and thorn scrub dominate at ground level.

Trees typically grow no higher than 40 ft (12 m) and are widely spaced.

The forest is relatively sparsely vegetated, with fewer species of flora.

***The dry season** sees the forest exploding in an outburst of color. Pink* pouí *blooms first, followed by bright orange* poró, *rose-colored* Tabebuia rosea, *vermilion* malinche, *and purple jacaranda.*

Parque Nacional Santa Rosa (see pp132–3) *protects the most important remnant of dry tropical forest in all Central America.*

***Guanacaste trees** spread their wide-reaching branches close to the ground, providing precious shade in the searing midday heat. Such dry forest species have evolved to withstand the long seasonal drought by shedding their leaves.*

Indio desnudo, *or naked Indian, is named for its distinct copper-red bark, which readily peels to reveal an olive-colored trunk. Naked Indian is also called the* gumbo-limbo.

***White-tailed deer** blend in well with the dun-colored grasses and dry forest. The best times to see them are dawn and dusk, when they emerge to search for food.*

***Thorny scrub**, such as acacia, have long spikes to prevent birds and animals from eating their leaves and seeds.*

Parque Nacional Santa Rosa ⓫

THE COUNTRY'S FIRST national park, inaugurated in 1971, Santa Rosa National Park covers 190 sq miles (492 sq km) of the Santa Elena Peninsula and adjoining land. It is divided into two sectors. To the north is the little-visited Murciélago Sector, with hidden beaches – notably Playa Blanca – accessed along a rugged dirt track. To the south, the much larger Santa Rosa Sector was the site of battles in 1856 and 1955, and boasts most of the sights of interest. The park protects the nation's largest stretch of tropical dry forest, as well as nine other distinct habitats. With 115 mammal species, including 20 types of bats, and 250 species of birds, the park is a superb wildlife-viewing area, especially in the dry season, when the deciduous trees shed their leaves.

Islas Murciélagos
The waters around these islands offer splendid scuba diving (see p252). *Manta rays, grouper, and other large species are common.*

Playa Nancite
This is one of two sites in Costa Rica where olive ridley turtles nest en masse in synchronized arribadas (see p141), *especially in September–October. Protected as a research site, it is off-limits to visitors except by permit.*

Crocodiles
The mangroves at the northern and southern ends of Playa Naranjo harbor crocodiles.

Witch's Rock, off Playa Naranjo, is renowned among surfers for the powerful, tubular waves that rise here and pump ashore.

Playa Naranjo
A gorgeous white-sand surfing beach, Playa Naranjo has campsites with basic facilities. It is reached by an arduous dirt road that often gets washed out in wet season – check with rangers before setting out for the beach.

Key

- Murciélago Sector
- Santa Rosa Sector

Tanquetas (armored vehicles) lie half-buried in the undergrowth as rusting relics of an ill-fated attack launched by Nicaraguan dictator Anastasio Somoza against Costa Rica in 1955.

Visitors' Checklist

Road Map A1. 22 miles (35 km) N of Liberia. *666-5051.* *Santa Rosa Sector: from Liberia; Murciélago Sector: from Santa Rosa park entrance, via Cuajiniquíl.* *tours to Playa Naranjo from Playa Tamarindo and Playas del Coco.* *8am–4pm daily for vehicles; 24 hrs for hikers.* *by reservation.* *by reservation.* www.acguanacaste.ac.cr

Sendero Indio Desnudo
Named for indio desnudo *(naked Indian) or gumbo- limbo trees, this short trail features a monument to the Costa Ricans who fought in the battles of 1856 and 1955.*

La Casona
Also called Hacienda Santa Rosa, this important monument is a replica built in 2001 after the 1663 original was destroyed by arsonists. The battle of 1856 against William Walker (see p45) *was fought outside the hacienda, which now functions as a historical museum.*

Centro de Investigaciones is the main center for tropical dry forest research in Costa Rica.

Sendero Los Patos leads to waterholes, which provide excellent opportunities for viewing peccaries and other mammals in the dry season.

0 km 2
0 miles 2

Key

- Pan-Am Highway
- Other road
- Trail
- Park boundary
- Visitor information
- Camping
- Viewpoint

The Contra Connection

Col. Oliver North

During the 1980s, the remote Murciélago Sector was utilized as a secret training ground for the CIA-backed Nicaraguan Contras in their battle to topple the Sandinista government *(see p46)*. An airstrip was illegally established here under the orders of Colonel Oliver North, a key player in the Iran-Contra scandal that shook the US in 1983–8. The road to the park entrance runs alongside the airstrip, which occupies land confiscated from Nicaraguan strongman Anastasio Somoza.

Visitors soaking up the sun on the wide gray-sand beaches of Tamarindo

Bahía Culebra ⓬

Road Map A2. 12 miles (19 km) W of Liberia.

Ringed by dramatic cliffs and fringed by beaches of varying hues, Bahía Culebra (Snake Bay) is the setting for Proyecto Papagayo, a controversial tourism project that has restricted access to the bay's sparkling waters. Spilling down the cliffs are big hotels, including the **Four Seasons Resort at Papagayo Peninsula** *(see p208)*. Pre-Columbian settlements on the bay await excavation. **Witch's Rock Canopy Tour** has ziplines and a walkway through the dry forest canopy.

Witch's Rock Canopy Tour
23 miles (37 km) W of Liberia.
666-1624. *8am–4pm daily.*

Playas del Coco ⓭

Road Map A2. 22 miles (35 km) SW of Liberia. *2,000.* *Fiesta Cívica (Jan); Festival de la Virgen del Mar (mid-Jul).*

This wide, silvery beach combines the allure of a traditional fishing community with a no-frills resort. Although not particularly attractive, the pelican-patrolled beach is a favorite with Costa Rican families, and has a lively nightlife. Local outfitters offer sportfishing and scuba trips to Islas Murciélagos *(see pp134)* and Isla Catalina, where schools of rays can be seen.

Environs: Secluded Playa Ocotal, west of Playas del Coco, has the region's best dive site. It is also a premier sportfishing destination. Playas Hermosa and Panamá, north of Coco, have exquisite settings, with Isla Catalina silhouetted dramatically at sunset.

Playa Flamingo ⓮

Road Map A2. 38 miles (62 km) SW of Liberia. *2,000.*

With gently curving white sands cusped by rugged headlands, the gorgeous Playa Flamingo justifies its official yet less common name, Playa Blanca (White Beach). The large marina is a sportfishing base. Deluxe villas dot the rocky headlands. Most of the hotels are upscale timeshare resorts and, despite its fine beach, Flamingo is shunned by the offbeat and party crowd.

Surfers heading for the water

Environs: North of Playa Flamingo, the estuary of Río Salinas opens out at modestly appealing Playa Penca, where roseate spoonbills, egrets, and a rich variety of other birdlife can be spotted in the mangroves.

Southwest of Flamingo is **Playa Conchal** (Shell Beach), with its shining sands; the diamond-like sparkle of the sands is caused by crushed seashells. The beach slopes gently into turquoise waters, which are ideal for snorkeling and other watersports. For a fee, visitors can access **Paradisus Playa Conchal Beach & Golf Resort** *(see p210)*, which boasts a championship golf course.

Tamarindo ⓯

Road Map A2. 11 miles (18 km) S of Flamingo. *3,800.* *International Festival of Music (Jul–Aug).*

Until recently a sleepy fishing village, Tamarindo has rapidly developed into the region's premier resort. This hip surfers' haven is also a center for sportfishing, diving, and snorkeling. Tamarindo is popular with backpackers, but also boasts a cosmopolitan selection of restaurants and boutique hotels.

The area lies within **Parque Nacional Marino Las Baulas** (Leatherback Turtle Marine National Park), inaugurated in 1990. It protects 85 sq miles (220 sq km) of ocean and 1,100 acres (445 ha) of beach – **Playa Grande** – a prime nesting site of leatherback turtles. Between October and April, as many as 100 leatherbacks can be seen on the beach. Pacific ridley, green, and hawksbill turtles occasionally nest here. **El Mundo de la Tortuga** is a captivating museum dedicated to the leatherback turtle.

The park also incorporates Playa Langosta, south of Tamarindo, and 990 acres (400 ha) of mangroves, which can be explored on boats.

Parque Nacional Marino Las Baulas
686-4967. *Oct–Feb: 24 hrs; Mar–Sep: 6am–6pm daily.* *compulsory on the beach; Oct–Feb: 6pm–6am daily.*

El Mundo de la Tortuga
Playa Grande. *653-0471.*
Oct–May: 4pm–6am.

Surfing Beaches of Northern Nicoya

Acclaimed as the "Hawaii of Latin America," Costa Rica offers world-class surfing and warm waters year-round. The greatest concentration of surfing beaches is in Northern Nicoya, where Pacific breakers pump ashore all year. Conditions are ideal between December and March, when the Papagayo winds kick up high waves. Dozens of beaches guarantee that surfers will find a fairly challenging ride on any day, while extremely varied tidal conditions provide breaks for every level of experience. Be warned, however: riptides are common and many surfers lose their lives every year; few beaches have lifeguards. Numerous villages and resorts have become surfers' havens and are heavily reliant on the waveboard trade, with scores of surf camps and surf shops.

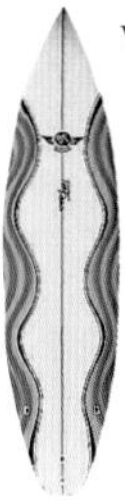

Surfing board

Playa Naranjo ①
This remote beach in the Golfo de Papagayo boasts a superb beach break, called Witch's Rock. Naranjo is accessed by 4WD or by boat from the resorts of Northern Nicoya.

Playa Grande ②
Consistently high waves pump ashore onto this long, easily accessible beach. It is protected as part of a prime nesting site of the leatherback turtle.

Tamarindo ③
The surf capital of Northern Nicoya, Tamarindo offers a rivermouth break, rocky point break, and beach breaks. It is also the gateway to nearby isolated surfing beaches such as Playas Langosta, Avellanas, and Negra.

Playa Nosara ④
Discovered only recently by surfers, Nosara has a fine beach break and a dramatic setting. It is backed by mangroves and has warm, rocky tidepools.

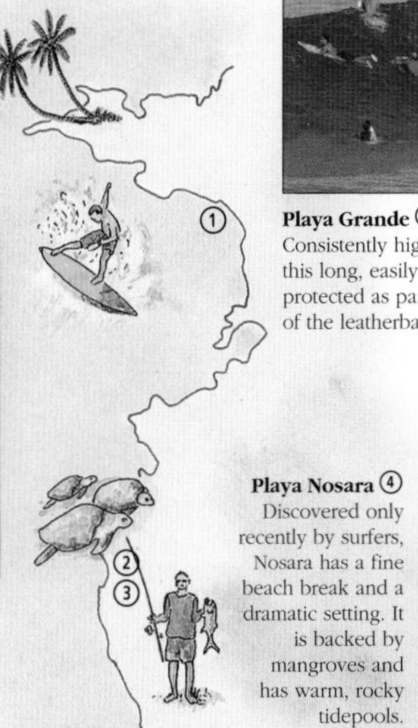
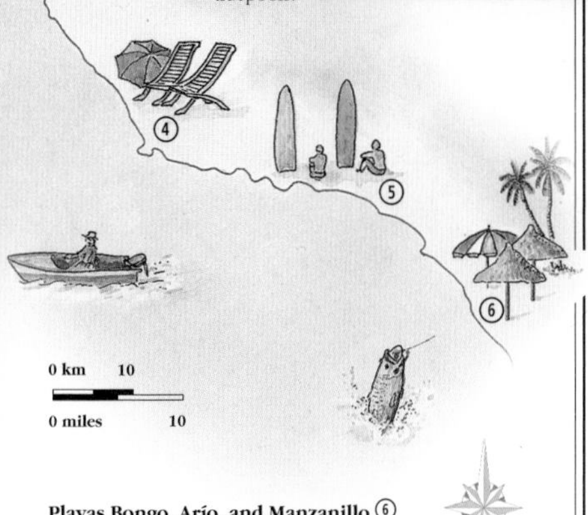

Playas Bejuco and San Miguel ⑤
Long slivers of silvery sand are washed by good surf. Marine turtles come ashore. These beaches are oriented to budget travelers.

Playas Bongo, Arío, and Manzanillo ⑥
All three are as off-the-beaten-track as possible in Costa Rica. Just getting there is half the fun. Cracking waves, combined with the solitude, guarantee surfer bliss. Facilities are virtually nonexistent.

Refugio Nacional de Vida Silvestre Ostional 16

Road Map A3. 34 miles (55 km) S of Tamarindo. *682-0470.* *from Santa Cruz and Nicoya via Nosara.* *24 hrs daily.* *compulsory for the beach.*

THE SETTING FOR one of the most remarkable occurrences in nature, Ostional National Wildlife Refuge protects 4 sq miles (10 sq km) of land and sea around Playa Ostional. The beach is one of less than a dozen worldwide where Pacific ridley turtles nest in synchronized *arribadas*. The best time to view them is during August and September. Green and leatherback turtles also nest here in smaller numbers. Ostional is the only place in Costa Rica where residents are legally allowed, under strict guidelines, to harvest eggs during the first 36 hours of an *arribada*.

Ostional is accessed by dirt roads that require 4WD during the wet season. The remote setting and the surrounding forests have shielded the area from development and there are few facilities for visitors. Personal contact with turtles is forbidden, as are flashlights and flash photography.

A participant in a surfing competition at Playa Guiones, Nosara

Nosara 17

Road Map A3. 3 miles (5 km) S of Ostional. *2,800.*

THIS ISOLATED community on the Nicoya coast comprises twin villages. **Bocas de Nosara**, 3 miles (5 km) inland, on the banks of Río Nosara, is a peasant hamlet where ox-carts still creak along dusty lanes. **Beaches of Nosara**, to the south, is a predominantly foreign settlement, with contemporary homes amidst forests near the shore. Several species of animals and birds can be frequently seen here at close range. Farther south, stunning **Playa Guiones** is a long, calm stretch of white sand and sun-warmed tide-pools in which monkeys can sometimes be seen enjoying a good soak. Strong tides rule out swimming, but the breakers are perfect for surfing. To the north, small **Playa Pelada** is encircled by steep cliffs. Nearby, **Reserva Biológica Nosara** protects 125 acres (50 ha) of tropical forest along the Río Nosara estuary. Over 250 bird species nest here, including wood storks, white-fronted parrots, and frigate birds.

Vultures, Nosara

Reserva Biológica Nosara
Bocas de Nosara. *682-0035.* *by appointment.* www.lagarta.com

Sámara 18

Road Map A3. 16 miles (26 km) S of Nosara. *2,700.* *at Carrillo.*

POPULAR WITH backpackers, surfers, and middle-class Costa Ricans, Sámara is the most southerly of the beach resorts developed for tourism. A giant strangler fig tree marks the southern end of Playa Sámara at Matapalo, where villagers eke out a living from the sea. There are few other sights of interest, and life revolves around lazing on the gray sands, or going surfing and riding. **Playa Carrillo**, 2 miles (3 km) south of Sámara, is a sportfishing center, while to the north, the **Flying Crocodile Lodge and Flying Center** offers flights by ultralight plane.

Beach sign, Sámara

Flying Crocodile Lodge and Flying Center
Esterones, 3 miles (5 km) N of Sámara. *656-8048.* *7am–3pm daily.* www.flying-crocodile.com

Islita 19

Road Map B3. 9 miles (14 km) S of Sámara. *1,000.* *to Sámara, then by jeep-taxi.*

SET IN THE LEE of the soaring Punta Islita, this charming village is known for the **Hotel Hacienda Punta Islita** *(see p208)*, a hilltop resort which houses the **Galería de Arte Contemporáneo Mary Anne Zürcher**. Artworks in varied media by established and local artists are available here. The hotel also fosters the **Museo de Arte Contemporáneo al Aire Libre** (Open Air Museum of Contemporary Art), spread around the village – houses, individual trees, and even the soccer field have been decorated by residents and hotel staff with murals and other spontaneous aesthetic expressions. Several rivers have to be forded along the rough dirt road linking Islita to Sámara. During the wet season, long detours via San Pedro to the east are often necessary.

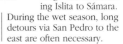

◁ **A farmhouse and ranch in the Cordillera de Guanacaste**

Arribadas of Olive Ridley Turtles

THE SYNCHRONIZED mass nestings called *arribadas* (arrivals), which are unique to the ridley turtle, are known to occur regularly at only nine beaches worldwide. Of these, two are in Costa Rica – Playa Nancite and Playa Ostional. *Arribadas* take place between April and December, peaking in August and September. Lasting between three and eight days, they happen at two- to four-week intervals, usually during the last quarter of the moon's cycle. On any one night, as many as 20,000 turtles congregate just beyond the breakers. Then, wave after wave of turtles storm ashore, even climbing over one another in a single-minded effort to find a nesting spot on the crowded sands. Millions of eggs are laid during each *arribada*, believed to be an evolutionary adaptation to ensure survival in the face of heavy predation.

Mosaic turtle

***Ridley turtles** come ashore in groups numbering up to 100,000 turtles during a single* arribada. *Ridleys nest every year, sometimes as often as three times a season.*

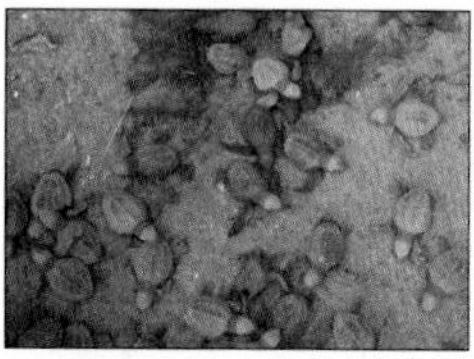

***Hatchlings** emerge together at night for the dangerous run to the sea and the safety it offers. Only about 1 percent survive to adulthood.*

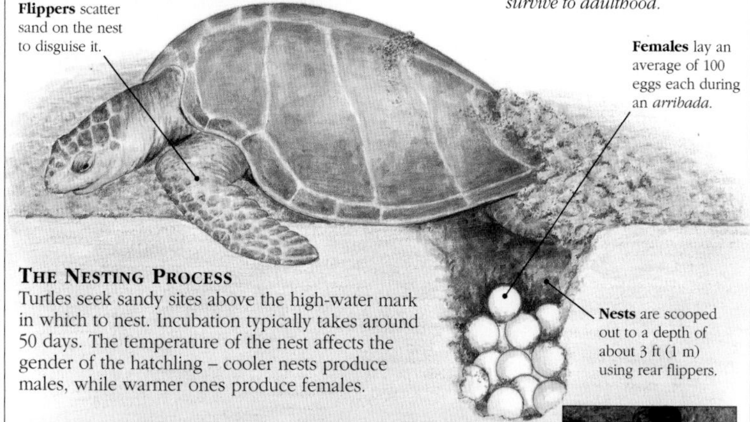

Flippers scatter sand on the nest to disguise it.
Females lay an average of 100 eggs each during an *arribada*.
Nests are scooped out to a depth of about 3 ft (1 m) using rear flippers.

THE NESTING PROCESS

Turtles seek sandy sites above the high-water mark in which to nest. Incubation typically takes around 50 days. The temperature of the nest affects the gender of the hatchling – cooler nests produce males, while warmer ones produce females.

***Scientists** tag ridley turtles during an* arribada *at Santa Rosa's Playa Nancite in an effort to track and study them.*

***Coatis**, as well as raccoons and vultures, dig up turtle nests to feast on the eggs; less than 10 percent of turtle eggs hatch.*

***Commercial harvesting** of eggs is legally done only by villagers of Ostional.*

Nicoya 20

Road Map A3. 44 miles (71 km) SW of Liberia. 21,000. *Fiesta de la Yegüita (Dec 12).*

Emanating sleepy colonial charm, Nicoya dates back to the mid-1600s, and is named after the Chorotega *cacique* (chief) who greeted the Spanish conquistador Gil González Davila in 1523. An advanced Chorotega settlement existed here in pre-Columbian times. Today, the town serves as the administrative center for the Nicoya Peninsula and bustles with the comings and goings of *campesinos* (peasants) and cowboys. Nicoya is also the gateway for Sámara and the Pacific beaches of the south-central Nicoya Peninsula.

Life centers around the old plaza, **Parque Central**. Built in 1644, the intimate, wood-beamed **Iglesia Parroquia San Blas**, located in the northeast corner of the plaza, has a simple façade inset with bells. Inside, a small museum has a display of historical artifacts and religious memorabilia.

The simple exterior of the Iglesia Parroquia San Blas in Nicoya

Environs: Nature lovers can head about 17 miles (27 km) northeast to **Puerto Humo**, a small riverside port town from where boats depart for Parque Nacional Palo Verde *(see p130)*. The mangrove-fringed banks of Río Tempisque in this area attract waterfowl and other birds. Crocodiles can sometimes be seen sunning themselves on the muddy banks. A 4WD is recommended for visitors who are driving themselves. Buses operate from Nicoya.

Santa Cruz 21

Road Map A2. 14 miles (22 km) N of Nicoya. 17,500. *Fiesta Patronal de Santo Cristo (mid-Jan); Fiesta de Santiago (Jul 25).*

Steeped in local tradition and heavily influenced by cowboy culture, Santa Cruz is Costa Rica's official La Ciudad Folklórica (National Folkloric City). Connected by Highway 160 to Tamarindo and the beaches of the north-central Nicoya Peninsula, this cultural center was founded in 1760. Although many of the wooden colonial edifices that once graced its historic core were destroyed in a recent fire, the overall ambience is charming. **Plaza de los Mangos** serves as a focal point for the city's festivals, which draw visitors from miles around to enjoy traditional *marimba* music and dance. *Topes* (horse shows) and *recorridos de toros* (bullfights) also take place here.

Ruined bell tower, Plaza Bernabela Ramos, Santa Cruz

The architectural highlight of Santa Cruz is the landscaped and tree-shaded **Plaza Bernabela Ramos**. On its east side is a modern church with fine stained-glass windows. Next to it is the ruined bell tower of a Colonial-style church, which was destroyed by an earthquake in 1950. The plaza is a pleasant spot to relax and admire the statues, including that of Chorotega *cacique* Diría in the southwest corner, and a *montador* (bull-rider) on a bucking bull in the northeast.

Statue of a bull-rider, Plaza Bernabela Ramos, Santa Cruz

Fiesta de la Yegüita

***The Virgin of Guadalupe* by Miguel Cabrera**

Also known as the Festival of the Virgin of Guadalupe, this fiesta blends Chorotega and Catholic traditions. According to legend, twin brothers were battling to death for the love of an Indian princess when a *yegüita* (little mare) intervened to stop the fight. The festival takes place every December and features traditional Costa Rican food, bullfights, rodeos, street processions, fireworks, music and dance, and ancient Indian rituals.

Guaitíl ㉒

Road Map A2. 7 miles (11 km) E of Santa Cruz. *1,500.*

THIS SMALL VILLAGE offers the most authentic display of traditional culture *(see pp32–3)* in Costa Rica. Although situated in the heart of an agricultural area, virtually the entire community derives its income by making ceramics in pre-Columbian style. Guaitíl sits on the cusp between cultures – even the contemporary pieces draw inspiration from traditional Chorotega designs.

Approximately 100 families are organized into several artists' cooperatives, including a children's cooperative. Headed by the matriarch of the family, almost every household has its traditional wood-fired, dome-shaped *horno* (oven) for firing pots and other ceramic objects. Visitors are welcome in the yards to watch artisans work the red clay dug from nearby riverbanks. The dusty lanes are lined with thatched stores and open-air shacks where the pottery is displayed.

Tourist demand has stoked native pride, and a regeneration of Chorotega culture is now spilling over into nearby villages as well.

CHOROTEGA POTTERY

Guaitíl artisans use the same simple tools as their ancestors did to craft pottery in the age-old manner, perpetuating their native traditions. The decorative bowls, pots, and clay figures are polished with *zukias* (ancient grinding stones), and blessed by shamans, after which totemic animal motifs in black, red, and white are painted on ocher backgrounds. The quintessential Guaitíl piece is a three-legged vase in the form of a cow. Although most pieces are traditional, some artisans work in a creative synthesis that blurs the line between the old and the new.

Clay figure from Guaitíl

Parque Nacional Barra Honda ㉓

Road Map B3. 11 miles (18 km) E of Nicoya. *659-1551.* *Nicoya–Santa Ana village (0.5 mile/1 km from park entrance), then by jeep-taxi.* *8am–4pm daily; last admission: noon; caving: 7am–1pm daily.*

EXCITING CAVING awaits visitors to this national park, established in 1974, which spreads over 9 sq miles (23 sq km). A tropical dry forest area, Barra Honda was formerly used for raising cattle and today is in the process of being reforested.

Hiking in the park is splendid. Trails lead to lookout points atop Cerro Barra Honda (1450 ft/442 m), a massif lifted up by powerful tectonic forces. Cerro Barra Honda is riddled with limestone caverns formed by the action of water over millions of years. Of the 40 caves discovered so far, 20 have been explored. **Santa Ana**, the largest cave, soars to a height of 790 ft (240 m). Inside **Cueva Terciopelo**, a dripstone formation called El Órgano (The Organ) produces musical tones when struck. **La Pozo Hediondo** (Stinking Well) is named for the droppings of the bats roosting here. Some caves have blind salamanders and blind fish, and most boast dramatic stalactites and stalagmites. Indigenous artifacts have been found in some caves.

Cave descents into Cueva Terciópelo are permitted from November to April; a licensed guide is compulsory. Spelunkers enter Terciópelo via a 100-ft (30-m) rappel. Access to the other caves requires prior permission.

Spelunking equipment and guides can be hired at **Proyecto Nacaome**, a cooperative. Hikers must report to the Los Laureles ranger station. A 4WD is needed to reach the park entrance. Jeep-taxis run from Nicoya.

Puente de Amistad con Taiwan across Río Tempisque on Hwy 18

ENVIRONS: Opened in 2003, **Puente de Amistad con Taiwan** (Friendship with Taiwan Bridge) is a dramatic suspension bridge over Río Tempisque. Replacing a now defunct ferry, it links Nicoya to the Pan-Am Highway.

A spelunker at Cueva Terciopelo, Parque Nacional Barra Honda

THE NORTHERN ZONE

THE NORTHERN PROVINCES *are Costa Rica's flatlands – a gentle landscape quilted in pastures, fruit plantations, and humid rainforest. This wide-open canvas is framed by a dramatic escarpment of mountains. The extreme north of this perennially wet region is a world of seasonally flooded lagoons and migratory waterfowl, while the mountains in the south are cloaked in dense forests, which are protected in a series of naional parks and wildlife reserves.*

The rolling *llanuras* (plains) form a triangle, narrow to the west and broadening eastward, which extends north from the base of the *cordilleras* (mountain ranges) to Río San Juan, on the Nicaraguan border. The scenery is nowhere more splendid than around Lake Arenal, located on a depression between the Guanacaste and Tilarán Mountains. Volcán Arenal looms ethereally over the waters. Its near-constant eruptions and other local attractions have given a boost to the nearby town of La Fortuna, now a base for various adventure activities.

At the time of the Spanish arrival, the Corobicí peoples occupied the lower flanks of the mountains and were at war with their Nicaraguan neighbors. During the colonial era, settlements were restricted to the main river courses, and were subject to constant plundering by pirates.

The region remained aloof from the rest of the country until the early 19th century, when a trade route was laid linking highland towns to a wharfside settlement – today's Puerto Viejo – which gave access to the Caribbean. Founded around that time, Ciudad Quesada grew to become the region's administrative center. The settlement campaign initiated in the 1950s led to the decimation of huge tracts of forest to make room for cattle farms as well as banana and citrus plantations. New settlements have since sprung up throughout the region.

Cloud-wreathed Volcán Arenal, the country's most active volcano

◁ **Arenal Botanical Gardens on the northern shore of Laguna de Arenal**

Exploring the Northern Zone

Stone figurine, Centro Neotrópico SarapiquíS

THE MAIN GATEWAY to the northern lowlands is Ciudad Quesada, a dairy town on the mountain flanks that fringe the region's southern border. La Fortuna, to the west, is a center for outdoor activities, from caving to horseback riding. The region's major attraction is Volcán Arenal, great for hiking and for soaking in the thermal waters of Tabacón. Nearby Lake Arenal offers fine fishing and world-class windsurfing. To the east of Ciudad Quesada are several private reserves – one of which boasts the thrilling Rainforest Aerial Tram. Boats depart the nondescript town of Puerto Viejo de Sarapiquí for nature cruises along Río Sarapiquí. Caño Negro Wildlife Refuge, in the far north, is a superb birding and angling destination.

SIGHTS AT A GLANCE

Towns and Cities
Ciudad Quesada 9
La Fortuna 1
Puerto Viejo de Sarapiquí 12

National Parks and Reserves
Parque Nacional Volcán Arenal 3
Refugio Nacional de Vida Silvestre Caño Negro 8
Refugio Nacional de Vida Silvestre Corredor Fronterizo 14

Areas of Natural Beauty
Arenal Hanging Bridges 5
Arenal Rainforest Reserve and Aerial Tram 6
Cavernas de Venado 7
Laguna de Arenal pp150–52 4
La Marina Zoológica 10
La Selva Biological Station 15
Rainforest Aerial Tram 18
Rara Avis 17
Sarapiquí Heliconia Island 16
Selva Verde 13
Tabacón Hot Springs Resort and Spa 2

Indigenous Site
Centro Neotrópico SarapiquíS 11

A cowboy at Selva Verde

Volcán Arenal shrouded in mist

See Also

- ***Where to Stay*** pp212–14
- ***Where to Eat*** pp234–5

The hot springs at Tabacón, near Volcán Arenal

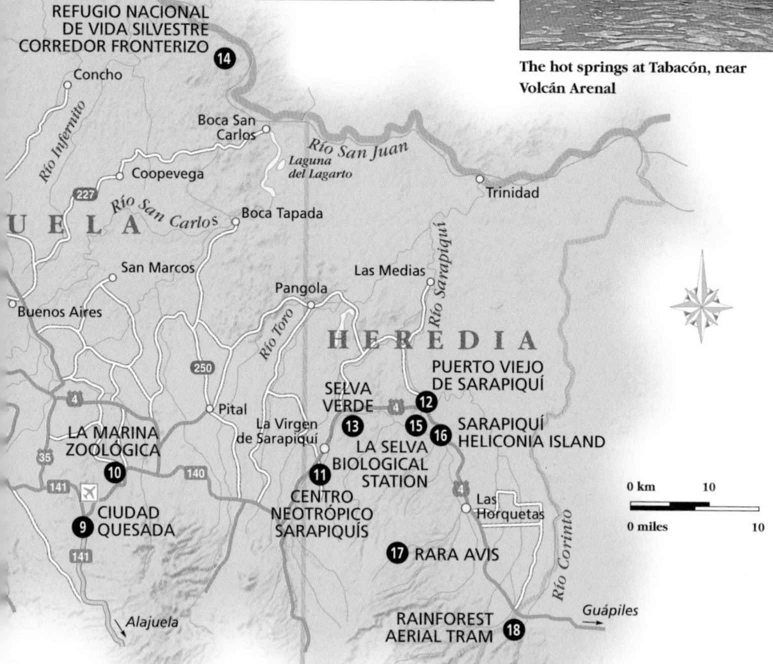

Key

- Major road
- Secondary road
- Minor road
- International border
- Provincial border
- Peak

Getting Around

Reached by charter planes, the towns of Upala and Los Chiles are access points for many of the region's tourist destinations. Flights to La Fortuna's airstrip have been cancelled since 2000 because of a couple of plane crashes. The town is linked by tourist buses with San José and key resorts beyond the region. Organized tours can be booked through tour operators and hotels. However, the best way of getting around is to rent a car. A 4WD is essential to reach Caño Negro and other sights away from main roads. Many roads are prone to landslides, especially along the north shore of Lake Arenal and those that link La Fortuna and Upala.

La Fortuna ❶

Road Map C2. 81 miles (131 km) NW of San José. *9,750.*

Volcán Arenal towers over this agricultural community and tourist hub, officially known as La Fortuna de San Carlos. Situated on a gentle slope, the picturesque town is laid out on a grid around a broad, landscaped plaza, which has a sculpture of an erupting volcano. A modern church stands on the plaza, its tall bell tower contrasting with Arenal behind.

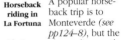

Horseback riding in La Fortuna

There are numerous restaurants and hotels that cater to the tourists who come here in search of adventure. Several agencies offer horseback rides, caving, fishing, biking, and rafting. A popular horseback trip is to Monteverde *(see pp124–8)*, but the ride is very demanding on the overworked horses, some of which have died on the trail.

Environs: The **Ecocentro Danaus Butterfly Farm and Tropical Garden** provides an educational introduction to the local fauna. It has a netted butterfly garden, a snake zoo, a frog garden, and a small lagoon stocked with waterfowl and caimans. **Arenal Mundo Aventura** is a 2-sq-mile (5-sq-km) wildlife refuge and ecotour center with trails, rappeling, and canopy tours. The **Albergue La Catarata** ecolodge also has a butterfly garden and raises dog-sized rodents called *tepescuintles*. Nearby, a steep, muddy trail leads to the base of **Catarata La Fortuna**, a refreshingly cool, ribbon-like 210-ft (70-m) high waterfall. Swimming in the pools at its base is unsafe after heavy rains. Instead, visitors can soak in thermal waters at **Baldi Termae Spa**, which has landscaped outdoor pools and a swim-up bar and restaurant. Southeast of La Fortuna on Highway 142, the **Hotel Bosques de Chachagua** *(see p212)*, is a

One of the many buses that run from La Fortuna to various sights

working cattle ranch with a 320-acre (130-ha) private forest reserve at the base of soaring mountains. The reserve, which also welcomes day visitors, offers horseback rides into the forest and has hiking trails as well.

Ecocentro Danaus Butterfly Farm and Tropical Garden
2 miles (3 km) E of La Fortuna. *460-8005.* *8am–3:30pm daily.*

Arenal Mundo Aventura
1 mile (1.6 km) S of La Fortuna.
479-9762. *8am–5pm daily.*
www.arenalmundoaventura.com

Albergue La Catarata
2 miles (3 km) SW of La Fortuna.
479-9612. *by donation.*
www.cataratalodge.com

Catarata La Fortuna
3 miles (5 km) SW of La Fortuna. *479-8360.* *8am–5pm daily.*

Baldi Termae Spa
3 miles (5 km) W of La Fortuna.
479-9652. *10am–10pm daily.*

Tabacón Hot Springs Resort and Spa ❷

Road Map C2. 8 miles (13 km) W of La Fortuna. *460-2020.* *from La Fortuna and Nuevo Arenal.* *10am–10pm daily.*
www.tabacon.com

Steaming-hot waters pour out from the base of Volcán Arenal and cascade through this lush, landscaped *balneario* (bathing resort). Río Tabacón feeds a series of therapeutic mineral pools with temperatures that range from 27° to 39°C (80°–102°F). Spa treatments are available. The main pool has a swim-up bar, and there is a splendid restaurant with views *(see p235)*. La Fuentes Termales, an affiliated *balneario* nearby, can be accessed from Tabacón Lodge via zipline.

Tabacón's location in the path of the main lava flow is considered dangerous. Along with Pueblo Nuevo, Tabacón was decimated in 1968 when Arenal erupted. Nonetheless, the resort is usually crowded, especially on weekends.

Environs: On the volcano's northern flank, **Jungla y Senderos Los Lagos** has crocodiles sloshing about in a pool, trails through primary forest, and horseback rides.

Jungla y Senderos Los Lagos
4 miles (6 km) W of La Fortuna.
479-8000. *6am–10pm daily.*

The landscaped pools of the *balneario* at Tabacón

A panoramic view of Volcán Arenal and the San Carlos Plains

Parque Nacional Volcán Arenal ❸

Road Map C2. 11 miles (18 km) W of La Fortuna. 461-8499. *to La Fortuna, then by jeep-taxi.* *8am–4pm daily.*

Encircling the country's most active volcano, Arenal Volcano National Park spreads over 45 sq miles (120 sq km). Rising from the San Carlos Plains, the majestic Arenal is one of Costa Rica's most rewarding sights. Pre-Columbian tribes considered it the sacred "Home of the Fire God." Arenal ceased activity between the 13th and 16th centuries, and stayed inactive until July 29, 1968, when an earthquake awakened the sleeping giant. The perfectly conical 5,400-ft (1,650-m) high volcano now smolders incessantly and minor eruptions occur almost daily. At night it can look like a firecracker as it spews out red-hot lava, which pours down its northwestern flank. Witnessing an eruption is a matter of luck, as clouds often conceal the upper reaches; the dry season is the best for viewing. Ask to be woken if there is a nocturnal eruption.

Trails cross a moonscape of smoking lava scree on Arenal's lower western slopes. Hikers should note, however, that access to areas within the park is restricted, and should observe the posted "no entry" zones. The volcano has already claimed several lives.

The park also includes the dormant 3,800-ft (1,150-m) high Volcán Chato to the east. **Arenal Observatory Lodge**, *(see p213)* midway up the western flank of Chato, has stunning views of Arenal and Lake Arenal. A museum provides an understanding of vulcanicity, and the restaurant offers grandstand views when Arenal erupts. Trails from the observatory lead through thick forests to the summit, where a jade-colored lake shimmers in the crater. Canoes can be hired here. The ranger station at the park entrance sells maps and also has restrooms. Tour companies and hotels in La Fortuna offer guided tours.

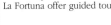

Sign at Arenal Observatory Lodge

Laguna de Arenal ❹

See pp150–51.

Arenal Hanging Bridges ❺

Road Map C2. 12 miles (19 km) W of La Fortuna. 479-8362. *to La Fortuna, then by jeep-taxi.* *7:30am– 4:30pm daily.* www.hangingbridges.com

A self-guided trail meanders through 620 pristine acres (250 ha) of primary forest and is punctuated by a series of 14 bridges suspended over ravines. The relatively easy, 2-mile (3-km) trail clings to the mountainside and offers close-up views of every level of the moist tropical forest, from ground to canopy. Guided walks include dawn birding and a night tour.

Arenal Rainforest Reserve and Aerial Tram ❻

Road Map C2. El Castillo, 14 miles (22 km) W of La Fortuna. *479-9944.* *7am–9pm daily.* *to La Fortuna, then by jeep-taxi.* *7:30am and 3:30pm.* www.arenalreserve.com

Aerial trams *(teleféricos)* whisk visitors up the northern slopes of the Cordillera de Tilarán at this private facility, opened in 2004. The open-air carriages climb steeply through rainforest to a *mirador* (lookout point) at 4,250 ft (1,300 m) from where visitors can enjoy fabulous views of Lake Arenal and the volcano. From the *mirador*, 2 miles (3 km) of ziplines connect treetop canopies and offer exhilarating rides across broad ravines.

Environs: The **Jardín de Mariposas/Castillo de Insectos** has a small, fascinating display of insects, scorpions, and snakes, as well as a netted butterfly garden and a medicinal herb garden.

Jardín de Mariposas/ Castillo de Insectos
El Castillo, 14 miles (22 km) W of La Fortuna. *479-8014.* *8am–4pm daily.*

Open-air *teleféricos* at the Arenal Rainforest Reserve & Aerial Tram

Laguna de Arenal ❹

Butterfly at Laguna de Arenal

Ringed by hills, with Volcán Arenal standing tall to the east, Lake Arenal has a breathtaking setting at an elevation of 1,800 ft (540 m). The 48-sq-mile (124-sq-km) lake fills a tectonic depression forming a gap between Tilarán and the Cordillera de Guanacaste, and was created in 1973 when the Instituto Costarricense de Electricidad (ICE) dammed the eastern end of the valley. The sole town is Nuevo Arenal, on the lake's north side. The easternmost shores are forest-clad, while huge swathes of verdant pasture lie to the south and west. The lake is swept by near-constant winds, providing windsurfers with world-class conditions. Archeologists have identified pre-Columbian settlements beneath the waters.

Lucky Bug Gallery
This small shop attached to Restaurante Willy's Caballo Negro (see p235) *sells an eclectic range of quality artwork and crafts.*

Lago de Coter
The small lake features an activity center offering kayaking, swimming, and birding (see p152).

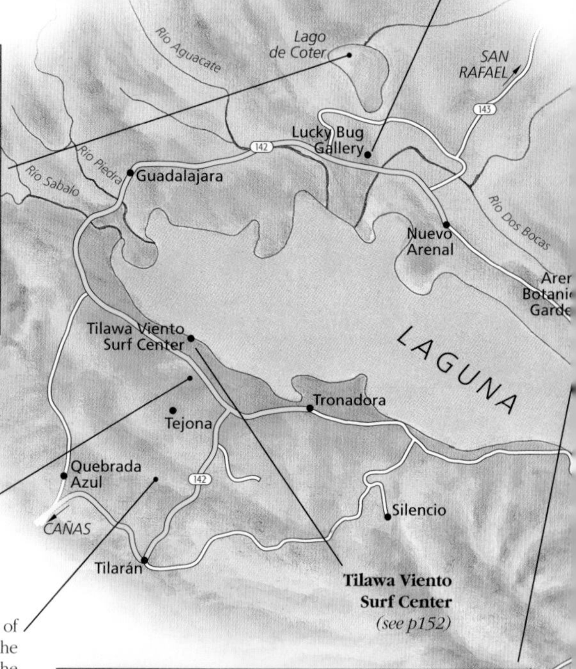

Hotel Tilawa Skateboard Park has good skateboarding facilities.

Tilawa Viento Surf Center *(see p152)*

Wind turbines line ridges of the Continental Divide on the exposed western side of the lake, supplying electricity to the national grid (see p152).

0 km 3

0 miles 3

Arenal Botanical Gardens
Started in 1991, this extensive private garden displays hundreds of tropical plant species, including several colorful flowering varieties. Also featured are a butterfly garden and a hummingbird sanctuary (see p152).

Key

- Major road
- Other road
- Parque Nacional Volcán Arenal boundary

The magnificent setting of Laguna de Arenal

Visitors' Checklist

Road Map B2.11 miles (18 km) from La Fortuna along Hwy 142.
from La Fortuna.
Hotel Tilawa Skateboard Park
695-5050. *dawn–sunset daily.* www.hotel-tilawa.com

Arenal Hanging Bridges
A series of suspension bridges are part of a 2-mile (3-km) self-guided interpretive trail through rainforest. The trail offers superb views of Volcán Arenal ❺

Presa Sangregado, the 288-ft (88-m) long, 184-ft (56-m) high earthen dam that created the lake, generates a large portion of the nation's hydroelectric power.

El Castillo
This community is a starting point for horseback rides to Monteverde via the Cordillera Tilarán. Other attractions include Jardín de Mariposas, which has a small museum displaying insects and reptiles, and a butterfly garden (see p149).

Arenal Rainforest Reserve and Aerial Tram
The Arenal Rainforest Reserve's "sky tram" consists of open-air carriages, which ascend forest-covered mountain slopes. Fabulous views of the lake and volcano can be seen ❻

Exploring Laguna de Arenal

LAKE ARENAL IS ENCIRCLED to the west and north by the winding Route 142, which links Tilarán with La Fortuna. East of Nuevo Arenal, the road deteriorates and is frequently blocked by landslides. A dirt road along the southeastern shore is often impassable and not recommended. The hotels and restaurants lining the northern shore make a pleasant break from driving. The greatest attractions of the area are the picture-postcard vistas, which can be best appreciated from Arenal's southwest shore. The lake is also a favored spot for sportfishing, windsurfing, and other watersports.

Tilawa Viento Surf Center on Lake Arenal

Nuevo Arenal

24 miles (39 km) W of La Fortuna.
2,200.

Replacing the old village, which was flooded in 1973 by the formation of the lake, this orderly town is a service center for the lake region. It has the only fuel station in the area, as well as a German bakery and an Italian restaurant. A dirt road, leading north through the Río Quequer Valley, links Nuevo Arenal with San Rafael on Highway 4.

View of the lake from Arenal Botanical Gardens

Arenal Botanical Gardens

2 miles (3 km) E of Nuevo Arenal.
385-4557. *9am–5pm daily.*
May–Nov: Sun.
www.junglegold.com

Spread over 7 acres (3 ha), this garden contains more than 2,500 species of tropical and subtropical flora from around the world, including orchids, bromeliads, and ferns. There are several varieties of heliconias, anthuriums, and ginger, which draw hummingbirds in profusion. However, there are few educational signs, and visitors are left to guess at the identity of many plants. Be sure to pick up a visitors' pamphlet at the entrance before setting out on the narrow and muddy self-guided trail that snakes up and down the steep hillside. A dense bamboo forest forms a graceful tunnel over the trail, which leads through a netted butterfly garden. Blue morphos, heliconids, and owl-eyes *(Caligno memnon)*, flit about here, and around a dozen species of snakes can be seen behind glass cases.

Tilawa Viento Surf Center

11 miles (18 km) SW of Nuevo Arenal. *695-5050.*
http://windsurfcostarica.com

Swept by steady, strong northeasterly winds between November and March, Lake Arenal is rated as one of the world's finest windsurfing sites. The Tilawa Viento Surf Center on the lake's western shore caters to all levels of windsurfers. Besides hiring out sailboards, it offers multi-day packages and beginners' and advanced lessons.

Rain Goddess

231-4299.
www.bluwing.com

Well stocked with *guapote* (rainbow bass) and other light-tackle game fish, Lake Arenal is considered a premier angling spot. Local hotels and tour operators offer fishing trips, as does the *Rain Goddess*. A 65-ft (20-m) cruise vessel with deluxe accommodations in wood-paneled cabins, it features multiday fishing packages.

Lago de Coter

4 miles (6 km) NW of Nuevo Arenal.

North of Lake Arenal, Lago de Coter occupies a basin in the Fila Vieja Dormida Mountains. The **Lake Coter Eco-Lodge** *(see p213)* is a center for activities such as canoeing, kayaking, horseback riding, and mountain biking. It also offers appealing accommodations. Over 350 species of birds have been recorded in the surrounding forests. A 3-sq-mile (9-sq-km) forest reserve nearby offers guided hiking and birding tours, as well as a zipline canopy tour.

WIND TURBINES

Electricity-generating wind turbines on Lake Arenal's shores

Rising over emerald pastures on the western shores of Lake Arenal, two parallel ridge crests are dotted with over 100 wind turbines, each 120-ft (35-m) high. Situated near the village of Tejona, which has some of the highest average wind speeds in the world, this wind farm is the largest in Central America, with a projected annual production of up to 70 MW. Electricity is sold to the state-owned ICE (Instituto Costarricense de Electricidad).

Volcanoes in Costa Rica

Located in one of the world's most volcanic zones, Costa Rica has seven active volcanoes, and at least 60 that are either dormant or extinct. Volcanoes are created by plate tectonics – that is, the movement of the interlocking plates making up the earth's crust that ride on the magma (molten rock) in the mantle. Most volcanoes occur at the boundaries where plates meet or move apart, with magma bursting through cracks in the plate. Lying between 100 and 150 miles (160–240 km) inland of the subduction zone of the Cocos and the Caribbean plates, Costa Rica's volcanoes are concentrated in the northwestern and central regions. Most are steep-sided cones formed by silica-rich magma, and are highly explosive, with Arenal being the most active.

"Poor man's umbrella," found on volcanic soil

The Formation of Costa Rica's Volcanoes

Costa Rica's landmass sits on the Caribbean plate, beneath which the east-moving Cocos plate is being forced to form a subduction zone. The intense pressure melts the rocks – this viscous magma wells up to create volcanoes.

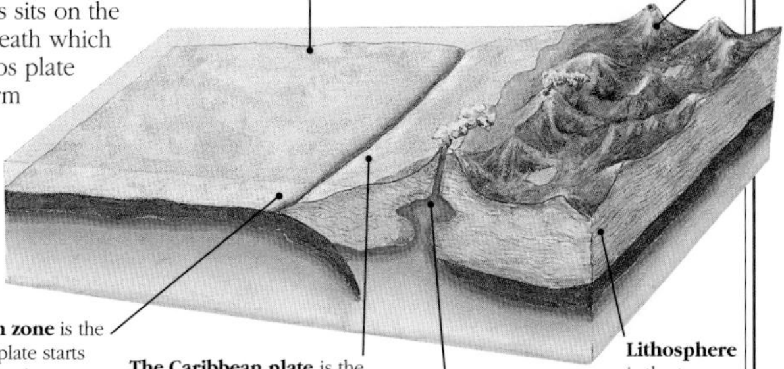

Cocos plate

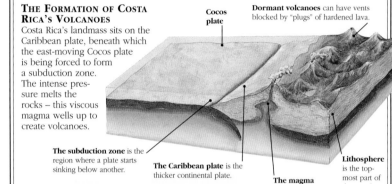

Dormant volcanoes can have vents blocked by "plugs" of hardened lava.

The subduction zone is the region where a plate starts sinking below another.

The Caribbean plate is the thicker continental plate.

The magma chamber feeds the volcano.

Lithosphere is the topmost part of the mantle.

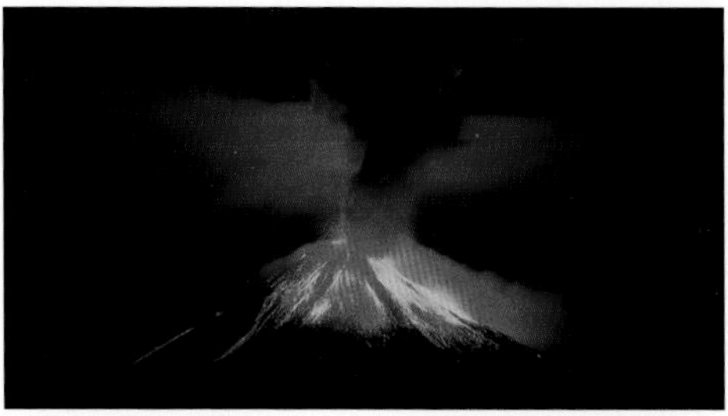

Volcanic eruptions *can be viewed at Arenal, which erupts every few hours during its active phases, oozing hot lava down its slopes. Lava blasted laterally from volcanoes appears as* nuées ardentes *(glowing clouds) – superheated avalanches of gas, ash, and rock that move downhill at astonishing speeds.*

Smoke and ash *are often steadily emitted by active volcanoes such as Volcán Arenal* (see p149). *Smoking cinder blocks can sometimes be seen rolling down the slopes.*

Bubbling mud pools *and fumaroles (vents of steam), formed from rainwater superheated from below, are features of volcanoes such as Miravalles* (see p131).

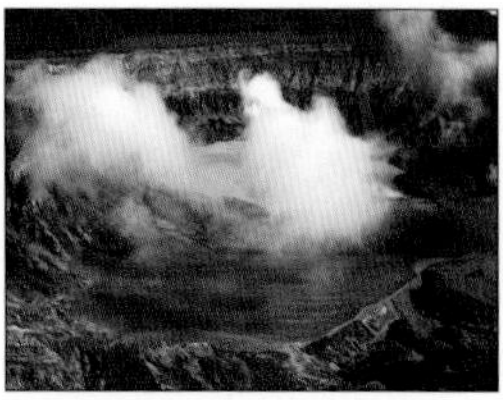

Calderas *are formed when the craters of volcanoes collapse, creating huge circular depressions. This caldera on 8,850-ft (2,700-m) high Volcán Poás is a mile (1.6 km) wide, still emits smoke, and contains a mineral lake* (see p90).

The wetlands of Refugio Nacional de Vida Silvestre Caño Negro

Cavernas de Venado 7

Road Map C2. 1 mile (1.6 km) W of Venado, 24 miles (39 km) NW of La Fortuna. *479-9390.* *from Ciudad Quesada.* *7am–8pm daily.* *8am and 1pm.*

Bioluminescent fungi help light the way for visitors scrambling through the underground passageways of these limestone caverns. Ten chambers, extending almost 2 miles (3 km), have been explored. Exquisite stalagmites, stalactites, and other subterranean formations fill the labyrinthine and narrow chambers, many of which contain marine fossils. **Cascada de La Muerte** is an underground waterfall that gushes during the wet season from May to November and after heavy rain. Bats flit about, blind fish swim in the underground streams, and small transparent frogs hop around in the ooze.

Guides lead 2-hour long explorations. Wilbert Solis, who owns the land on which the caves are located, supplies safety helmets, flashlights, and rubber boots. Come prepared to get covered in mud, and bring a change of clothes.

Agencies in La Fortuna offer tours. Venado is also accessible by a dirt road that begins at Toad Hall *(see p234)*, on the north shore of Lake Arenal. The village offers basic accommodation.

Refugio Nacional de Vida Silvestre Caño Negro 8

Road Map C1. 65 miles (105 km) NW of La Fortuna. *471-1309.* *from Upala.* *from Los Chiles.* *8am–4pm daily.*

One of the most important wetland conservation areas in Costa Rica, Caño Negro Wildlife Refuge protects over 38 sq miles (98 sq km) of marshlands, lagoons, and *yolillo* palm forest. The majority of visitors come to fish for champion-size snook and tarpon, which thrive in Río Frío and other watercourses that feed Lago Caño Negro, a 3-sq-mile (9-sq-km) seasonal lake. Rare ancient garfish also inhabit the tannin-stained waters. The short dry season from December to April is best for viewing crocodiles, caimans, and the large mammals that gather near permanent bodies of water. Monkeys and tapirs are numerous, although jaguars and other cats are more elusive. Lucky visitors may also see large flocks of migratory birds and waterfowl, including jabiru storks, Nicaraguan grackles, roseate spoonbills, and the largest colony of neotropic cormorants in Costa Rica.

Neotropic cormorant

Caño Negro village, on the west bank of Lago Caño Negro, is the only community within the reserve. The park headquarters are located here, as are several lodges that offer guided tours and arrange fishing licenses. Boats can also be rented in nearby Los Chiles, and agencies in San José offer tours, especially during the July–March fishing season. Much of the region floods in the wet season and access along the rough dirt roads can be a challenge.

Ciudad Quesada 9

Road Map C2. 59 miles (95 km) NW of San José. *36,350.* *Catuzon, S of the plaza, 479-9106.* *Sat.* *Feria del Ganado (Apr).*

An important market center serving the local dairy and cattle industries, Ciudad Quesada is set amid pastures atop the mountain scarp of the Cordillera de Tilarán, at an elevation of 2,130 ft (650 m). The town, known locally as San Carlos, is the administrative center for the region, and is famous throughout Costa Rica for its annual cattle fair and *tope* (horse show). It has grown rapidly since the 1950s, when the government initiated the settlement of the relatively uninhabited northern lowlands. Visitors might stop here to admire the landscaped town plaza and the work of numerous *talabarterías* (saddle-makers).

Environs: Highway 140 slopes east, passing **Termales del Bosque**, where visitors can soak in thermal mineral

Mineral spring pools at Termales del Bosque, Ciudad Quesada

springs and have mud baths. Hiking trails lace botanical gardens, and horseback rides and a zipline canopy tour are also on offer. Nearby, **Hotel Occidental El Tucano** *(see p212)* has a full-service spa, as well as hot springs and hiking trails that lead into a forest reserve.

Termales del Bosque
4 miles (6 km) E of Ciudad Quesada.
460-4740. *7am–10pm daily.*
www.termalesdelbosque.com

La Marina Zoológica ⑩

Road Map C2. 6 miles (10 km) E of Ciudad Quesada. *474-2202.* *from Ciudad Quesada.* *8am–4pm daily.*

This private, non-profit zoo takes in orphaned animals as well as others rescued by the park service. Here, visitors can get close to animals that are rarely seen in the wild. Its numerous inhabitants include jaguars, agoutis, monkeys, peccaries, and snakes, as well as macaws, toucans, and many other bird species. Tapirs are bred for release into the wild.

Shaman healing table and stones, Museo de Cultura Indígena

Centro Neotrópico SarapiquíS ⑪

Road Map D2. La Virgen de Sarapiquí, 29 miles (47 km) N of Alajuela. *761-1004.* *San José–Puerto Viejo de Sarapiquí.* *7am–8pm daily.* www.sarapiquis.org

This broad-ranging ecological center on the banks of Río Sarapiquí offers an enriching insight into indigenous cultures *(see pp32–3)*. The state-of-the-art **Museo de Cultura Indígena**, housed in a huge round *palenque* (thatched structure), is dedicated to Costa Rica's living indigenous communities and the preservation of their artifacts. Its impressive exhibits include a large collection of masks, bark cloth paintings, and other decorative, domestic, and ritual objects, including shamanic healing sticks. Educational signs describe the indigenous peoples' spirit-filled animistic concept of nature. An air-conditioned theater shows audio-visual presentations, including a 15-minute documentary.

The **Parque Arquealógica Alma Alta**, set in an orange orchard, is centered around four indigenous tombs, dating from the 15th century, and a representation of a pre-Columbian village. Indian guides offer fascinating tours of **Chester's Field Botanical Gardens**. Named for the naturalist Chester Czepulos (1916–92), the gardens have about 500 native species of plants known since pre-Columbian times for their medicinal use. An excellent illustrated booklet helps those planning to explore alone. The center has a quality restaurant, hotel, library, and conference center.

Parque Arquealógica Alma Alta at the Centro Neotrópico SarapiquíS

Environs: The center adjoins the **Tirimbina Rainforest Reserve**, which protects 750 acres (300 ha) of mid-elevation premontane forest. It can be reached from Centro Neotrópico SarapiquíS by a 855-ft (260-m) long suspension bridge across Río Sarapiquí. A 325-ft (100-m) canopy walkway features among Tirimbina's 5 miles (8 km) of trails. Guided tours include a special "World of Bats" night walk. The reserve's Education Center, which is on Tirimbina Island in the middle of the river, is used for scientific investigation and has a library on tropical ecology.

Hacienda Pozo Azul is a working cattle ranch which offers whitewater rafting trips and canopy tours. Accommodation is available at Magsasay Lodge, adjoining Parque Nacional Braulio Carrillo *(see p91)*. The nearby **Snake Garden** lets visitors get nose-to-nose with 70 snake species.

Tirimbina Rainforest Reserve
761-1579. *7am–5pm Mon–Fri, 7am–4pm Sat–Sun.*
www.tirimbina.org

Hacienda Pozo Azul
La Virgen de Sarapiquí. *761-1360.* *9am–5pm daily.*
www.haciendapozoazul.com

Snake Garden
La Virgen de Sarapiquí. *761-1059.* *9am–5pm daily.*

Horseback riding at Hacienda Pozo Azul, a working ranch

Puerto Viejo de Sarapiquí ⓬

Road Map D2. 52 miles (84 km) N of San José. *16,300.*

POSITIONED at the base of the Cordillera Central, on the banks of Río Sarapiquí, Puerto Viejo has functioned as an important river port since colonial days. Before the opening of the Atlantic Railroad in 1890, the town was the main gateway between San José and the Caribbean Sea. While the port trade has reduced, *pangas* (water-taxis) still connect the town to Parque Nacional Tortuguero *(see p167)* and Barra del Colorado via Río San Juan. Boats also set out on nature excursions.

Banana trees cover most of the Llanura de San Carlos flatlands around Puerto Viejo. **Bananero La Colonia**, a processing factory in the middle of banana fields, welcomes visitors.

Bananero La Colonia
3 miles (5 km) SE of Puerto Viejo. *768-8683.* *by appt.*
www.bananatourcostarica.com

Water-taxis on Río San Juan at Puerto Viejo de Sarapiquí

A verdant trail in the rainforests of Selva Verde

Selva Verde ⓭

Road Map D2. 5 miles (8 km) W of Puerto Viejo de Sarapiquí. *766-6800.* *San José–Puerto Viejo via Vara Blanca.* *6am–4pm daily.*
www.selvaverde.com

ONE OF THE country's best private reserves, the 470-acre (190-ha) Selva Verde (Green Forest) reserve adjoins Parque Nacional Braulio Carrillo *(see p91)*. A prime destination for birders, the virgin low-elevation rainforest is home to over 420 bird species, including eight species of parrots. Ocelots, sloths, capuchin monkeys, and mantled howler monkeys are among the 120 species of mammals to be seen. Poison-dart frogs are numerous, as are snakes, although these are difficult to spot. Several of Selva Verde's 500 species of butterflies can be seen in a netted butterfly garden.

Guided canoe trips are offered on Río Sarapiquí, which runs through Selva Verde. Naturalist guides can be hired, and maps are provided for the well-maintained trails. The reserve also has a lodge with comfortable rooms.

Refugio Nacional de Vida Silvestre Corredor Fronterizo ⓮

Road Map C1. Bahía Salinas to Punta Castillo. *283-8004.*

INTENDED AS a biological corridor, the 230-sq-mile (590-sq-km) Frontier Corridor National Wildlife Refuge protects a wide strip of Costa Rican territory along the border with Nicaragua, from Bahía Salinas on the west coast to Punta Castillo on the east. The eastern part of the refuge runs along Río San Juan. Lined with virgin rainforest, this broad river flows 120 miles (195 km) east from Lake Nicaragua to Punta Castillo, and has long been disputed by the two nations.

Pangas link Puerto Viejo de Sarapiquí to Trinidad village, at the confluence of Ríos Sarapiquí and San Juan. The river trip through the reserve is splendid for spotting sloths, crocodiles, and myriad birds, including oropendolas and rare chestnut-bellied herons.

ENVIRONS: Boca San Carlos, 24 miles (39 km) upstream of Trinidad on Río San Juan, has an airstrip and can also be reached by a dirt road. It is a gateway for river journeys into Nicaragua. Nearby, **Laguna del Lagarto** is a private reserve protecting 2 sq miles (5 sq km) of virgin rainforest and swamps. Elusive manatees inhabit the lagoons and a nature lodge offers a good base for wildlife viewing. The restored, 17th-century, mossy hilltop fort of **Fortaleza de la Inmaculada Concepción**, near the Nicaraguan hamlet of El Castillo, 25 miles (40 km) upstream of Boca San Carlos, is worth a visit. Its small museum recalls the days when Spanish defenders fought back pirates and an English invasion fleet led by Lord Nelson.

Laguna del Lagarto
10 miles (16 km) S of Boca San Carlos. *289-8163.*
http://lagarto-lodge-costa-rica.com

FRESHWATER SHARKS

The presence of sharks in freshwater Lake Nicaragua has been a puzzle for centuries. In the 1970s, scientists tagged individual sharks with electronic monitors and found that they migrate along Río San Juan between the Caribbean Sea and the lake, a distance of 106 miles (169 km). These euryhaline sharks, capable of living in both fresh- and saltwater, are even able to navigate rapids.

Bull shark in the waters of Lake Nicaragua

Costa Rica's Snakes

Costa Rica has more than 160 species of *serpientes* or *culebras*, of which only 22 are venomous. Snakes slither about in habitats ranging from savanna to montane rainforest; there are also pelagic species found in the sea. While many species are flamboyantly colored, most are camouflaged in shades of green and brown. Most snakes are nocturnal creatures and, therefore, seldom seen. They rarely strike unless threatened, and chances of the casual visitor being bitten are slim – most bites are inflicted on field laborers. Hikers should keep an eye on the trails and look carefully before parting foliage or placing their hands on branches or in holes. Sturdy shoes that protect the ankles are recommended.

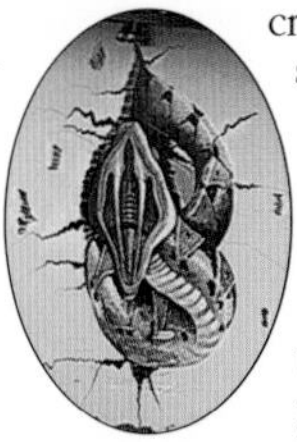

Mural at the Snake Garden, La Virgen

Snake Species

Costa Rica's snakes belong to nine families, including Elapidae (coral snakes), Boidae (boas), and Viperidae (vipers). Most other snakes belong to the Colubridae family.

Serpentarios *(snake farms) permit visitors to view and handle snakes in safe environments with experienced handlers.*

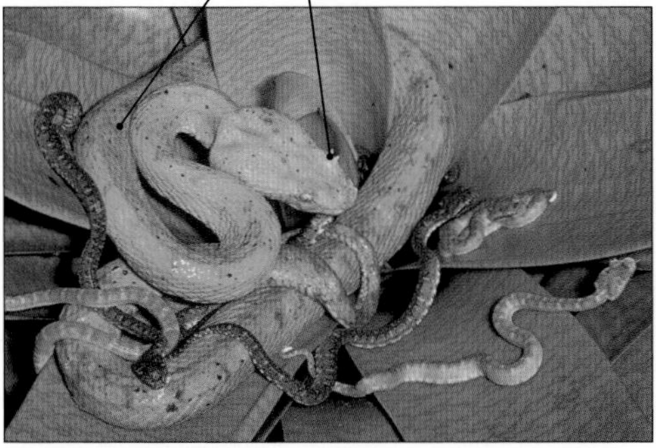
Camouflage is provided by the eyelash viper's banana-yellow or lime-green skin.
Hood-like scales above its eyes give this viper its name.

Eyelash vipers (bocaracá) *are highly venomous, with syringe-like fangs. Their upper jaws have heat sensors capable of detecting and tracking warm-blooded prey in complete darkness.*

Pencil-thin, with long, pointed snouts, vine snakes rarely grow more than a foot (30 cm) long.

Vine snakes (bejuquillo) *are commonly found inside bromeliads, from where they ambush frogs and birds. Their I-beam bodies support them as they negotiate branches in search of prey.*

The fer-de-lance (terciopelo), *camouflaged by its brown and gray skin, inhabits grasslands and riverbanks. Fast-moving and aggressive, this massive snake is responsible for the majority of fatal snake bites in Costa Rica.*

Coral snakes (corál) *are very venomous. Costa Rica has four species, brightly colored in bands of red, black, and white or yellow.*

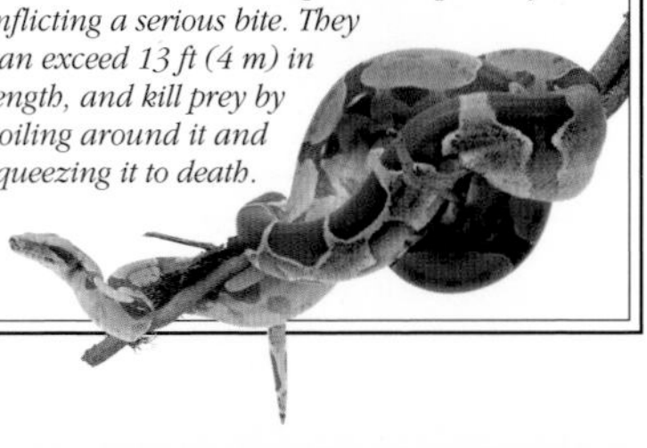

Boas (boa) *are relatively shy, and although non-venomous, have large teeth capable of inflicting a serious bite. They can exceed 13 ft (4 m) in length, and kill prey by coiling around it and squeezing it to death.*

Broad-billed motmot, La Selva Biological Station

La Selva Biological Station ⓯

Road Map D2. 2 miles (3 km) S of Puerto Viejo. *766-6565.* *OTS shuttles from Puerto Viejo & San José.* *8am–5pm by appt.* www.ots.ac.cr

Created by the scientist Dr. Leslie Holdridge in 1954, La Selva Biological Station has been run as a private research facility by the Organization of Tropical Studies (OTS) since 1968. Scientific research at this 6-sq-mile (15-sq-km) reserve spans physiological ecology, soil science, and forestry, with over 1,000 tree species in the Holdridge Arboretum.

The predominant habitat is a vast swathe of lowland and premontane rainforest at the base of Parque Nacional Braulio Carrillo *(see p91)*. Snakes, although profuse, are rarely seen. More noticeable are poison-dart frogs, enameled in gaudy colors, and more than 500 species of butterflies, including neon blue morphos. Elusive jaguars and other big cats prowl the forests, preying on monkeys, coatis, and deer, which are among La Selva's 120 mammal species. Leafcutter ants are underfoot everywhere, carrying their scissored cargos. About half of Costa Rica's bird species have been sighted here; the annual 24-hour La Selva Christmas Bird Count has become a pilgrimage for ornithologists from around the world. A basic bird-watching course is offered on Saturday mornings.

Access to the reserve is restricted to 65 people at any given time, and although it is open to the public by reservation, scientists and students get priority. Over 31 miles (50 km) of boardwalk trails crisscross La Selva, but precipitation can exceed 157 inches (400 cm) in a year, and many trails are muddy. The gift shop has self-guiding booklets. OTS offers guided excursions from San José that include transport. Dormitory lodging is offered on a space-available basis.

Sarapiquí Heliconia Island ⓰

Road Map D2. 5 miles (8 km) S of Puerto Viejo. *762-0520.* *San José– Puerto Viejo de Sarapiquí via PN Braulio Carrillo.* *8am–5pm daily, by appointment.* www.heliconiaisland.com

This beautifully laid-out garden on the banks of Río Puerto Viejo was created in 1992 by the American naturalist Tim Ryan. Hundreds of tropical plant species grow amid the lush 5-acre (2-ha) lawns. Also known as the Sarapiquí Botanical Garden, the garden specializes in heliconias, of which it has more than 80 species from around the world. Various species of gingers thrive here, and also a superb collection of bamboos and orchids. Equally impressive are the palms, which include the traveler's palm, native to Madagascar. It is so named because in an emergency, travelers can drink the water that is stored in its stalk.

Tropical heliconia

Hummingbirds hover as they sip nectar. Violaceous trogons and orange-chinned parakeets are among the more than 200 species of birds drawn to the exotic flora. Rare green macaws nest in *almendro* (almond) trees and are frequently sighted.

Ryan leads tours, imparting fascinating trivia on tropical plant ecology. The torchlit nighttime tours are especially rewarding. The river has calm stretches safe for swimming.

Poison-Dart Frogs

A colorful poison-dart frog

The rainforests of Central and South America are inhabited by poison-dart frogs *(Dendrobates pumilio)*, so named because Indians use their poison to tip their arrows and blow-darts. About 65 separate species exist, although only three species are deadly to humans. The frogs, which are no more than an inch (3 cm) long, produce the bitter toxin in their mucous glands and advertise this with flamboyant colors – mostly vivid reds, greens, and blues – to avoid being eaten by predators. Thus, unusually for frogs, they are active by day amongst the moist leaf litter. Several species of non-toxic frogs mimic their coloration. In captivity, poison-dart frogs tend to lose their toxicity, which they derive from their principal diet of ants and termites.

Rara Avis 17

Road Map D2. 17 miles (27 km) S of Puerto Viejo. 764-3131. *San José–Las Horquetas.* www.rara-avis.com

THIS WORLD-FAMOUS rainforest reserve was among the first private reserves in Costa Rica. Adjoining Parque Nacional Braulio Carrillo and La Selva, the 4-sq-mile (10-sq-km) Rara Avis is perched on the remote northeast slopes of Volcán Chato at an elevation of 2,300 ft (700 m).

The brainchild of entrepreneur Amos Bien, who created it in 1983, Rara Avis pioneered the notion of generating income through ecologically sustainable ventures in protected primary forests. Its selective farming projects include a butterfly farm and philodendron and orchid cultivation.

Trails wander through pristine mid-elevation rainforest. The biodiversity is impressive, from anteaters, spider monkeys, and porcupines to boa constrictors, coral snakes, red-eyed tree frogs, elusive jaguars and pumas, and almost 400 species of birds, including the umbrella bird, sunbitterns, and the endangered great green macaw. A rappeling system lets you get eye-to-eye with canopy dwellers such as toucans and capuchin monkeys. The park has several waterfalls, but caution is required when swimming in the pools that form at their base.

Porcupine in Rara Avis

Rara Avis is accessed by a daunting track that is often knee-deep in mud. Transfers from Las Horquetas, on Highway 4, are by tractor-drawn canopied trailer, a bumpy 9-mile (14-km) journey that takes 3 hours. Come prepared for heavy rainfall, which averages more than 200 inches (500 cm) per year. Rubber boots are provided for hikers. Overnight stays are strongly recommended; accommodation is in a choice of rustic lodges.

BANANAS

Ripening fruit at a banana plantation

Costa Rica is the world's seventh largest banana producer and its second largest exporter. Plantations cover 195 sq miles (500 sq km) of the nation. Massive tracts of protected rainforest are felled each year to plant bananas, and many chemicals are used to maintain output. When washed out to sea, these chemicals kill fish, poison the waters, and foster the growth of plants that choke estuaries and corals. As a result of environmental campaigns, the banana industry now follows more ecologically sensitive practices.

Rainforest Aerial Tram 18

Road Map D3. Hwy 32, 25 miles (40 km) NE of San José. 257-5961. *San José–Guápiles.* *9am–4pm Mon; 7am–4pm Tue–Sun.* www.rainforestram.com

OFFERING A dramatic excursion into the forest canopy, this automated exploration system was conceived by the American naturalist Dr. Donald Perry while he was involved in scientific investigation at Rara Avis. Inaugurated in 1994, the Rainforest Aerial Tram, also called "El Teleférico," is the highlight of a 875-acre (355-ha) private nature reserve on the eastern edge of Parque Nacional Braulio Carrillo. Visitors ride in open gondolas that silently skim the floor of the rainforest and then soar above the trees on a 2-mile (3-km) circuit. The 90-minute tour is preceded by a video, which describes the construction of the $2 million system, and the flora and fauna to be seen. A naturalist guide accompanies each gondola to assist visitors in spotting and identifying wildlife. Howler and white-faced monkeys are frequently seen at close quarters, as are anteaters, iguanas, sloths, and even eyelash vipers, blending almost imperceptibly with the foliage. Early morning and late afternoon are the best times to spot wildlife, but visitors should keep in mind that the main aim of the journey is to learn about rainforest ecology.

Trails lead to Río Corinto, and guided birding trips are offered. Accommodations are in the form of cabins. Tour agencies nationwide offer package excursions.

Rainforest Aerial Tram gondola at the start of its tour

THE CARIBBEAN

UNIQUE WITHIN THE COUNTRY *for its Afro-Caribbean culture, this region is steeped in traditions brought by Jamaican forebears, which lend a colorful, laid-back charm to the ramshackle villages that sprinkle the coast. One of Costa Rica's wettest regions, it extends along 125 miles (200 km) of the Caribbean coastline between the Nicaraguan and Panamanian borders. Stunning beaches line the shore, and primordial rainforest merges with swampy lagoons in the north and rises into the rugged Talamanca Mountains in the south.*

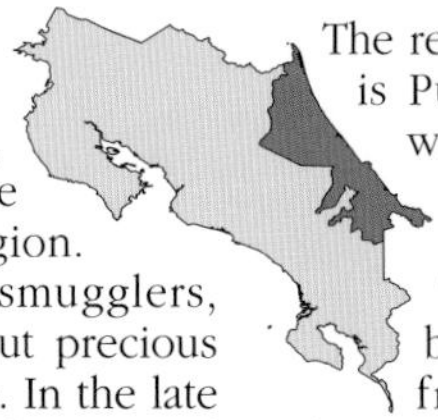

After the closure of the port of Puerto Limón to trade in 1665 *(see p43)*, the Spanish made little attempt to settle the region. This drew pirates and smugglers, who induced slaves to cut precious hardwoods for illicit trade. In the late 19th century, Jamaican laborers and their families arrived to build the Atlantic Railroad and work on banana plantations. Succeeding generations adopted a subsistence life of farming and fishing, which continues in today's Creole culture. Inland, descendants of the original indigenous tribes live in relative isolation in designated reserves in the Talamanca foothills, clinging to shamanism and other traditional practices.

The region's only significant town is Puerto Limón, located midway down the coast. Northward, flatlands extend to the Nicaraguan border. The coastal strip is backed by swampy jungles and freshwater lagoons that culminate in Tortuguero National Park and Barra del Colorado National Wildlife Refuge. A network of canals, created in the 1960s to link Puerto Limón with Barra, opened up this otherwise virtually inaccessible region. South of Puerto Limón, the shore is lined with stupendous beaches. The communities of Cahuita and Puerto Viejo are popular with surfers and a predominantly young crowd seeking offbeat adventure.

Brightly colored wooden house in the village of Cahuita

◁ **Palms lining the surfing beach Playa Chiquita, near Puerto Viejo de Talamanca**

Exploring the Caribbean

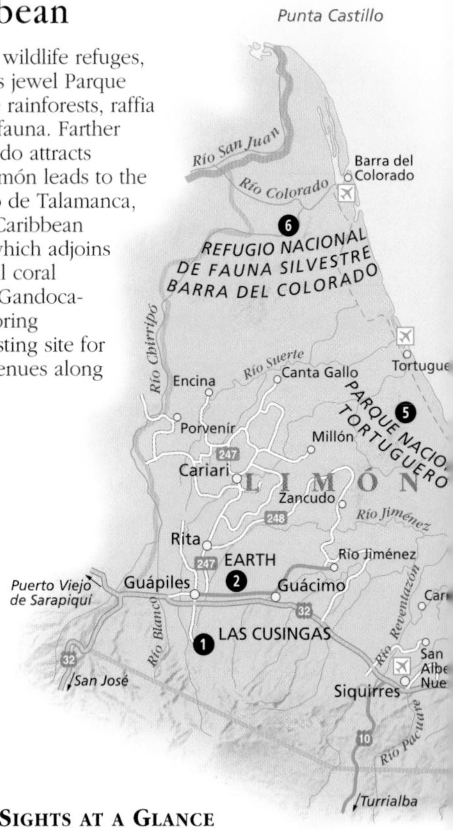

With several national parks and wildlife refuges, the humid Caribbean has as its jewel Parque Nacional Tortuguero, with its dense rainforests, raffia palm swamps, and exotic range of fauna. Farther north, rain-sodden Barra del Colorado attracts anglers. The port town of Puerto Limón leads to the villages of Cahuita and Puerto Viejo de Talamanca, vibrant centers of indigenous Afro-Caribbean culture. Parque Nacional Cahuita, which adjoins Cahuita village, also protects a small coral reef. Fine beaches extend south to Gandoca-Manzanillo, a coastal wetland harboring manatees and also an important nesting site for marine turtles. Many horticultural venues along Highway 32 exhibit tropical flora.

Entrance to a house in Puerto Limón

Sights at a Glance

Towns and Cities
Cahuita 9
Puerto Limón 3
Puerto Viejo de Talamanca 11

National Parks and Reserves
Parque Nacional Cahuita 10
Parque Nacional Tortuguero 5
Refugio Nacional de Fauna Silvestre Barra del Colorado 6
Refugio Nacional de Vida Silvestre Gandoca-Manzanillo 12
Reserva Biológica Hitoy-Cerere 8

Areas of Natural Beauty
Aviarios del Caribe Wildlife Refuge 7
EARTH 2
Las Cusingas 1

Tour
Canal de Tortuguero Tour p166 4

Indigenous Sites
Indigenous Reserves 13

See Also

- ***Where to Stay*** pp214–16
- ***Where to Eat*** pp235–6

Key

- Major road
- Secondary road
- Minor road
- International border
- Provincial border
- Canal

Beach at Puerto Viejo de Talamanca

A picker cushioning a large bunch of bananas, Cahuita

Getting Around

Highway 32, linking San José to Puerto Limón, is heavily trafficked, particularly along the mountainous sections. A bus service provides easy access to Cahuita and Puerto Viejo de Talamanca. No roads penetrate to Tortuguero and Barra del Colorado, but both villages have airstrips serviced by daily scheduled flights from San José. Another popular option is to journey by canal – tour operators can make arrangements. An infrequent bus service connects the indigenous reserves along rough dirt roads – an uncomfortable, albeit cheap, ride.

Green honeycreeper, one of the species of birds found in Las Cusingas

Las Cusingas ❶

Road Map D3. 2 miles (3 km) S of Hwy 32, 37 miles (59 km) E of San José. *San José–Guápiles, then by jeep-taxi or hiking.* *710-2652.* *8:30am–4:30pm daily.*

THIS BOTANICAL garden, spread over 35 acres (14 ha) near the less-than-appealing town of Guápiles, undertakes scientific investigation into tropical flora, fruits, and more than 80 species of medicinal plants. Hummingbirds, parrots, and scores of other birds flock to feed on the nectar and seeds. There are two short forest trails, one of which leads to Río Santa Clara and 10 sq miles (26 sq km) of protected forest. The visitor center, which includes a library, offers an introduction to reforestation, conservation, tropical ecology, and the use of medicinal plants.

Guided tours are offered, each about 2 hours long. A rustic family-size cabin with a wood-fired oven can be rented, and visitors can dine with the friendly Tico owners.

ENVIRONS: Acclaimed American-born artist Patricia Erickson welcomes visitors to her studio **Gallery at Home**, which displays her vibrant paintings inspired by scenes of Caribbean family life. To get there, turn south at Río Blanco; the studio is a short way down, on the left. Next door, her husband Brian's **Muebles de Bamboo** offers a chance to watch bamboo furniture being made, using 32 different species grown in a bamboo garden.

Located on the borders of Parque Nacional Tortuguero and Refugio Nacional de Fauna Silvestre Barra del Colorado *(see p167)*, **Finca La Suerte** offers superb opportunities for wildlife-viewing in a variety of habitats, including rainforests and marshes. Poison-dart frogs *(see p158)* and monkeys are particularly abundant. This private educational and research center specializes in residential workshops in tropical ecology, and offers overnight accommodation. It can be accessed from Guápiles by buses that pass through the community of Cariari.

Gallery at Home
330 yd (300 m) S of Hwy 32, 4 miles (6 km) W of Guápiles. *710-1958.* *by appointment.*

Finca La Suerte
La Primavera, 27 miles (43 km) NE of Guápiles. *710-8005.* *9am–5pm daily.* www.lasuerte.org

EARTH ❷

Road Map D2. 7 miles (12 km) E of Guápiles. *713-0000.* *San José–Puerto Limón.* *9am–4pm daily.* www.earth.ac.cr

ONE OF THE world's leading tropical research centers, the Escuela de Agricultura de la Región Tropical Húmeda (Agricultural College of the Humid Tropical Region) focuses on ecologically sustainable practices. Founded in 1990, the center offers university degrees. EARTH operates its own experimental banana plantation, banana processing plant, and paper-making plant that uses banana skins. There are guided tours and nature trails through a 990-acre (400-ha) primary rainforest; horses can also be hired.

ENVIRONS: More than 600 species of tropical flowers, including several varieties of heliconia, paint the landscape in riotous color at **Costa Flores**. Spread over 300 acres (120 ha), it is the world's largest commercial farm for tropical flowers. A 12-mile (19-km) long monorail system is used for picking and taking the blooms to the hangar-sized packing area. Hummingbirds, the sole pollinators of heliconia, zoom around the landscaped gardens, which is dotted with ponds.

Heliconia, Costa Flores

Costa Flores
9 miles (14 km) E of Guápiles. *716-6430.* *8am–4pm Mon–Fri, Sat–Sun by appointment.* www.costafloresgarden.com

Sign for EARTH, a center for tropical research

Bust of Don Balvanero Vargas in Puerto Limón's Parque Vargas

Puerto Limón ❸

Road Map F3. 100 miles (160 km) E of San José. *85,000.* *Black Culture Festival (Sep); Día de las Culturas (Oct 12).*

Located in the bay where Christopher Columbus and his son Fernando anchored in 1502, the port town of Puerto Limón had its origins in early colonial days. Used by pirates and smugglers for trading mahogany and other tropical hardwoods, the settlement thrived on this illicit traffic under the nose of the Spanish authorities. The town has a large Chinese population, whose forebears arrived during the 1880s as indentured laborers for the construction of the Atlantic Railroad. A small Chinese cemetery at the entrance to the town honors this Asian heritage. Today, the port handles most of the nation's sea trade; the main highway into town is crowded with container trucks throughout the day. The maritime facilities have been expanded to serve cruise ships plying the Caribbean coast.

Columbus supposedly landed at **Isla Uvita**, half a mile (1 km) offshore. His landfall is commemorated by a bronze bust, which was unveiled in 1992, in time for the 500th anniversary of his arrival in the Americas. The bust faces **Parque Vargas**, a tiny tree-shaded park named after Don Balvanero Vargas, a former governor of Limón province. The park, which features a bust of Don Vargas, is at the east end of the pedestrian-only Avenida 2 (also known as El Bulevar). Nearby, a beautiful mural by artist Guadalupe Alvarez depicts local history since pre-Columbian days.

Puerto Limón has some intriguing architecture, with pretty filigreed iron balconies in the style of New Orleans. To the west of Parque Vargas, the cream-colored stucco Belle Epoque **Alcadía** (Town Hall) is a fine example. Other structures are classics of the Caribbean vernacular style, made of wood and painted in lively tropical pastels, with broad balconies on stilts beneath which locals gather to play dominoes. Visit the lively **Mercado Central**, to the north of the museum, for everything from pigs' heads to freshly caught fish.

Detail of mural by Guadalupe Alvarez near Parque Vargas

Shoppers outside Mercado Central in Puerto Limón

Nocturnal bar-life in Puerto Limón is lively and colorful but somewhat seedy, and there is drug trading. Visitors should generally be cautious; avoid Parque Vargas at night.

Environs: Local surfers find their fun off **Playa Bonita**, 2 miles (3 km) north of town. This gold-sand beach gets crowded on weekends with Limonenses, as the town's inhabitants are known. Swimming in the south end of the bay is dangerous. A mile (1.6 km) to the north of Playa Bonita, **Moín** is where Costa Rica's crude oil is processed and bananas loaded for shipment to Europe and North America. Boats leave from here for Tortuguero *(see p167)*.

Mercado Central

Calles 3/4 and Aves Central/2.
6am–6pm daily.

Carnaval

In the second week of October, Puerto Limón erupts into kaleidoscopic color for Carnaval *(see p37)*, a week-long Caribbean Mardi Gras celebration culminating on Día de las Culturas (Columbus Day). Special buses bring revelers from San José, and the city packs in as many as 100,000 visitors. Live reggae, salsa, and calypso get everyone dancing. Other amusements include beauty contests, bull-running, *desfiles* (parades), street fairs, and firework displays. The highlight is the Grand Desfile, a grand parade of flamboyant costumes and floats held on the Saturday before October 12. Most events take place on the docks.

Extravagantly dressed dancers at Carnaval

Canal de Tortuguero Tour ❹

Kingfisher

TRAVEL ALONG THE Caribbean seaboard became possible with the building of the Tortuguero canal system in 1966–74. Four canals make up this 65-mile (105-km) long aquatic highway, which connects the port of Moín to Barra del Colorado village, and is lined with rainforest. Narrow in places, when the looming forest seems to close in on the water, the canal offers a thrilling boating experience, with sightings of caimans and river turtles, and birds such as aricaris and kingfishers.

A tourist boat moving through the Tortuguero Canal

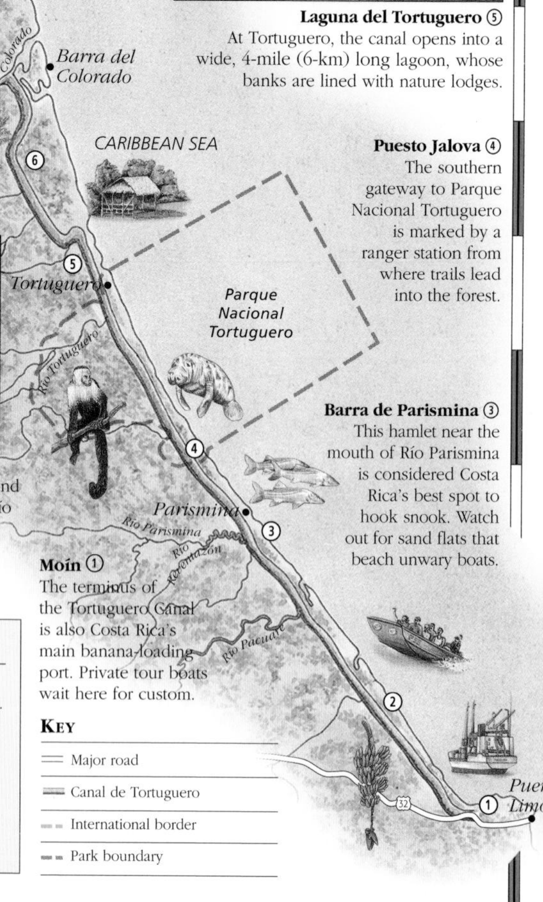

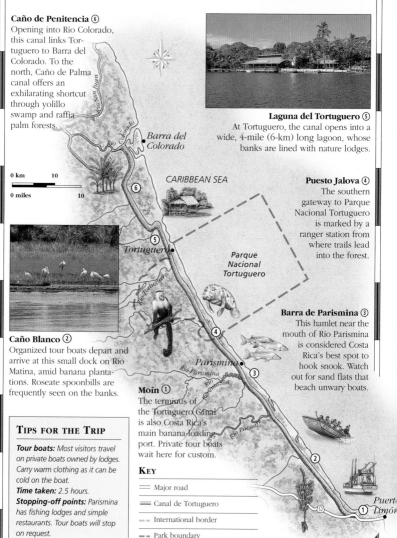

Caño de Penitencia ⑥
Opening into Río Colorado, this canal links Tortuguero to Barra del Colorado. To the north, Caño de Palma canal offers an exhilarating shortcut through yolillo swamp and raffia palm forests.

Laguna del Tortuguero ⑤
At Tortuguero, the canal opens into a wide, 4-mile (6-km) long lagoon, whose banks are lined with nature lodges.

Puesto Jalova ④
The southern gateway to Parque Nacional Tortuguero is marked by a ranger station from where trails lead into the forest.

Caño Blanco ②
Organized tour boats depart and arrive at this small dock on Río Matina, amid banana plantations. Roseate spoonbills are frequently seen on the banks.

Barra de Parismina ③
This hamlet near the mouth of Río Parismina is considered Costa Rica's best spot to hook snook. Watch out for sand flats that beach unwary boats.

Moín ①
The terminus of the Tortuguero Canal is also Costa Rica's main banana-loading port. Private tour boats wait here for custom.

KEY

- Major road
- Canal de Tortuguero
- International border
- Park boundary

TIPS FOR THE TRIP

Tour boats: *Most visitors travel on private boats owned by lodges. Carry warm clothing as it can be cold on the boat.*
Time taken: *2.5 hours.*
Stopping-off points: *Parismina has fishing lodges and simple restaurants. Tour boats will stop on request.*

A guide escorting a tour group through Parque Nacional Tortuguero

Parque Nacional Tortuguero ❺

Road Map E2. 32 miles (52 km) N of Puerto Limón. *709-8086.* *from Pavona, Moín, and Caño Blanco.* *5:30am–6pm daily; last admission: 4pm.*

Created to protect the most important nesting site of the green turtle in the Western Hemisphere, the 73-sq mile (190-sq km) Tortuguero National Park extends along 14 miles (22 km) of shoreline and 19 miles (30 km) out to sea. The Canal de Tortuguero runs through the park, connecting a labyrinth of deltas, canals, and lagoons.

With 11 distinct life zones ranging from raffia palm forest to herbaceous swamps, the park offers one of the most rewarding nature experiences in the country. Although trails start from the ranger stations at the northern and southern ends of the park, this watery world is best seen by boat: the wide canals allow grandstand wildlife viewing, and silent approaches on the water permit unusually close contact with the fauna. River otters, caimans, and howler, spider, and white-faced monkeys are easily sighted, as are birds such as oropendolas, toucans, and jacamars and other waterfowl. A guide is strongly recommended to avoid getting lost in the waterways and to identify wildlife that might otherwise be missed.

For most visitors, the star attraction is the green turtle, which nests between June and November. Three other species of marine turtles also come ashore throughout the year, although in lesser numbers. Entry to the beach is strictly regulated at night – only two tour groups are allowed each night, escorted by guides from the local cooperative.

Note that there are no roads to the park; access is by boat or small planes that land at Tortuguero village.

Environs: The villagers of **Tortuguero**, to the north of the park at the junction of Laguna del Tortuguero and the Canal de Tortuguero, traditionally made their living by lumbering or by culling turtles. Today, tourism is a major source of employment, and locals have learned a new ethic as conservationists. The **John H. Phipps Biological Station and Natural History Visitor's Center** has a small, but good display on ecology. **Cerro Tortuguero** (390 ft/ 119 m), 3 miles (5 km) north of the village, offers good views over the area.

John H. Phipps Biological Station and Natural History Visitor's Center
550 yd (500 m) N of Tortuguero village. *711-0680.* *10am–noon and 2–5:30pm Mon–Sat; 2–5:30pm Sun.*

Refugio Nacional de Fauna Silvestre Barra del Colorado ❻

Road Map E2. 21 miles (34 km) N of Tortuguero. *711-1201.* *from Tortuguero, Puerto Viejo de Sarapiquí, and Pavona.* *8am–4pm daily.* *included with PN Tortuguero.*

Connected to Parque Nacional Tortuguero by Caño de Penitencia, this 350-sq-mile (910-sq-km) refuge extends north to the border with Nicaragua. Despite abundant wildlife, the flooded marshes, teeming rainforest, and vast raffia palm forests are virtually untapped as a wilderness destination. Crocodiles as well as birds such as jabiru storks and endangered great green macaws can be spotted, while tapirs, jaguars, and manatees inhabit the deep forests and swamps. The refuge's many rivers have populations of tarpon, snook, and garfish, and lodges catering to fishing enthusiasts are centered around Barra del Colorado at the mouth of Río Colorado.

Manatees

The endangered West Indian manatee *(Trichechus manatus)*, or sea cow, is found in lagoons and coastal habitats. With front flippers and a paddle-like tail, this hairless gray-brown mammal resembles a tuskless walrus. It feeds primarily on aquatic vegetation such as water hyacinths. Spending most of its time submerged, it is rarely seen. However, increasing encounters with manatees in Tortuguero and Barra del Colorado suggest that the population may be increasing.

West Indian manatee *(Trichechus manatus)*

Aviarios del Caribe Wildlife Refuge ❼

Road Map F3. 22 miles (35 km) S of Puerto Limón. 750-0775. *Puerto Limón–Cahuita.* *6am–3pm daily, by appointment.* www.ogphoto.com/aviarios

COMPRISING WETLAND habitat at the Río Estrella delta, this private reserve features the world's only center dedicated to sloth research and rescue. Named for the two-toed sloth that is the center's mascot, the **Buttercup Sloth Center** looks after dozens of sloths, reintroducing into the wild those believed capable of rehabilitation.

The 185-acre (75-ha) reserve has trails through the tropical humid forest, and it is possible to canoe through freshwater lagoons and marshes, which are home to river otters and river turtles. Poison-dart frogs are easily seen. Rooms are available in a wooden lodge.

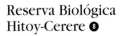

Poison-dart frog, Aviarios del Caribe Wildlife Refuge

Reserva Biológica Hitoy-Cerere ❽

Road Map F3. 28 miles (45 km) S of Puerto Limón and 12 miles (20 km) SW of Hwy 36 at Penshurst. 798-3170. *from Puerto Limón to Finca 12, further by jeep-taxi.* *8am–5pm daily.* www.sinac.go.cr

LYING NEAR the head of the Río Estrella valley and extending up the western flanks of the Talamanca Mountains, the 38-sq-mile (100-sq-km) Hitoy-Cerere Biological Reserve appeals to hardy hikers and nature lovers. It offers pristine rainforest habitats fed by heavy rainfall. July, August, November, and December are the wettest months, when rivers thunder down the steep slopes. Large mammals thrive amid the dense forests, including all six of Costa Rica's cat species *(see p113)*. Lucky visitors might even spot the extremely rare harpy eagle. Note that this isolated refuge offers minimal infrastructure.

One of Parque Nacional Cahuita's many beaches

ENVIRONS: Reserva Selva Bananito, bordering Parque Internacional de La Amistad *(see p179)*, protects 5 sq miles (13 sq km) of ecologically sustainable farmland and rainforest. Overnight stays in the Caribbean-style lodge are recommended. **Orquídeas Mundo** raises and breeds rare hybrid orchids. Botanist Pierre Dubois offers guided tours.

Reserva Selva Bananito
22 miles (35 km) SW of Puerto Limón. 253-8118. www.selvabananito.com

Orquídeas Mundo
Penshurst, 22 miles (31 km) S of Puerto Limón. 750-0789. *8am–4pm daily.* orchidpierre@yahoo.com

Cahuita ❾

Road Map F3. 27 miles (43 km) S of Puerto Limón. *5,300.* *Southern Caribbean Music Festival (Mar–Apr); Carnavalito Cahuita (early Dec).*

WITH ITS dreadlocked Rastafarian culture, Cahuita (an Indian word for "mahogany point") is the most colorful village in Costa Rica. Sandwiched between sea and mountain, this hamlet is full of character, thanks to its Afro-Caribbean inhabitants, who live in bright wooden houses, some of which stand on stilts over the sandy streets. Locals speak a patois English infused with a lilting accent, and the spicy cuisine *(see p222)* owes much to Jamaican heritage. Cahuita's slow rhythm appeals to travelers who want to be immersed in its laid-back culture. North of the village are the black sands of palm-fringed **Playa Negra**.

Locals outside a snack bar in Cahuita village

Parque Nacional Cahuita ❿

Road Map F3. 27 miles (43 km) S of Puerto Limón. 755-0461. *Puerto Limón–Cahuita.* *8am–4pm daily.* *at Puerto Vargas ranger station; by donation at Kelly Creek station.*

SITUATED IMMEDIATELY south of Cahuita, this 4-sq-mile (10-sq-km) park was created in 1970 to protect marshlands, mangroves, and tropical rainforest. Wildlife abounds, and nature trails provide an easy means of spotting armadillos, rodent-like agoutis, and anteaters, as well as toucans, and green macaws. Crocodile-like caimans can be seen in freshwater rivers, while parrot fish, lobsters, and green turtles swim around a depleted coral reef off Playa Blanca. Swimming off Playa Vargas, farther to the south, is inadvisable; waves pummel the long beach where marine turtles nest. A 4-mile (6-km) long trail connects Cahuita village's Kelly Creek ranger station to the one at Puerto Vargas, but note that Río Perozoso has to be waded across en route.

◁ **Along the Canal de Tortuguero, Parque Nacional Tortuguero**

Costa Rica's Marine Turtles

SURVIVORS FROM the age of the dinosaur, turtles have remained virtually unchanged in their physiology for 200 million years. Marine turtles (Chelonidae) can travel great distances, using their powerful flippers for propulsion, and often cross entire oceans to feed, mate, and lay eggs. Males spend their whole lives at sea, while adult females return to land to lay eggs once every two or three years. Most nest at their natal beach and return to it often to lay eggs at intervals of several weeks. Costa Rica is one of the world's premier turtle-watching sites, and regulates entry of visitors to the major nesting sites. However, the country's turtle species remain under threat: illegal poaching of turtles and eggs continues, and hatchlings fall prey to other wildlife.

A turtle-shaped planter made of rubber tire

TURTLE SPECIES

Five of the world's seven marine turtles species nest year-round along Costa Rica's coasts. The Caribbean coast is especially rich in turtle life.

Eggs are golf-ball sized and often illegally harvested.

Thick skin, rather than a shell, encases the skeleton.

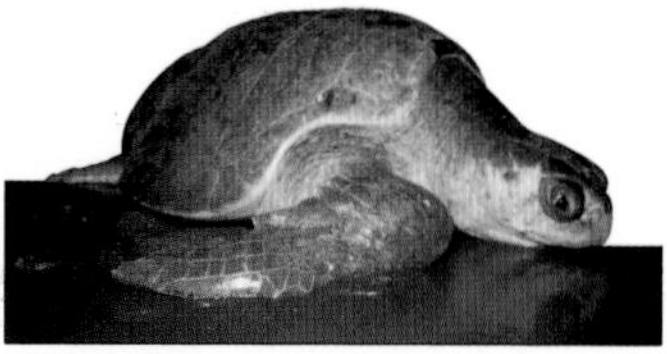

***Pacific/olive ridley turtles**, the smallest of the marine turtles, synchronize their egg-laying. Tens of thousands nest at Playas Ostional and Nancite* (see p141).

***The leatherback turtle**, although found across the world's oceans, is critically endangered. With the male weighing up to 2,000 lbs (905 kg), this is world's largest reptile. It nests at several beaches in Costa Rica, most importantly at Playa Grande* (see p136).

***Green turtles**, once abundant, were decimated in the 19th century by hunting. Now, Tortuguero is an important nesting site* (see p167).

***Loggerhead turtles**, seen in fewer numbers in Costa Rica than other turtles, prefer the Caribbean coast, and are found in Tortuguero.*

TURTLE	BEST PLACES TO SEE	NESTING SEASONS
Green	PN Tortuguero (C) Playa Grande (P)	Jun–Nov May–Aug
Hawksbill	Gandoca-Manzanillo (C)	Mar–Aug
Leatherback	Gandoca-Manzanillo (C) Playa Grande (P)	Feb–Apr Oct–Apr
Loggerhead	PN Tortuguero (C)	Year-round
Olive ridley	Playa Ostional and Playa Nancite (P)	Apr–Dec

C – Caribbean, P – Pacific

***Hawksbill turtles**, hunted for their beautiful shells, rarely grow beyond 36 inches (92 cm) and nest singly. They are most easily spotted at Gandoca-Manzanillo Wildlife Refuge* (see p172).

Puerto Viejo de Talamanca ⓫

Road Map F3. 8 miles (13 km) S of Cahuita. *4,000.* *750-0398 (Talamanca Association for Ecotourism & Conservation/ATEC).* *Southern Caribbean Music Festival (Mar–Apr).*

One of the Caribbean coast's best surfing areas, Puerto Viejo de Talamanca is also a must-visit destination for offbeat travelers in Central America. Little more than a collection of stilt-legged shacks a decade ago, it has since expanded rapidly. Although electricity arrived in 1996, followed by a paved road in 2001, the village retains an earthy, laid-back quality.

Surfers come here between December and March to test their skills against the reef break La Salsa Brava, which can attain heights of up to 21 ft (6.5 m). The palm-fringed black sands of **Playa Negra** curl north from town. North of the beach, **Finca la Isla Botanical Garden** is an excellent place to explore the coastal rainforest along well-kept trails. Bromeliads are a specialty of this 12-acre (5-ha) garden, which also grows exotic fruits and ornamental plants. A self-guided booklet is available.

Puerto Viejo has some of the best budget accommodation in Costa Rica, as well as colorful, unpretentious eateries. Open-air bars and discos come alive at night, with revelers spilling onto the sands.

Environs: A string of lovely surfing beaches – **Playa Cocles**, **Playa Uva**, and **Playa Chiquita** – runs south from Puerto Viejo to the hamlet of Manzanillo. A paved road lined with hotels and *cabinas* *(see p197)* lies along the shore, with forested hills rising inland. Horseback rides are offered by **Seahorse Stables**. The **Mariposario**, a butterfly garden, sits on a ridge overlooking Playa Uva. Public transport in these areas is limited, but bicycles, scooters, and cars can be rented in Puerto Viejo.

Detail of a statue at a lodge in Puerto Viejo

Finca la Isla Botanical Garden

0.5 mile (1 km) NW of Puerto Viejo. *750-0046.* *10am–4pm Fri–Mon.* http://greencoast.com/garden.htm

Seahorse Stables

2 miles (3 km) S of Puerto Viejo. *750-0468.* *by appointment.* www.costaricahorsebackriding.com

Mariposario

4 miles (6 km) S of Puerto Viejo. *750-0086.* *8am–4pm daily.*

Tucuxí Dolphin

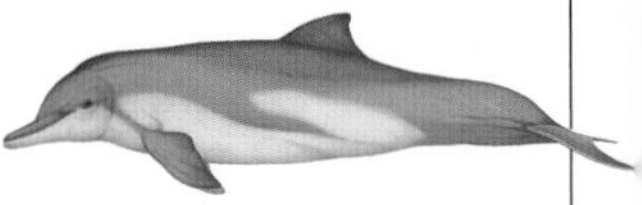

Tucuxí dolphin

The rare *tucuxí* dolphin *(Sotalia fluviatilis)* – pronounced "too koo shee" – lives in the freshwater rivers and lagoons of Gandoca-Manzanillo and similar environments. This small species grows to 6 ft (2 m) in length and is blue-gray with a pink belly and long snout. It is shy and generally avoids boats, but is known to interact with its larger sea-going cousin, the bottle-nosed dolphin.

Refugio Nacional de Vida Silvestre Gandoca-Manzanillo ⓬

Road Map F4. 8 miles (13 km) S of Puerto Viejo. *759-9001.* *from Puerto Viejo de Talamanca.* *8am–4pm daily.*

Enclosing a mosaic of habitats, Gandoca-Manzanillo Wildlife Refuge is a mixed-use park occupied by settlements whose inhabitants live in harmony with the environment. Created in 1985, this 32-sq-mile (83-sq-km) reserve extends out to sea, protecting a coral reef and 17 sq miles (44 sq km) of marine habitat where several species of turtles breed. The Costa Rican conservation society **Asociación ANAI** runs a volunteer program for those who are keen to assist with research and protection of turtles.

The beach at Refugio Nacional de Vida Silvestre Gandoca-Manzanillo

On land, the refuge has mangrove swamp, rare *yolillo* palm swamp and *cativo* forest, and tropical rainforest, all swarming with wildlife. Manatees and *tucuxí* inhabit the lagoons and estuaries. The waters are also important breeding grounds for sharks, game fish, and lobsters.

A coastal trail and several inland ones – often overgrown and muddy – afford unparalleled opportunities for spotting mammals and an astounding diversity of birds, amphibians, and reptiles. The coast trail leads to Punta Mona (Monkey Point) and **Punta Mona Center**, an educational institution and organic farm.

Environs: A local farmers' cooperative, **ASACODE** (Asociación Sanmigueleña de Conservación y Desarrollo) offers guided trips into a private 620-acre (250-ha) reserve adjoining Gandoca-Manzanillo Wildlife Refuge. **Finca Lomas**, run by ANAI, is an experimental farm inside the reserve.

Green iguanas raised on Reserva Indígena KeköLdi

Asociación ANAI
Manzanillo. 750-0020.
www.anaicr.org

Punta Mona Center
3 miles (5 km) SE of Manzanillo.
352-4442. *8am–5pm daily.*
http://puntamona.org

ASACODE
San Miguel, 9 miles (14 km) W of Gandoca. *751-2261.* *7am–5pm.*

Indigenous Reserves 13

Road Map F4. *to Bribri, then by jeep-taxi.* *750-0191 (ATEC).*

The indigenous Bribri and Cabécar peoples inhabit a series of fragmented reserves on the Caribbean slopes of the Talamanca Mountains, surviving primarily through subsistence agriculture. These two related groups have managed to retain much of their culture, native languages, animistic dances, and shamanistic practices *(see pp32–3)*.

The most accessible reserve is the **Reserva Indígena KeköLdi**, spread across 14 sq miles (36 sq km) in the hills southwest of Puerto Viejo. The reserve's local conservation projects includes a farm where green iguanas are bred. The farm is located off the main road near Hone Creek, a 30-minute walk from Puerto Viejo. Farther south, beyond the regional administrative center of Bribri, is the **Reserva Indígena Talamanca-Bribri**. Centered on Shiroles, 11 miles (18 km) southwest of Bribri, this reserve encompasses the Valle de Talamanca, a broad basin carpeted by plantations of bananas – a source of ongoing unrest among ill-paid workers. Trips to communities within the reserve are offered by **Albergue Finca Educativa Indígena**, an educational center and tourist lodge in Shiroles.

From Bambú, 6 miles (10 km) west of Bribri, a trip by dug-out canoe down Río Yorkín leads to **Reserva Indígena Yorkín**, where visitors housed in traditional lodgings gain an appreciation of indigenous culture.

Another reserve in this area is **Reserva Indígena Talamanca-Cabécar**, reached from Shiroles along rugged dirt roads that push up the valley of Río Coén. This remote settlement of the San José Cabécar is considered the most important center of shamanism and Indian culture. From here, a trail crosses the Talamancas and drops to Buenos Aires on the western slopes. Do not attempt this multiday hike without a local guide. Guided hikes and overnight visits to the reserves are arranged by the Talamanca Association for Ecotourism and Conservation (ATEC) in Puerto Viejo de Talamanca. Note that independent travel to all reserves is officially illegal and is discouraged; contact ATEC for permission. The only place where a permit to visit is not required is the iguana farm in the Reserva Indígena KeköLdi.

Inside a house in the Reserva Indígena KeköLdi

Albergue Finca Educativa Indígena
Shiroles. *248-2538.* *by appointment.*

Shamanism

The Bribri and Cabécar have a spirit-filled, animist vision of the world in which the shaman-healer – called *awá* by the Bribri and *jawá* by the Cabécar – is the central authority in the community. Shamanic tools include magic stones, *seteé* (medicine collars), *uLú* (healing canes), and a whole pharmacy of medicinal herbs. These are used along with ritual song and dance to cure a person who is ill, or to restore harmony within the community.

Instrument used in ritual music

A Bribri shaman feather

THE SOUTHERN ZONE

FROM WORLD-CLASS SURFING *and sportfishing to hardy mountain bikes and scuba diving with hammerhead sharks, Costa Rica's remote south is a setting for splendid adventures. Pre-Columbian relics lie smothered in jungles that offer some of the finest wildlife viewing in the nation. The country's largest indigenous communities live in isolated mountain retreats in this region.*

Spanish conquistadors marched into the region to conquer the nomadic Chibchas and Diquis tribes, and to search in vain for gold. The coastal area remained isolated and neglected throughout the colonial period and beyond. In 1938, the United Fruit Company arrived, and planted bananas across the valleys of the Sierpe and Coto-Colorado Rivers; banana plantations are still the economic mainstay of the region. To the north, the shore is hemmed by the thickly forested Fila Costanera Mountains, while waves crash upon gray-sand beaches. Farther south, the Peninsula de Osa is deluged with rains that feed a huge swathe of emerald green rainforest. The peninsula hooks around Golfo Dulce – a calm bay attracting dolphins and whales, as well as sportfishing boats from the town of Golfito. Isla del Caño floats on the horizon offshore. Considered sacred by pre-Columbian tribes, it contains ancient burial sites. To the southwest, uninhabited Isla del Coco is surrounded by teeming sealife.

The Talamancas, in the northeast of the region, rise to 12,530 ft (3,820 m) at the top of Cerro Chirripó. Here, the Boruca and Guaymí peoples struggle to maintain their cultures in remote communities threatened by logging and other commercial interests. Thick forests carpet the rugged peaks, forming a virginal environment where jaguars, tapirs, and other endangered species thrive. Between the two mountain ranges, the fertile Valle de El General is a breadbasket of agricultural produce.

A hiker surveying the vast expanse of Parque Nacional Chirripó

◁ **A school of jackfish circling round in the waters off Isla del Coco**

Exploring the Southern Zone

THE JUNGLED SHORE OF the Southern Zone is peppered with some of the country's finest beaches, including those at Bahía Drake, Zancudo, and Parque Nacional Marino Ballena. Surfers flock to Dominical and Pavones, while Golfito is a base for sportfishing. Whales and dolphins cavort in offshore waters, especially around Isla del Caño, while experienced divers can swim with hammerhead and whale sharks at remote Isla del Coco. Along the coast lie the rainforests of Parque Nacional Corcovado (on the Peninsula de Osa) and lesser-known sites such as the forest reserves Terraba-Sierpe and Barú. To the north, Chirripó offers an exciting hike to the summit.

0 km 20
0 miles 20

Kayaking in Reserva Forestal del Humedad Nacional Terraba-Sierpe

KEY

- Pan-American Highway
- Major road
- Secondary road
- Minor road
- International border
- Provincial border
- △ Peak

SIGHTS AT A GLANCE

Towns and Cities
Dominical 8
Golfito 16
Palmar 11
Pavones 18
San Isidro de El General 2
Zancudo 17

National Parks and Reserves
Parque Internacional La Amistad 5
Parque Nacional Chirripó pp180–81 4
Parque Nacional Isla del Coco 19
Parque Nacional Marino Ballena 9
Parque Nacional Piedras Blancas 15
Refugio Nacional de Vida Silvestre Barú 7
Reserva Biológica Isla del Caño 13
Reserva Forestal del Humedad Nacional Terraba-Sierpe 12

Areas of Natural Beauty
Cerro de la Muerte 1
Las Cruces Biological Station 6
Peninsula de Osa pp188–91 14
Valle del Río Chirripó 3

Indigenous Site
Reserva Indígena Boruca 10

Lush vegetation fringing aquamarine waters at Bahía Drake

Colorful blooms outside a house near Parque Nacional Chirripó

Getting Around

Palmar, Puerto Jiménez, Golfito, and Ciudad Neily have domestic airports, while charter planes serve smaller airstrips. Major tourist sights can be reached from San José by long-distance bus. Local buses are the main form of transportation in this region, although more remote sights are accessible only by jeep-taxi or cheap but uncomfortable *colectivos* (pickup trucks).

Highway 2 (the Pan-American Highway) is paved, as is Highway 16 through the Valle de Coto Brus, but most connecting routes are potholed dirt roads that are covered with mud after rains. Many nature lodges on the Osa Peninsula and the Golfo Dulce shores can be reached only by water-taxi.

See Also

- ***Where to Stay*** pp216–19
- ***Where to Eat*** pp236–7

Winding road in the valley of Cerro de la Muerte

Cerro de la Muerte ❶

Road Map D4. 31 miles (50 km) S of Cartago. *San José–San Isidro.*

CERRO BUENAVISTA is popularly called Cerro de la Muerte (Mountain of Death), after the peasants who died of exposure while taking their produce to San José before the Pan-Am Highway was built across it. The **Casa Refugio de Ojo de Agua**, a refuge hut at Km 76, has exhibits on the pioneers.

The highway, connecting San José with the Valle de El General, passes below the actual summit (11,500 ft/ 3,500 m), which is buffeted by high winds. The vegetation is Andean *páramo* (grassland), with shriveled species that have adapted to the cold, boggy conditions. When the clouds part, there are superlative views to be had.

About 4 miles (6 km) short of San Isidro, a giant statue of Christ offers blessings to motorists on the hair-raising road. This stretch of the Pan-Am Highway requires great caution – avoid it at night.

ENVIRONS: Quetzals can be spotted at **Reserva Bosque Nubioso Iyök Amí**, a cloud forest reserve.

Reserva Bosque Nubioso Iyök Amí

Pan-Am Hwy at Km 80. *772-0222.* *8am–4pm daily.* www.iyokami.com

San Isidro de El General ❷

Road Map E4. 51 miles (82 km) S of Cartago. *41,200.* *Selva Mar, Calle 1 and Aves 2/4, 771-4582.* *Día de San Isidro Labrador (May 15).*

THIS PEACEFUL market town sits at the base of Cerro de la Muerte and is the administrative center for Valle de El General. For tourists, it serves as a refueling stop and a base for exploring Chirripó and Parque Internacional La Amistad. The only sights of interest in town are the small **Museo Regional del Sur** (Museum of the Southern Region), with exhibits on local history and culture, and the modern, concrete cathedral on the east side of the plaza. Built in 1967, the cathedral has stained-glass windows and a simple altar, which is dominated by a mural of San Isidro Labrador, patron saint of San Isidro.

ENVIRONS: Bird-lovers are in for a treat at **Los Cusingos Neotropical Bird Sanctuary**. Administered by the Tropical Science Center of Costa Rica, this 350-acre (142-ha) refuge for birds was founded by the eminent American ornithologist, Dr. Alexander Skutch (1904–2004), co-author of the authoritative *Birds of Costa Rica*. More than 300 bird species have been noted in this sanctuary. Indian petroglyphs dot the grounds.

Museo Regional del Sur

Calle 2 and Ave 1. *771-8453.* *8am–noon & 1–4:30pm Mon–Fri.*

The striking modern cathedral of San Isidro de El General

Los Cusingos Neotropical Bird Sanctuary

Quizarrá de Pérez Zeledón, 9 miles (14 km) SE of San Isidro. *200-5472 (Tropical Science Center).* *7am–4pm Tue–Sun, by appt.*

Works of art at the Museo el Pelicano, Valle del Río Chirripó

Valle del Río Chirripó ❸

Road Map E4. 6 miles (10 km) E of San Isidro. *from San Isidro.*

THIS VALLEY IS scythed from the Talamanca Mountains by the turbulent Río Chirripó. Trout swim in the river's sparkling waters, and rapids provide kayaking thrills. A wonderful place to stop in the valley is the fruit-and-coffee *finca*, **Rancho La Botija** *(see p219)*, a popular destination for locals on weekends. Its attractions include an antique *trapiche* (sugarcane mill), restaurant, and accommodation. Nearby, the roadside **Piedra de los Indios** (Rock of the Indians) bears pre-Columbian petroglyphs as well as some modern graffiti.

The scenery grows more dramatic and the climate more alpine as the road climbs into the mountains to reach **San Gerardo de Rivas**, which has hot springs. This hamlet perches over the river gorge and is the gateway to Parque Nacional Chirripó. Close by, **Museo el Pelicano** is a curiosity for its inspired stone and timber art by coffee farmer Rafael Elizondo Basulta. A steep track, strewn

Variety of flora at the Chirripó Cloudbridge Reserve

with boulders, leads past the trailhead to the summit of Cerro Chirripó and ends at the **Chirripó Cloudbridge Reserve**. The locally endemic parrot mountain snake can be seen at this private reserve; there are also some good hiking trails.

Museo el Pelicano
Canaan, 10 miles (16 km) E of San Isidro. *390-4194.*

Chirripó Cloudbridge Reserve
San Gerardo de Rivas, 12 miles (20 km) E of San Isidro. *771-1866.*
8am–4pm daily.
www.cloudbridge.org

Parque Nacional Chirripó ❹

See pp180–81.

Parque Internacional La Amistad ❺

Road Map F4. *to Guácimo, 66 miles (107 km) SE of San Isidro, then by jeep-taxi.* *San Isidro HQ, Calle 2 and Aves 4/6, 771-3155; Estación Altamira, 31 miles (50 km) SE of Buenos Aires, 730-0846.*
8am–4pm daily.

Extending into Panama, the International Friendship Park is contiguous with other protected areas that form the Reserva de la Biosfera La Amistad (Amistad Biosphere Reserve). It sprawls over 675 sq miles (1,750 sq km) of the rugged Talamanca Mountains, and ranges from elevations of 490 ft (150 m) to 11,650 ft (3,550 m) atop Cerro Kamuk. This enormous park spans eight "life zones," from low montane rainforest to swampy high-altitude grassland. The diverse wildlife includes five cat species and the endangered harpy eagle.

With permits and a guide, experienced hikers can cross the Talamancas on a trail that starts from the town of Buenos Aires, 38 miles (61 km) southeast of San Isidro, and leads to Reserva Indígena Talamanca-Cabécar *(see p173)*.

The main ranger station, a hostel, and an ecology exhibition are at **Estación Altamira**, the recommended entry point. All the official access points require 4WD.

Environs: East of Buenos Aires, **Reserva Biológica Durika**, a 3-sq-mile (9-sq-km) forest reserve, operates as a self-sufficient holistic community. Guided hikes, vegetarian meals, and rustic accommodation are on offer. Reached via the small hill town of San Vito, southeast of Buenos Aires, **La Amistad Lodge** *(see p218)* is a good base for exploring the southern Talamancas. This cozy lodge, part of a cattle and organic coffee estate, provides access to the reserve Zona Protectorado Las Tablas. Horseback rides and guided birding hikes to two mountain camps are offered.

Reserva Biológica Durika
11 miles (18 km) N of Buenos Aires.
730-0657.
www.durika.org

Las Cruces Biological Station ❻

Road Map F5. 4 miles (6 km) S of San Vito. *773-4004.* *San Vito–Ciudad Neily.* *8am–4pm daily.*
www.ots.ac.cr

One of the world's leading tropical research and educational centers, Las Cruces is run by the Organization of Tropical Studies (OTS). The center is surrounded by a 580-acre (235-ha) mid-elevation forest, in which an incredible diversity of birds and mammals can be easily seen along 6 miles (10 km) of trails. Clouds envelop the reserve, nourishing the multitude of ferns, palms, bromeliads, orchids, and ornamentals laid out in the 25-acre (10-ha) **Wilson Botanical Gardens**, designed by distinguished Brazilian landscaper Roberto Burle-Marx. A riot of color in even the rainiest of weather, the collection extends to greenhouses, where varieties of tropical plants are propagated.

Ferns, Las Cruces Biological Station

The Resplendent Quetzal

Resplendent quetzal

Costa Rica is home to the most striking of the quetzal species *(see p26)* – the resplendent quetzal – one of the most beautiful tropical birds. The male bird has iridescent green feathers, blood-red chest, and 24-inch (60-cm) tail feathers; the female is less flamboyant. Pre-Columbian cultures worshiped the quetzal as a living depiction of Quetzalcoatl, the plumed serpent god. The male's tail feathers, used in ceremonies, were considered more precious than gold; only nobles and priests were allowed to wear them.

Parque Nacional Chirripó ❹

Red-tailed hawk

COSTA RICA'S HIGHEST mountain, Cerro Chirripó (12,530 ft/3,820 m) is enfolded in the 194-sq-mile (502-sq-km) Chirripó National Park. Part of the Amistad Biosphere Reserve, the park protects three distinct "life zones" in rugged, virgin territory where wildlife flourishes with minimal interference from humans. As many as 60 percent of all wildlife species in Costa Rica are found here, including all six types of wild cats *(see p113)* and many endemic species of flora and fauna. Glacial activity some 35,000 years ago carved small U-shaped valleys and deposited moraines, still visible today. Spring is the best time for hiking, although weather is always unpredictable, with frequent fog and rain.

KEY

Parque Nacional Chirripó

Area of park illustrated

Cloud Forest

Almost constantly shrouded in mist, the forests above 8,200 ft (2,500 m) are typified by dwarf blueberry trees festooned with epiphytes and mosses. Monkeys and quetzals are found in plenty.

The ranger station in San Gerardo de Rivas sells trail maps. Visitors must report here before setting out on the hike to the summit.

Sendero Termometro, leading into cloud forest, is one of the steepest stretches of the trail.

HIKING IN THE PARK

Most visitors hike to the summit along a well-marked trail that ascends 8,200 ft (2,500 m) from the trailhead, near San Gerardo de Rivas. The 20-mile (32-km) hike to the top and back normally takes two days, with an overnight stay near the summit. Hire guide-porters in San Gerardo. An alternative route is from Herradura via Cerro Uran.

Hikers in Parque Nacional Chirripó

KEY

- Minor road
- Park boundary
- Trail
- Viewpoint
- Visitor information
- Peak

Serene Lago San Juan, Parque Nacional Chirripó

Visitors' Checklist

Road Map E4. 12 miles (19 km) NE of San Isidro de El General.
to San Gerardo de Rivas, 2 miles (3 km) from the park.
Ranger station, San Gerardo de Rivas; 771-3155 (Park office, San Isidro de El General).
7:30am–5pm daily; by appointment. No more than 40 people allowed at a time.
May. mandatory.
by reservation.

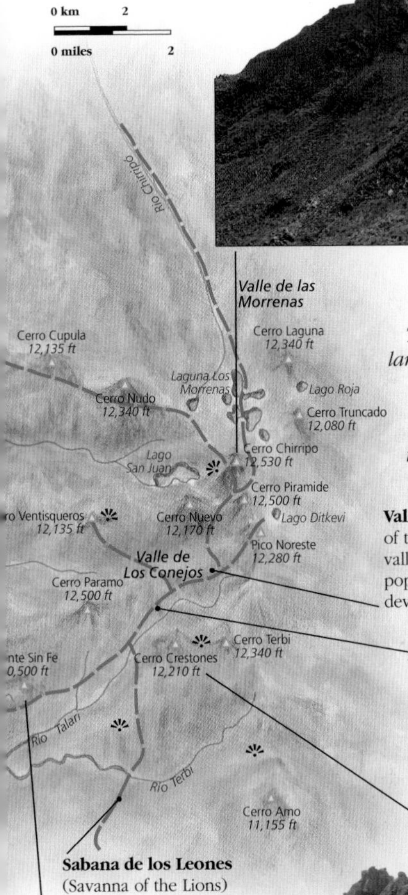

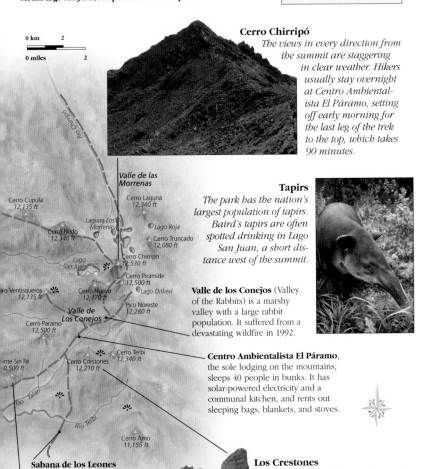

Cerro Chirripó
The views in every direction from the summit are staggering in clear weather. Hikers usually stay overnight at Centro Ambientalista El Páramo, setting off early morning for the last leg of the trek to the top, which takes 90 minutes.

Tapirs
The park has the nation's largest population of tapirs. Baird's tapirs are often spotted drinking in Lago San Juan, a short distance west of the summit.

Valle de los Conejos (Valley of the Rabbits) is a marshy valley with a large rabbit population. It suffered from a devastating wildfire in 1992.

Centro Ambientalista El Páramo, the sole lodging on the mountains, sleeps 40 people in bunks. It has solar-powered electricity and a communal kitchen, and rents out sleeping bags, blankets, and stoves.

Sabana de los Leones (Savanna of the Lions) is named for the pumas frequently seen on the southern slopes.

Monte Sin Fe (Faithless Mountain) is reached by a steep uphill section called La Cuesta del Agua.

Los Crestones
Marking the end of a steep 1.2-mile (2-km) long climb called La Cuesta de los Arrepentidos (Repentants' Hill), these dramatic vertical rock formations were considered a sacred site by pre-Columbian Indians.

Zipline tour in Refugio Nacional de Vida Silvestre Barú

Refugio Nacional de Vida Silvestre Barú 7

Road Map D4. 2 miles (3 km) N of Dominical. *787-0003. Dominical–Quepos. 7am–5:30pm daily.* www.haciendabaru.com

A FORMER CATTLE ranch and cocoa plantation, the 815-acre (330-ha) Hacienda Barú has varied habitats, including 2 miles (3 km) of beach that draw nesting hawksbill and olive ridley turtles. Turtle eggs are collected and incubated in a nursery for release. Barú has more than 310 bird species and several mammal species, such as jaguarundis and the arboreal kinkajous. There are butterfly and orchid gardens. Guided tree-climbing, canopy tours, kayak trips through the mangroves, hikes, horseback rides, and overnight stays in treetop tents are also on offer.

Dominical 8

Road Map D4. 18 miles (29 km) SW of San Isidro de El General. *1,400.*

THE QUINTESSENTIAL surfer's destination, this offbeat village thrives on the backpacker trade: the community consists mostly of foreign surfers who settled here and set up shop. Its long brown beach extends south from the mouth of Río Barú to the fishing hamlet of Dominicalito. Experienced surfers, who are drawn by the beach, reef, and rivermouth breaks, should watch out for the riptides.

ENVIRONS: The thickly forested mountains south of Dominical, the Fila Costanera, are also called **Escaleras** (Staircase). Here, **Bella Vista Lodge** *(see p217)* offers horseback rides and accommodation in a Colorado-style lodge with magnificent views. Nearby, **Finca Brian y Emilia** is a small fruit farm where visitors can learn about exotic fruits and enjoy splendid birding, hearty *campesino* (peasant) food, back-to-basics accommodation, and a log-fired riverside hot tub.

Highway 243 winds through the Río Barú valley, connecting Dominical to San Isidro. Tour companies offer trips to **Las Cascadas Nauyaca** (also called Cascadas Santo Cristo or Cascadas Don Lulo), a dramatic, two-tiered waterfall, which is a 4-mile (6-km) horseback ride away from the highway. The entrance fee includes a visit to "Don" Lulo's mini-zoo.

Finca Brian y Emilia
Escaleras, 3 miles (5 km) SE of Dominical. *396-6206. by appointment.*

Las Cascadas Nauyaca
Platanillo, 6 miles (10 km) E of Dominical. *787-0198. 8am.* www.ecotourism.co.cr/nauyacawaterfalls

Surfers wading into the sea at the beach at Dominical

Parque Nacional Marino Ballena 9

Road Map D4. 11 miles (18 km) S of Dominical. *743-8236. from Dominical. 6am–6pm daily; 24 hrs on Easter and Christmas.* www.sinac.go.cr

CREATED TO protect the nation's largest coral reef, Whale Marine National Park stretches for 8 miles (13 km) along the shore of Bahía de Coronado, and extends 9 miles (14 km) out to sea. It is named after the humpback whales that gather in the warm waters to breed in the dry season between December and April.

The park incorporates **Las Tres Hermanas** and **Isla Ballena**, which are important nesting sites for frigate birds, brown boobies, and pelicans. Hawksbill and olive ridley turtles nest on the quiet, palm-fringed beaches in the wet season. Kayaking and scuba diving trips can be arranged.

ENVIRONS: To the north, **Refugio Nacional de Vida Silvestre Rancho Merced** offers city-slickers a chance to play cowhand; it also functions as a wildlife refuge. Nearby, **Reserva Biológica Oro Verde**, a family-run farm in the Fila Tinamaste Mountains, is known for its birding. Marine turtles nest at **Playa Tortuga**. Inland, the twin hamlets of **Tortuga Abajo** and **Ojochal** make a good base for exploring the area. **Manglar Sur**, the Mississippi-style riverboat, offers tours of the Terraba-Sierpe mangrove forests *(see p184)*.

Signage for RNVS Rancho Merced

Refugio Nacional de Vida Silvestre Rancho Merced
Uvita, 11 miles (18 km) S of Dominical. *823-5858.*

Reserva Biológica Oro Verde
2 miles (3 km) NE of Uvita. *743-8072.* www. costarica-birding-oroverde.com

Manglar Sur
Tortuga Abajo, 7 miles (11 km) S of Uvita. *304-1717. daily by reservation.* www.manglarsur.com

Costa Rica's Tropical Flowers

A LUXURIANT HOTHOUSE of biodiversity, Costa Rica nurtures over 15,000 known plant species, including 800 types of ferns. Varieties of tropical flowers such as cannas, plumerias, and begonias flourish in the warm and humid regions, as do bromeliads and other epiphytes, which draw moisture and oxygen from the air.

Orchid bloom

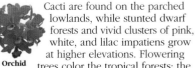

Cacti are found on the parched lowlands, while stunted dwarf forests and vivid clusters of pink, white, and lilac impatiens grow at higher elevations. Flowering trees color the tropical forests: the poinciana flames with vermilion blossoms, and the jacaranda drops its violet-blue, bell-shaped blooms to form spectacular carpets in spring.

Heliconias *are known for their unusual bracts. The lobster-claw heliconia* (right) *has a yellow-tipped red bract. Costa Rica's 30 native species of heliconia thrive in areas with plenty of moisture.*

Bracts are flowerheads atop huge stems that can grow up to 25 ft (8 m).

Large leaves indicate that the heliconia is related to the banana plant.

Passion flowers *emanate a foul smell to attract pollinators, especially Heliconiinae butterflies.*

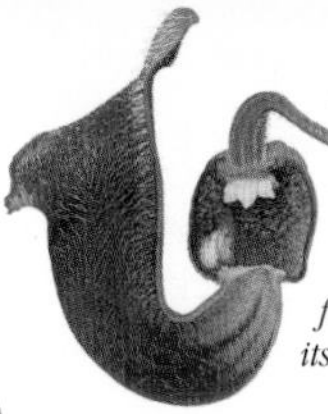

The Aristolochia*, or "Dutchman's pipe," gives off a fetid odor resembling that of rotting flesh. This draws flies, its principal pollinators.*

Bromeliads *collect water in their tightly wrapped, thick, waxy leaves. Falling leaf matter decays inside this whorl, providing nutrients for the plant and creating a self-contained ecosystem.*

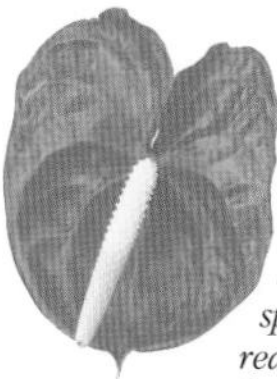

Anthuriums *have a distinctive heart-shaped spathe – usually red, white, or greenish – from which the flower spike protrudes.*

Ginger lilies *have large, hyacinth-like flowers rich in nectar. Introduced from Asia, these shoulder-high plants are common in landscaped gardens.*

The bird of paradise *flowers from a dramatic spathe with bright orange sepals and vivid blue petals. Set at right angles to the stem, the spathe looks like a bird's head.*

ORCHIDS

Detail of a mural showing various orchids

More than 1,400 species of orchids grow in Costa Rica, from sea level to the heights of Chirripó *(see p81)*. The greatest numbers are found at mid-level elevations, below 6,000 ft (1,830 m). Orchids range from the 0.03-inch (1-mm) wide liverwort orchid *(Platystele jungermannioides)*, the world's smallest flower, to others with pendulous 3-ft (1-m) long petals. All varieties of these flowers have three petals and three sepals. Some have evolved unique features to attract specific pollinators: for example, the markings on certain orchids are visible only to insects that can see in the ultraviolet spectrum.

Reserva Indígena Boruca ⓾

Road Map E5. 22 miles (35 km) SW of Buenos Aires. *from Buenos Aires.* *Fiesta de los Diablitos (Dec 31–Jan 2).*

THIS IS ONE of several indigenous reserves – inhabited by the Boruca and Bribri – in the mountains hemming the Valle de El General. Located in the Fila Sinancra Mountains, the reserve is known for its Fiesta de los Diablitos, as well as its carved *jícaras* (gourds) and balsa-wood *mascaras* (masks). The women use traditional back-strap looms to weave cotton purses and shawls. The ridge-top drive to the hamlet of **Boruca** offers great views of the Río Terraba gorge. Local culture is showcased in the **Museo Comunitario Boruca**.

Reserva Indígena Térraba and **Reserva Indígena Curré** flank the Boruca reserve. **Reserva Indígena Cabagra**, home to the Bribri, can be accessed from the town of Brujo, 7 miles (11 km) southeast of Buenos Aires. With visitors demonstrating a growing interest in indigenous cultures, these remote communities are gradually opening up to tourism.

Museo Comunitario Boruca

Boruca, 25 miles (40 km) SW of Buenos Aires. *730-2468.* *by request.*

Palmar ⓫

Road Map E5. 78 miles (125 km) SE of San Isidro de El General. *9,900.*

SITTING AT THE foot of the Río Terraba valley, at the intersection of Costanera Sur and the Pan-Am Highway, Palmar is the service center for the region. The town straddles Río Terraba, which flows west through the wide Valle de Diquis. Pre-Columbian *esferas de piedra* (stone spheres) and a centenarian steam locomotive are displayed in the plaza of Palmar Sur. Palmar Norte is the town's modern quarter.

Reserva Forestal del Humedad Nacional Terraba-Sierpe

Reserva Forestal del Humedad Nacional Terraba-Sierpe ⓬

Road Map E5. 11 miles (18 km) W of Palmar. *786-7825 (Cámara de Turismo de Osa).* *8am–4pm Mon–Sat.*

CREATED TO protect the nation's largest stretch of mangrove forest and swamp, the Terraba-Sierpe National Humid Forest Reserve covers an area of 85 sq miles (220 sq km) between the deltas of the Sierpe and Terraba Rivers. Countless channels crisscross this vitally important ecosystem, which fringes 25 miles (40 km) of coastline.

Visitors kayaking in these quiet channels can see a variety of wildlife, including basilisk lizards, iguanas, crocodiles, and caimans, as well as monkeys, coatis and crab-eating raccoons. The birding is excellent. Guided boat and kayak tours are offered from Ciudad Cortés, 4 miles (6 km) west of Palmar, and Sierpe, 9 miles (14 km) south of Palmar.

Reserva Biológica Isla del Caño ⓭

Road Map D5. 12 miles (19 km) W of Bahía Drake. *735-5036 (PN Corcovado).* *tours from Bahía Drake, Manuel Antonio & Dominical.* *8am–4pm daily.* www.sinac.go.cr

THRUST FROM the sea by tectonic forces, the 805-acre (325-ha) uninhabited Isla del Caño was named a protected reserve in 1976, along with 10 sq miles (26 sq km) of surrounding waters. It is administered as part of Parque Nacional Corcovado *(see p191)*. Struck more frequently by lightning than any other spot in Costa Rica, it was considered sacred by the pre-Columbian Diquis peoples.

The coral-colored beaches are great for sunbathing. In the shallows, coral reefs teem with lobsters and fish, while dolphins, whales, and manta rays swim in the warm waters farther out. Diving is permitted in designated zones *(see p252)*. Terrestrial wildlife is relatively limited, although the lucky hiker might come across four-eyed foxes, brown boobies, and ospreys.

Mossy pre-Columbian tombs and granite *esferas* (spheres) are scattered along a trail running from the beachfront ranger hut to a lookout point. The trail winds past milk trees *(Brosimum utile)*, named for their drinkable milky latex.

Overnight stays are not permitted. Many lodges in the area offer day trips.

FIESTA DE LOS DIABLITOS

At midnight on December 31, the Boruca gather to reenact the war between their ancestors and the Spanish conquistadors. At the sound of a conch shell, men dressed in burlap sacking and devil masks pursue a fellow tribesman dressed as a bull. The *diablitos* (devils) drink *chicha* (corn beer) and perform theatrical skits recalling tribal events. After three days, the bull is symbolically killed, metaphorically freeing the tribe from colonial repression.

Borucas in devil masks

The Mangroves of Coastal Costa Rica

COSTA RICA'S SHORES contain five of the world's 65 species of mangroves – black, buttonwood, red, tea, and white. Mangroves are woody halophytes – plants able to withstand immersion in saltwater – and form swampy forests in areas inundated by tides. These communities are of vital importance to the maritime ecosystem, fostering a wealth of wildlife.

Crab found in mangroves

The tangled roots buffer the action of waves, preventing coastal erosion. They also filter out the silt washed down by turbulent rivers: the accumulated mud extends the land out to sea. Threatened by the country's coastal development, this fragile ecosystem is now legally protected, with the Terraba-Sierpe reserve being the largest tract.

THE MANGROVE ECOSYSTEM

Mangroves grow in mud so dense that there is little oxygen, and nutrients supplied by decomposing leaf litter lie close to the surface. Hence, most plants develop interlocking stilt roots that rise above the water to draw in oxygen and food.

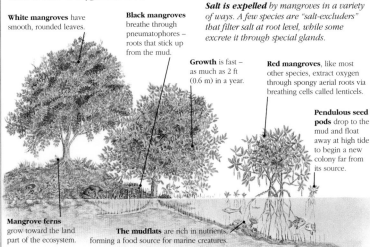

***Salt is expelled** by mangroves in a variety of ways. A few species are "salt-excluders" that filter salt at root level, while some excrete it through special glands.*

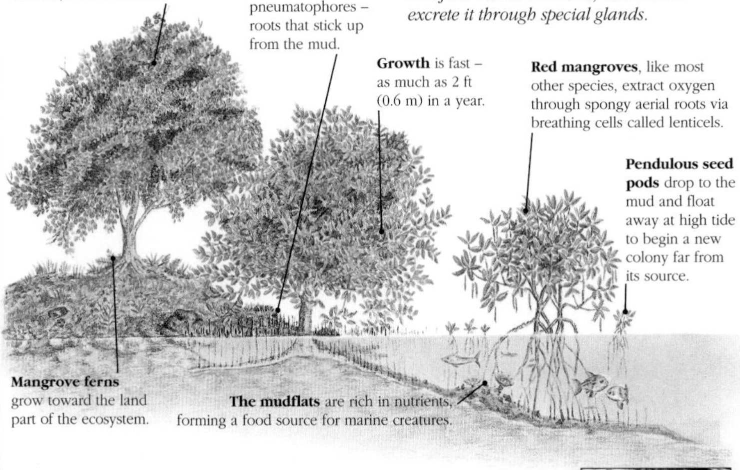
White mangroves have smooth, rounded leaves.
Black mangroves breathe through pneumatophores – roots that stick up from the mud.
Growth is fast – as much as 2 ft (0.6 m) in a year.
Red mangroves, like most other species, extract oxygen through spongy aerial roots via breathing cells called lenticels.
Pendulous seed pods drop to the mud and float away at high tide to begin a new colony far from its source.
Mangrove ferns grow toward the land part of the ecosystem.
The mudflats are rich in nutrients, forming a food source for marine creatures.

THE RICH FAUNA OF THE MANGROVES

The microorganisms that grow in the nutrient-rich muds foster the growth of larger creatures such as shrimps and other crustaceans, which in turn attract various species of mammals, reptiles, and birds.

***Aquatic nurseries** for oysters, sponges, and numerous fish species, including sharks and stingrays, thrive in the tannin-stained waters. The roots protect baby caimans and crocodiles from predators.*

***Larger species**, such as raccoons, coyotes, snakes, and wading birds forage for small lizards and crabs.*

***Birds**, such as frigate birds and pelicans, and endemic species such as the yellow mangrove warbler roost atop mangroves.*

Peninsula de Osa ⓮

Scarlet macaw

Washed by warm Pacific waters on three sides, the isolated Osa Peninsula curls around the Golfo Dulce. The peninsula was a center for the pre-Columbian Diquis culture, whose skill as goldsmiths sent Spanish conquistadors on a futile search for fabled gold mines. Deluged by year-round rains, much of this rugged area remains uninhabited and trackless, and is covered with virgin rainforest. About half of Osa is protected within Parque Nacional Corcovado, the largest of the parks and reserves that make up the Corcovado Conservation Area. Those with a taste for adventure are richly rewarded with majestic wilderness and some of the most spectacular wildlife-viewing in the nation.

Bahía Drake
With a beautiful setting, Drake Bay is great for scuba diving and sportfishing centered on the small village of Agujitas (see p190).

Playa San Josecito
Backed by rainforest, this is a beautiful golden sand beach with accommodations. Access is by boat or hiking trail.

Refugio Nacional de Vida Silvestre Punta Río Claro, located inland of Punta Marenco, protects more than 400 bird species, four monkey species, and prime rainforest habitat adjoining Corcovado (see p190).

0 km 5
0 miles 5

Parque Nacional Corcovado
Sprawling Corcovado National Park protects one of the last original tracts of the Pacific coast's tropical rainforest in Meso-America. La Leona (left) *is one of its four ranger stations. Crocodiles, tapirs, jaguars, and scarlet macaws are found in the park in large numbers* (see p191).

◁ **A flock of brown pelicans at Parque Nacional Corcovado**

Logging

The peninsula's large stands of precious hardwoods, such as mahogany, have suffered from excessive logging. Although restrictions have been placed on the activities of lumber companies, the cutting of protected tree species continues unabated.

Logging truck

Visitors' Checklist

Road Map E5. SW Costa Rica. *12,000.* *at Puerto Jiménez; airstrips at Carate, PN Corcovado, and Bahía Drake.* *to Puerto Jiménez or La Palma, then take a jeep-taxi to the park or hike (from La Palma to Los Patos).* *to Bahía Drake, then walk or take another boat to the park; or to Puerto Jiménez.*

Dolphins
Dolphins and humpback whales are frequently seen playing in the Golfo Dulce (Sweet Gulf).

Key

- Main road
- Trail
- Park boundary
- Airstrip
- Camping
- Visitor information

Puerto Jiménez
The only town of significance on the Osa Peninsula, this is the starting point for visits to Corcovado, and a center for biking, surfing, and similar activities, including kayaking through nearby mangroves (see p190).

Playa Platanares
A vital nesting site for marine turtles, the beach is fringed by wildlife-rich forest. A coral reef offshore is good for snorkeling.

Dos Brazos, a former gold mining center, welcomes visitors for gold-panning trips with community members.

Carate, the gateway to Corcovado, is accessed by chartered planes and a rugged dirt track.

Laguna Pejeperrito is inhabited by caimans, crocodiles, and waterfowl.

Cabo Matapalo is popular with surfers.

Exploring Peninsula de Osa

Ranger station, Parque Nacional Corcovado

THE LUSH RAINFORESTS of Corcovado lie at the heart of the Osa Peninsula. Although tourism to the region is booming, travel into the interior is still a challenge. Highway 245 follows the eastern shore and a feeder road now links Rincón to Bahía Drake, but the only guaranteed access to the western shores is by boat or by small plane. Wilderness lodges line the coast.

Along the shore of sweeping Bahía Drake

Bahía Drake

Rocky cliffs and forested hills provide a compelling setting for the scalloped Drake Bay. Sir Francis Drake is said to have anchored his *Golden Hind* here in March 1579. In 2003, a dirt road was cut from Rincón, on Golfo Dulce, to Bahía Drake (pronounced "DRA-cay"), but the route is often impassable in wet weather, even for 4WD vehicles. Most visitors still arrive by boat from Sierpe *(see p184)*. The small village of **Agujitas**, toward the bay's southern end, survives largely on subsistence farming and fishing. The women, however, have another source of income: the traditionally made *molas* (reverse-appliqué cloths).

Dolphin- and whale-watching trips on the bay are popular. Snorkeling is good in the southern bay, where the canyon of Río Agujitas can be explored by kayak. There are several budget accommodation options, as well as lodges that offer scuba diving and sportfishing. One such is **Jinetes de Osa** *(see p216)*, which features snorkeling along with scuba diving and deep-sea angling. Among its other attractions are zipline tours and a treetop observation walkway.

From Agujitas, a coastal trail leads south for 8 miles (13 km), via **Playas Cocalito**, **Caletas**, and **San Josecito**, to Parque Nacional Corcovado, passing by the **Refugio Nacional de Vida Silvestre Punta Río Claro**. This 2-sq-mile (5-sq-km) nature reserve adjoins Corcovado, and is home to much the same species of wildlife as can be seen in Corvocado. Guided hikes can be booked at Punta Marenco Lodge nearby. Crocodiles and tapirs are frequently sighted while canoeing on **Laguna Chocuaco**, to the east of Agujitas; the local community cooperative offers trips.

Colorful hand-stitched *molas* by the women of Agujitas village

Refugio Nacional de Vida Silvestre Punta Río Claro

Playa Caletas, 4 miles (6 km) S of Agujitas. *258-1919 (San José).* *8am–5pm daily.* www.puntamarenco.com

Puerto Jiménez

6,200.

The only settlement of significance on the peninsula, this dusty village is popular with backpackers. In the 1980s, Puerto Jiménez briefly blossomed on income from local gold and had a reputation as a "Wild West" frontier town, where carrying a gun was considered a good idea and prostitutes were paid with gold nuggets. Today, the town thrives on tourist money.

Various adventure activities are offered by local operators. Kayakers flock to the mangroves extending east along the shore of the Golfo Dulce to the estuary of Río Platanares. Home to crocodiles, caimans, freshwater turtles, and river otters, this ecosystem is protected within the 555-acre (225-ha) **Refugio Nacional de Vida Silvestre Preciosa Platanares**. The refuge lies along the shores of the lovely **Playa Platanares**, which has a small coral reef good for snorkeling. The beach is a nesting site for five species of marine turtles, best sighted from May to December. A small *vivero* (nursery) raises hatchlings for release into the jade-green waters.

The shore south of Puerto Jiménez is lined with beaches. **Cabo Matapalo**, at the tip of the peninsula, and **Playa Sombrero** offer great surfing.

Refugio Nacional de Vida Silvestre Preciosa Platanares

2 miles (3 km) E of Puerto Jiménez. *735-5007.* *by donation.*

Locals on the main street of Puerto Jiménez

The Corcovado Lodge Tent Camp on the beach at Parque Nacional Corcovado

Parque Nacional Corcovado

25 miles (40 km) SW of Puerto Jiménez. *735-5036.* *8am–4pm daily.* www.sinac.go.cr

Considered the crown jewel among the protected regions of the humid tropics, this 165-sq-mile (425-sq-km) park was created in 1975 to preserve the largest Pacific coast rainforest in the Americas, as well as 20 sq miles (52 sq km) of marine habitat. Corcovado (meaning "hunchback") has eight distinct zones, including herbaceous swamps, flooded swamp forest, and montane forest. The area receives up to 158 inches (400 cm) of rainfall per year, with torrential rains from April to December.

Wildlife viewing is splendid and among the most diverse in Costa Rica. The park has over 400 species of birds, including the endangered harpy eagle, and the largest population of scarlet macaws in Central America; birdwatchers are guaranteed sightings. Jaguars are spotted more frequently here than at any other park in the nation, as are tapirs. Both species are often seen on the beaches, especially around dusk. Corcovado is known for its large packs of peccaries – menacing wild hogs that should be avoided. The endangered *titi* (squirrel monkey) is also found here. There are over 115 species of amphibians and reptiles. Poison-dart frogs *(see p158)* are easily seen in their gaudy livery, but the elusive lime-green red-eyed tree frog and Fleischmann's transparent frog are harder to spot. The fortunate might witness green, hawksbill, leatherback, or Pacific ridley turtles crawling ashore to nest. However, the park is understaffed and the wildlife is under threat by poachers.

Small biplane used for transport within Osa

Although there are hotels and organized tours close by, the park is best suited to self-sufficient hikers who enjoy rugged adventures. There are four official entry points and ranger stations. **San Pedrillo**, to the west, is linked by a trail from Bahía Drake. **Los Patos**, to the east, can be reached from La Palma, 12 miles (19 km) northwest of Puerto Jiménez. **La Leona**, to the south, is 1 mile (1.6 km) west of the airstrip at Carate, a hamlet 25 miles (40 km) west of Puerto Jiménez; visitors must then hike or ride a horse from Carate. **Sirena**, the main ranger station, is 10 miles (16 km) northwest of La Leona and 16 miles (26 km) southeast of San Pedrillo. Poorly marked trails connect the stations; it is wise to hire a guide.

The coastal San Pedrillo–La Leona trail passes the dramatic 100-ft (30-m) high **Cascada La Llorona**. Be prepared to ford rivers inhabited by crocodiles on this two-day hike. The trail's northern section is open only from December to April. The San Pedrillo–Los Patos trail allows access to **Laguna Corcovado**, where tapirs and jaguars are often sighted.

There is no scheduled air service to the airstrips near the park, but air-taxis are offered by charter companies.

Interesting attractions close to Parque Nacional Corcovado include the 105-acre (43-ha) wetlands **Humedal Lacustrino Laguna Pejeperrito**, 2 miles (3 km) east of Carate, and the 865-acre (350-ha) **Refugio Nacional de Vida Silvestre Pejeperro**, 2.5 miles (4 km) farther east. They are little visited, but offer good opportunities for spotting birds, as well as crocodiles.

Gold Mining

Oreros (gold panners) had sifted for gold in the rivers of the Osa Peninsula since pre-Columbian days. When the United Fruit Company *(see p41)* pulled out of the region in 1985, unemployed workers flooded the peninsula, leading to a latter-day gold rush. This short-lived gold rush caused major damage: trees were felled, river banks dynamited, and exposed soils sluiced. After violent clashes with the authorities, the *oreros* were ousted in 1986. Some still work the outer margins of Corcovado, while others earn their income leading gold hunts for tourists.

Nuggets of gold

Parque Nacional Piedras Blancas ⓯

Road Map E5. 28 miles (46 km) SE of Palmar. *741-1173.* *from Golfito.* *8am–4pm daily.*

SPLIT OFF from Parque Nacional Corcovado in 1991, this 55-sq-mile (140-sq-km) park protects the forested mountains to the north of Golfo Dulce. Local conservation efforts are centered on the village of La Gamba, where a cooperative runs the **Esquinas Rainforest Lodge** *(see p218)*, which breeds the rodent-like *tepezcuintles* and offers hikes.

The emerald forests spill over the beaches – Playa Cativo and Playa San Josecito, which has the botanical garden **Casa de Orquídeas**, known for its encyclopedic collection of orchids and ornamentals. Lining the shores are wilderness lodges. Boat trips, including water-taxi rides, from Puerto Jiménez and Golfito to the two beaches make for pleasant excursions.

Casa de Orquídeas
Playa San Josecito, 6 miles (10 km) N of Puerto Jiménez. *776-0012.*

Sign of the colorful botanical garden, Casa de Orquídeas

Golfito ⓰

Road Map F5. 48 miles (77 km) SE of Palmar. *10,900.*

A SPORTFISHING base, port, and administrative center for the southern region, dilapidated Golfito (Small Gulf) unfurls along 4 miles (6 km) of shoreline. Established by the United Fruit Company in 1938, the town's reign as the nation's main banana shipping port ended when the company pulled out of the region in 1985. The legacy of "Big Fruit" can be seen in the intriguing architecture of Zona Americana, the north end of

Stilt-legged house in Zona Americana, Golfito

town, which has stilt-legged wooden houses. An antique locomotive sits in the small plaza of Pueblo Civíl, the town center. The **Museo Marino** nearby is worth a peek for its collection of corals and seashells.

On weekends and holidays, Golfito is flooded with Ticos drawn to the Depósito Libre (Free Trade Zone) shopping compound created in 1990 to revive the town's fortunes.

The forested hills east and north of town are protected within **Refugio Nacional de Vida Silvestre Golfito**.

Museo Marino
Hotel Centro Turístico Samoa, just N of Pueblo Civíl. *775-0233.* *7am–11am daily.*

Refugio Nacional de Vida Silvestre Golfito
E of Golfito. *775-1210.* *8am–4pm daily.* *with local operators.*

Zancudo ⓱

Road Map F5. 6 miles (10 km) S of Golfito (41 miles/66 km by road). *water-taxi from Golfito.*

THIS HAMLET on the east shore of Golfo Dulce is known for its stupendously beautiful gray sand beach, caressed by breezes and surf. The 4-mile (6-km) long strip of sand is a spit, projecting from the shore. A mangrove swamp inland of the beach is good for spotting crocodiles, caimans, and waterfowl. Sportfishing centers offer superb river-mouth and deep-water fishing *(see p251)*, while tarpon and snook can be hooked from the shore.

Pavones ⓲

Road Map B5. 7 miles (12 km) S of Zancudo. *water-taxi from Golfito.*

KNOWN IN the surfing world for its consistent 0.5-mile (1-km) 3-minute break, this small fishing village has blossomed in recent years due to the influx of young surfers. The waves peak between April and October. Coconut palms lean over the beautiful, rocky coastline.

ENVIRONS: Marine turtles nest along the shore. At **Punta Banco**, 6 miles (10 km) south of Pavones, the local community participates in the Tiskita Foundation Sea Turtle Restoration Project, which has a nursery to raise baby turtles for release. Nearby, **Tiskita Lodge** *(see p218)* offers fabulous vistas from its hillside perch. This rustic nature lodge is part of a large fruit farm that lures a wealth of bird- and animal life. Guided hikes are offered into a private reserve, where waterfalls tumble through majestic rainforest.

Reserva Indígena Guaymí, 9 miles (14 km) south of Punta Banco, is the remote mountain home of the Guaymí. Visits are discouraged.

A surfer wading ashore at Pavones

Parque Nacional Isla del Coco ⓳

NAMED A NATIONAL PARK in 1978, the world's largest uninhabited island is a UNESCO World Heritage Site. Of volcanic origin, the 9-sq-mile (23-sq-km) island is a part of the Galapagos chain. Torrential rainfall feeds spectacular waterfalls that cascade to the sea, while dense premontane moist forest carpets the land. The fragile ecosystem protects endemic fauna such as the Pacific dwarf gecko and Cocos anole, as well as 70 endemic plant species. A highlight is the huge colonies of seabirds, including magnificent frigate birds, noddies, and white terns. With waters of astounding clarity, the island is a world-renowned dive site *(see p252)*.

VISITORS' CHECKLIST

310 miles (500 km) SW of the mainland. *with dive operators (a 36-hr journey).* *256-7476 (Fundación Amigos de La Isla del Coco).* *daily. Permit required to step ashore, which the dive operator will arrange.* **Dive Operators** *Undersea Hunter: 228-6535; Okeanos Aggressor: see p253.* www.cocosisland.org

Isla del Coco, the "Dinosaur Island" of *Jurassic Park*

Bahía Chatham
The main anchorage has etchings carved into the cliff-face by sailors. Many of these date back centuries.

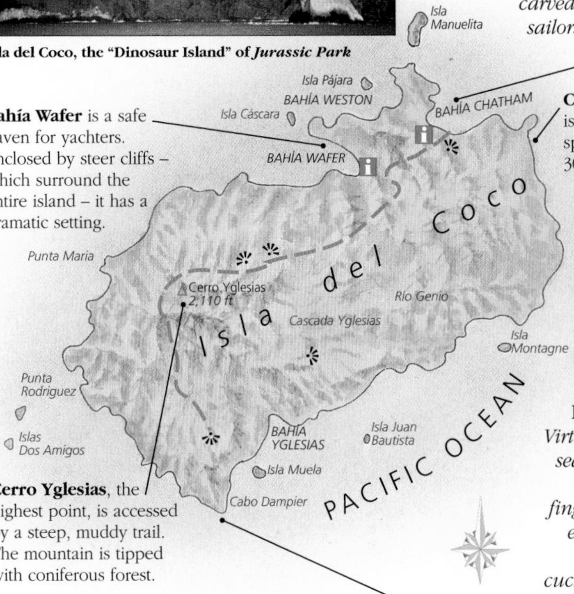

Bahía Wafer is a safe haven for yachters. Enclosed by steer cliffs – which surround the entire island – it has a dramatic setting.

Coral reefs around the island contain 18 coral species and more than 300 species of fish.

Cerro Yglesias, the highest point, is accessed by a steep, muddy trail. The mountain is tipped with coniferous forest.

Red-footed Boobies
Virtually unafraid, these seabirds allow humans to approach within fingertip distance. Birds endemic to the island include the Cocos cuckoo and Cocos finch.

0 km 1
0 miles 1

KEY

- Trail
- Viewpoint
- Peak
- Visitor information

Hammerhead Sharks
Congregating in their hundreds, these sharks provide an exhilarating experience for scuba divers. Also drawn by the huge fish population around the island are white-tipped sharks.

Travelers' Needs

Where to Stay

Sign outside Orosi Lodge *(see p205)*

Costa Rica has an excellent selection of accommodations covering the entire country, with a wide choice for every budget. Even the remotest corners have inexpensive *cabinas* (cabins). The country's forté is the wilderness nature lodge, many in extraordinary settings, where guests can view wildlife without leaving their hammocks. Also on offer are special-interest lodgings catering to a particular activity, such as surfing or sportfishing. Hotels range from self-catering *apartotels* (apart-hotels) to world-class luxury resorts and boutique hotels, which reflect the individuality of their owners. Recent years have seen an explosion in the number and quality of backpackers' hotels. Costa Rican hotels rarely use the star-grading system. Instead, the country has adopted the Certificate for Sustainable Tourism (CST) system, which grades hotels by their cultural and ecological sensitivity, such as level of energy efficiency.

A warmly welcoming room at the upscale Four Seasons *(see p208)*

Chain Hotels

Costa Rica's many chain hotels span a range of prices. The **Enjoy Group** offers all-inclusive options, in which all meals, entertainment, and facilities are provided for a set room rate at its Fiesta beach resorts. International chains such as **Best Western**, **Choice Hotels**, and **Quality Inn** are well-represented in the low- and mid-range brackets. **Occidental** and **Marriott** offer reliable service and quality. **Four Seasons** represents the deluxe end.

Daily room cleaning, linen change, and private bathrooms with showers are standard, and all chain hotels have a restaurant and bar. However, visitors should be aware that standards among budget-oriented chain hotels vary considerably and may not conform to their equivalents in North America or Europe. The more expensive options usually offer a gourmet restaurant, gym, and casino or nightclub, and sometimes tour agency and boutique shops.

Boutique Hotels

A pleasant accommodation option is the range of intimate boutique hotels, which are characterized by a charming originality and hospitality. Ranging from upscale, family-run bed-and-breakfasts to architectural stunners in the midst of coffee plantations to beach hotels inspired by a Balinese aesthetic, these exquisite lodgings can be found throughout the country.

Capitán Suizo, one of Costa Rica's many boutique hotels *(see p212)*

Most of the boutique hotels are the creation of foreign entrepreneurs with artistic vision, and with few exceptions benefit from the owners' hands-on management. They are usually lower priced than many chain hotels of similar standard and represent excellent value. Many boutique hotels offer gourmet dining, a spa, and a range of activities and excursions.

Wilderness Lodges

Nature lovers can choose between several 100 wilderness lodges in the country. The majority are located close to, or within, national parks and wildlife reserves, or otherwise offer immediate access to regions of natural beauty. Guided hikes and other wilderness-related activities are available at these lodges.

Accommodations range from basic to modestly upscale, although all have a degree of rusticity in common. The focus is on the nature experience, rather than the amenities offered. Several lodges have attained international fame; advance bookings are recommended

◁ **Hotel balcony in San José, with a lovely view of surrounding hills**

Bathroom in Shawandha Lodge at Puerto Viejo ***(see p215)***

for these. Many of the more simple lodges, including those located within indigenous reserves, are run by community cooperatives. These offer opportunities to appreciate local culture and experience nature from the local perspective. **Cooprena** is a promotion and booking agent representing many such ecolodges.

Budget Hotels

The country has thousands of simple budget accommodations called *cabinas*, which cater to the mass of Tico (Costa Rican) travelers and backpackers. Usually the term refers to a row of hotel rooms, but it is used loosely and can cover a variety of accommodation types. *Cabina* is at times used interchangeably with *albergue*, *hospedaje*, or *posada*, three terms for "lodging." *Albergue* normally refers to simple rural lodges, and *hospedaje* and *posada* are usually akin to bed-and-breakfasts.

It is acceptable to ask to inspect rooms before taking them. Services and furnishings are minimal, and bathroom accouterments are usually limited to soap and towels; bring your own sink plug and wash cloth. Many cheaper *cabinas* require that visitors share bathrooms. Be prepared for cold water only; where hot water is available, it is typically heated by inefficient electric elements that can give you a shock if touched. You may be asked to place toilet paper in a basket to avoid blocking the toilet drain. Theft is a common problem in *cabinas*. Take a padlock, and check that doors and windows are secure and that there are no holes or cracks that can be used by peeping toms.

Several budget hotels operate as members of International Youth Hostel Federation (IYHF). Most are run to a very high standard and have clean, single-sex dormitories. Some also have co-ed dorms. **Hostelling International Costa Rica** is the representative of the IYHF in Costa Rica and can make reservations for hostels all over the country.

Apartotels and Motels

Ticos are fond of *apartotels*, which are basic self-catering apartments with kitchens or kitchenettes and a small living and dining room; they are usually offered on long-term rentals. Rarely do they have restaurants or other facilities. San José has a large number of *apartotels*; they are also found in other towns and the major beach resorts.

Motels should not be confused with their North American or European equivalents. Found across the nation, they are no-frills places of convenience used mainly by lovers and rented by the hour. Overnight stays are usually permitted, even for singles. Occasionally they can prove useful at night in locations where few other options exist.

Casa de Las Tías ***(see p202)*****, Escazú**

Corcovado Lodge Tent Camp, featuring luxury tents ***(see p216)***

Camping

Visitors can camp in many of the national parks and wildlife refuges, including at ranger stations, where water, toilets, and occasionally showers are usually available. Some ranger stations prepare meals by arrangement; if not, carry your own provisions. A mosquito net and waterproof tent are also essential items to carry.

Outside the reserves, camping facilities are few except at major beach resorts. On weekends and public holidays, Tico families flock to beaches, where they camp on the sands. Avoid this illegal practice and restrict your camping to designated sites. Hammocks can be bought or rented and hung almost anywhere. Campers always need to beware of theft and should never leave items unguarded.

Pool at Hotel Villa Caletas *(see p207)*, of the Small Distinctive Hotels

Hotel Groups

Several local hotel groups represent member hotels that market themselves jointly based on their similarities. Six of the finest boutique hotels of the country form the **Small Distinctive Hotels of Costa Rica**. This group offers a distinctive ambience in their excellent accommodations, which are located in diverse regions ranging from the capital city to mountains and beaches. **Small Unique Hotels** is another group of six quality hotels situated in strategic spots around the country; all offer topnotch service. Several Swiss-and German-owned hotels are marketed under the **Charming & Nature Hotels of Costa Rica** umbrella.

Specialized Lodging

Many places cater for a specific activity. Several nature lodges, for instance, are dedicated exclusively to sportfishing, and offer all-inclusive packages. Usually these are in remote locations accessible solely by boat. Other resorts specialize in scuba diving, and offer diving lessons for beginners. Visitors planning more advanced diving will need to provide proof of their qualifications. Budget-oriented "surf camps" are often found at Costa Rica's many beaches. Some are quite sophisticated and offer various options, from outdoor dormitories with hammocks to private air-conditioned rooms. There are also plenty of health-oriented hotels, which range from rustic lodges to luxurious yoga retreats.

Many tour operators offer specialist tours for those interested in a particular activity *(see p248)*. By far the largest focus is on nature tourism: packages usually include stays at wilderness lodges and pre-arranged hikes, birding, and similar nature excursions.

Booking

It is best to book your accommodation well ahead of your visit, particularly if you are traveling during the dry season (December–April). This is especially true around Christmas, New Year, and Easter, and during special local events, such as Carnaval in Puerto Limón. Reservations are also recommended for travelers following a pre-planned route. Advance bookings for *cabinas* are not as critical except at the peak times.

Many hotels in Costa Rica have a reputation for not honoring reservations, and for not issuing refunds. It is, therefore, advisable to make reservations through a travel agency or tour operator. If making a booking yourself, never send your request by mail, as the postal service is unreliable. Instead, use the phone or fax, or book online using the hotel websites. If a deposit is required you can pay by credit card. In all cases, make sure that you obtain a written confirmation of your reservation.

Los Sueños Marriott Ocean & Golf Resort *(see p207)*, set amid sprawling grounds in Playa Herradura

El Sano Banano Beach Hotel *(see p207)* in Montezuma

Prices and Payments

Regardless of hotel type, prices will be higher in the dry season than in the wet season (May–November). The more expensive hotels usually charge an additional premium for the peak season, which is the Christmas–New Year holidays, as well as for Easter. Rates can also vary according to the type of room. Hotels that depend on business travelers often have reduced rates for weekends and long stays. Tour operators may also be able to offer special deals that you may find difficult to obtain yourself. Many hotels offer discount schemes, such as special rates for surfers.

A 16.39 percent tax is added to lodgings in tourist hotels. This is not always included in the advertised rate. Traveler's checks and credit cards are accepted in most hotels, with the exception of many budget hotels, which will only accept cash. Most places accept payment in US dollars.

Tipping

It is customary to leave a *propina* (tip) for the hotel staff at the end of your stay. The amount will depend on the type and quality of service, as well as the length of your stay. Use your discretion. In general, it is normal to tip bellboys $1 and chambermaids $1 or more. Visitors should be aware that hotel wages among service staff in Costa Rica are often quite low and that tips in dollars often amount to a significant part of such workers' livelihoods.

Disabled Travelers

Only the more recently built hotels have access and purpose-built facilities for disabled travelers, including bathrooms with wheelchair access. Many wilderness lodges have level trails designed for wheelchairs. Hotel staff in all parts of Costa Rica will do everything they can to assist disabled travelers. **Vaya con Silla de Ruedas** (Go With Wheelchairs) provides services for disabled travelers, including recommendations for appropriate lodgings.

The lobby of Hotel Grano de Oro *(see p203)* in San José

Directory

Chain Hotels

Best Western
0800-011-0063.
www.bestwestern.com

Choice Hotels
0800-011-0517.
www.choicehotels.com

Enjoy Group
296-6263.
www.fiestaresort.com

Four Seasons
696-0000.
www.fourseasons.com/costarica

Marriott
298-0844.
marriott.com

Occidental
248-2323.
www.occidental-hoteles.com

Quality Inn
0800-011-0517.
www.qualityinn.com

Wilderness Lodges

Cooprena
248-2538.
www.turismoruralcr.com

Youth Hostels

Hostelling International Costa Rica
Calles 29/31 and Ave Central, 1002 San José.
234-8186.
www.hicr.org

Hotel Groups

Charming & Nature Hotels of Costa Rica
www.charminghotels.net

Small Distinctive Hotels of Costa Rica
258-0150.
www.distinctivehotels.com

Small Unique Hotels
www.costa-rica-unique-hotels.com

Disabled Travelers

Vaya con Silla de Ruedas
PO Box 54, 4150 Sarchí.
454-2810.
www.gowithwheelchairs.com

Choosing a Hotel

Most of the hotels and resorts in this guide have been selected across a wide price range for facilities, good value, and location. The prices listed are those charged by the hotel, although discounts may be available through agencies. The hotels are listed by area. For map references for San José, see pages 78–9.

PRICE CATEGORIES
For a standard double room per night in the tourist season, including tax and service:

$ Under $25
$$ $25–40
$$$ $40–80
$$$$ $80–140
$$$$$ Over $140

SAN JOSÉ

CITY CENTER Casa Ridgway $
Calle 15 and Aves 6 bis/8 ***Tel*** *222-1400* ***Fax*** *233-6168* ***Rooms*** *13* ***Map*** *2 E4*

Located close to the Museo Nacional in downtown San José, Casa Ridgway is a peaceful hostel operated by a Quaker organization. With spacious dorms and private rooms, as well as a communal kitchen, this hostel is good value for money. Also on offer is a library and a TV lounge. **www.amigosparalapaz.org**

CITY CENTER Costa Rica Backpackers $
Calles 21/23 and Ave 6 ***Tel*** *221-6191* ***Fax*** *223-2406* ***Rooms*** *16* ***Map*** *2 F4*

On the eastern edge of downtown, this secure backpackers' hostel is run to high standards by French owners. It has both private rooms and dorms, plus a self-service kitchen, TV lounge, Internet rooms, and tour planning facilities. Its swimming pool is set in a lush garden. **www.costaricabackpackers.com**

CITY CENTER Kap's Place $$
Calle 19 and Aves 11/13 ***Tel*** *221-1169* ***Fax*** *256-4850* ***Rooms*** *18* ***Map*** *2 E2*

In a quiet locality close to Barrio Amón, this rambling converted home has a cozy family atmosphere and is enlivened by colorful decor. Each room is distinct, and some have TVs. Guests can use the kitchen, and a terrace garden has hammocks to laze in. Free Internet access is available. **www.kapsplace.com**

CITY CENTER Pensión de la Cuesta $$
Calles 11/15 and Ave 1 ***Tel*** *256-7946* ***Fax*** *255-2896* ***Rooms*** *9* ***Map*** *2 D3*

This converted Victorian home is located in a peaceful area near Parque Nacional. The 80-year old wooden house is brightly decorated and adorned with plants. Guests have use of the kitchen, and there's a TV lounge. The lodge also arranges daily tours, transfers, and 4WD rentals. **www.suntoursandfun.com/lacuesta**

CITY CENTER Gran Hotel $$$
Calle 3 and Ave 2 ***Tel*** *256-7575* ***Fax*** *256-9393* ***Rooms*** *94* ***Map*** *1 C4*

Built in 1899, the Gran Hotel is considered a historic monument, and boasts a fabulous location for sightseeing. The lobby casino offers non-stop excitement. Open round the clock, the patio café is a great place to listen to *marimba* music and watch the world go by. **www.granhotelcr.com**

CITY CENTER Hotel Don Carlos $$$
Calle 9 bis and Ave 9 ***Tel*** *221-6707* ***Fax*** *255-0828* ***Rooms*** *36* ***Map*** *2 D2*

Located in the heart of Barrio Amón and once the residence of two former presidents, Don Carlos is a part of San José's heritage. Its maze of quiet corridors, decorated with artwork and pre-Columbian motifs, lead into garden settings. There is a splendid souvenir store. **www.doncarloshotel.com**

CITY CENTER Hotel Kekoldi $$$
Calles 5/7 and Ave 9 ***Tel*** *248-0804* ***Fax*** *248-0767* ***Rooms*** *10* ***Map*** *2 D2*

Decorated in bright pastels and saturated with sunlight, this renovated Art Deco house enjoys a fine location in the heart of historic Barrio Amón. Its elegant rooms are well appointed, and it has a small private Japanese garden. Tours, transfers, and car rentals can be arranged. **www.kekoldi.com**

CITY CENTER Hotel Presidente $$$
Calles 7/9 and Ave Central ***Tel*** *222-3022* ***Fax*** *221-1205* ***Rooms*** *100* ***Map*** *2 D4*

Steps away from Plaza de la Cultura, this hotel has a casino, rooftop Jacuzzi and sauna, and an excellent street-front café and restaurant. The best suite in the house offers an 8-person Jacuzzi, an open-air shower, and spectacular views from oversized windows. **www.hotel-presidente.com**

CITY CENTER Hotel Santo Tomás $$$
Calles 3/5 and Ave 7 ***Tel*** *255-0448* ***Fax*** *222-3950* ***Rooms*** *20* ***Map*** *1 C3*

Located near the Museo de Jade, this former Victorian mansion has Neoclassical decor. A delightful restaurant *(see p225)* opens into a garden with a small pool and Jacuzzi. Guests can take advantage of safe deposit boxes and Internet facilities. A tropical buffet breakfast is included in the rates. **www.hotelsantotomas.com**

Key to Symbols *see back cover flap*

CITY CENTER Britannia Hotel $$$$

Calle 3 and Ave 11 ***Tel*** *223-6667* ***Fax*** *223-6411* ***Rooms*** *23* ***Map*** *1 C2*

This restored mansion in Barrio Amón dates from 1910 and was built by a Spanish coffee baron. Stained-glass windows, mosaic tile floors, and period furnishings help create a warm atmosphere. A modern annex is similarly decorated and has lush courtyards. **www.hbritannia.com**

CITY CENTER D'Raya Vida Villa $$$$

Calle 15 bis and Ave 11 ***Tel*** *223-4168* ***Fax*** *223-4157* ***Rooms*** *4* ***Map*** *2 E2*

This gracious Southern plantation-style mansion is now a bed-and-breakfast with stylish furnishings and splendid artwork. A quiet garden room with a fountain and a sunny, glass-enclosed den are ideal for relaxation. The hotel offers free transfers from the airport. **www.rayavida.com**

CITY CENTER Hotel Amón Plaza $$$$

Calle 3 bis and Ave 11 ***Tel*** *257-0191* ***Fax*** *257-0284* ***Rooms*** *87* ***Map*** *2 C2*

This modern hotel in Barrio Amón offers good service and excellent facilities. The elegant lobby is well appointed with objects of art. The hotel also has a disco, a conference center, a spa, and an upscale open-air roadside restaurant. All rooms have a wireless Internet connection. **www.hotelamonplaza.com**

CITY CENTER Hotel Balmoral $$$$

Calles 7/9 and Ave Central ***Tel*** *222-5022* ***Fax*** *221-7826* ***Rooms*** *112* ***Map*** *2 D3*

The modern Balmoral hotel is suitable for business travelers and tourists. The decor is uninspired, but it is located close to major sights and offers a wide range of services, including a business center and conference rooms. There is a casino for those who want to try their luck. **www.balmoral.co.cr**

CITY CENTER Hotel Fleur de Lys $$$$

Calle 13 and Aves 2/4 ***Tel*** *223-1206* ***Fax*** *257-3637* ***Rooms*** *31* ***Map*** *2 D4*

A well-kept establishment close to the Museo Nacional, this restored Victorian mansion exudes charm. Individually furnished rooms are elegant and have wrought-iron and wicker beds. Atrium gardens contain lush tropical plants. A laundry service and Internet access are offered. **www.hotelfleurdelys.com**

CITY CENTER Hotel Villa Tournon $$$$

Barrio Tournon, E of "La Republica" ***Tel*** *233-6622* ***Fax*** *222-5211* ***Rooms*** *80* ***Map*** *2 D1*

Located north of Barrio Amón, this modern hotel features modern artwork, polished hardwood floors, and rich fabrics in the guest rooms, all of which also have cable Internet connections. The piano bar and restaurant are excellent. A business center and conference rooms are also available. **www.hotel-costa-rica.com**

CITY CENTER Hotel Aurola Holiday Inn $$$$$

Calle 5 and Ave 5 ***Tel*** *222-2424* ***Fax*** *255-1171* ***Rooms*** *200* ***Map*** *2 D3*

The Aurola Holiday Inn is a 17-story, modern building on Parque Morazán. Some of its rooms have breathtaking views of volcanoes and the city. The hotel has a spacious, elegant lobby, as well as a casino, gym, and sauna. Also on offer are facilities for business travelers. **www.aurola-holidayinn.com**

CITY CENTER Radisson Europa Hotel and Conference Center $$$$$

Calle 3 and Ave 15 ***Tel*** *257-3257* ***Fax*** *257-8192* ***Rooms*** *107* ***Map*** *1 C1*

This is a contemporary business hotel on the northern edge of downtown with international levels of service. The facilities on offer include a casino, gym, wireless high-speed Internet, six conference rooms, and shops. **www.radisson.com/sanjosecr**

EAST OF CITY CENTER Hostal Toruma $

Calles 29/31 and Ave Central ***Tel*** *224-4085* ***Fax*** *224-4085* ***Rooms*** *18*

The residence of a former president of Costa Rica, this youth hostel is spotlessly clean and run to high standards. Both dormitories and private rooms are available. Breakfast is included, and there is a guest kitchen. There is also an Internet café and a travel desk to assist visitors. **www.toruma.com**

EAST OF CITY CENTER Hotel 1492 $$$

Calles 31/33 and Ave 1, No. 2985 ***Tel*** *225-3752* ***Fax*** *280-6206* ***Rooms*** *10*

Named after the year that Columbus landed in the New World, this is a charming, atmospheric bed-and-breakfast hotel in a Colonial-style house. Setting Hotel 1492 apart are its personalized service, a cozy lounge with a fireplace, and wine and cheese served on a garden patio. **www.hotel1492.com**

EAST OF CITY CENTER Hotel Don Fadrique $$$

Calle 37 and Ave 8 ***Tel*** *225-8186* ***Fax*** *224-9746* ***Rooms*** *20*

In a quiet, upscale corner of San Pedro, two elegant historic homes have been joined together and converted into an intimate hotel. Vibrant artwork and pastel-colored interiors are hallmarks. Some rooms have their own secluded gardens. **www.hoteldonfadrique.com**

EAST OF CITY CENTER Boutique Hotel Jade $$$$

N of Autos Subaru dealership, Barrio Dent ***Tel*** *224-2455* ***Fax*** *224-2166* ***Rooms*** *29*

Close to the Universidad de Costa Rica, this two-story hotel has public areas boasting lively contemporary decor. It features a cigar bar and a superb restaurant *(see p225)*. Each room has Internet access and a minibar. The hotel is a member of Small Unique Hotels of Costa Rica *(see p198)*. **www.hotelboutiquejade.com**

EAST OF CITY CENTER Hôtel Le Bergerac $$$$

Calle 35, S of Ave Central **Tel** *234-7850* **Fax** *225-9103* **Rooms** *19*

Set in a former colonial home in San Pedro, this hotel exudes a classical European aesthetic and has a fine French restaurant *(see p225)*. Many of the spacious, wood-floored rooms have their own private garden patios. The hotel has a reputation for excellent service. **www.bergerachotel.com**

EAST OF CITY CENTER Hotel Milvia $$$$

NE of Centro Comercial M&N, San Pedro **Tel** *225-4543* **Fax** *225-7801* **Rooms** *9*

Hotel Milvia is a small, intimate hotel housed in a 1930s wooden home in a quiet residential area. Sitting rooms and a tropical garden are great for relaxation. Hardwood floors, spacious rooms, and bathrooms featuring hand-painted decorative tilework add to its elegance. **www.hotelmilvia.com**

ESCAZÚ Casa de Las Tías $$$

San Rafael de Escazú **Tel** *289-5517* **Fax** *289-7353* **Rooms** *5*

This bed-and-breakfast is housed in a sprawling Victorian-style cedar house, set amidst lush gardens within walking distance of Escazú. The atmosphere is cozy and tranquil. The hosts are a delight and provide gourmet breakfasts. **www.hotels.co.cr/casatias.html**

ESCAZÚ Costa Verde Inn $$$

Barrio Rosa Linda, San Miguel de Escazú **Tel** *228-4080* **Fax** *289-8591* **Rooms** *18*

Polished hardwoods are a feature of this delightful bed-and-breakfast hotel, which has a cozy lounge warmed by a log fire. Each room is individually decorated. Guests can take relaxing swims in the pool, and the lush garden is perfect for lazing in a hammock. **www.costaverdeinn.com**

ESCAZÚ Posada El Quijote $$$

Off Calle del Llano, San Miguel de Escazú **Tel** *289-8401* **Fax** *289-8729* **Rooms** *10*

Exquisite gardens, complete with a brook running through them, and stupendous views through the floor-to-ceiling windows are the highlights of this contemporary hilltop hotel. Each of its nine rooms has hand-crafted wood furniture and private baths. No children allowed. **www.quijote.co.cr**

ESCAZÚ Villa Escazú $$$

W of Banco Nacional, San Miguel de Escazú **Tel** *289-7971* **Fax** *289-7971* **Rooms** *6*

This is a Swiss-style chalet with a veranda on three sides for great views. Surrounded by verdant gardens, it has a charming rustic atmosphere; log fires add to the cozy ambience inside. An upstairs veranda has rockers, and the studio apartment has a kitchen and TV. **www.hotels.co.cr/vescazu.html**

ESCAZÚ Apartotel María Alexandra $$$$

NW of El Cruce, San Rafael de Escazú **Tel** *228-1507* **Fax** *289-5192* **Rooms** *14*

This offers modern apartments and twin-level units with elegant furnishings, close to the center of Escazú. The amenities include a swimming pool, sauna, fitness center, and mini-golf, as well as a travel agency, and Harley-Davidson authorized rentals for biking aficionados. **www.mariaalexandra.com**

ESCAZÚ The Alta Hotel $$$$$

Alto de las Palomas, 2 miles (3 km) W of Escazú **Tel** *282-4160* **Fax** *282-4162* **Rooms** *23*

Set on a hillside with great views, this elegant hotel blends Colonial and contemporary styles. Graciously appointed rooms have deep Roman-style tubs. The gourmet restaurant, La Luz *(see p226)*, has however struggled for consistency. **www.thealtahotel.com**

ESCAZÚ Hotel Real Intercontinental $$$$$

Autopista Prospero Fernández and Blvd Camino Real **Tel** *289-7000* **Fax** *289-8989* **Rooms** *261*

This opulent hotel, 1 mile (1.6 km) west of San Rafael de Escazú, offers deluxe amenities and is popular with business travelers. The spa includes a beauty salon, fitness center, and swimming pool. A floodlit tennis court, shops, tour agency, and a business center are among its other amenities. **www.iccostarica.gruporeal.com**

ESCAZÚ Tara Resort Hotel $$$$$

San Antonio de Escazú **Tel** *228-6992* **Fax** *228-9651* **Rooms** *41*

Originally a stately private home, this antebellum-style mansion enjoys a splendid mountainside location. Furnished with antiques, it can be imposing. It has rooms and villas, as well as a gym, a full-service spa, tennis, croquet, and an excellent restaurant *(see p226)*. **www.tararesort.com**

WEST OF CITY CENTER Gaudy's Backpackers $

Calles 36/38 and Ave 5 **Tel** *258-2937* **Fax** *258-2937* **Rooms** *13*

On a quiet residential street close to Paseo Colón, this clean backpackers' hostel is in a converted middle-class home. It has mixed dorms and private rooms with bathrooms. Also on offer are free tea and coffee, a lounge with cable TV, and a free Internet connection. There is no curfew. **www.backpacker.co.cr**

WEST OF CITY CENTER La Mariposa Azúl $

Calles 40/42 and Ave 4 **Tel** *258-7878* **Fax** *258-7878* **Rooms** *5*

Across the road from Parque Sabana, La Mariposa Azúl is clean, quiet, and secure. This simply furnished backpackers' hostel offers a choice of private rooms and dorms, with facilities such as a full kitchen, Internet access, and TV. Several restaurants are a short walk away. **www.lamariposaazul.com**

Key to Price Guide *see p200* **Key to Symbols** *see back cover flap*

WEST OF CITY CENTER Classic Hotel B&B $$

Calle 20 and Aves 3/5 ***Tel*** *223-4316* ***Fax*** *257-3123* ***Rooms*** *13*

This clean and secure option is close to the Coca-Cola bus terminal. Rooms are pleasantly decorated, and it also has a large dormitory for backpackers, as well as a charming garden. The hotel offers facilities such as Internet access. There is no curfew or lockout. **www.costaricabackpackerstravel.com**

WEST OF CITY CENTER Apartotel La Sabana $$$

Calle 44, N of Avenida las Américas ***Tel*** *220-2422* ***Fax*** *231-7386* ***Rooms*** *25*

Located next to Parque Sabana, this modern *apartotel* offers rooms, studios, and apartments. As part of its Business Express service, it provides an office within the room, complete with ergonomic chair. Other amenities include babysitting services upon request and a sauna. **www.apartotel-lasabana.com**

WEST OF CITY CENTER Barceló Rincón del Valle $$$

S of Sabana Sur ***Tel*** *231-4927* ***Fax*** *231-5924* ***Rooms*** *20*

Polished hardwoods and pleasing contemporary decor are the attractions of this modern hotel. Its proximity to Parque Sabana, the Museo de Ciencias Naturales "La Salle," and other San José attractions make it a good base from which to explore. **www.barcelo.com**

WEST OF CITY CENTER Hotel Cacts $$$

Calles 28/30 and Ave 3 bis, No. 2845 ***Tel*** *221-2928* ***Fax*** *221-8616* ***Rooms*** *33*

In a hilly residential area, this rambling hotel has ultra-clean rooms with simple decor; those in a modern annex are gloomy. Some rooms have shared bathrooms, while the deluxe rooms have TVs. Breakfast is served on a rooftop terrace. The hotel also has a travel service. **www.tourism.co.cr/hotels/cacts**

WEST OF CITY CENTER Hotel Rosa del Paseo $$$

Calles 28/30 and Paseo Colón ***Tel*** *257-3225* ***Fax*** *223-2776* ***Rooms*** *18*

Facing onto Paseo Colón, this converted century-old Caribbean-Victorian stucco home has many historic features, such as Italian mosaic floors and old English furniture. Rooms are situated around two garden patios, and breakfast is served outside. There is also a crafts store. **www.rosadelpaseo.com**

WEST OF CITY CENTER Best Western Irazú $$$$

Barrio La Uruca ***Tel*** *232-4811* ***Fax*** *231-6485* ***Rooms*** *350*

Best Western Irazú is a comfortable modern hotel on the northwestern fringe of the city. Its amenities include tennis courts, a casino and bar, a travel agency, and a shopping mall. Shuttles connect the hotel to downtown and to the international airport. **www.bestwesterncostarica.com**

WEST OF CITY CENTER Hotel Grano de Oro $$$$

Calle 30 and Aves 2/4 ***Tel*** *255-3322* ***Fax*** *221-2782* ***Rooms*** *35*

Combining exquisite decor and exemplary service with a peaceful location, this colonial-era mansion enjoys a loyal clientele. It has rooftop Jacuzzis and a splendid gourmet restaurant *(see p226)*. Well managed by Canadian owners, it is a member of Small Distinctive Hotels of Costa Rica *(see p198)*. **www.hotelgranodeoro.com**

WEST OF CITY CENTER Hotel Parque del Lago $$$$

Calles 40/42 and Ave 2 ***Tel*** *257-8787* ***Fax*** *223-1617* ***Rooms*** *40*

This is a well-kept modern establishment close to Parque Sabana. Popular with business travelers, it has an elegant bar, and its public areas are decorated with tropical hardwoods, colonial tile work, and details from traditional Costa Rican architecture. **www.parquedellago.com**

WEST OF CITY CENTER Quality Hotel Centro Colón $$$$

Calle 38 and Ave 3 ***Tel*** *257-2580* ***Fax*** *257-2582* ***Rooms*** *103*

Located near Parque Sabana, this twin-tower high-rise hotel offers contemporary elegance. Amenities include a casino, nightclub, and coffee shop, as well as a tour agency, business center, and souvenir shop. **www.hotelcentrocolon.com**

WEST OF CITY CENTER Tryp Corobicí $$$$$

Autopista General Cañas, Sabana Norte ***Tel*** *232-0618* ***Fax*** *231-5698* ***Rooms*** *203*

A landmark hotel with dramatic architecture and soaring atrium, this is popular with business travelers. The hotel has spacious rooms and abundant facilities including a casino, two restaurants and a bar, a travel agency, and a free shuttle service. **www.trypcorobici.solmelia.com**

THE CENTRAL HIGHLANDS

ALAJUELA Hotel II Millenium B&B $$$

Río Segundo de Alajuela, 1 mile (1.6 km) SE of Alajuela ***Tel*** *430-5050* ***Fax*** *441-2365* ***Rooms*** *12*

A favorite of backpackers, this simple but well-run, pleasant hostel has private rooms with baths as well as dorms. The owners offer a free 24-hour airport pickup service. The hostel also arranges day trips to nearby places of interest. Internet facilities are available. **www.bbmilleniumcr.com**

ALAJUELA Hotel Los Volcanes $$$

Calle Central and Ave 3 **Tel** *441-0525* **Fax** *440-8006* **Rooms** *11*

This restored 1920s home is rich in hardwoods and has lovely wrought-iron beds in all the rooms. Some rooms are around a patio. The hotel offers Internet facilities and a free airport shuttle service, and also has a travel agency. **www.montezumaexpeditions.com/hotel.htm**

ALAJUELA Orquideas Inn $$$$

Cruce de Grecia y Poás, 2 miles (3 km) W of Alajuela **Tel** *433-9346* **Fax** *433-9740* **Rooms** *28*

At the base of Volcán Poás, this atmospheric hacienda-style building sits in sprawling lush grounds. The comfortable rooms have brightly colored decor. Fountains feed the pool, which has a wooden sundeck. The bar draws its own clientele. **www.orquideasinn.com**

ALAJUELA Pura Vida Hotel $$$$

Cruce de Tuetal Norte y Sur, 0.5 mile (1 km) N of Alajuela **Tel** *441-1157* **Fax** *441-1157* **Rooms** *7*

Originally a coffee *finca* (farm) set amid verdant hillside gardens, this family-run bed-and-breakfast has independent *casitas* (cottages) in distinct styles. The open-air restaurant serves gourmet meals. The owners' dogs have the run of the place. **www.puravidahotel.com**

ALAJUELA Xandari $$$$$

Tacacori, 3 miles (5 km) N of Alajuela **Tel** *443-2020* **Fax** *442-4847* **Rooms** *21*

A superb boutique hotel with visionary contemporary design set in its own coffee *finca* (farm) in the hills above Alajuela. Spacious guest villas have rippling ceilings, artwork, and fabulous views. Apart from a restaurant *(see p227)*, the hotel boasts a spa. Trails lead through bamboo groves to a waterfall. **www.xandari.com**

ATENAS Hotel Vista Atenas $$

2 miles (3 km) W of Atenas **Tel** *446-4272* **Fax** *446-4272* **Rooms** *9*

Located on the eastern slope of a hill, this pleasant hotel overlooks the entire central valley and has fabulous views of Poás, Barva, and Irazú Volcanoes. It offers accommodations in cabins or rooms and gourmet European meals in the restaurant. **www.vistaatenas.com**

ATENAS El Cafetal Inn $$$$

Santa Eulalia, 3 miles (5 km) N of Atenas **Tel** *446-5785* **Fax** *446-7028* **Rooms** *16*

This friendly country inn is located on a coffee *finca* with nature trails. The spectacular two-story house with rounded glass corner alcoves overlooks the Río Colorado valley and coffee and sugarcane fields. The live-in owners are charming conversationalists. Choose from rooms or cottages. **www.cafetal.com**

BOSQUE DE PAZ RESERVE Bosque de Paz Lodge $$$$$

9 miles (14 km) E of Zarcero **Tel** *234-6676* **Fax** *225-0203* **Rooms** *12*

A two-story riverstone-and-timber building on the edge of the rainforest, this lodge has terra-cotta floors and wrought-iron beds. There is also a library with natural history books and research documents on the reserve. Meals are included in the price. Reservations are required. **www.bosquedepaz.com**

GRECIA Posada Mimosa $$$$

Rincón de Salas, 2 miles (3 km) S of Grecia **Tel** *494-5868* **Fax** *494-5868* **Rooms** *10*

This appealing family-run property is sprawled over several acres of forest and sugarcane fields, with great views over the valley. The swimming pool is spectacularly situated. A selection of rooms and cabins, all of a good standard, are available. **www.mimosa.co.cr**

HEREDIA Hotel Bougainvillea $$$$

Santo Domingo de Heredia, 2 miles (3 km) SE of Heredia **Tel** *244-1414* **Fax** *244-1313* **Rooms** *81*

This reasonably priced hotel is managed to high standards. Original pieces of specially commissioned modern art are scattered through the hotel. Rooms have views either of the mountains or of the San José skyline. The hotel offers tennis, swimming, and a jogging track, as well as a well-known restaurant *(see p227)*. **www.bougainvillea.co.cr**

HEREDIA Finca Rosa Blanca Country Inn $$$$$

Santa Barbara de Heredia, 4 miles (6 km) NW of Heredia **Tel** *269-9392* **Fax** *269-9555* **Rooms** *9*

This fabulous family-run hotel on a coffee farm is an architectural delight inspired by Spanish architect Antoni Gaudí. Each guest room has unique decor and gourmet meals are served *(see p228)*. Horseback rides, bungee jumping, and whitewater rafting can be arranged. **www.fincarosablanca.com**

LA DAMITA Genesis II Eco-Lodge $$$

22 miles (35 km) S of Cartago **Tel** *381-0739* **Rooms** *4*

In the heart of a cloud forest *(see p96)*, this rustic nature lodge offers no-frills comfort and a range of activities. Guests have a choice of rooms or cabins; camping is also possible. Bathrooms are shared in an effort to conserve water. There's a common kitchen. **www.genesis-two.com**

LA GARITA Hotel La Rosa de América $$$

Barrio San José, 3 miles (5 km) W of Alajuela **Tel** *433-2741* **Fax** *433-2741* **Rooms** *12*

Located at an elevation of 3,000 ft (915 m) between La Garita and Alajuela, La Rosa de América is an intimate, reasonably priced hotel. Rooms are available in cabins set amid lush gardens. The American family who owns it keeps it spotlessly clean. **www.larosadeamerica.com**

LA GARITA Martino Resort & Spa $$$$

Hwy 3, 2 miles (3 km) E of Pan-Am Hwy **Tel** *433-8382* **Fax** *433-9052* **Rooms** *42*

Manicured lawns, sumptuous hardwoods, and Romanesque-style statuary are hallmarks of this gracious family-run hotel. Facilities include a casino, tennis court, a modern gym and full-service spa, and a cigar bar and gourmet restaurant *(see p228)*. **www.hotelmartino.com**

LOS ANGELES CLOUD FOREST RESERVE Villablanca Cloud Forest Hotel $$$$

San Ramón **Tel** *461-0300* **Fax** *461-0302* **Rooms** *34*

Perched atop the Continental Divide at the edge of a cloud forest, this recently renovated colonial-era farmstead offers charming cottages warmed by log fires. Horseback rides, hikes, and bird-watching tours over 5 sq miles (12 sq km) of dairy pasture and cloud forest are a specialty. **www.villablanca-costarica.com**

MONTE DE LA CRUZ Hotel Chalet Tirol $$$

6 miles (10 km) NE of Heredia **Tel** *267-6222* **Fax** *267-6373* **Rooms** *23*

Designed in the style of a Swiss alpine village, this mountain retreat has a fine restaurant *(see p228)*. Choose from modern hotel rooms or rustic yet cozy chalets. Trails lead into cloud forest, and its facilities include tennis courts, a sauna, and meeting and convention facilities.

OROSI Orosi Lodge $$$

SW of the plaza, Orosi village **Tel** *533-3578* **Fax** *533-3578* **Rooms** *6*

This charming family-run hotel is a minute's walk from hot spring pools, and is well placed for other local attractions such as Casa el Soñador. It offers rooms with kitchenettes, private baths, and terraces. It is known for its excellent café, which also has Internet facilities *(see p228)*. **www.orosilodge.com**

OROSI Rancho Río Perlas Resort & Spa $$$$

1 mile (1.6 km) W of Orosi **Tel** *533-3341* **Fax** *533-3085* **Rooms** *52*

Surrounded by lush gardens, the secluded valley setting is a plus point for this modern chain hotel. Thermal waters feed the pool and spa. Fishing outings to the five ponds in the surrounding area can be organized for keen anglers.

POÁS Siempre Verde Bed & Breakfast $$$

Doka Estate, 7 miles (11 km) N of Alajuela **Tel** *449-5562* **Fax** *239-0445* **Rooms** *4*

Scenically situated within a vast coffee plantation, this warm, friendly hotel is a peaceful retreat from the bustle of the cities. Siempre Verde provides breakfast, as well as meals for special events such as conferences and private parties. **http://dokaestate.com**

SALISPUEDES Finca Eddie Serrano $$$

Km 80 on the Pan-Am Hwy **Tel** *381-8456* **Rooms** *16*

Quetzals are found in plenty at Finca Eddie Serrano *(see p96)*, also known as Albergue Mirador de Quetzales. Located near Genesis II, this rustic timber lodge has simple log cabins offering awesome views, and is perfect for keen birders. The rates include breakfast and dinner. **ww.exploringcostarica.com/mirador/quetzales.html**

SAN GERARDO DE DOTA Trogon Lodge $$$

5 miles (8 km) W of the Pan-Am Hwy **Tel** *293-8181* **Fax** *239-7657* **Rooms** *23*

Situated amid lush gardens at an elevation of 7,000 ft (2,135 m) in the Valle de San Gerardo, this wooden lodge enjoys a marvelous setting next to the clear waters of Río Savegre. It offers trout fishing, as well as hiking, horseback rides, and mountain biking. **www.grupomawamba.com**

TURRIALBA Hotel Wagelia $$$

Calles 2/4 and Ave 4 **Tel** *556-1566* **Fax** *556-1596* **Rooms** *18*

This is a centrally located hotel with modest furnishings and a reasonably priced restaurant. It has a tour agency and can organize rafting and kayaking on Río Pacuare and visits to attractions such as Guayabo and Volcán Turrialba. **www.hotelwagelia.com**

TURRIALBA Hotel Casa Turire $$$$$

Hacienda Atirro, 5 miles (8 km) SE of Turrialba **Tel** *531-1111* **Fax** *531-1075* **Rooms** *16*

Situated on the shores of Lake Angostura, this delightful boutique hotel has spacious rooms and an elegant restaurant *(see p229)*. Activities include visits to sugarcane, coffee, and macadamia nut processing centers. It is a member of Small Distinctive Hotels of Costa Rica *(see p198)*. **www.hotelcasaturire.com**

TURRIALBA Rancho Naturalista $$$$$

Tuís, 9 miles (14 km) E of Turrialba **Tel** *433-8278* **Fax** *433-4925* **Rooms** *11*

Perched on a mountainside, this homely wilderness ranch is considered one of the finest birding lodges in the country. They have an extensive trail system and resident guides. Visitors can choose between cottages or rooms. Meals and guided hikes are included in the price.

VARA BLANCA Poás Volcano Lodge $$$$

14 miles (22 km) N of Alajuela **Tel** *482-2194* **Fax** *482-2513* **Rooms** *11*

This mountaintop farmstead is now a cozy family-run hotel standing amid cattle pastures with stupendous views. Guests are offered log fires, down comforters, and home-baked caraway bread. There is also a games room, a gift shop, a small library, and an art gallery. **www.poasvolcanolodge.com**

VARA BLANCA Peace Lodge $$$$$

Montaña Azul, 15 miles (24 km) N of Alajuela **Tel** *225-0643* **Fax** *225-1082* **Rooms** *17*

Located at the La Paz Waterfall Gardens, the lodge's dramatic deluxe decor includes natural wood beams, hardwood flooring, hand-crafted canopy beds, fireplaces, and garden bathrooms and riverstone showers in spacious rooms. Each room boasts a Jacuzzi and oversized balcony. **www.waterfallgardens.com**

VOLCÁN TURRIALBA Volcán Turrialba Lodge $$$$

12 miles (19 km) NW of Turrialba **Tel** *273-4335* **Fax** *273-0703* **Rooms** *22*

This simple mountain lodge is situated between Turrialba and Irazú Volcanoes, perfect for horseback rides and hiking. Of particular interest is the Volcán Turrialba Tour, a unique opportunity to descend to the floor of a major volcanic crater. A 4WD is required to access the lodge. **www.volcanturrialbalodge.com**

THE CENTRAL PACIFIC AND SOUTHERN NICOYA

JACÓ Hotel Cocal and Casino $$$

Calle Cocal **Tel** *643-3067* **Fax** *643-1201* **Rooms** *43*

Conveniently located, this is a lively low-rise beachfront hotel. With two swimming pools and a poolside bar, an open-air restaurant that serves good international cuisine, and a casino, the hotel is popular with small tour groups. Children are not allowed. **www.hotelcocalandcasino.com**

JACÓ Hotel Poseidon $$$$

Calle Bohio **Tel** *643-1642* **Rooms** *14*

The gourmet restaurant *(see p229)* is the highlight of this two-story hotel with modest furnishings. The upstairs rooms are better. All rooms have minibars. The hotel can arrange tours and activities. **www.hotel-poseidon.com**

JACÓ Vista Guapa Surf Camp $$$$

1 mile (1.6 km) NW of Jacó **Tel** *643-2830* **Fax** *643-3242* **Rooms** *6*

Set on a hillside, this surfers' hotel has simply but comfortably furnished bungalows, with great views of the ocean. Guests can watch TV in the communal lounge. While there is no restaurant as such, breakfast and dinner are available in the main house. The hotel specializes in surfing packages. **www.vistaguapa.com**

JACÓ Hotel Club del Mar $$$$$

Hwy 34, 1 mile (1.6 km) S of Jacó **Tel** *643-3194* **Fax** *643-3550* **Rooms** *31*

This modern beachfront hotel has rooms and self-catering villas around a huge pool with a tapas bar. There is a lush garden and a full-service spa. The focus is on watersports, with swimming, surfing, and canoeing on offer. Kayaks can also be rented. **www.clubdelmarcostarica.com**

MALPAÍS Malpaís Surf Camp & Resort $

S of Carmen **Tel** *640-0031* **Fax** *640-0061* **Rooms** *16*

This well-run surfers' camp has several types of accommodations, from camping and cabins with shared bathrooms to poolside rooms and rustic bungalows with their own facilities. It offers various forms of recreation, such as horseback riding, mountain biking, and surf fishing, as well as surfing tours. **www.malpaissurfcamp.com**

MALPAÍS Funky Monkey Lodge $$$

Playa Santa Teresa, 1 mile (1.6 km) N of Carmen **Tel** *640-0317* **Fax** *640-0272* **Rooms** *4*

Located close to the beach, this is a delightful rustic lodge. Wooden bungalows have partially open-air showers, kitchenettes, and verandas with hammocks. The bar-restaurant specializes in sushi. The lodge rents out surf boards, and can arrange hiking, fishing, and diving trips. **www.funky-monkey-lodge.com**

MALPAÍS Hotel Milarepa $$$$

Playa Santa Teresa, 3 miles (5 km) N of Carmen **Tel** *640-0023* **Fax** *640-0168* **Rooms** *4*

This intimate beachfront hotel is operated by live-in French owners. With an Asian aesthetic, the bungalows sit on the sands and have antique four-poster beds and partly open-air bathrooms. The restaurant serves gourmet cuisine. **www.milarepahotel.com**

MALPAÍS Star Mountain Eco-Resort $$$$

1 mile (1.6 km) E of Malpaís **Tel** *640-0101* **Fax** *640-0102* **Rooms** *5*

A family-run ecological lodge, Star Mountain Eco-Resort is surrounded by forests adjoining Parque Nacional Cabo Blanco. Highlights are the colorful decor and a delightful tropical ambience. The hotel's open-air restaurant looks over lush grounds. Closed September–November. **www.starmountaineco.com**

MALPAÍS Florblanca Resort $$$$$

Playa Santa Teresa, 3 miles (5 km) N of Carmen **Tel** *640-0232* **Fax** *640-0226* **Rooms** *10*

A serene beachfront deluxe resort with a Balinese motif. Spacious villas feature bathrooms open to the sky and tasteful furnishings, while the alfresco Nectar Bar & Restaurante offers gourmet food *(see p229)*. Guests can learn yoga and martial arts. A member of Small Distinctive Hotels of Costa Rica *(see p198)*. **www.florblanca.com**

Key to Price Guide *see p200* **Key to Symbols** *see back cover flap*

MANUEL ANTONIO Didi's B&B $$$

1 mile (1.6 km) S of Quepos ***Tel*** *777-0069* ***Fax*** *777-2863* ***Rooms*** *3*

This small and charming family-run bed-and-breakfast, with comfortable rooms, is set in the midst of verdant rainforest. The garden boasts a water pool and a bar. The hotel is operated by gracious Italian hosts who cook gourmet organic meals by request. **www.didiscr.com**

MANUEL ANTONIO Nature's Beachfront Aparthotel $$$$

Playa Espadilla, 3 miles (5 km) S of Quepos ***Tel*** *777-1473* ***Fax*** *777-1475* ***Rooms*** *5*

This homely cottage hotel enjoys a stupendous beachfront setting and easy access to the popular Parque Nacional Manuel Antonio. The simply furnished rooms include a backpackers' studio and a suite. Restaurants are a 3-minute walk along the beach. **www.maqbeach.com/natures.html**

MANUEL ANTONIO Hotel La Mariposa $$$$$

3 miles (5 km) S of Quepos ***Tel*** *777-0355* ***Fax*** *777-0050* ***Rooms*** *56*

A venerable hotel with a magnificent hilltop setting, Hotel La Mariposa has fantastic views of the ocean and the rainforests of Parque Nacional Manuel Antonio. Rooms vary from Mediterranean-style cottages to contemporary suites. The restaurant is renowned *(see p230)*. Free shuttles to the beach. **www.hotelmariposa.com**

MANUEL ANTONIO Hotel Si Como No Resort $$$$$

3 miles (5 km) S of Quepos ***Tel*** *777-0777* ***Fax*** *777-1093* ***Rooms*** *61*

This is an upscale contemporary hotel with a choice of restaurants *(see p230)*. It boasts a multimedia theater, Internet café, spa, two pools, and a host of activities. Original rooms have a Disneyesque feel; newer rooms are more elegant. **www.sicomono.com**

MANUEL ANTONIO Makanda by the Sea $$$$$

3 miles (5 km) S of Quepos ***Tel*** *777-0442* ***Fax*** *777-1032* ***Rooms*** *11*

Makanda offers great forest and ocean views from spacious deluxe villas in harmony with their surroundings. Forest trails lead to a secluded beach with pre-Columbian fish traps. There is an infinity pool, and a romantic open-air restaurant serves gourmet cuisine *(see p230)*. **www.makanda.com**

MONTEZUMA Horizontes de Montezuma $$$

1 mile (1.6 km) N of Montezuma ***Tel*** *642-0534* ***Fax*** *642-0625* ***Rooms*** *7*

A gracious plantation-style hilltop lodging with a huge veranda, this hotel has delightful, sparkling-white decor. It offers intensive as well as short-term Spanish language courses. The hotel can make arrangements with local tour operators for various activities. **www.horizontes-montezuma.com**

MONTEZUMA El Sano Banano Beach Hotel $$$$$

Playa Grande, 0.5 mile (1 km) E of Montezuma ***Tel*** *642-0638* ***Fax*** *642-0631* ***Rooms*** *14*

Set amid lush palm-shaded gardens, this attractive hotel is reached by a beach walk. It features various types of accommodations, including beach suites and bungalows, all with an exquisite and creative aesthetic. The landscaped pool is a highlight. **www.elbanano.com**

PLAYA HERMOSA Cabinas Las Arenas $$

Hwy 34 ***Tel*** *643-3508* ***Fax*** *643-3508* ***Rooms*** *10*

Sitting over the shore, this surfers' guesthouse has charming wooden cabins and also permits camping. The restaurant is appealingly rustic, and there is a souvenir shop. Various tour reservations are offered. **www.cabinaslasarenas.com**

PLAYA HERMOSA Terraza del Pacífico $$$$

1 mile (1.6 km) S of Jacó ***Tel*** *643-3222* ***Fax*** *643-3424* ***Rooms*** *42*

Although it promotes itself as a surfers' hotel, Terraza del Pacifico is a modern beachfront option with broad appeal. It offers rooms and suites (with kitchenettes), as well as a pool for children. Canopy tours and dolphin-watching trips can be arranged. **www.terrazadelpacifico.com**

PLAYA HERRADURA Hotel Villa Caletas $$$$$

2 miles (3 km) N of Playa Herradura ***Tel*** *637-0505* ***Fax*** *637-0303* ***Rooms*** *36*

Combining a sublime mountaintop location and stunning decor, this French-run hotel exudes luxury. Its restaurants are acclaimed *(see p230)*, and it has a full-service spa. Live concerts are held in the classical amphitheater set in the cliff-face. A member of Small Distinctive Hotels of Costa Rica. **www.hotelvillacaletas.com**

PLAYA HERRADURA Los Sueños Marriott Ocean & Golf Resort $$$$$

1 mile (1.6 km) W of Hwy 34 ***Tel*** *630-9000* ***Fax*** *630-9090* ***Rooms*** *201*

This grand beachfront hotel boasts a marina, a golf course in the lap of nature, a casino, business facilities, and a choice of restaurants *(see p230)*. Tastefully done-up suites have superb views of the ocean and mountains surrounding the resort, as well as minibars and 24-hour service. **www.marriott.com/sjols**

PUNTARENAS Hotel Tioga $$$$

Calles 17/19 and Ave 4 ***Tel*** *661-0271* ***Fax*** *661-0127* ***Rooms*** *52*

Established in 1959, this venerable hotel facing the Gulf of Nicoya is close to several good restaurants and bars. Rooms are adequate rather than inspired; some have only cold water. Hotel Tioga has a small casino, and the enclosed pool in the atrium courtyard has an island with a large tree. **www.hoteltioga.com**

PUNTARENAS Fiesta Resort and Casino $$$$$

Playa Puntarenas, 5 miles (8 km) E of Puntarenas **Tel** 663-0808 **Fax** 663-0856 **Rooms** 204

Part of the Enjoy Group *(see p196)*, this lively all-inclusive beach resort has a casino and several pools, bars, and restaurants. Sports facilities include tennis, volleyball, mini-golf, and watersports. Also on offer are live entertainment at night and a kids' club. The resort gets crowded on weekends. **www.fiestaresort.com**

QUEPOS Hotel Villa Romántica $$$$

On the road leading to Parque Nacional Manuel Antonio **Tel** 777-0037 **Fax** 777-0604 **Rooms** 15

This two-story Colonial-style hotel with lush gardens is conveniently located: it is close to Parque Nacional Manuel Antonio and a short walk away from downtown, with easy access to shops, bars, and restaurants. Rooms for up to four people are available. They have either air conditioning or ceiling fans. **www.villaromantica.com**

SAVEGRE Albergue El Silencio $$

El Silencio, 25 miles (40 km) SE of Quepos **Tel** 380-5581 **Fax** 777-1938 **Rooms** 10

Part of Coopesilencio *(see p116)*, this rustic ecolodge is run by the local community. Located amid primary forest and including a butterfly garden, Albergue El Silencio has quaint timber-and-thatch cabins. The ecolodge offers various activities. **www.turismoruralcr.com**

SAVEGRE Rafiki Safari Lodge $$$$$

19 miles (30 km) SE of Quepos **Tel** 777-2250 **Fax** 777-5327 **Rooms** 9

Set in a deep river valley, this African-style lodge has luxurious safari tents with fully appointed bathrooms. The lodge offers nature trips, as well as kayaking and whitewater rafting. A highlight is its South African *braai* (barbecue). **www.rafikisafari.com**

TAMBOR Tambor Tropical $$$$$

0.5 (1 km) SW of the airstrip **Tel** 683-0011 **Fax** 683-0013 **Rooms** 20

A modern beachside hotel, Tambor Tropical features hexagonal two-story hardwood cabins in tranquil landscaped grounds. The hotel offers a spa and yoga classes. Among the many activities available for guests are boat trips, sportfishing, and horseback riding. **www.tambortropical.com**

TAMBOR Tango Mar Resort $$$$$

3 miles (5 km) SW of Tambor **Tel** 683-0001 **Fax** 683-0003 **Rooms** 38

Tango Mar boasts a cliffside setting overlooking a splendid beach. Choose from amongst modern hotel rooms, romantic thatched cabins, and villas. The resort has a nine-hole golf course, as well as stables and a yoga and spa center. **www.tangomar.com**

GUANACASTE AND NORTHERN NICOYA

BAHÍA CULEBRA Four Seasons Resort at Papagayo Peninsula $$$$$

Punta Mala, 27 miles (43 km) W of Liberia **Tel** 696-0000 **Fax** 696-0500 **Rooms** 165

Visitors get the best of all worlds at this deluxe chain resort: a fabulous hilltop location, excellent facilities, and fine service. It offers three swimming pools, a full-service spa, tennis, and a championship golf course designed by Arnold Palmer. **www.fourseasons.com/costarica**

BAHÍA SALINAS Eco-Playa Resort $$$$

Playa La Coyotera, 10 miles (16 km) W of La Cruz **Tel** 228-7146 **Fax** 289-4536 **Rooms** 36

Home to an advanced windsurfing center, this beachfront resort has a windswept location and spacious, well-appointed rooms. Guests can visit nearby Refugio Nacional de Vida Silvestre Isla Bolaños by kayak or boat. Also on offer are tours to Nicaragua's colonial cities and to Lake Nicaragua. **www.ecoplaya.com**

ISLITA Hotel Punta Islita $$$$$

Punta Islita, 10 miles (16 km) S of Carrillo **Tel** 231-6122 **Fax** 231-0715 **Rooms** 32

This remote hillside hotel offers a variety of accommodations. Most of them have canopy beds and offer great views. The hotel has the gourmet 1492 Restaurante *(see p231)*, a spa, and a beach club, and offers kayaking, canopy tours, and an ATV adventure ride along mountain trails and the shore. **www.hotelpuntaislita.com**

LIBERIA Hotel Guanacaste $$

Calle 12 and Aves 1/3 **Tel** 666-0085 **Fax** 666-2287 **Rooms** 26

Part of the Costa Rican youth hostel chain *(see p197)*, this well-run hostel is popular with budget travelers, including local truck drivers. It is well placed for beaches and Rincón de la Vieja, Santa Rosa, Guanacaste, and Lomas Barbudal National Parks. **www.hicr.org**

LIBERIA Best Western Hotel & Casino El Sitio $$$

Hwy 21, W of Pan-Am Hwy **Tel** 666-1211 **Fax** 666-2059 **Rooms** 52

This modern hotel has spacious rooms around an atmospheric courtyard with two pools. It also has gift stores, a tour desk, and a casino for those who wish to try their luck. It is the perfect jumping-off point for visiting Pacific beaches, national parks, and volcanoes. **www.bestwestern.com**

MONTEVERDE Pensión Santa Elena $$

Santa Elena, E of bus stop ***Tel*** *645-5051* ***Fax*** *645-5051* ***Rooms*** *24*

In the heart of Santa Elena, this popular and friendly budget hotel appeals to backpackers. Bright and inviting private rooms and budget dorms are available. The hotel offers a short cut tour to Volcán Arenal, and also has a tourist information bureau. **www.pensionsantaelena.com**

MONTEVERDE Arco Iris Lodge $$$

Santa Elena, NE of bus stop ***Tel*** *645-5067* ***Fax*** *645-5022* ***Rooms*** *12*

Albergue Arco Iris is a superbly run budget hotel in the center of Santa Elena. Amid well-tended lawns are a dozen delightful stone-and-timber cottages built by craftsmen using locally available material. The hotel is well placed for both the Monteverde and Santa Elena Reserves. **www.arcoirislodge.com**

MONTEVERDE El Sol Retreat & Spa $$$

3 miles (5 km) SW of Santa Elena ***Tel*** *645-5838* ***Fax*** *645-5042* ***Rooms*** *3*

This eccentric hotel combines fantastic rustic decor and a fabulous mountainside position. The German-Spanish hosts offer their guests gourmet organic meals, holistic treatments, horseback rides, a spa with a sauna and pool, and six well-trained horses for rides. **www.elsolnuestro.com**

MONTEVERDE El Sapo Dorado $$$$

Cerro Plano, 0.5 mile (1 km) E of Santa Elena ***Tel*** *645-5010* ***Fax*** *645-5180* ***Rooms*** *30*

This hillside hotel has accommodations in lovely stone-and-timber cottages. Some suites offer the coziness of a fireplace, while others have open-air terraces overlooking the Gulf of Nicoya. El Sapo Dorado also boasts one of Monteverde's premier restaurants *(see p232)*. **www.sapodorado.com**

MONTEVERDE Monteverde Lodge $$$$

SE of Santa Elena ***Tel*** *257-0766* ***Fax*** *257-1665* ***Rooms*** *27*

A contemporary hotel set in exquisite gardens at the edge of Costa Rica's best-known cloud forest, Monteverde Lodge offers spacious rooms, a family-size Jacuzzi, and fine dining. Operated by Costa Rica Expeditions, it specializes in birding and nature hikes. **www.costaricaexpeditions.com**

NICOYA Hotel De Lujo Río Tempisque $$$

Hwy 21, 1 mile (1.6 km) N of Nicoya ***Tel*** *686-6650* ***Fax*** *686-6650* ***Rooms*** *30*

Located next to the main highway, this modern family-run hotel offers its guests comfortable rooms set in lush landscaped grounds. Solidly built, the rooms feature hardwood ceilings and clean, tiled bathrooms with oversize showers, and amenities such as coffee-makers and microwaves.

NOSARA Blew Dog Surf Camp $$

Beaches of Nosara, SW of Hwy 160, N end of Playa Guiones ***Tel*** *682-0080* ***Rooms*** *8*

This interestingly named surfers' hotel is located just a few minutes away from Playa Guiones. It has simply appointed yet comfortable cabins and a dormitory, as well as a lively bar with games. Turtle tours to Ostional, kayaking, sportfishing trips, and yoga and pilates are all on offer. **www.blewdogs.com**

NOSARA Hotel Café de Paris $$$

Beaches of Nosara, 4 miles (6 km) S of the airstrip ***Tel*** *682-0087* ***Fax*** *682-0089* ***Rooms*** *17*

What started as a great French-run bakery has expanded into an open-air restaurant *(see p232)*, bar, and hotel featuring a range of accommodations. The architecture of the hotel makes the most of the tropical breezes. A range of activities is available. Closed October. **www.cafedeparis.net**

NOSARA Lagarta Lodge $$$

Punta Nosara, 2 miles (3 km) S of Boca Nosara ***Tel*** *682-0035* ***Fax*** *682-0135* ***Rooms*** *6*

A Swiss-run hilltop hotel whose main appeal lies in the wonderful coast or hill vista that every room offers, as well as the restaurant and bar. Rooms are comfortable, although uninspired. Trails lead into Reserva Biológica Nosara, and canoeing, and bird- and turtle-watching trips are offered. **www.lagarta.com**

NOSARA Villa La Ventana B&B $$$$

Beaches of Nosara, 0.5 mile (1 km) E of Hwy 160 ***Tel*** *682-0316* ***Fax*** *682-0316* ***Rooms*** *3*

Sumptuous furnishings, a spectacular hilltop position, and a view of the ocean from every room and balcony are the most attractive aspects of this deluxe villa. Each suite comes with a wrought-iron canopied four-poster bed and private bath. **www.villalaventana.com**

PLAYA CARRILLO Guesthouse Casa Perico $

0.5 mile (1 km) NE of Puerto Carrillo ***Tel*** *656-0061* ***Rooms*** *4*

Casa Perico is a simple budget hotel with a hilltop setting and a great ocean view. It offers dorm rooms and a communal kitchen. The hotel is a two-minute walk from the beach, and scuba diving and horseback rides can also be arranged.

PLAYA CARRILLO El Sueño Tropical $$$

1 mile (1.6 km) SE of Puerto Carrillo ***Tel*** *656-0151* ***Fax*** *656-0152* ***Rooms*** *12*

Set amid vast beautiful gardens, this comfortable Italian-run hotel has two swimming pools, a dozen rooms, and a thatched hilltop restaurant *(see p232)*. Each room is decorated with bamboo and tropical pastels. Free transfers to Playa Carrillo's airstrip are available. **www.elsuenotropical.com**

PLAYA CARRILLO Hotel Guanamar $$$$

S of Playa Carrillo **Tel** *656-0054* **Fax** *656-0001* **Rooms** *41*

Sportfishing is the forté of this recently renovated hillside hotel. Hardwood decks encourage leisurely walks, and spectacular views are to be had from almost anywhere on the property. The hotel offers comfortable rooms, a small casino, and a broad range of activities. **www.hotelguanamar.com**

PLAYA CONCHAL Paradisus Playa Conchal Beach & Golf Resort $$$$$

Playa Brasilito, 2 miles (3 km) SW of Flamingo **Tel** *654-4123* **Fax** *654-4181* **Rooms** *302*

This deluxe all-inclusive resort nestles up to a sparkling white beach and is known for its championship golf course. The spacious rooms are elegantly appointed. Meals can be expensive but local restaurants are a short distance away. **www.solmelia.com**

PLAYA FLAMINGO Mariner Inn $$$

By the marina, central Playa Flamingo **Tel** *654-4081* **Fax** *654-4024* **Rooms** *12*

A favorite of yachting enthusiasts, this small two-story inn is conveniently located next to the marina. The lively open-air Spreader Bar has great views and is where anglers, divers, and surfers can relax and watch the activity at the marina from the comfort of leather rockers.

PLAYA FLAMINGO Flamingo Marina Resort $$$$

Atop hill, S of central Playa Flamingo **Tel** *654-4141* **Fax** *654-4035* **Rooms** *123*

This rambling hotel is perched on a lush hilltop close to the unspoiled expanse of Playa Flamingo. In addition to tropical breezes and spectacular views, it offers comfortable rooms, swimming pools, bars, and restaurants. It also has a boutique, dive shop, and activity center. **www.flamingomarina.com**

PLAYA GRANDE Hotel Bula Bula $$$$

S of El Mundo de la Tortuga, S end of Playa Grande **Tel** *653-0975* **Fax** *653-0978* **Rooms** *10*

This low-rise hotel offers intimate rooms with delightful decor and private baths. The open-air restaurant is run by a professional chef and opens on to lush gardens *(see p233)*. Also on offer are turtle tours and aquatic activities, as well as visits to Guaitíl and Arenal and Rincón de la Vieja Volcanoes. **www.hotelbulabula.com**

PLAYA GRANDE Hotel Las Tortugas $$$$

W of El Mundo de la Tortuga, N end of Playa Grande **Tel** *653-0423* **Fax** *653-0458* **Rooms** *11*

Situated right next to Parque Nacional Marino Las Baulas, this ecologically sensitive hotel is popular with surfers. Rooms facing the turtle-nesting beach lack ocean views as turtles are sensitive to light. However, the amiable atmosphere and excellent restaurant make up for this *(see p233)*. **www.tamarindo.com/tortugas**

PLAYA GRANDE Hotelito Si Si Si $$$$

1 mile (1.6 km) S of El Mundo de la Tortuga **Tel** *653-0715* **Fax** *653-0982* **Rooms** *4*

This stunning beachfront villa has a surfeit of marble. Each room has its own private terrace opening on to the pool and Jacuzzi. The hotel has a lively thatched beach bar, volleyball, tennis, and kayaking, and can arrange for a crab stampede during the wet season (May–November). **www.hotelitosisisi.com**

PLAYA HERMOSA Hotel La Finisterra $$$

Atop hill, W of main road, S end of Playa Hermosa **Tel** *672-0293* **Fax** *672-0227* **Rooms** *10*

Known for its fine dining *(see p233)*, this hilltop hotel also offers the best views in the region. The spacious rooms include private bathrooms. Breakfast is included in the price. Among other activities, guests can tour Río Bebedero in Parque Nacional Palo Verde in a *panga* (water-taxi) or explore the Río Tempisque estuary. **www.finisterra.net**

PLAYA HERMOSA Villas del Sueño $$$

W of main road, S end of Playa Hermosa **Tel** *672-0026* **Fax** *672-0026* **Rooms** *14*

Friendly Canadian hosts oversee this well-run hotel. It offers both spacious rooms and self-contained villas. There is gourmet dining in the open-air restaurant, which offers live music *(see p233)*. Activities include hiking, kayaking, rafting, and visits to Guaítil. **www.villadelsueno.com**

PLAYA NEGRA Hotel Playa Negra $$$

11 miles (18 km) S of Tamarindo **Tel** *658-8034* **Fax** *658-8035* **Rooms** *10*

This beachfront hotel resembles an African kraal with delightfully colorful, round, thatched bungalows. Their high roofs and multiple windows ensure that the breeze cools them naturally. Each bungalow has an attached bath. There is a large swimming pool and a restaurant *(see p233)*. Closed October. **www.playanegra.com**

PLAYA NEGRA Pablo's Picasso $$$

S of Los Pargos **Tel** *658-8158* **Rooms** *11*

Located near one of the premier surfing spots of Costa Rica and aimed mainly at surfers and backpackers, this budget hotel offers dorms and simple *cabinas* *(see p197)*. It also has a restaurant *(see p233)* and a bar with a pool table and videos. The rates include breakfast. Tamarindo is a short drive away. **http://pablosplayanegra.com**

PLAYA OCOTAL El Ocotal Beach Resort & Marina $$$$$

2 miles (3 km) SW of Playas del Coco **Tel** *670-0321* **Fax** *670-0083* **Rooms** *71*

Commanding a hilltop with spectacular views, this modern hotel specializes in scuba diving and sportfishing but is a splendid option for everyone. Also on offer are snorkeling, mountain biking, kayaking, tennis, and horseback riding. **www.ocotalresort.com**

PLAYA OSTIONAL Pacha Mama $

Limonal, 2 miles (3 km) NE of Ostional ***Tel*** *371-7941* ***Fax*** *228-5173* ***Rooms*** *35*

This no-frills spiritual retreat deep in the hills above Ostional operates as a commune, and offers guests the option of camping as well as thatched cottages. Meditation sessions, yoga, and silent retreats are offered. The minimum stay is one week. **www.pacha-mama.org**

PLAYA OSTIONAL Tree Tops Bed & Breakfast $$$$

San Juanillo, 3 miles (5 km) N of Ostional ***Tel*** *682-8098* ***Fax*** *682-8298* ***Rooms*** *1*

The owners rent out one room in their thatched home overlooking a cove surrounded by wildlife-rich forest. Guests are welcomed as family, and the meals served are delicious. Activities include swimming with turtles, riding, and sportfishing.

PLAYAS DEL COCO Hotel Puerta del Sol $$$$

SE of the plaza ***Tel*** *670-0195* ***Fax*** *670-0650* ***Rooms*** *10*

Decorated in warm tropical pastels, this small, intimate hotel is run with panache by its Italian owners. It is acclaimed for Sol y Luna, its open-air gourmet restaurant *(see p233)*. Just a few minutes away from Playas del Coco fishing village, the hotel offers diving, sportfishing, and boat tours.

PLAYAS DEL COCO Rancho Armadillo $$$$

1 mile (1.6 km) SE of Playas del Coco ***Tel*** *670-0108* ***Fax*** *670-0441* ***Rooms*** *6*

This hacienda-style hotel offers a tranquil setting amid expansive grounds. There is delightful decor in the spacious rooms, all of which have "rainforest" showers. The owner, a former chef, prepares meals by request. **www.ranchoarmadillo.com**

RINCÓN DE LA VIEJA Buena Vista Mountain Lodge & Adventure Center $$$

17 miles (27 km) NE of Liberia via Cañas Dulces ***Tel*** *661-8158* ***Fax*** *661-8158* ***Rooms*** *80*

This ecolodge, a former cattle ranch, is known for the range of activities it offers. Accommodation is in stone-and-timber cabins, and a rustic open-air restaurant serves *típico* (typical) meals, made using the lodge's own produce. **www.buenavistacr.com**

RINCÓN DE LA VIEJA Hacienda Lodge Guachipelín $$$

14 miles (22 km) NE of Liberia via Curubandé ***Tel*** *666-8075* ***Fax*** *442-1910* ***Rooms*** *40*

At the center of a working cattle and horse farm, this down-to-earth, cozy hotel is perfectly situated for exploring Parque Nacional Rincón de la Vieja on horseback. The hotel's wide, inviting verandas are great for spending a somnolent afternoon. **www.guachipelin.com**

RINCÓN DE LA VIEJA Rincón de la Vieja Lodge $$$

17 miles (27 km) NE of Liberia via Curubandé ***Tel*** *661-8198* ***Fax*** *661-8198* ***Rooms*** *22*

Close to the park entrance, and the nearest hotel to the volcano, this nature lodge has rustic wooden dorms, cabins, and bungalows spread throughout landscaped grounds. About 70 percent of the lodge's vast grounds are part of a reserve. The rates include meals. **www.rincondelaviejalodge.com**

SÁMARA Hotel Belvedere $$$

Playa Sámara, NE of soccer field ***Tel*** *656-0213* ***Fax*** *656-0215* ***Rooms*** *12*

This cozy hotel on the hillside, close to the beach, has Swiss-style chalets, some with air conditioning and king-size beds. The lush gardens contain a Jacuzzi and a swimming pool, which look out on to the ocean. Breakfast, included in the rate, is served on the terrace.

SÁMARA Hotel Casa del Mar $$$

Playa Sámara, E of soccer field ***Tel*** *656-0264* ***Fax*** *656-0129* ***Rooms*** *17*

This small, two-story bed-and-breakfast is run to high standards by its French-Canadian owners. The rooms have simple furnishings. There are hammocks and lounge chairs for relaxing in the tropical garden or by the Jacuzzi. Nearby is a 5-mile (8-km) long beach for quiet walks. **www.casadelmarsamara.com**

SANTA CRUZ Hotel La Calle de Alcala $$$

SE of Plaza de los Mangos ***Tel*** *680-0000* ***Fax*** *680-1633* ***Rooms*** *29*

Hotel La Calle de Alcala is an intimate modern hotel with delightful decor and an appealing open-air bar and restaurant. The air-conditioned rooms have attached bathrooms. Among the amenities it offers are a swimming pool and Jacuzzi, and two conference rooms.

TAMARINDO Cabinas Arco Iris $$

E of Parque Central ***Tel*** *653-0330* ***Fax*** *653-0330* ***Rooms*** *5*

Liberal use of batiks, rich tropical colors such as mango, payapa, and peach, and counter-culture elements infuse this off-beat gem with irresistible charm. Karate and yoga are taught, and tattoos and massages are offered. There is a communal kitchen. **www.hotelarcoiris.com**

TAMARINDO Hostel La Botella de Leche $$

SW of Plaza Colonial ***Tel*** *653-0944* ***Rooms*** *12*

This centrally air-conditioned modern hostel for surfers and backpackers offers exceptional value. Guests can choose from dorms or private rooms. There is a communal kitchen, lockers, and Internet access, and surfboard rental is offered. **www.labotelladeleche.com**

TAMARINDO Luna Llena $$$$

SE of Iguana Surf **Tel** 653-0082 **Fax** 653-0120 **Rooms** 13

This brightly colored, intimate hotel is run to professional standards by its Italian owners. Stone pathways run between conical thatched cottages, whose comfortable rooms exude good taste. All the cottages have private bathrooms. **www.hotellunallena.com**

TAMARINDO Cala Luna Hotel & Villas $$$$$

1 mile (1.6 km) W of central Tamarindo **Tel** 653-0214 **Fax** 653-0213 **Rooms** 38

Rich earth colors and polished hardwoods grace this deluxe hotel with a New Mexico theme. Guests can choose to stay in rooms or villas. Each room has a patio terrace. The villas have their own private pool, parking, and kitchen. Typical Guanacastecan cuisine *(see p223)* is on offer in the restaurant. **www.calaluna.com**

TAMARINDO Capitán Suizo $$$$$

0.5 mile (1 km) SW of Plaza Colonial **Tel** 653-0075 **Fax** 653-0292 **Rooms** 30

This luxurious beachfront hotel is set in lush gardens that have a free-form swimming pool. The elegant rooms use plenty of natural stone and hardwood. The open-air restaurant is one of the area's finest *(see p234)*. The hotel is a member of Small Distinctive Hotels of Costa Rica *(see p198)*. **www.hotelcapitansuizo.com**

TAMARINDO Sueño del Mar Bed & Breakfast $$$$$

Playa Langosta, 0.5 mile (1 km) S of Tamarindo **Tel** 653-0284 **Fax** 653-0558 **Rooms** 6

This colonial-era home has been converted into a gracious family-run bed-and-breakfast. Rooms boast timber beams, terra-cotta tiles, and exquisite furnishings. Delicious breakfasts are served in the garden, which opens onto the beach. **www.sueno-del-mar.com**

TAMARINDO Tamarindo Diría $$$$$

E of Plaza Colonial **Tel** 653-0032 **Fax** 653-0208 **Rooms** 127

With a beachfront location in the center of Tamarindo, this upscale resort has a beautiful aesthetic. The restaurant is set under a tall *matapalo* tree on Tamarindo beach. The hotel also has two bars and a small casino. Among other activities, it offers tennis, golf, turtle-watching, and jungle boat rides. **www.hotel-tamarindo-diria-info.com**

TILARÁN Hotel El Sueño $$

N of the plaza **Tel** 695-5347 **Fax** 695-5347 **Rooms** 15

This is a clean, well-run hotel with a friendly ambience and no-frills rooms at bargain prices. It is well placed as a pleasant stop en route to and from Laguna de Arenal. Rooms, all on the second floor, surround a skylit courtyard. No meals are offered, but there's a restaurant below.

TILARÁN La Carreta Hotel $$

E of the plaza **Tel** 695-6593 **Fax** 695-6654 **Rooms** 6

Some of the charm of this hotel has gone since the departure of the original owner, but it still retains its delightful, individually themed rooms: one room has an Oriental motif. Rooms in the front section are to be preferred over newer rooms overlooking the courtyard garden, which has a hot tub.

THE NORTHERN ZONE

CAÑO NEGRO Hotel Caño Negro Fishing Club $$$

NW of Caño Negro village **Tel** 656-0071 **Fax** 656-0260 **Rooms** 14

This sportfishing lodge on the edge of Lago Caño Negro has spacious modern cabins set in a former citrus orchard. In addition to sportfishing packages, the lodge offers horseback tours and nature excursions. A souvenir shop is located on the grounds, and fishing tackle is available for sale. **www.canonegro.com**

CHACHAGUA Hotel Bosque de Chachagua $$$$

6 miles (10 km) SE of La Fortuna **Tel** 239-6464 **Fax** 239-6868 **Rooms** 30

At the base of a mountain range, the Chachagua Rainforest Lodge is housed in a working cattle ranch located in a private rainforest reserve. Comfortable and spacious cabins are set amid lovely gardens, and an open-air restaurant overlooks a corral. **www.chachaguarainforesthotel.com**

CIUDAD QUESADA Hotel Occidental El Tucano $$$$

5 miles (8 km) E of Ciudad Quesada **Tel** 460-6000 **Fax** 460-1692 **Rooms** 87

Sitting on the lower slopes of the thickly forested Cordillera Central, this spa resort hotel is famed for its thermal treatments. Rooms are generously appointed. Among its other facilities are a casino, tennis, mini-golf, and hiking trails. **www.occidentalhotels.com**

LA FORTUNA Gringo Pete's Hostel $

SE of the plaza **Tel** 479-8521 **Fax** 479-8521 **Rooms** 5

This rambling backpackers' hostel has colorful decor, and offers both dorms (one open-air) and private rooms. Guests can use the communal kitchen, and there's a barbecue grill. Facilities include lockers, hammocks and sofas in a simple lounge, as well as a travel service.

LA FORTUNA Luigi's Hotel $$$

2 blocks W of the plaza **Tel** *479-9636* **Fax** *479-9898* **Rooms** *20*

This two-story hotel on the north edge of town has comfortable rooms with verandas. Special packages are offered for groups. With one of the best restaurants in town *(see p234)*, Luigi's Hotel also has a small casino and Internet access for guests. **www.luigislodge.com**

LA VIRGEN DE SARAPIQUÍ Rancho Leona $

On the banks of Río Sarapiquí **Tel** *761-1019* **Rooms** *5*

Appealing to backpackers, this simple, offbeat hotel hangs over the banks of Río Sarapiquí. Some of the rooms have bunks. The lodge boasts a small spa. The main activity here is kayaking, with the owner leading kayak trips. Spanish language courses are also offered. **www.rancholeona.com**

LA VIRGEN DE SARAPIQUÍ Centro Neotrópico SarapiquíS Ecolodge $$$$

N of La Virgen de Sarapiquí **Tel** *761-1004* **Fax** *761-1415* **Rooms** *36*

Part of a broad-based ecological center *(see p155)*, this classy contemporary hotel boasts architecture inspired by traditional indigenous building techniques, and corresponding earthy interiors. The fine open-air restaurant and bar has the rainforest close at hand. **www.sarapiquis.org**

LAGUNA DE ARENAL Chalet Nicholas $$$

1 mile (1.6 km) W of Nuevo Arenal **Tel** *694-4041* **Fax** *695-5387* **Rooms** *3*

This bargain-priced, three-story bed-and-breakfast offers intimate rooms. Chalet Nicholas is run by welcoming hosts, who serve organic meals and arrange horseback rides. Trails lead into an adjacent forest reserve. **www.chaletnicholas.com**

LAGUNA DE ARENAL Lake Coter Eco-Lodge $$$

4 miles (6 km) NW of Nuevo Arenal **Tel** *289-6060* **Fax** *288-0123* **Rooms** *46*

This nature lodge is known for its wide range of activities, including kayaking, canoeing, freshwater fishing, hiking, horseback riding, and bird-watching. The duplex cabins are preferred over standard rooms, particularly for the views of Volcán Arenal as well as Arenal and Coter Lakes. **www.ecolodgecostarica.com**

LAGUNA DE ARENAL Mystica Lodge $$$

10 miles (16 km) W of Nuevo Arenal **Tel** *692-1001* **Rooms** *6*

The charming Italian owners tend this intimate hotel with care. Rooms have a romantic aesthetic, and verandas offer splendid views. Gourmet meals are served at the restaurant, which is dominated by a baker's oven *(see p234)*. There is also a small souvenir shop. **www.mysticalodge.com**

LAGUNA DE ARENAL Villa Decary $$$$

2 miles (3 km) E of Nuevo Arenal **Tel** *383-3012* **Fax** *694-4330* **Rooms** *8*

Originally a coffee farm, this modern bed-and-breakfast hotel overlooking tranquil Lake Arenal has a pleasing home-away-from-home feel. It is popular with birders as well as gay travelers. Bird books and binoculars are available for guests. **www.villadecary.com**

LAGUNA DE ARENAL Hotel La Mansion Inn $$$$$

5 miles (8 km) E of Nuevo Arenal **Tel** *692-8018* **Fax** *692-8019* **Rooms** *16*

This deluxe option, with a spectacular hillside location, boasts an elegant restaurant *(see p235)*. Rooms are graciously appointed, and have broad verandas with rocking chairs. The suites and deluxe rooms have TVs and minibars. Horseback rides are included in the rates, and rowboats are available. **www.lamansionarenal.com**

LAS HORQUETAS Rara Avis $$$

9 miles (14 km) W of Las Horquetas **Tel** *764-3131* **Fax** *764-4187* **Rooms** *18*

One of Costa Rica's original nature lodges and private rainforest reserves *(see p159)*, Rara Avis is deep in the rainforest. The rustic accommodations include a bare-bones treetop cabin. Rates are for a two-night stay and include meals. **www.rara-avis.com**

MUELLE Tilajari Resort Hotel and Country Club $$$$

12 miles (19 km) NW of Ciudad Quesada **Tel** *469-9091* **Fax** *469-9095* **Rooms** *76*

An expansive multifaceted resort on the banks of the Río San Carlos, Tilajari Resort Hotel and Country Club is popular for business meetings. The hotel has a wide range of excursions and facilities, including a gift shop, tennis courts, and botanical and butterfly gardens. **www.tilajari.com**

PARQUE NACIONAL VOLCÁN ARENAL Arenal Observatory Lodge $$$$

5 miles (8 km) SE of park entrance **Tel** *692-2070* **Fax** *290-8427* **Rooms** *35*

Spectacularly located on the flanks of Volcán Chato, this modern ecolodge offers dramatic views of Volcán Arenal from its rooms as well as its pleasant restaurant *(see p235)*. Accommodations range from bunks in cabins to luxury rooms and a four-bedroom farmhouse. Guided hikes are offered. **www.arenal-observatory.co.cr**

PN VOLCÁN ARENAL Montaña de Fuego Resort & Spa $$$$

4 miles (6 km) W of La Fortuna **Tel** *460-1220* **Fax** *460-1455* **Rooms** *50*

The comfortable wooden cabins of this luxury hotel have large picture windows opening to the volcano. Trails lace the lush gardens. Helicopter tours are available, as well as activities such as horseback riding and whitewater rafting. The resort has a souvenir shop and a full-service spa. **www.montanadefuego.com**

PARQUE NACIONAL VOLCÁN ARENAL Volcano Lodge $$$$

4 miles (6 km) W of La Fortuna ***Tel*** *460-6080* ***Fax*** *460-6020* ***Rooms*** *62*

Located on the north side of Volcán Arenal, this modern hotel offers splendid vistas toward the volcano from its two-bedroom cottages; rockers are provided on the patio. Furnishings are comfortable, albeit unremarkable. The restaurant serves fine meals. **www.volcanolodge.com**

PUERTO VIEJO DE SARAPIQUÍ Posada Andrea Cristina $$

0.5 mile (1 km) W of Puerto Viejo ***Tel*** *766-6265* ***Fax*** *766-6265* ***Rooms*** *4*

This comfortable bed-and-breakfast is set in a forested garden, which draws varieties of wildlife. The lodge is run to high standards by an active conservationist and his wife, who cooks excellent meals. The naturalist owner takes guests on informative tours to nearby attractions. **www.andreacristina.com**

PUERTO VIEJO DE SARAPIQUÍ La Selva Biological Station $$$$

2 miles (3 km) S of Puerto Viejo ***Tel*** *766-6565* ***Fax*** *766-6535* ***Rooms*** *10*

The lodge at this well-known biological station *(see p158)*, operated by the Organization of Tropical Studies (OTS), offers dormitories as well as private rooms. The rates include set meals at fixed hours. Reservations are essential at La Selva, which appeals mainly to nature lovers. **www.ots.ac.cr**

PUERTO VIEJO DE SARAPIQUÍ Selva Verde $$$$$

5 miles (8 km) W of Puerto Viejo ***Tel*** *766-6800* ***Fax*** *766-6011* ***Rooms*** *45*

A world-renowned ecolodge and private reserve *(see p156)*, Selva Verde specializes in birding and nature hikes. The adventure activities have educational components, and there are conservation programs for student or teacher groups. The spacious rooms have canopied verandas, and the room rate includes food. **www.selvaverde.com**

THE CARIBBEAN

BARRA DEL COLORADO Río Colorado Lodge $$$$$

W of Barra del Colorado Sur airstrip ***Tel*** *710-6879* ***Fax*** *231-5987* ***Rooms*** *18*

Built on stilts at the mouth of Río Colorado, this sportfishing lodge offers well-equipped fiberglass fishing boats with knowledgeable guides and a well-stocked tackle shop. Among its other attractions are a small zoo, games room, and boat tours into the nearby rainforest. **www.riocoloradolodge.com**

BARRA DEL COLORADO Silver King Lodge $$$$$

W of Barra del Colorado Sur airstrip ***Tel*** *711-0708* ***Fax*** *711-0708* ***Rooms*** *10*

Adjoining Río Colorado Lodge and rising over a swampy riverfront, this all-wood sportfishing lodge has spacious cabins linked by boardwalks. Several fishing packages are on offer. The lodge is closed mid-June through August, and also from mid-November through December. **www.silverkinglodge.net**

CAHUITA Alby Lodge $$

SE of bus stop and plaza ***Tel*** *755-0031* ***Fax*** *755-0031* ***Rooms*** *4*

Run by an Austrian, the lodge is situated amid lawns close to the beach. It features charming thatched and stilt-legged cabins, spaced well apart for privacy. Each small, simply appointed cabin has a hammock, plus mosquito nets over the bed. Guests can make use of a communal kitchen. **www.albylodge.com**

CAHUITA Atlantida Lodge $$$

Playa Negra 1 mile (1.6 km) N of Cahuita village ***Tel*** *755-0115* ***Fax*** *755-0213* ***Rooms*** *30*

This lodge is set in verdant grounds a stone's throw from the beach. Thatch and bamboo roofs add to the tropical feel, as do hammocks in the open-air restaurant. This modestly priced hotel with duplex cabins is conscientiously run by French-Canadian owners. **www.atlantida.co.cr**

CAHUITA El Encanto Bed & Breakfast Inn $$$

Playa Negra, 0.5 mile (1 km) N of Cahuita village ***Tel*** *755-0113* ***Fax*** *755-0432* ***Rooms*** *7*

Set in a serene garden infused with a Buddhist aesthetic, this is a delightful family-run hotel. Tasteful fabrics and art pieces grace the rooms, which vary in size. The hotel organizes several activities such as kayak tours, horseback riding, snorkeling, scuba diving, and dolphin-watching. **www.elencantobedandbreakfast.com**

CAHUITA Kelly Creek Cabins & Restaurant $$$

E of bus stop, next to Kelly Creek ranger station ***Tel*** *755-0007* ***Rooms*** *4*

Located adjacent to the entrance of Parque Nacional Cahuita, this beachfront hotel has spacious wooden cabins with broad verandas. A surf break at one end of the lovely beach is great for surfing. The open-air restaurant serves Spanish fare; an excellent barbeque is also available. **www.hotelkellycreek.com**

CAHUITA Magellan Inn $$$

Playa Negra, 3 miles (5 km) N of Cahuita village ***Tel*** *755-0035* ***Fax*** *755-0035* ***Rooms*** *6*

The exquisite grounds and gourmet cuisine *(see p235)* are the top draws at this family-run hotel at the far north end of Cahuita. All rooms have verandas overlooking a sunken pool and the beautiful gardens. The clean beaches of Cahuita are within walking distance. **allcostaricatravel.com/magellan.html**

Key to Price Guide *see p200* **Key to Symbols** *see back cover flap*

GUÁPILES Casa Río Blanco Ecolodge $$$

Río Blanco, 4 miles (6 km) W of Guápiles ***Tel*** *710-4124* ***Fax*** *710-4124* ***Rooms*** *6*

This delightful riverside bed-and-breakfast at the edge of the forest is run by a charming couple. Cabins boast rich and calming decor. It offers nature trails and splendid wildlife viewing – over 300 species of birds have been recorded in the surrounding forests. **www.casarioblanco.com**

PUERTO LIMÓN Hotel Park $$$

Calle 1 and Ave 3 ***Tel*** *758-3476* ***Fax*** *758-4364* ***Rooms*** *32*

This clean, well-run hotel has one of the town's best restaurants plus secure parking (a requirement in this town). Although fairly simple, the rooms are adequate. It's worth paying extra for an oceanfront room with balcony. Locals are drawn to the bar.

PUERTO VIEJO DE TALAMANCA Chimúri Beach Cottages $$

Playa Negra, 1 mile (1.6 km) W of Puerto Viejo ***Tel*** *750-0119* ***Fax*** *750-0119* ***Rooms*** *3*

This enclave of wooden cabins, of which two are two-story, offers a peaceful beachside retreat a 20-minute walk from the village. Mauricio Salazar, the friendly Bribri owner, offers excursions to Reserva Indígena KeköLdi *(see p173)*. **http://greencoast.com/chimuri.htm**

PUERTO VIEJO DE TALAMANCA Kaya's Place $$

Playa Negra, W of Puerto Viejo ***Tel*** *750-0690* ***Fax*** *750-0713* ***Rooms*** *26*

This creatively conceived two-story hotel, built of wood in an Afro-Caribbean style, is run by Rastafarians. Located steps from the beach, the hotel has a large terrace where guests can enjoy superb views of the ocean from hammocks. Movies are screened in the lounge. **www.kayasplace.com**

PUERTO VIEJO DE TALAMANCA Playa Punta Uva Cabinas $$

Punta Uva, 3 miles (5 km) E of Puerto Viejo ***Tel*** *750-0431* ***Rooms*** *3*

This cozy, charming lodging is set in a lush palm-shaded garden edging up to the sands. The multilingual Dutch owner is a welcoming conversationalist, and tends with care the gingerbread-trimmed cabins, constructed from exotic local hardwoods. **www.puntauva.com**

PUERTO VIEJO DE TALAMANCA Rockings J's $$

E of the Puerto Viejo bus stop, on the road to Manzanillo ***Tel*** *750-0657* ***Rooms*** *10*

This is a well-run and popular surfers' hostel with a choice of accommodations, including camping, canopied hammocks, dorms, and private rooms. The ambience is lively and colorful. Surf boards and bicycles can be rented. **www.rockingjs.com**

PUERTO VIEJO DE TALAMANCA Casa Verde Lodge $$$

SE of the Puerto Viejo bus stop ***Tel*** *750-0015* ***Fax*** *750-0047* ***Rooms*** *13*

Superbly run by a Swiss owner, this clinically clean hotel with spacious rooms offers a solid budget-priced bargain. It boasts a gift store and poison-dart frog display, and also arranges tours. Several eateries serving excellent local and international cuisine are just a few blocks away. **www.cabinascasaverde.com**

PUERTO VIEJO DE TALAMANCA La Costa de Papito $$$

Playa Cocles, 1 mile (1.6 km) E of Puerto Viejo ***Tel*** *750-0704* ***Fax*** *750-0080* ***Rooms*** *10*

Located in front of the white expanse of Playa Cocles and surrounded by tropical gardens on the edge of a forest, this hotel has spacious hardwood cabins with endearing jungly decor, huge verandas, and attached baths. Breakfast is served on the verandas or in the main house. **www.greencoast.com/papito.htm**

PUERTO VIEJO DE TALAMANCA Shawandha Lodge $$$$

Playa Chiquita, 3 miles (5 km) E of Puerto Viejo ***Tel*** *750-0018* ***Fax*** *750-0037* ***Rooms*** *11*

Gracious contemporary decor in spacious thatched cabins highlight this romantic resort, which extends up to the rainforest. The open-air restaurant is acclaimed for its French-inspired cuisine *(see p236)*. **www.shawandhalodge.com**

PUERTO VIEJO DE TALAMANCA Samasati Nature Retreat $$$$$

Hone Creek, 2 miles (3 km) W of Puerto Viejo ***Tel*** *224-1870* ***Fax*** *224-5032* ***Rooms*** *18*

Nestled high in forested hills, this rustic hotel specializes in yoga and holistic practices. Choose from simple cabins with shared bathrooms, bungalows, or self-contained two-story houses. Wildlife viewing is fabulous. A 4WD is required to get there. **www.samasati.com**

SELVA BANANITO RESERVE Selva Bananito Lodge $$$$$

16 miles (26 km) SW of Puerto Limón ***Tel*** *253-8118* ***Fax*** *280-0820* ***Rooms*** *11*

Close to Reserva Biológica Hitoy-Cerere, this rustic rainforest lodge has stilt-legged cabins, splendid for nature viewing and active adventures. Basic meals, included in rates, are served family style. A 4WD is essential for access. **www.selvabananito.com**

TORTUGUERO Miss Junie's $$

N of public dock, Tortuguero village ***Tel*** *711-0683* ***Rooms*** *12*

A simple two-story hotel run by a delightful hostess who serves Caribbean soul food *(see p236)*. Set close to the lagoon, the rooms have wicker furnishings, ceramic floors, shuttered windows with screens, and ceiling fans. Each has hot water in private bathrooms.

TORTUGUERO Tortuga Lodge & Gardens $$$$

3 miles (5 km) N of Tortuguero village ***Tel*** *257-0766* ***Fax*** *257-1665* ***Rooms*** *27*

Spacious rooms are on offer at this well-run eco- and sportfishing lodge with lush grounds. Top-class nature guides are on hand to take guests on turtle- or other wildlife-watching trips. It has family-style dining. Various packages are available. **www.costaricaexpeditions.com**

TORTUGUERO Laguna Lodge $$$$$

1 mile (1.6 km) N of Tortuguero village ***Tel*** *225-3740* ***Fax*** *283-8031* ***Rooms*** *80*

This riverside ecolodge specializing in nature excursions has butterfly and botanical gardens, and an atmospheric restaurant overhanging the waters. Package rates include transfers, buffet meals, and nature tours. Fishing trips with experienced guides are available on request. **www.lagunatortuguero.com**

THE SOUTHERN ZONE

BAHÍA DRAKE Jinetes de Osa $$$$

S of Agujitas ***Tel*** *236-5637* ***Fax*** *241-2906* ***Rooms*** *9*

Specializing in scuba diving, this hotel stands amid rainforest on the beach. The rooms, although simple, are clean and comfortable. Rates include meals in an open-air restaurant, and fresh bread and fresh produce supplement the hotel's Mexican and Italian cuisine. **www.costaricadiving.com**

BAHÍA DRAKE Aguila de Osa Inn $$$$$

0.5 mile (1 km) S of Agujitas ***Tel*** *296-2190* ***Fax*** *232-7722* ***Rooms*** *13*

Tucked away in a canyon at the mouth of Río Agujitas, this lodge specializes in scuba diving and sportfishing. Spacious yet simply furnished rooms stairstep a steep hillside. Included in the room rate are quality meals served at the open-air restaurant *(see p236)*. **www.aguiladeosainn.com**

BAHÍA DRAKE La Paloma Lodge $$$$$

Playa Cocalito, 1 mile (1.6 km) S of Agujitas ***Tel*** *239-2801* ***Fax*** *239-0954* ***Rooms*** *11*

La Paloma is a deluxe family-run clifftop hotel set amidst lush grounds with dramatic sunset views. The spacious and cozy cabins have wide balconies with hammocks. A range of activities are offered, including night hikes, all of which are covered by the room rate. The lodge is closed in October. **www.lapalomalodge.com**

CABO MATAPALO Buena Esperanza $$$

Playa Sombrero, 10 miles (16 km) S of Puerto Jiménez ***Tel*** *735-5531* ***Fax*** *735-5648* ***Rooms*** *3*

A colorful and offbeat charmer, this hotel appeals mainly to the surfing and backpacker set. Its communal rooms have shared bathrooms, which are open to the elements. Buena Esperanza has a bar-restaurant that is very popular and usually filled to capacity.

CABO MATAPALO Bosque del Cabo $$$$$

12 miles (19 km) S of Puerto Jiménez ***Tel*** *735-5206* ***Fax*** *735-5206* ***Rooms*** *12*

This family-run clifftop hotel combines simplicity with luxury. The surrounding forest abounds in wildlife, and scarlet macaws nest on the property. The open-air, solar-powered restaurant serves delicious food, which is included in the room rate. Yoga, a canopy tour, and various excursions are on offer. **www.bosquedelcabo.com**

CABO MATAPALO Lapa Ríos $$$$$

9 miles (14 km) S of Puerto Jiménez ***Tel*** *735-5130* ***Fax*** *735-5179* ***Rooms*** *16*

Set in a private nature reserve, this deluxe jungle lodge is superb for birding and wildlife viewing. The lodge offers breathtaking ocean vistas and the airy and open bamboo bungalows have great romantic appeal. The gourmet restaurant *(see p236)* is set beneath a *palenque* (soaring circular thatched cover). **www.laparios.com**

CARATE Corcovado Lodge Tent Camp $$$$

1 mile (1.6 km) W of Carate ***Tel*** *257-0766* ***Fax*** *257-1665* ***Rooms*** *20*

On the edge of Parque Nacional Corcovado, this beachfront camp has a splendid safari-style jungle atmosphere. Bathrooms are shared, and guests eat in a restaurant with a thatched roof. The most popular camp activity is wildlife watching from a canopy platform. Meals are included in the room rate. **www.costaricaexpeditions.com**

CARATE Lookout Inn $$$$

0.5 mile (1 km) E of Carate ***Tel*** *735-5431* ***Fax*** *735-5431* ***Rooms*** *8*

This three-story hotel has a splendid hillside location good for spotting scarlet macaws. A wooden staircase takes guests up the mountainside to spectacular ocean views. A range of activities is offered, and guests can even try panning for gold in Río Carate. Room rates include meals. **www.lookout-inn.com**

CARATE Luna Lodge $$$$$

0.5 mile (1 km) N of Carate ***Tel*** *380-5036* ***Rooms*** *15*

This peaceful rainforest lodge offers guests a choice of airy thatched cabins and safari-style tents. A traditional, conical, thatched restaurant-bar enjoys a spectacular setting. Meals are included in the rates. A variety of tours are available. A 4WD is required for access. **www.lunalodge.com**

Key to Price Guide *see p200* **Key to Symbols** *see back cover flap*

CIUDAD NEILY Hotel Andrea $$

23 miles (37 km) E of Golfito ***Tel*** *783-3784* ***Fax*** *783-1057* ***Rooms*** *45*

Located in the heart of Ciudad Neily, this modern Colonial-style hotel has comfortable rooms and a fine restaurant *(see p236)*. The room rates are a bargain considering the amenities the hotel offers. **www.hotelvillabosque.com**

DOMINICAL Cabinas San Clemente $$

W from the soccer field ***Tel*** *787-0026* ***Fax*** *787-0158* ***Rooms*** *16*

This is a friendly hostel aimed at surfers, located just a few steps away from the beach. Some rooms have air conditioning and hot water, and some of the newer rooms have wraparound verandas. Fully furnished houses are also offered. The hostel's popular bar and grill *(see p236)* is a short walk away.

DOMINICAL Refugio Nacional de Vida Silvestre Barú $$$

2 miles (3 km) N of Dominical ***Tel*** *787-0003* ***Fax*** *787-0057* ***Rooms*** *6*

This wildlife refuge *(see p182)* has modestly furnished cabins, each with a beautiful view of the forest and located within a short walk of the beach. Camping is an option. A wide selection of activities is available, from spending a night in the jungle to bird-watching hikes. **www.haciendabaru.com**

DOMINICAL Hotel Roca Verde $$$$

0.5 mile (1 km) S of Dominical ***Tel*** *787-0036* ***Fax*** *787-0013* ***Rooms*** *10*

The highlights of this small hotel near the beach are the charming *cabinas* (cottages) and an open and airy bar and restaurant with frequent live music, very popular with the surf crowd *(see p236)*. Kayaking, canopy tours, sportfishing, and biking are on offer. **www.rocaverde.net**

DOMINICAL Villas Río Mar Jungle & Beach Resort $$$$

0.5 mile (1 km) N of Dominical ***Tel*** *787-0052* ***Fax*** *787-0054* ***Rooms*** *40*

Set on the banks of Río Barú and surrounded by tropical forests, this hotel has recently renovated thatched bungalows in lush gardens. There is a large swimming pool with a wet bar and a Jacuzzi, a tennis court, and a romantic restaurant housed in a *palenque*. **www.villasriomar.com**

ESCALERAS Bella Vista Lodge $$$

4 miles (6 km) SE of Dominical ***Tel*** *388-0155* ***Rooms*** *5*

Bella Vista is a horse ranch perched on a dramatic mountaintop. The wooden cabins have bathrooms and porches with hammocks. The rooms in the lodge have private bathrooms, and share other facilities. Horseback rides are available. **www.bellavistalodge.com**

ESCALERAS Pacific Edge $$$

3 miles (5 km) S of Dominical ***Tel*** *787-8010* ***Fax*** *787-8080* ***Rooms*** *4*

With a dramatic location 600 ft (183 m) up on a ridge, this delightful hotel is surrounded by primary forests perfect for birding. Simple cabins have charming touches. The hotel is well placed for both Marino Ballena and Manuel Antonio National Parks. **www.pacificedge.info**

GOLFITO La Purruja Lodge $$

2 miles (3 km) SE of Golfito ***Tel*** *775-1054* ***Rooms*** *5*

This well-run hotel has spacious rooms at bargain prices. Set amid beautifully tended gardens, its cabins provide easy access to the rainforest to the rear. Tents are permitted. Excellent bird-watching is on offer in the hotel premises and the surrounding area. **www.purruja.com**

GOLFITO Hotel Centro Turístico Samoa $$$

N of Pueblo Civil ***Tel*** *775-0233* ***Fax*** *775-0573* ***Rooms*** *14*

This clean and modestly furnished waterfront hotel has spacious rooms. The hotel marina has facilities for sailboats and sportfishing boats. The lively bar and restaurant have excellent views of the marina and the surrounding gulf *(see p237)*. The hotel also contains the Museo Marino *(see p192)*. **www.samoadelsur.com**

GOLFITO Banana Bay Marina $$$$

S of the plaza ***Tel*** *775-0838* ***Fax*** *775-0735* ***Rooms*** *4*

Banana Bay Marina is a small contemporary hotel with delightful decor. Its quiet, comfortable rooms look out on to the marina and have private bathrooms. The Bilge Bar & Grill is one of the best in town *(see p236)*, and the hotel also offers Internet access. **www.bananabaymarina.com**

LAS CRUCES Las Cruces Biological Station $$$$

4 miles (6 km) S of San Vito ***Tel*** *773-4004* ***Fax*** *773-3665* ***Rooms*** *12*

This research center *(see p179)* has spacious and airy wooden cabins overlooking lush forest. All cabins have balconies and private baths. There are refectory-style meals in a dining room with views of the Talamanca Mountains. Guided nature hikes are on offer. Reservations are essential. **www.ots.ac.cr**

LOS PATOS Albergue Ecoturístico Cerro de Oro $$$

6 miles (10 km) W of La Palma, 3 miles (5 km) S of Rincón ***Tel*** *248-2538* ***Fax*** *248-1659* ***Rooms*** *8*

Located on the border of Parque Nacional Corcovado, this ecotourism project is run by a small local gold miners' cooperative. The back-to-basics hostel has only cold water. Camping is permitted. Guided hikes and horseback trips are offered, including a Gold Tour and a Medicinal Herb Tour.

OJOCHAL Finca Bavaria $$$

0.5 mile (1 km) E of Playa Ballena ***Tel*** *(49) 863-0216 (Germany)* ***Rooms*** *5*

This German-run property is set in hilltop gardens. The spacious rooms have bamboo decor and a romantic aesthetic. Ocean views can be enjoyed from the terraces. There are nature trails for guests who wish to enjoy the solitude of the surroundings. **www.finca-bavaria.de**

OJOCHAL Villas Gaia $$$

Playa Tortuga, 0.5 mile (1 km) W of Ojochal ***Tel*** *244-0316* ***Fax*** *244-0316* ***Rooms*** *12*

Providing easy access to Playa Tortuga and the Terraba-Sierpe mangrove ecosystem, this colorful property offers scuba diving and other activities, plus a gourmet restaurant *(see p237)*. The hilltop swimming pool offers spectacular views of ocean sunsets. **www.villasgaia.com**

OJOCHAL The Lookout at Turtle Beach $$$$$

Playa Tortuga, 0.5 mile (1 km) W of Ojochal ***Tel*** *378-7473* ***Rooms*** *10*

Offered for group rentals only, this luxury option is set in lovely landscaped hilltop grounds. There is delightful pastel decor in the *casitas* (cottages), which have private patios and splendid views. Gourmet meals are on offer, and a range of activities is available. **www.hotelcostarica.com**

PARQUE INTERNACIONAL LA AMISTAD Finca Anael $$

Reserva Biológica Durika, 11 miles (18 km) E of Buenos Aires ***Tel*** *730-0657* ***Fax*** *730-0657* ***Rooms*** *9*

A simple lifestyle is the hallmark of this ecologically sustainable mountain farm. Accommodation is in rustic cabins, with meals being included in the room rates. The *finca* (farm) can arrange guided nature hikes. A 4WD is required for access. **www.durika.org**

PARQUE INTERNACIONAL LA AMISTAD La Amistad Lodge $$$$

Las Mellizas, 17 miles (27 km) NE of San Vito ***Tel*** *228-8671* ***Fax*** *289-7858* ***Rooms*** *10*

This alpine coffee farm adjoining La Amistad is a good base for exploring the reserve. The rooms and cabins, although simple, are comfortable. The lodge specializes in nature hikes and horseback riding, including to two high-mountain camps. It can be reached only by a 4WD. **www.laamistad.com**

PAVONES Cabinas La Ponderosa $$$

2 miles (3 km) S of Pavones, on the road to Punta Banco ***Tel*** *824-4145* ***Rooms*** *6*

This is a popular beachfront surfers' hostel with comfortable, casual cabins. All cabins have private bathrooms, outdoor sitting area, and either fans or air conditioning. Volleyball, basketball, horseback rides, and forest trails are also available for those who want break from surfing. **www.cabinaslaponderosa.com**

PAVONES Casa Siempre Domingo Bed & Breakfast $$$

1 mile (1.6 km) S of Pavones ***Tel*** *820-4709* ***Rooms*** *4*

A bargain-priced family-run bed-and-breakfast set in lush gardens. The elevation and open interiors allow for constant breezes and the tropical decor adds to the ambience. Miles of secluded beaches lend themselves to quiet walks, and trails lead into rainforest. **www.casa-domingo.com**

PAVONES Tiskita Lodge $$$$$

Punta Banco, 3 miles (5 km) S of Pavones ***Tel*** *296-8125* ***Fax*** *296-8133* ***Rooms*** *16*

This rustic hilltop ecolodge is part of a fruit farm and forest reserve fabulous for viewing wildlife. "Rainforest" bathrooms are made of river stones. Meals, served family-style in the open-air farmstead, and guided nature hikes are included. Closed mid-September to mid-October. **www.tiskita-lodge.co.cr**

PIEDRAS BLANCAS Esquinas Rainforest Lodge $$$$$

Las Gambas, 6 miles (10 km) NE of Golfito ***Tel*** *775-0140* ***Fax*** *775-0140* ***Rooms*** *14*

Adjoining Parque Nacional Piedras Blancas, this pleasant ecolodge has comfortable rooms with private bathrooms and terraces. Guided nature hikes, Golfo Dulce kayak tours, and other activities are offered. The rates include meals made from the hotel's own fresh produce. **www.esquinaslodge.com**

PIEDRAS BLANCAS Playa Nicuesa Rainforest Lodge $$$$$

Playa Nicuesa, 9 miles (14 km) NW of Golfito ***Tel*** *735-5237* ***Rooms*** *8*

This is an atmospheric ecolodge nestled between ocean and rainforest reserve, adjoining Piedras Blancas. All rooms have canopied beds and garden showers. Electricity is provided by solar power. Rates include meals. Access is only by boat – a 20-minute journey from Golfito. **www.nicuesalodge.com**

PIEDRAS BLANCAS Rainbow Adventures Lodge $$$$$

Playa Cativo, 9 miles (14 km) NW of Golfito ***Tel*** *831-5677* ***Rooms*** *12*

Backed by pristine forest, this intimate, tucked-away three-story beachfront ecolodge is constructed of beautiful native hardwoods, and furnished with antiques and handwoven rugs. The freshwater pool is fed by local streams. Access is by boat only. Meals and transfers are included. **www.rainbowcostarica.com**

PLAYA PLATANARES Pearl of the Osa $$$$

2 miles (3 km) E of Puerto Jiménez ***Tel*** *735-5205* ***Fax*** *735-5205* ***Rooms*** *8*

This two-story hotel has simple furnishings, lively pastel decor, and a fabulous beachfront setting. The Pearl has a few *palapas* (beach shacks) for the use of its guests, and its shaded open-air bar-restaurant is a great place to relax. **www.pearloftheosa.com**

PLAYA PLATANARES Iguana Lodge $$$$$

2 miles (3 km) E of Puerto Jiménez ***Tel*** *735-5205* ***Fax*** *735-5205* ***Rooms*** *8*

Adjacent to Pearl of the Osa, this sibling property has luxurious bamboo-and-log bungalows; some have garden showers. The rates include gourmet meals; dinner is served under a soaring thatched roof. The lodge also has a Japanese bathhouse. **www.iguanalodge.com**

PLAYA SAN JOSECITO Casa Corcovado Jungle Lodge $$$$$

8 miles (13 km) S of Bahía Drake ***Tel*** *256-3181* ***Fax*** *256-7409* ***Rooms*** *14*

Close to the northern border of Corcovado, this luxurious jungle-themed hotel has thatched cabins with exquisite decor. Excursions and gourmet meals are offered. Access is solely by boat. Closed September to mid-November. **www.casacorcovado.com**

PUERTO JIMÉNEZ Parrot Bay Village $$$$

E of Puerto Jiménez ***Tel*** *735-5180* ***Fax*** *735-5568* ***Rooms*** *8*

Enjoying a lush oceanfront setting, this hotel has eight private wooden cabins centered within a botanical garden in a mangrove lagoon. The nearby beach has warm, calm waters. Activities include dolphin- and whale-watching, kayaking through the mangroves, sportfishing, and hiking. **www.parrotbayvillage.com**

RINCÓN Suital Lodge $$$

4 miles (6 km) NE of Rincón ***Tel*** *826-0342* ***Fax*** *826-0342* ***Rooms*** *3*

This is a rustic wooden lodge with individual stilt-legged cabins set in a forest clearing. All have private bathrooms and balconies. Close by are about 3 miles (5 km) of forest trails and a peaceful beach. Other activities include kayaking on Río Esquinas and horseback riding. **www.suital.com**

SAN GERARDO DE RIVAS Cabinas Roca Dura $

9 miles (14 km) NE of San Isidro ***Tel*** *771-1866* ***Rooms*** *9*

Roca Dura is a backpackers' delight. Built into the rock-face and named accordingly, the hotel has basic and draughty yet distinctive rooms. The bedrock makes up one of the walls at the entrance, as well as in one of the bedrooms. The hotel also has a simple restaurant.

SAN GERARDO DE RIVAS Río Chirripó Mountain Retreat B&B $$$

8 miles (13 km) NE of San Isidro ***Tel*** *771-7065* ***Rooms*** *8*

A fabulous riverside location, rich decor, and tasteful furnishings combine to make this bargain-priced bed-and-breakfast an irresistible option. All rooms have private baths and a deck overlooking the river. There are also some roofed camping platforms for the more adventurous. **www.riochirripo.com**

SAN ISIDRO DE EL GENERAL Rancho La Botija $$$

4 miles (6 km) NE of San Isidro de El General ***Tel*** *770-2147* ***Fax*** *770-2146* ***Rooms*** *11*

This charming family-run hotel is set within coffee plantations and orchards. The land falls within an archeological zone, and a Tour of the Trails is offered. A 110-year old *trapiche* (sugarcane press) dominates the atmospheric restaurant. There is also an observatory. **www.ecotourism.co.cr/docs/labotija**

SIERPE Veragua River Lodge $$$

1 mile (1.6 km) NE of Sierpe ***Tel*** *788-8111* ***Fax*** *786-7460* ***Rooms*** *7*

Veragua River Lodge is a peaceful and isolated riverside hotel with whimsical charm. The Italian artist owner has converted the two-story house into an intimate hotel with delightful tropical decor. All the rooms are comfortable and spacious.

UVITA Toucan Hotel $

E of Hwy 34, Central Uvita ***Tel*** *743-8140* ***Rooms*** *10*

This is a well-run budget hostel near Parque Nacional Marino Ballena. One room has air conditioning, three others share a bathroom, and there's also a cabin. Guests have the use of a communal kitchen, laundry, and TV room. Internet access is offered. **www.tucanhotel.com**

UVITA Balcón de Uvita $$$

0.5 mile (1 km) NE of Uvita ***Tel*** *743-8034* ***Fax*** *743-8034* ***Rooms*** *3*

Known for its gourmet restaurant with Thai and Indonesian cuisine *(see p237)* and an incredible ocean view, this small family-run hotel has a magnificent hillside setting surrounded by forest. Nearby Playa Uvita is excellent for snorkeling, surfing, kayaking, and swimming. **www.balcondeuvita.com**

ZANCUDO Cabinas Sol y Mar $$$

1 mile (1.6 km) S of Zancudo village ***Tel*** *776-0014* ***Rooms*** *5*

This charming American-run hotel is always abuzz with karaoke, beach golf, and other activities. The restaurant specializes in Californian cuisine *(see p237)*. The rooms are enlivened by Guatemalan fabrics. Camping is permitted, and a two-bedroom house can also be rented. Closed October. **www.zancudo.com**

ZANCUDO Roy's Zancudo Lodge $$$$

N of Zancudo village ***Tel*** *776-0008* ***Fax*** *776-0011* ***Rooms*** *20*

This highly respected sportfishing lodge enjoys a windswept oceanfront setting. The rooms are comfortable and well tended, and there are a swimming pool and large hot tub close to the ocean. The lodge provides tackle and lure for anglers, as well as fly rods. Closed October. **www.royszancudolodge.com**

Where to Eat

Remarkably cosmopolitan, the restaurants in San José and a few other cities offer a wealth of dining options. These span the globe, from Peruvian to Indian, with French and Italian cuisine being well represented. In the countryside, food is based on traditional staples – rice and beans, accompanied by pork or chicken and tropical vegetables. Regional variations are prevalent, especially along the nation's eastern seaboard, where Afro-Caribbean dishes are infused with coconut milk and spices. Hot spices are rarely used elsewhere in Costa Rica. Small snack shops, called *sodas*, are found throughout the country, as are fast-food chain outlets, both US and local. Roadside fruit stalls are ubiquitous, with fresh fruits being an important part of the local diet *(see p222)*. Some vegetarian restaurants exist in San José and other major cities, and most other establishments will feature at least one vegetarian dish.

A chef at San José's Hotel Grano de Oro

Alfresco seating at the Restaurant Grano de Oro *(see p226)*, San José

Restaurants and Bars

The capital city offers by far the greatest choice of places to eat, with a variety of cuisines for every budget and taste. Many of the finest gourmet restaurants are in deluxe hotels. There are a number of internationally renowned eateries presided over by award-winning chefs. Most of these specialize in conventional international cuisine. Hotels usually have their own restaurants, which in wilderness areas may be the only places to eat in the vicinity. In *hospedajes* (B&Bs), the owners may be willing to prepare meals for an extra fee. The cheapest places to eat local dishes are the family-run *sodas*, small snack counters serving fixed-price menus and *casados* (set lunches, often referred to as *plato del día, plato ejecutivo*, or *comida corrida*).

Working-class males visit *cantinas* – neighborhood bars often identified by their Wild West-style swing doors – where *bocas (see p222)* are served. Drunken bar brawls are frequent and women will generally not feel comfortable in these places. Visitors should stick to recommended bars in urban areas. Hotel staff can advise you of places to avoid.

Chain Restaurants

All the principal American fast-food chains are conspicuous in Costa Rica, including Burger King, KFC, Pizza Hut, and McDonald's. There are also several homegrown companies, such as Burguí and Rosti Pollo, which compete with their US counterparts.

The main cities have a good selection of chain cafés, which serve light snacks and sometimes inexpensive buffets. An excellent option is Spoons, found in larger cities in the Central Highlands – it offers a wide range of sandwiches, salads, and hot meals at low prices. Musmanni is a nationwide *panadería* (bakery) chain selling freshly baked breads, confectionery, and sandwiches. Mexican fare is the specialty of Antojitos, which has outlets around San José. Bagelman's features bagels, sandwiches, and breakfast specials, while Pops is the local ice cream chain.

Local Eating Habits

For the most part, Ticos (Costa Ricans) follow North American eating habits, with some differences. The typical *desayuno* (breakfast) consists of *gallo pinto (see p222)* served with fresh fruit juice and milky coffee. Males often take a shot of whisky with their breakfast. Extended families usually come together on weekends for brunch. Many businesses close at noon for *almuerzo* (lunch), which might last as long as 2 hours. The *merienda* (mid-afternoon coffee break) is still popular.

A bar in the village of Ojochal, near Dominical

El Sano Banano Village Restaurant & Café *(see p230)*, Montezuma

Most restaurants close by 11pm, as the local preference is for early dining. Ticos are leisurely in their dining, and often linger at the table after finishing their meal, which can be frustrating if the restaurant is full. Many eateries close on Sunday.

Ticos rarely invite friends and acquaintances to dine at home, and prefer to extend invitations to restaurants. They seldom arrive at an appointed hour, except for important businesses occasions, and it is considered rude to arrive on time if invited for *cena* (dinner) in a private home.

Paying and Tipping

Fixed-price menus such as *casados* normally offer better value than their à la carte equivalents. At *sodas*, it is possible to have a wholesome cooked meal for around 800 colones. In elegant restaurants, a three-course dinner with wine might cost around 13,000 colones per person. *Sodas* have no tax – in other places, the prices shown on menus usually include a 13 percent sales tax. An additional 10 percent service charge is often automatically added to your bill. Feel free to challenge this charge if service has been poor, and tip extra only if you have been well attended to.

Credit cards are accepted by most restaurants in cities and major resorts, but expect to pay in cash in rural areas, small restaurants, and *sodas*. VISA is the widely accepted card, followed by MasterCard and American Express; few places take Diners Club or traveler's checks.

Food Hygiene

Food is normally of a high standard nationwide, and tap water in most regions is trustworthy. However, it is still worth taking precautions. Drink only bottled water, fruit juices, or processed drinks. Bottled water is sold in all restaurants, hotels, and supermarkets. In restaurants and bars, order drinks without ice *(sin hielo)*.

Cocktail menu, Ricky's Bar, Cahuita

Salads, vegetables, and fruits pose little problem, except in the Caribbean, Puntarenas, and Golfito, where hygiene can be questionable. To play safe, you may wish to avoid salads and uncooked vegetables, and to peel all fruits, especially those bought from open-air markets and urban fruit stalls. Across the nation, milk and dairy products are pasteurized and are no cause for concern. Take care to avoid undercooked shellfish, meat, and fish.

Children

Costa Ricans love children and most restaurants welcome them. High-chairs are usually available, and many restaurants offer child portions; some even have special kids' menus. Many eating places, especially fast-food outlets and rural roadside cafés, have children's playgrounds.

Alcohol

Restaurants are usually licensed to sell beers and spirits, including *guaro*, the popular alcohol of choice. The more elegant restaurants serve a variety of international wines, although outside the Central Highlands quality often suffers due to poor storage. Sale of alcohol is not permitted during election periods and three days (Thursday–Saturday) preceding Easter; nonetheless, Ticos stock up in advance, and the days before elections see heavy drinking.

Smoking

Smoking is popular in Costa Rica, and it is common for diners to light up between or even during courses. Many restaurants now have non-smoking sections, but these are rarely in separate rooms.

The kitchen of the Iguana Lodge, Playa Platanares *(see p219)*

What to Eat in Costa Rica

At Costa Rica's *ferias de agricultores* (farmers' markets), stalls are piled with glistening fruit, including exotics such as guayaba, marañon, and papaya. Tomatoes, peppers, and squash add their own bouquets and hues, as does a pot-pourri of herbs and spices. Pasture-fed cattle provide beef and fresh milk, while poultry roams free until ready for the pot. The warm waters off Costa Rica's shores deliver fresh fish and crustaceans glistening with brine. Caribbean and Creole are the main culinary styles.

Ripe papayas

One of the many *sodas* (food-stalls) found all over Costa Rica

Caribbean Cuisine

Making the most of local spices, cuisine along Costa Rica's Atlantic seaboard bears the zesty imprimatur of Jamaica, thanks to the many islanders who settled in the region. The sea's fresh bounty, such as shrimp and lobster, finds its way into curries and stews enlivened with chilies, ginger, and Scotch bonnet peppers. In Tortuguero, green turtle has long been a favorite meat, popularly used in stews, along with mackerel. *Pargo* (red snapper) is often "jerked" – spiced up with mouth-searing peppers and grilled over coals.

Akee – a small yellow fruit whose flesh has the texture and appearance of scrambled eggs – is a key ingredient at breakfast. The milk of the versatile coconut forms a base ingredient for cooking and in cocktails, while providing invigorating refreshment

A selection of fresh seafood available in Costa Rica

Costa Rican Dishes and Specialties

Scotch bonnet peppers

Gallo pinto (fried rice and black beans) is the dish most associated with Costa Rica. It is commonly served as breakfast with scrambled eggs and slabs of local Monteverde cheese. At lunch it becomes *arroz con pollo*, with lightly seasoned stewed chicken or pork. This forms the basis of *casados* (set meals), served with vegetables such as carrots, yucca, cabbage, onions, *plátanos* (fried plantain), and a simple salad of lettuce, tomatoes, and hearts of palm. Rice dishes are enlivened by a splash of *Lizano*, a mildly spicy sauce of vegetables and fruits. Countryfolk still favor traditional stews such as *sopa de mondongo*, made from tripe and vegetables, and a spicy meatball soup called *sopa de albondigas*, from Guanacaste. Main meals are often preceded by *bocas*, tasty tidbits such as tortillas with cheese. Turtle eggs on offer may have been illegally harvested.

***Ceviche** is raw chunks of white fish marinated in citrus juice with garlic, onion, and red and green peppers, served on crackers or lettuce leaves.*

Well-stocked grocery store in San José

when drunk fresh from the shell. Local fruits such as citrus, papaya, and guava are jellied and candied with sugar, coconut, and cocoa.

Guanacastecan Specialties

From the heartland of *comida criolla* (Creole cuisine), Guanacastecan fare revolves around *maíz* (sweet corn), introduced in pre-Columbian times by indigenous peoples. Succulent yellow sweet corn is eaten as a vegetable – cooked, boiled, or grilled – and, following ancient recipes, is ground into flour to form the base for tortilla and *tamale* dough. *Arroz* (rice) was brought by the Spanish from Asia. Today, it is a major crop in the lowlands and forms the chief accompaniment to the nation's cuisine. Brahma cattle graze the pastures, producing highly prized steaks and ground beef. The seas off Nicoya are famous for game fish, such as the flavorful dorado or mahi-mahi. Playa Flamingo and Tamarindo are the most important centers for sport-fishing, while the port town of Puntarenas has a large shrimping fleet.

Vegetables at a *feria de agricultores* (farmers' market)

On the Menu

Arreglados (nationwide). Puff pastries filled with cheeses and/or meats.

Akee and codfish (Caribbean). Akee, blended with salted codfish and served with callaloo (similar to spinach) and fried dumplings called Johnny Cakes.

Cajetas (nationwide). A thick, nougat-like dessert made of coconut milk and sugar, which is laced with orange peel and other fruits.

Chorreadas (Guanacaste). Large corn tortillas served like pancakes and topped with *natilla* (sour cream).

Empañadas (nationwide). Savory turnover pastries filled with minced meat, potatoes and onions, or cheese and beans.

Pan bon (Caribbean). Dark bread spiced up with nutmeg and sweetened with caramelized sugar and candied fruits.

Rundown (Caribbean). Mackerel simmered in coconut milk with vegetables.

Tamales (nationwide). Steamed corn-dough pastries stuffed with minced beef and wrapped in banana leaves.

***Filete de pescado grillé**, grilled fillet of* corvina *(sea bass), is traditionally served with* ajo *(buttered garlic), rice, and mixed vegetables.*

***Olla de carne**, a dish from Guanacaste, is a meat-and-vegetable stew with pumpkin-like chayote, corn, plantain, potatoes, and yuca.*

***Tres leches** comprises layers of dense sponge cake soaked in condensed milk, evaporated milk, and cream, and topped with whipped cream.*

Choosing a Restaurant

The restaurants in this guide have been selected, as far as possible, for the quality of the food and atmosphere. However, in some parts of Costa Rica there are few restaurants that can be recommended. In such cases, places have been suggested that offer at least good value. For map references for San José, see pages 78–9.

PRICE CATEGORIES
For a three-course meal for one (excluding wine), including tax and service:

- $ Under $10
- $$ $10–15
- $$$ $15–20
- $$$$ $20–30
- $$$$$ Over $30

SAN JOSÉ

CITY CENTER La Criollita $
Calles 7/9 and Ave 7 ***Tel*** *256-6511* **Map** *2 D3*

This delightful eatery on the edge of Barrio Amón is suffused with sunlight filtering through a *vidriera* (stained-glass panel). Songbirds visit the lush outdoor patio. The large menu includes full breakfasts, snack lunches, and simple but well-executed entrées. It is popular with a business clientele at lunch. Closed Sunday.

CITY CENTER Mama's Place $
Calles Central/2 and Ave 1 ***Tel*** *223-2270* **Map** *1 B3*

Attracting workers at lunchtime, this small, no-frills family-run diner in the heart of downtown specializes in filling *casados* (set meals) and Italian pastas and salads. *Típico* (typical) dishes are displayed behind glass, cafeteria-style. The Italian family running the place fusses over their clientele. Closed Sunday.

CITY CENTER Restaurante Vishnu $
Calles 1/3 and Ave 1 ***Tel*** *290-0119* **Map** *1 C3*

This is a splendid budget option for vegetarians, with an extensive menu and large portions. It focuses on health food, including vegetarian burgers, salads, fruit juices, and filling *casados*. The owners have similar restaurants downtown and throughout San José. The eatery is kept spotlessly clean.

CITY CENTER Balcón de Europa $$
Calle 9 and Aves Central/1 ***Tel*** *221-4841* **Map** *2 D3*

An informal, timeless restaurant in the heart of downtown, with wood-paneled walls and serving hearty pastas and other dishes conjured up by the French-born chef-owner. The decor includes framed proverbs and historical prints. Closed Saturday.

CITY CENTER Café de la Posada $$
Calle 17 and Ave 2 ***Tel*** *257-9414* **Map** *2 E4*

A delightful bohemian café-restaurant run by Argentinians. Creative fare includes *empañadas* (stuffed turnovers), salads, quiches, and omelettes, as well as cappuccinos and delicious desserts, enjoyed to the accompaniment of jazz and classical music. Diners can sit outside under large umbrellas in a pleasant pedestrian precinct.

CITY CENTER La Cocina de Leña $$
Centro Comercial El Pueblo, Barrio Tournon ***Tel*** *256-5353* **Map** *2 D1*

Tucked away amidst the narrow alleys of the El Pueblo complex, this invitingly rustic restaurant is decorated in the style of a quintessential Costa Rican farmstead and is considered *the* place to enjoy traditional fare. The menu also includes corn dishes.

CITY CENTER Spoon $$
Calles 5/7 and Ave Central, plus various other locations throughout San José ***Tel*** *224-0328* **Map** *1 C3*

Clean and simple cafeteria-style venue popular for its bargain-priced *casados* and various dishes such as salads, sandwiches – including *lapices* (submarines) – and local favorites. Delicious baked goods attest to the chain's origins as a bakery.

CITY CENTER Aya Sofya $$$
Calle 21 and Ave Central ***Tel*** *221-7185* **Map** *2 F4*

Housed in a former colonial structure, this folksy Turkish restaurant with a touch of the Levantine serves traditional regional staples, including *dolmades* (stuffed grape leaves), kebabs, and baklava, made by a chef from Turkey. Belly dancers perform on weekends. Closed Sunday.

CITY CENTER Café Mundo $$$
Calle 15 and Ave 9 ***Tel*** *222-6190* **Map** *2 E2*

This converted mansion with plenty of historical character provides a pleasant environment for enjoying dishes from an eclectic menu spanning salads to steaks. The restaurant, which has several dining rooms, a bar, and a tree-shaded patio, doubles as an art gallery.

Key to Symbols *see back cover flap*

CITY CENTER Café Parisien $$$

Parque Mora Fernández, Ave 2 ***Tel*** *221-4000* ***Map*** *1 C4*

An inviting 24-hour patio restaurant known for its splendid position in front of the Teatro Nacional, and for the comings and goings of itinerant musicians and hawkers. The simple *arroz con pollo* (chicken with rice) is cheap and filling, and a buffet is offered. Usually, there is a pianist playing.

CITY CENTER Tin Jo $$$

Calle 11 and Aves 6/8 ***Tel*** *221-7605* ***Map*** *2 D4*

This homely restaurant spans the Orient with its wide-ranging menu featuring regional dishes from China, India, Indonesia, Japan, and Thailand. The cuisine is filling and tasty, rather than gourmet. The decor bears minimal Asiatic motifs, but the moodily dark ambience is appealing.

CITY CENTER Restaurante El Oasis $$$$

Hotel Santo Tomás, Calles 3/5 and Ave 7 ***Tel*** *255-0448* ***Map*** *2 D3*

Attached to Hotel Santo Tomás *(see p200)*, this charming restaurant has a pleasantly airy atmosphere enhanced by colonial tilework and a 19th-century period feel, and opens on to a courtyard garden with a water cascade. Seafood and meats such as filet mignon are well prepared, and the dessert list is impressive.

CITY CENTER Bakéa $$$$$

Calle 7 and Ave 11 ***Tel*** *221-1051* ***Map*** *2 D2*

This relative newcomer has hip contemporary decor and a creative nouvelle menu that appeals to the city's chic crowd. The young chef-owner, a Costa Rican trained in Paris, has yet to deliver consistent quality, but on good nights the food is delicious. Closed Sunday and open for lunch only on Monday.

EAST OF CITY CENTER Bagelman's $

Calle 33 and Ave 2 ***Tel*** *224-2432*

Specializing in sandwiches, bagels, and baked goods, this clean modern option resembles a tastefully decorated fast-food restaurant in ambience. The breakfasts, including *gallo pinto (see p222)*, are an attractive bargain, but the menu also features omelettes and other American favorites. There is an outlet in Escazú as well.

EAST OF CITY CENTER Café Ruiseñor $$

Calles 41/43 and Ave Central ***Tel*** *225-2562*

Separated from the buzz of traffic by a wide grassy strip, this airy brasserie in the Los Yoses district is an excellent place to lunch on soups, salads, and nouvelle seafood and meat dishes. The cappuccinos and espressos are good. Choose indoor or shaded patio dining. Closed Sunday.

EAST OF CITY CENTER Ave Fenix $$$

Ave Central, Los Yoses ***Tel*** *225-3362*

An excellent Chinese restaurant with an extensive menu and an authentically Oriental ambience, including Chinese staff. The large portions come at reasonable prices. Exotic dishes are highlighted by a creative use of original sauces, such as maraschino cherries and lime juice.

EAST OF CITY CENTER Île de France $$$$

Hôtel le Bergerac, Calle 35, S of Ave Central ***Tel*** *234-7850*

Inventive French dishes along with well-known classics such as *vichysoisse* are the hallmark of this intimate restaurant inside the Hôtel le Bergerac *(see p202)*. A large wine selection and delicious desserts round out the pleasing dining experience, which can be enjoyed in an airy courtyard patio.

EAST OF CITY CENTER Jürgen's Grill $$$$$

Boutique Hotel Jade, N of Autos Subaru dealership, Barrio Dent ***Tel*** *283-2239*

Situated in the Boutique Hotel Jade *(see p201)*, this fashionable restaurant exudes contemporary elegance. The menu of predominantly nouvelle dishes is invitingly creative and the ambience appealing, although the service is somewhat formal and a dress code applies. The bar has a cigar lounge. Closed Sunday.

ESCAZÚ Bouzouk $$

Calle 2, San Miguel de Escazú ***Tel*** *289-3217*

This colorful Greek restaurant – the only one in Costa Rica – is run by Greek-Canadians and offers a contemporary and vibrant ambience enhanced by live music. Daily food specials complement the set menu of staples such as *dolmades* and Greek salad. Closed Monday.

ESCAZÚ Giacomin $$

Calle del Llano, San Rafael de Escazú ***Tel*** *288-3381*

Light snacks and baked goods, from croissants to *paninis*, are offered at this café specializing in exquisite home-made chocolates and gourmet coffees. Enjoy your temptations in the air-conditioned café or on a terrace overlooking a landscaped garden. Closed Sunday.

ESCAZÚ Lunas y Migas $$

Centro Comercial Trejos Monte, San Rafael de Escazú ***Tel*** *288-2774*

This tiny gourmet deli-bakery is recommended for its scrumptious croissants, delicious quiches, pizzas, pastas, Argentinian *empañadas*, and desserts, as well as the cappuccinos and espressos served by congenial hosts, who are recent Argentinian transplants.

ESCAZÚ Le Monastère $$$$

4 miles (6 km) W of Escazú **Tel** *289-4404*

Located high above Santa Ana, this fashionable restaurant in a former chapel plays on the monastic theme. Waiters dress as monks, and Gregorian music fills the historic hallways and dining rooms. The French cuisine includes *escargot*, and sea bass with crab, caviar, and champagne. Closed Sunday.

ESCAZÚ Atlanta Dining Room $$$$$

Tara Resort Hotel, San Antonio de Escazú **Tel** *228-6992*

This renowned restaurant, in the Tara Resort Hotel *(see p202)*, draws Costa Rica's social elite. Antique furnishings add to the formal, even aloof, antebellum atmosphere. The menu features well-known Continental favorites, from lobster bisque to grilled beef with shrimp and béarnaise sauce.

ESCAZÚ El Invernadero $$$$$

Ave 5, W of Calle León Cortes San Miguel de Escazú **Tel** *228-0216*

A classy restaurant tucked away in the heart of a residential area of San Miguel de Escazú, El Invernadero serves Costa Rican and Italian gourmet nouvelle dishes. The *tilapia chile dulce* (fish in brandy and red pepper sauce) is recommended. Bring a jacket or sweater against the chilly air-conditioning. Closed Sunday.

ESCAZÚ La Luz $$$$$

The Alta Hotel, Alto de las Palomas, 2 miles (3 km) W of Escazú **Tel** *282-4160*

High ceilings and elegant contemporary decor in mock-Tudor style characterize this upscale restaurant in the Alta Hotel *(see p202)*. Inventive nouvelle gourmet cuisine makes the most of local ingredients, although the food quality has famously gone through periods of ups and downs.

WEST OF CITY CENTER Sabor Nicaragüense $

Calle 20 and Aves Central/1 **Tel** *248-2547*

Situated close to the Coca Cola bus terminal, this clean and well-run family-operated restaurant serves Nicaraguan fare, as well as Costa Rican staples at budget prices. Although air-conditioned, it also has a small outdoor area facing the tumultuous street.

WEST OF CITY CENTER Antojitos $$

W of Sabana Oeste, Rohrmoser **Tel** *231-5564*

A lively Mexican restaurant serving all the traditional favorites, along with steaks and grilled meats, as well as excellent margaritas. Mariachis sometimes entertain diners. Antojitos has outlets throughout the city. The chain is extremely popular with locals and can get noisy.

WEST OF CITY CENTER Machu Picchu $$

Calle 32 and Aves 1/3 **Tel** *222-7384*

Extremely popular seafood restaurant with superb service. The fare includes quality Peruvian dishes, from *ceviche* (marinated raw fish or shellfish) to the *picante de mariscos* seafood casserole. Meals are best accompanied with the *pisco sour* house drink. Peruvian art and posters enliven the place. Closed Sunday.

WEST OF CITY CENTER Marisquería La Princesa Marina $$

Sabana Oeste, SW corner of Parque Sabana **Tel** *232-0481*

Good, simple dishes from the sea are served at this no-frills restaurant on the west side of Parque Sabana. This canteen-style option is always lively and very popular with the working-class crowd for its filling portions. The *ceviche* appetizer is recommended, as is the *corvina al ajillo* (garlic sea bass) as a main dish.

WEST OF CITY CENTER Lubnan $$$

Calles 22/24 and Paseo Colón **Tel** *257-6071*

Small and popular Lebanese restaurant with authentic Levantine dishes such as *falafel* and *shish kebabs*, served by waiters wearing red vests and fezes. Hookahs are passed around and prove popular with the young crowd, which flocks here for the quasi-party atmosphere. Closed Monday.

WEST OF CITY CENTER La Bastille $$$$

Calle 22 and Paseo Colón **Tel** *255-4994*

A long-standing fixture, this elegant and semi-formal restaurant on a busy thoroughfare serves highly regarded French cuisine from the hands of Chef Hans Pulfer. Service, however, is aloof, and although not required, a jacket and other dressy attire is not out of place. Closed Sunday.

WEST OF CITY CENTER La Masía de Triquell $$$$

Calle 44, Sabana Norte **Tel** *296-3528*

A large and elegant restaurant, in Edificio Casa España, specializing in Spanish dishes, including paella and seafoods such as *corvina a la vizcaína* (sea bass with sautéed spinach). Service is professional and somewhat formal. Reservations are required.

WEST OF CITY CENTER Restaurant Grano de Oro $$$$$

Hotel Grano de Oro, Calle 30 and Aves 2/4 **Tel** *255-3322*

One of the city's finest restaurants, this elegant option is in San José's premier boutique hotel *(see p203)* and attracts the social and business elite. Superb French-inspired dishes blend Costa Rican influences, and the desserts alone justify dining here. The filling breakfasts include healthy options. The staff are efficient and courteous.

Key to Price Guide *see p224* **Key to Symbols** *see back cover flap*

THE CENTRAL HIGHLANDS

ALAJUELA Jalapeños Comida Tex-Mex $

Calle 2 and Aves Central/1 ***Tel*** *430-4027*

This lively restaurant draws a loyal clientele of local expatriate residents. The menu ranges from hamburgers and omelettes to Tex-Mex staples such as *tostadas* (tortillas with fillings), corn nachos, and *huevos rancheros* (a breakfast favorite made with tortillas and eggs).

ALAJUELA Xandari $$$$

Tacacori, 3 miles (5 km) N of Alajuela ***Tel*** *443-2020*

Magnificent views across the valley from the open-air balcony are a highlight at this romantic restaurant, located in a superlative boutique hotel set amid coffee plantations *(see p204)*. Gourmet health-conscious dishes using fresh local ingredients are complemented by a robust wine list and estate-grown coffee.

ATENAS C@fé K-puchinos $$

NE corner of the plaza

This colonial-era adobe home houses an Internet café. The Spanish owners serve light snacks such as *tortillas española*, and Iberian-inspired nouvelle dishes, such as salmon in wine sauce. The large wine list also includes sangría. With gourmet coffees, it makes a pleasant breakfast spot.

ATENAS Mirador del Cafetal $$

Hwy 3, 5 miles (8 km) W of Atenas ***Tel*** *446-7361*

Tasty, simple food is served at this roadside restaurant with magnificent views over coffee fields and mountain valleys. The vast menu features filling breakfasts, plus indigenous dishes such as *tamales (see p223)*, as well as smoothies, cappuccinos, and daiquiris.

CIUDAD CARIARI Antonio Ristorante Italiano $$$

6 miles (10 km) NW of San José ***Tel*** *293-0622*

An elegant and modern restaurant, Antonio Ristorante Italiano specializes in well-prepared Italian dishes, from gnocchi to a splendid spaghetti with squid. Inexpensive *casados* (set meals) are a lunchtime bargain. The service is excellent. It has a piano bar.

CIUDAD CARIARI Sakura $$$$

Ribera de Belén, 0.5 (1 km) SE of San Antonio de Belén ***Tel*** *298-0000*

Quality Japanese fare is served in authentically Oriental surroundings adjoining the Japanese-owned Hotel Herradura. It has a sushi bar, teppanyaki grills where guests can watch their food being prepared, and tatami rooms with private chefs. An indoor pond is stocked with koi.

HEREDIA Azzurra $

Calles 2/4 and Ave 2 ***Tel*** *260-9083*

A favorite of local expatriate residents, this intimate café near the central plaza serves omelettes and *gallo pinto (see p222)* breakfasts, as well as salads, sandwiches, and delicious ice cream sundaes, all at bargain prices. A splendid casual spot to catch up on local gossip from English-speaking residents.

HEREDIA Spoon $

Plaza Heredia, Calle 9 and Ave 6 ***Tel*** *260-1333*

This small yet clean café on the edge of downtown is noted for its inexpensive *casados*, salads, snacks, desserts, and delicious baked goods, all served cafeteria-style. It is highly popular with university students as a breakfast and lunch spot.

HEREDIA Hotel Bougainvillea $$$

Santo Domingo de Heredia, 2 miles (3 km) SE of Heredia ***Tel*** *244-1414*

This clean and well-lit restaurant in Hotel Bougainvillea *(see p204)* is adorned with appealing artwork. It serves Continental dishes along with local fare of superior quality. The service is always professional, overseen by a conscientious and capable owner. The weekend brunch is popular with locals in the know.

HEREDIA Le Petit Paris $$$

Calle 5 and Aves Central/2 ***Tel*** *262-2524*

In the heart of town, this compact and intimate restaurant occupies a converted home. The traditional French cuisine – chicken *à la Normandie* is typical – is well-prepared and tasty, and the wide-ranging menu includes salads, sandwiches, and pastries. Crêpes are a specialty. There are art exhibits, and live jazz is hosted on Wednesdays.

HEREDIA Restaurante Don Próspero $$$

Santa Lucía, 0.5 mile (1 km) N of Heredia ***Tel*** *260-2748*

Part of the Café Britt coffee processing site *(see p92)*, this informally elegant open-air restaurant has a health-conscious menu featuring organically grown vegetables, plus delicious desserts and a wide variety of coffee drinks. Although best enjoyed as part of an inclusive tour, casual diners are also welcome.

HEREDIA Finca Rosa Blanca Country Inn $$$$$

Santa Barbara de Heredia, 4 miles (6 km) NW of Heredia ***Tel*** *269-9392*

Gourmet meals served at this deluxe boutique hotel *(see p204)* are fixed-price, four-course delights. Their accomplished chef uses estate-grown ingredients in nouvelle temptations of award-winning quality. The erudite and congenial owners sometimes dine with guests at the massive hand-crafted hardwood table. Reservations essential.

LA GARITA Fiesta del Maíz $

Hwy 3, 0.5 mile (1 km) W of Pan-Am Hwy ***Tel*** *487-5757*

This popular roadside restaurant specializes in traditional corn-based items, such as *chorreadas* (corn fritters) and *tamales (see p223)*, served in a no-frills environment. A favorite of locals, it gets packed on weekends, when *gallo pinto (see p222)* and other local favorites are also offered. Closed Monday–Thursday.

LA GARITA Restaurante Le Gourmet $$$$

Martino Resort & Spa, Hwy 3, 2 miles (3 km) E of Pan-Am Hwy ***Tel*** *433-8382*

Sumptuous restaurant situated in the Martino Resort & Spa *(see p205)*, with a curved balcony overlooking the pool that offers an option for outdoor dining . Health-conscious Italian fare utilizes fresh vegetables and fruits from the hotel's own gardens. The restaurant is open until 3am.

MONTE DE LA CRUZ Hotel Chalet Tirol $$$$

Monte de la Cruz, 6 miles (10 km) NE of Heredia ***Tel*** *267-6222*

Located in a Swiss-inspired hotel *(see p205)*, this cozy, wood-beamed alpine restaurant has a log fire and candlelit dining at night. While the focus is on traditional French dishes, the menu also features creative dishes using Costa Rican ingredients, such as shrimp in fennel and Pernod sauce.

OROSI Orosi Lodge $

SW of the plaza, Orosi village ***Tel*** *533-3578*

Located in a small lodge *(see p205)* tucked into the southeast corner of the village, this small café has a charming ambience. It serves light breakfasts, pizzas, snacks, and cookies and ice cream sundaes. A juke box and table football are on hand for rainy days. It also offers Internet connectivity.

SABANA REDONDA Restaurante Jaulares $$

12 miles (19 km) N of Alajuela ***Tel*** *482-2155*

This restaurant on the cool mid-elevation slopes of Volcán Poás, designed as a rustic farmstead, serves traditional dishes, steaks, and seafood. Pizzas are fired in a traditional wood-burning *horno* (oven). Take a sweater for chilly nights. Live music on weekends draws in the crowds.

SABANA REDONDA Las Fresas $$$$

11 miles (18 km) N of Alajuela ***Tel*** *482-2620*

Delectable Italian-inspired fare in a charming and elegant mountainside restaurant with a log fire. The combination of an invitingly warm ambience and exceptionally well-prepared and presented cuisine draws a clientele from far afield. The sea bass with garlic cream sauce is recommended. The wine list spans the globe.

SAN ANTONIO DE BELEN El Rodeo $$$

4 miles (6 km) S of Alajuela ***Tel*** *293-3909*

An appealing rusticity, with saddles and other equestrian paraphernalia, lend this airy timber-beamed restaurant a unique ambience. Authentic Costa Rica cuisine, such as corn tortillas with sliced tongue, and more imaginative dishes such as tenderloin in jalapeño cream, draw an appreciative clientele.

SAN JOSÉ DE LA MONTANA Las Ardillas $$$

6 miles (10 km) N of Heredia ***Tel*** *260-2172*

This wood-and-stone lodge set amid pines has a delightfully rustic ambience enhanced by a huge hearth with blazing logs on chilly days and at night. It specializes in roasted meat dishes, prepared in a wood-burning oven, and seafood, but also has local favorites.

SAN PABLO DE LEÓN CORTÉS Bar Restaurante Vaca Flaca $$

25 miles (40 km) SE of San José

Situated in a pine forest along the Ruta de los Santos *(see p97)*, this rustic restaurant has a wonderful warm ambience. The decor includes cowhide seats, cowboy hats, mounted deer heads, and old rifles. Simple traditional dishes are served, as are burgers, sandwiches, and the restaurant's own brand of coffee.

SAN RAMÓN Valle Escondido Lodge $$$

9 miles (14 km) N of San Ramón ***Tel*** *452-1150*

Boasting views down the valley, this glass-enclosed restaurant is recommended more for its stunning mountain setting than for its cuisine. Italian dishes predominate on the wide-ranging menu, which also features local favorites such as *corvina al ajillo* (garlic sea bass).

SANTA MARÍA DE DOTA La Casona de Sara $

E of Beneficio Coopedota ***Tel*** *541-2258*

Overseen by a charming matriarch, this simple family-run restaurant serves hearty *típico* fare from the open kitchen, where you are welcome to peek into the simmering pots to make your selection. Be sure to try the fresh fruit *batidos*, also called *refrescos* (shakes).

SARCHÍ Restaurante Las Carreteras $$$

Adjacent to Fábrica de Carretas Joaquín Chaverri, Sarchí Sur **Tel** *454-1633*

A homely and airy restaurant in the heart of this artisans' center melds a rustic charm with a contemporary setting. The extensive menu ranges from soups, salads, and burgers to Italian dishes and local favorites. Outdoor dining is an option on sunny days.

TURRIALBA Café Gourmet $

Calles 2/4 and Ave 4 **Tel** *556-9689*

This charming café, in an old wooden home one block from the main street, offers *gallo pinto* breakfasts, light snacks, and exquisite desserts as well as teas and gourmet coffees. It has a small shaded patio open to the street. Closed Sunday.

TURRIALBA Hotel Casa Turire $$$$

Hacienda Atirro, 5 miles (8 km) SE of Turrialba **Tel** *531-1111*

Opening on to a lavishly landscaped courtyard with fountains, this elegant restaurant in a classy boutique hotel *(see p205)* has a wide-ranging menu of locally inspired dishes highlighted by scrumptious desserts and estate-grown coffee. Dishes are creatively presented and filling, albeit not gourmet.

VARA BLANCA Restaurante Colbert $$

14 miles (22 km) N of Alajuela **Tel** *482-2776*

Views down the mountain are reason enough to dine at this French-run bakery and café, which serves crêpes, light snacks, confections, and nouvelle Costa Rican cuisine *à la français*, such as tilapia fish in tomato sauce. Sitting atop the Continental Divide, it is often shrouded in clouds.

THE CENTRAL PACIFIC AND SOUTHERN NICOYA

JACÓ Bar Restaurante Colonial $$

Calle Bohío and Ave Pastro Díaz **Tel** *643-3326*

A spacious and airy tropical-themed restaurant with a skylight, a large bar, and shaded outdoor dining. It offers an ambitious menu with light fare, including bar snacks, and fresh seafood with a nouvelle twist – mussels in garlic and olive oil are typical.

JACÓ Lighthouse Point Steak and Seafood House $$$

Hwy 34 and El Bulevar **Tel** *643-3083*

A creatively conceived 24-hour roadside diner with a lively bar, fully stocked souvenir store, and eclectic decor that includes surf boards hanging from the walls and ceiling. The expansive international menu ranges from filling American breakfasts to sushi and *casados* (set meals). It offers free hotel transfers.

JACÓ Hotel Poseidon Bar y Restaurante $$$$

Hotel Poseidon, Calle Bohío **Tel** *643-1642*

Located in Hotel Poseidon *(see p206)*, this restaurant is known for its hearty breakfasts and creative fusion fare, such as spicy peanut jumbo prawns. Oriental throw rugs, wooden carvings, and stone walls provide a warm ambience, enhanced by live jazz. The open-wall plan lets in the tropical breezes.

JACÓ Pacific Bistro $$$$

Calle Las Palmeras and Ave Pastro Díaz **Tel** *643-3083*

Situated on the main street, this gourmet restaurant serves Asia-Pacific fusion cuisine with a focus on fresh seafood. Spicy Indonesian shrimp noodles are a signature dish. Professionally trained chef Kent Green proves adept in the kitchen. Patrons can choose from indoor or patio dining.

MALPAÍS Playa Boa Restaurant $$$

Hotel Trópico Latino, 0.5 mile (1 km) N of Carmen **Tel** *640-0062*

Associated with the pleasant Hotel Trópico Latino, this beachfront restaurant is known for its creative nouvelle dishes in a romantic, suitably tropical-themed setting. Imaginatively blending fresh local ingredients with international spices and liquors, the menu proffers such temptations as fish of the day in coconut sauce.

MALPAÍS Rancho Itauna $$$

Playa Santa Teresa, 1 mile (1.6 km) N of Carmen **Tel** *640-0095*

Renowned for its full moon and New Year parties, this small, unpretentious, and colorful restaurant serves international cuisine from around the globe, but with an emphasis on Brazilian dishes. It occasionally has live music and parties, and hosts a traditional barbecue every Thursday evening.

MALPAÍS Nectar Bar and Restaurante $$$$

Florblanca Resort, Playa Santa Teresa, 3 miles (5 km) N of Carmen **Tel** *640-0232*

Outstanding menu and atmosphere at the fashionable Florblanca Resort *(see p206)*. Gourmet, Asian-inspired fusion dishes are presented with flair, and the airy beachfront setting is enhanced at night by candlelight. The curvilinear bar serves sushi and plays a wide variety of music, from classical to jazz.

MANUEL ANTONIO Café Milagro $$$

3 miles (5 km) S of Quepos ***Tel*** *777-0794*

A small roadside café with a charming ambience and simple furnishings in various tropical pastels. Sandwiches and pastries and a large selection of coffees and teas can be enjoyed on the shady patio to the rear. The café also has a souvenir store. Closed Sunday and during evenings in the low season.

MANUEL ANTONIO Mar y Sombra $$$

Playa Espadilla Sur ***Tel*** *777-0003*

Good, simple food is served at this open-air beachfront restaurant with tables under palm trees. The simple concrete tables and benches spill onto the beach, but it also has a covered restaurant where live music is played. The menu features burgers, seafood, and *típico* dishes, including *gallo pinto* *(see p222)*.

MANUEL ANTONIO Restaurante Gato Negro $$$

Hotel Casitas Eclipse, 3 miles (5 km) S of Quepos ***Tel*** *777-1728*

Situated in an elegant hotel, the airy restaurant has a warm, romantic ambience with splendid views. With a large wine list, the eating place has a Mediterranean-inspired menu. The choice of pastas is extensive, and many Italian favorites (such as tagliatelle) are featured.

MANUEL ANTONIO Barba Roja $$$$

2 miles (3 km) S of Quepos ***Tel*** *777-0331*

A venerable restaurant on a ridgecrest with splendid views and long-standing reputation. Seafood and steaks are its focus, although the menu ranges toward Mexican fare, and light snacks and filling breakfasts are offered. The bar draws a nightly crowd for the sunsets enjoyed alfresco. Closed Monday.

MANUEL ANTONIO Claro Que Si $$$$$

Hotel Si Como No Resort, 3 miles (5 km) S of Quepos ***Tel*** *777-0777*

This fine-dining restaurant with contemporary sophistication is located in an upscale hotel *(see p207)*. An engaging seafood menu, combining local ingredients with Caribbean and international flavors, is complemented by a large wine list. Healthy, mouthwatering winners include the avocado salad and the seafood and spinach ravioli.

MANUEL ANTONIO La Mariposa $$$$$

Hotel La Mariposa, 3 miles (5 km) S of Quepos ***Tel*** *777-0355*

Located in a venerable hotel *(see p207)*, this acclaimed restaurant serves French-inspired cuisine in the open air, with unsurpassed views over the national park. Ranging from local staples such as *gallo pinto*, to tempting entrées, including chicken breast in mustard and French wine sauce, the inventive menu has plenty of appeal.

MANUEL ANTONIO Sunspot Poolside Bar and Grill $$$$$

Makanda by the Sea, 3 miles (5 km) S of Quepos ***Tel*** *777-0442*

Acclaimed and intimate open-air gourmet restaurant with a romantic poolside setting located in a deluxe hotel with dramatic decor and ocean vistas *(see p207)*. Fresh ingredients and creative flare are hallmarks of the nouvelle menu, with many dishes prepared on the grill. Gourmet pizzas are a signature dish. Closed October.

MONTEZUMA El Sano Banano Village Restaurant & Café $$$

W side of the plaza ***Tel*** *642-0638*

This natural-food restaurant in the heart of the village boasts an international menu and is known for its fresh fruit juices. The scrambled tofu breakfast and curried veggies are popular items. Movies, free with dinner, are screened nightly. The restaurant prepares boxed lunches.

PLAYA HERMOSA Jammin Restaurante $

Hwy 34, 2 miles (3 km) S of Jacó ***Tel*** *643-1853*

Popular with the surfing crowd and decorated in trademark black, red, and green, this atmospheric Rastafarian-themed café is built with rough-hewn timbers. Its menu includes American breakfasts and snacks such as *quesadillas* (stuffed fried tortillas) and *ceviche* (marinated raw fish or shellfish).

PLAYA HERRADURA Steve N' Lisa's Paradise Café $$

1 mile (1.6 km) S of Parque Nacional Carara ***Tel*** *637-0168*

Sandwiched between Highway 32 and the ocean, this long-standing and popular open-air roadside diner has a small terrace overlooking the surf. A large menu of light snacks and international dishes includes burgers, tuna melt sandwiches, and cooked meals from pastas to seafood.

PLAYA HERRADURA El Mirador and El Anfiteatro $$$$$

Hotel Villa Caletas, 2 miles (3 km) N of Playa Herradura ***Tel*** *637-0606*

The sublime mountaintop setting at the renowned Hotel Villa Caletas *(see p207)* sets these two fine-dining eateries apart. Gourmet nouvelle dishes evoke the best of fusion cuisine and the classical-themed mood is inviting. A patio with fine views is suited to breakfasts and luncheons. Live concerts are offered in a classical amphitheater.

PLAYA HERRADURA El Nuevo Latino $$$$$

Los Sueños Marriott Ocean & Golf Resort, 1 mile (1.6 km) W of Hwy 34 ***Tel*** *630-9000*

Seafood and gourmet Latin fusion dishes highlight the menu in this elegant, yet informal, restaurant with pool views at the Los Sueños Marriott Ocean & Golf Resort *(see p207)*. Recommended appetizers include lobster and shrimp croquettes, followed perhaps by imaginative entrées such as plantain-crusted red snapper.

Key to Price Guide *see p224* **Key to Symbols** *see back cover flap*

PUNTARENAS La Caravelle V $$$

Paseo de las Turistas, Calle 21/23 ***Tel*** *661-2262*

Snug air-conditioned restaurant run by a Belgian couple who offer gourmet French-inspired fare using local ingredients. Recommended dishes include cream of lobster soup, and *corvina* with palmito purée and white wine sauce. The wood-paneled walls are hung with French-themed prints. Closed Monday.

PUNTARENAS La Yunta Steakhouse V $$$

Paseo de los Turistas ***Tel*** *661-3216*

A venerable two-story wooden home on the main oceanfront drag, this hotel has a shaded windswept veranda overlooking the Gulf of Nicoya. The menu includes grilled steaks, as well as seafood such as the signature *corvina tropical* (sea bass with tropical fruit sauce), all well prepared and offered in filling portions.

QUEPOS Dos Locos V $$

W of the bus station ***Tel*** *777-1526*

This Mexican restaurant has lively decor playing on the cactus and sombrero theme. Open walls lend an airy tropical feel. Its acclaimed regional fare includes expected staples, from *chimichangas* (deep-fried burritos) and *flautas* (cylindrical stuffed tortillas) to *quesadillas*. American breakfasts are also served.

QUEPOS El Gran Escape V $$$$

W of the bus station ***Tel*** *777-0395*

Immensely popular and often packed restaurant in an old two-story wooden building open to refreshing tropical breezes. The wide-ranging menu goes from light snacks to fresh seafood, steaks, and locally inspired coconut curry chicken. There is a sushi bar upstairs.

TAMBOR Restaurante Arrecife V $$$$

Hotel Costa Coral, 1 mile (1.6 km) W of the airstrip ***Tel*** *683-0105*

This clean restaurant boasts colorful contemporary decor. It has an extensive menu of light snacks and seafood, from *ceviche* and *corvina* with heart-of-palm sauce to burgers and chicken in orange sauce. The bar has karaoke and a large-screen TV.

GUANACASTE AND NORTHERN NICOYA

CAÑAS Restaurante Rincón Corobicí V $$

Pan-Am Hwy, 3 miles (5 km) N of Cañas ***Tel*** *669-6262*

Overhanging Río Corobicí, this airy, multidecked roadside restaurant offers a fine vantage point to watch whitewater rafters. The broad-ranging menu features local staples, including seafood – the garlic sea bass is particularly good. The home-made lemonade is a perfect antidote to the mid-summer heat.

CURUBANDÉ Posada el Encuentro Inn V $$$

6 miles (10 km) NE of Liberia ***Tel*** *382-0815*

This gracious and homely restaurant, in an exquisite bed-and-breakfast hotel run by a charming brother and sister team, features Costa Rican and international dishes served in delightfully airy surroundings. Guests can dine on a patio offering magnificent views. Reservations essential.

ISLITA 1492 Restaurante V $$$$$

Hotel Punta Islita, 6 miles (10 km) S of Carrillo ***Tel*** *661-4044*

A romantic and elegant gourmet restaurant under soaring thatch at the deluxe Hacienda Punta Islita resort *(see p208)* enjoys a fabulous hilltop setting and coastal vistas. Chef Lizbeth Molina Muñoz conjures local ingredients into mouthwatering treats influenced by Pacific Rim and European tastes. The service is excellent.

LIBERIA Café Europa V $$

Hwy 21, 12 miles (19 km) W of Liberia ***Tel*** *668-1081*

Small roadside café-bakery offering delicious pastries and breads baked onsite by the German owner. Burgers and German-inspired hot dishes such as breaded veal cutlets are also served. The restaurant can get stuffy; if the weather permits, opt to sit outside.

LIBERIA Restaurante Paso Real V $$$

Calles Central/2 and Ave Central ***Tel*** *666-3455*

Situated over the plaza, this spacious restaurant offers quality seafood, including calamari and lobster dishes, along with *casados* (set meals) and more. A small balcony permits outdoor dining. Service is prompt and courteous. The lively bar has a large-screen TV.

MONTEVERDE Moon Shiva V $$$

2 miles (3 km) E of Santa Elena ***Tel*** *645-6270*

Located at the Bromelias Art Gallery, this offbeat restaurant fuses Costa Rican ingredients with fare inspired by the Middle East, but the menu also features popular non-Hispanic snacks and desserts, as well as cappuccinos. World music plays, adding to the hip, somewhat "alternative" ambience.

MONTEVERDE Restaurant Morphos $$$

Santa Elena village ***Tel*** *645-5607*

In the heart of Santa Elena, this restaurant is built with natural stones and timbers, and has furniture made of rough-hewn logs. It has *casados* (set meals), but the menu also offers burgers, salads, and sea bass Dijon, as well as ice cream sundaes and fresh fruit *batidos* or *refrescos* (shakes). It can be packed, day or night.

MONTEVERDE Garden Restaurante $$$$

Monteverde Lodge, SE of Santa Elena ***Tel*** *645-5057*

Airy restaurant overlooking lush gardens. The menu highlights creative Costa Rican cuisine, such as shredded duck *empañadas* (stuffed turnovers), and coconut and macadamia-crusted sea bass, supported by a large wine list. A cozy bar with a log fire adjoins the restaurant. Service is swift and efficient.

MONTEVERDE El Sapo Dorado $$$$$

Cerro Plano, 0.5 mile (1 km) E of Santa Elena ***Tel*** *645-5010*

Recognized for its wholesome health-food dishes, this elegant restaurant attached to the El Sapo Dorado hotel *(see p209)* has a delightful ambience and an open-air terrace. The inventive menu includes dishes such as tofu with vegetarian primavera, and shrimp in Sambuca sauce, as well as delicious desserts.

NOSARA Pizzería Giardino Tropicale $$

Beaches of Nosara, 4 miles (6 km) S of the airstrip ***Tel*** *682-0258*

A rustic thatched restaurant with several wooden decks beneath shade trees. As the name suggests, it is known for its pizzas fired in a traditional wood-fired oven, but the menu also features seafood, including carpaccio of *corvina* (sea bass) and daily specials.

NOSARA Café de Paris $$$

Beaches of Nosara, 4 miles (6 km) S of the airstrip ***Tel*** *682-0087*

Centrally located within a lovely hotel *(see p209)*, this French-run, open-air restaurant has an eclectic menu, from light snacks, including crêpes and omelettes, to creative nouvelle cuisine, such as chicken breast in green pepper sauce. Enjoy your meals beneath a conical thatched roof supported by stripped and glazed tree trunks.

NOSARA Luna Bar and Grill $$$

Playa Pelada, Beaches of Nosara ***Tel*** *682-0122*

Tucked in a cove, this atmospheric beachfront bar with a hip groove offers gourmet snacks such as sushi rolls and lentil soup. It has a west-facing terrace for enjoying the spectacular sunsets. World music draws patrons on to the dance floor.

NOSARA Marlin Bill's $$$

Beaches of Nosara, 4 miles (6 km) S of the airstrip ***Tel*** *682-0458*

Situated at the main junction of the unpaved coast road, this elevated open-air eatery highlights American favorites, from pork loin chops and blackened tuna salad to Key lime pie. It is very popular with locals, who congregate at the bar, which also has a TV.

PLAYA CARRILLO El Sueño Tropical $$$

1 mile (1.6 km) SE of Puerto Carrillo ***Tel*** *656-0151*

An unpretentiously elegant restaurant with a soaring thatched roof and quintessential tropical motif set in a comfortable hotel *(see p209)*. The owners – three brothers from Verona, Italy – prepare mouthwatering treats such as *ravioli de pescado*, and are usually on hand to fuss over guests. An adjacent pool is handy for cooling off.

PLAYA CONCHAL Bar y Restaurante Camarón Dorado $$

N of plaza, Brasilito ***Tel*** *654-4028*

Edging on to the sands, this colorful yet rustic, no-frills restaurant has a suitably expansive menu of seafood, as well as some very filling salads such as the mixed *camarón dorado* – a veritable smorgasbord of meats, cheeses, and shellfish.

PLAYA CONCHAL Condor Lodge and Beach Resort $$$

SW of Playa Conchal ***Tel*** *653-8950*

Located atop a hill with stupendous views over the beach and beyond, this restaurant offers the option of dining on an open terrace. The menu features local and international staples, but guests come primarily for the unbeatable views. It has a swimming pool, and a bar and casino upstairs.

PLAYA CONCHAL Restaurante Las Playas $$$

Hotel Brasilito, NW corner of the plaza, Brasilito ***Tel*** *654-4596*

Open to the elements, this windswept restaurant in the Hotel Brasilito is splendidly situated just a few steps from the beach. A huge international menu includes classic German dishes, seafood, and steaks. The place for breakfasts, it offers warm croissants, *huevos rancheros* (a breakfast favorite made with tortillas and eggs), and more.

PLAYA FLAMINGO Marie's Restaurante $$$

W of the marina ***Tel*** *654-4136*

Airy country-style restaurant decorated with a maritime motif and a wood-fired oven. It caters to sailors with a menu of international favorites – from fish and chips to burritos – served on an open, tree-shaded veranda. A wide choice of coffee drinks and ice cream sundaes are reason enough to choose Marie's, named after the English-born hostess.

PLAYA GRANDE The Great Waltini's $$$

Hotel Bula Bula, S of El Mundo de la Tortuga, S end of Playa Grande ***Tel*** *653-0975*

This small restaurant in delightful Hotel Bula Bula *(see p210)* has a shaded deck overlooking a landscaped garden. Snacks and gourmet fusion dishes from the hands of a professional chef are served. Consider the shrimp and crab-cakes followed by duckling with red wine and raspberry reduction. The eatery hosts a rib night each Wednesday.

PLAYA GRANDE Hotel Las Tortugas $$$$

W of El Mundo de la Tortuga, N end of Playa Grande ***Tel*** *653-0423*

Situated close to the beach within Hotel Las Tortugas *(see p210)*, this restaurant serves light meals such as burgers and salads, as well as steaks and seafood. The owners boast of their apple pie and ice cream, and with good reason. There is a shaded wooden deck, and the service and mood are relaxed and friendly.

PLAYA HERMOSA Hotel La Finisterra $$$$

Atop the hill, W of the main road, S end of Playa Hermosa ***Tel*** *670-0293*

Recherché French-Costa Rican cuisine served on the hilltop terrace of La Finisterra *(see p210)*. Dishes such as filet mignon with peppercorn sauce have earned the chef a regional reputation for excellence. Sushi is served on Friday evenings. Closed Tuesday.

PLAYA HERMOSA Villas del Sueño $$$$

S end of Playa Hermosa ***Tel*** *672-0026*

Elegance is a keyword at this open-air restaurant of the well-run Villas del Sueño *(see p210)*. Live bands perform in high season. Gourmet meals focus on fresh seafood such as mahimahi and shrimp in cream sauce, but also include such dishes as tenderloin in brandy and three-pepper sauce.

PLAYA NEGRA Café Playa Negro $$

S of Los Pargos Plaza ***Tel*** *658-8143*

Small, charming Internet café in the village center, a short walk from the beach. The Peruvian-born owner-chef offers a wide selection of light food, from pancakes and French toast to *ceviche* (marinated raw fish or shellfish), quiches, and pastas. Leave room for the lemon pie or an iced fresh fruit *batido* (shake).

PLAYA NEGRA Hotel Playa Negra $$$

11 miles (18 km) S of Tamarindo ***Tel*** *658-8034*

This shaded thatched restaurant has a breezy oceanfront setting in Hotel Playa Negra *(see p210)*. It offers French-inspired dishes plus *gallo pinto (see p222)* breakfasts and international lunch staples such as burgers. It has a pool table in the bar, and the hotel's swimming pool is open to diners.

PLAYA NEGRA Pablo's Picasso $$$

S of Los Pargos ***Tel*** *658-8158*

Located in a hotel *(see p210)*, this rustic restaurant with a barefoot ambience serves jumbo burgers, pastas, and *típico* (typical) dishes plus filling American breakfasts, including pancakes. It boasts a pool table and movies at the bar with oversize wooden chairs. Popular with the surfing crowd.

PLAYA OCOTAL Father Rooster Bar & Grill $$$

2 miles (3 km) W of Playas del Coco ***Tel*** *670-1246*

Situated on the sands, this rustic restaurant is centered on a lively bar of rough-hewn timbers, which serves killer cocktails. The menu focuses on bar foods, such as burgers and *quesadillas* (stuffed fried tortillas). Activities include volleyball, and the mood is almost always party-hearty.

PLAYAS DEL COCO Louisiana Bar and Grill $$$

S of the plaza ***Tel*** *670-0882*

On the main drag, this breeze-swept upstairs restaurant with balcony specializes in spicy hot Cajun food and local seafood, many of them quite creative, such as squid with olives and onions. The *ceviche* appetizer is recommended. It is popular with the younger crowd. Closed Thursday.

PLAYAS DEL COCO Restaurante Sol y Luna $$$

Hotel Puerta del Sol, SE of the plaza ***Tel*** *670-0195*

Opening on to an exquisitely landscaped garden in Hotel Puerta del Sol *(see p211)*, this intimate restaurant has Romanesque decor and a menu of Italian staples prepared by a professional chef. An extensive wine list and delicious coffee drinks and desserts, including tiramisu, round off the menu.

SÁMARA El Delfin $$$

E of the soccer field ***Tel*** *656-0418*

High-quality restaurant fringing the beach, with a romantic candlelit ambience and French-influenced menu that also extends to pastas, pizzas, and ice cream sundaes. The French owner is on hand to ensure consistent quality and take care of guests.

TAMARINDO Lazy Wave $$

Hotel Pasatiempo, S of Plaza Colonial ***Tel*** *653-0737*

With a dead tree at its heart, this open-air restaurant draws a young, high-energy crowd. The seafood menu favors the health-conscious and offers a daily selection of fusion dishes, such as wasabi-crusted tuna. Eclectic dishes such as *jambalaya* (a kind of paella) are also available occasionally. Closed Sunday.

TAMARINDO Panadería La Laguna del Cocodrilo $$

E of Tamarindo Diría and Plaza Colonial ***Tel*** *653-0065*

Situated in front of a lagoon with crocodiles, this congenial bakery-café produces superb pastries and *empañadas* (stuffed turnovers) and is known for its all-you-can-eat breakfast buffet. The French owners deliver consistently light croissants and sweet and savory tarts.

TAMARINDO Stella's Fine Dining $$$$

S of Plaza Colonial ***Tel*** *653-0127*

An intimate restaurant serving gourmet seafood, steaks, and vegetarian dishes under thatch. Wood-fired pizzas, Wiener schnitzel, and Thai fish curry exemplify the global reach of the menu. The extensive wine and beer list is similarly international. Free transfers are offered to and from guests' hotels.

TAMARINDO Capitán Suizo $$$$$

0.5 mile (1 km) SW of Plaza Colonial ***Tel*** *653-0075*

Fine nouvelle cuisine served in an airy, colorful, and tranquil beachfront restaurant with a poolside bar, located within the luxurious Capitán Suizo hotel *(see p212)*. Creative dishes fuse European influences and Costa Rican ingredients – sea bass in mango sauce and tilapia fish in caper sauce are typical of the menu, which changes daily.

TAMARINDO El Jardín del Edén $$$$$

SE of Tamarindo Diría and Plaza Colonial ***Tel*** *653-0137*

Overlooking a landscaped swimming pool, floodlit at night, this thatched restaurant is appealing for its exquisitely romantic atmosphere. Gourmet Mediterranean-inspired dishes include lobster in lemon sauce, and jumbo shrimp in whiskey. Fresh-baked pastries and *gallo pinto (see p222)* are served at breakfast.

THE NORTHERN ZONE

CHACHAGUA Coco Loco Art Gallery and Café $$$

6 miles (10 km) SE of La Fortuna ***Tel*** *468-0990*

A charming roadside café with inventive decor, outdoor patios, and splendid art galleries. The international menu, prepared by the live-in German owners, includes sandwiches (the BLT is recommended) and Mediterranean-inspired salads, all at fair prices. Select from various gourmet coffees and teas, plus fresh fruit smoothies.

LA FORTUNA Choza de Laurel $

W of the plaza ***Tel*** *479-9231*

A rustic restaurant in the style of an old farmhouse, with a wood-fired *horno* (oven) and beams adorned with cloves of garlic. Inexpensive *casados* (set meals) and local dishes are the focus, as well as rotisserie chicken and other grilled meats. The *plato especial* (mixed plate) is popular.

LA FORTUNA Restaurante Luigi $$$

Luigi's Hotel, 2 blocks W of the plaza ***Tel*** *479-9636*

Flambée dishes are a specialty of this elegant restaurant, but the menu also includes local seafood and other internationally recognized dishes, such as beef stroganoff, along with pizzas and pastas. Attached to Luigi's Hotel *(see p213)*, this spacious eatery opens onto a pleasant roadside terrace.

LA FORTUNA Soda La Cascada $$$

N of the plaza ***Tel*** *479-9145*

With a huge circular thatched roof, La Cascada dominates the town square. Open-sided and airy, it has a pleasingly informal ambience. Mid-priced Western favorites are served, as are pastas, pizzas, and Costa Rican staples, from *gallo pinto* to *corvina al ajillo* (garlic sea bass). An upstairs bar has a large-screen TV and disco.

LAGUNA DE ARENAL Tom's Pan $$

Nuevo Arenal, SE of the plaza ***Tel*** *694-4547*

This rustic, German-run bakery-café on the main drag in town serves baked dishes hot from the oven. It also offers international favorites, including American breakfasts, as well as lasagne and sauerkraut. There are only a few tables and chairs on the shaded terrace out front.

LAGUNA DE ARENAL Mystica Lodge $$$

10 miles (16 km) W of Nuevo Arenal ***Tel*** *692-1001*

Located in the intimate Mystica Lodge *(see p213)*, this Italian restaurant is colorful by day and romantic by night. It has exquisite decor: informally elegant place settings, rough-hewn timber furniture, tropical pastels, and flowers on every table. Pizzas are the specialty, but the raviolis and other dishes, prepared in the open kitchen, are all top-notch.

LAGUNA DE ARENAL Toad Hall $$$

5 miles (8 km) E of Nuevo Arenal ***Tel*** *692-8020*

Café-style balcony dining with splendid lake views is offered at this art gallery serving organic salads, foccacia sandwiches, scrumptious desserts, and gourmet coffees and teas. The decor is colorful, the setting sublime, and the simple dishes prepared by the live-in owners are tasty and filling.

Key to Price Guide *see p224* **Key to Symbols** *see back cover flap*

LAGUNA DE ARENAL Hotel La Mansion Inn $$$$

5 miles (8 km) E of Nuevo Arenal ***Tel*** *692-8018*

This is an elegant and airy restaurant with rustic country decor and fine views of the lake, set in a deluxe hotel *(see p213)*. Gourmet dishes fuse international and Costa Rican cuisines, and soups, sandwiches, and light snacks are also served. The atmospheric bar, in the shape of a ship's prow, is a fine spot for postprandial cocktails.

LAGUNA DE ARENAL Restaurante Willy's Caballo Negro $$$$

1 mile (1.6 km) W of Nuevo Arenal ***Tel*** *694-4515*

The owner's German origins show in the menu of this delightful café overlooking a pond with waterfowl. Its schnitzels are well known, but eggplant Parmesan and veal cutlet in spicy onion and bell pepper sauce exemplify more inventive fare. Reservations are necessary. Its art store, the Lucky Bug Gallery, is renowned.

PARQUE NACIONAL VOLCAN ARENAL Arenal Observatory Lodge $$$$

5 miles (8 km) SE of the park entrance ***Tel*** *692-2070*

Spectacular views of Volcán Arenal are the main draw of this restaurant, which is located in a modern ecolodge *(see p213)* on the upper flanks of Volcán Chato. Its menu melds international influences with local ingredients: the chicken in curry sauce and the various tilapia dishes are recommended. Service is courteous and efficient.

TABACÓN Balneario Tabacón $$$

8 miles (13 km) W of La Fortuna ***Tel*** *460-6229*

Situated over steaming hot springs with dramatic volcano views, this airy restaurant offers Costa Rican staples and a wide choice of quality international dishes, from *gallo pinto* to burgers and French onion soup. The *corvina* in apple and chile pepper sauce is recommended. Service is efficient.

THE CARIBBEAN

CAHUITA Miss Edith's $$

NW of Cahuita Plaza ***Tel*** *755-0248*

Spicy Caribbean classics such as "rundown" *(see p223)* are featured at this colorful restaurant attached to the home of the eponymous owner. The family prepares meals in an open kitchen, and patrons dine on a shaded and colorful terrace. Home-made ice cream is served on weekends, and the herb teas are worth trying.

CAHUITA Cha Cha Cha $$$

W of Cahuita Plaza ***Tel*** *394-4153*

A wide-ranging menu spans the globe at this charmingly rustic restaurant painted white with blue trim and lit by candles and fairy-lights. Grilled squid salad, fajitas, and spicy coconut honey wings are typical appetizers. Entrées range from filet mignon to sea bass with shrimp and basil sauce. Closed Monday.

CAHUITA Casa Creole $$$$

Magellan Inn, Playa Negra, 3 miles (5 km) N of Cahuita village ***Tel*** *755-0035*

Attached to the Magellan Inn *(see p214)*, this informally elegant open-air restaurant specializes in creative nouvelle cuisine fusing Asian, European, and Caribbean flavors. The spiced shrimp Martinique in Creole sauce is a signature dish. Candlelit dining adds to the romance, and the creative cocktails are splendid. By reservation only.

GUÁCIMO Restaurant Río Palmas $$

Hwy 32, 1 mile (1.6 km) E of Guácimo ***Tel*** *760-0330*

The special feature of this welcoming roadside restaurant are its forest trails good for spotting poison-dart frogs. The menu features the standard Costa Rican fare, as well as international dishes. The dining is in the open air beneath a red-tile roof, but is set back from the busy highway.

MANZANILLO Bar y Restaurante Maxi $

Manzanillo village ***Tel*** *759-9061*

This no-frills restaurant in a two-story wooden structure draws a young party crowd and is always lively, even at lunch. Quality seafood snacks and dishes cooked Caribbean-style as well as filling *típico* (typical) dishes are served, including on the beach by request.

PLAYA COCLES La Pecora Nera $$$$$

1 mile (1.6 km) E of Puerto Viejo ***Tel*** *750-0490*

An unpretentious yet world-class restaurant where mouthwatering gourmet Italian fare belies the offbeat locale. Delicious gnocchis, bruschetta, pizzas, and calzones feature on the wide-ranging menu. The Italian owner-chef Ilario Giannono and his family fuss over patrons. Closed Monday.

PUERTO LIMÓN Restaurante Brisas del Caribe $$

Calles 0/1 and Ave 2 ***Tel*** *758-0138*

This clean and airy downtown restaurant, on the north side of Parque Vargas, is the best in town. It is known for its seafood dishes but the locals flock there especially for its lunchtime *casados* and for its large buffet of *típico* fare, served cafeteria-style.

PUERTO LIMÓN Restaurante La Salamander $$

Calle 2 and Ave 3

A stylish little café in a renovated century-old structure in the heart of the city, La Salamander has a surprisingly bohemian air. On the menu are Costa Rican staples, sandwiches, and desserts, as well as tea and cappuccinos. An upstairs bar has pool tables.

PUERTO VIEJO DE TALAMANCA Café Rico $$

NE of the soccer field ***Tel*** *750-0510*

This rustic open-air café in a two-story structure of rough-hewn timbers serves hearty, health-conscious breakfasts and lunches on the palm-fringed ground floor. This is the place for granola with fruit and yogurt, sandwiches and scrambles, or *huevos rancheros* (a breakfast favorite made with tortillas and eggs). Closed Monday and Tuesday.

PUERTO VIEJO DE TALAMANCA Salsa Brava $$$

E of Puerto Viejo village ***Tel*** *750-0241*

This informal rainbow-hued thatched restaurant has a lovely beachfront setting and an international menu featuring *ceviche* (marinated raw fish or shellfish), Caesar salad with chicken teriyaki, ice cream sundaes, and sangría. The Spanish owners provide filling portions. It has counter dining and a roadside patio. Closed Monday.

PUERTO VIEJO DE TALAMANCA Shawandha Lodge $$$$

Playa Chiquita, 3 miles (5 km) E of Puerto Viejo ***Tel*** *750-0018*

A delightful ambience pervades this classy restaurant attached to a romantic lodge *(see p215)*. The Tico chef fuses tropical flavors into tantalizing French-Caribbean dishes. A typical dinner might comprise avocado and palmito salad, lobster *à la Normandie*, and mango mousse.

TORTUGUERO Miss Junie's $$

N of the public dock, Tortuguero village ***Tel*** *710-0523*

Named for a village matriarch who serves delicious Caribbean dishes, such as jerk chicken, and lobster in curry and coconut milk, on the porch of her home-turned-lodge *(see p215)*. She also bakes *pan bon* (bread laced with caramelized sugar) and ginger cakes. Not open for breakfast. Reservations needed.

THE SOUTHERN ZONE

BAHÍA DRAKE Aguila de Osa Inn $$$

0.5 mile (1 km) S of Agujitas ***Tel*** *296-2190*

This circular, thatched restaurant of the Aguila de Osa Inn *(see p216)* is perhaps the best in the area, and most dishes are filling and flavorful, albeit not gourmet. Seafood, including sushi, dominates the menu, which also ranges to pastas. It has splendid bay views, best enjoyed from the relaxing sofas with a cocktail in hand.

CABO MATAPALO Lapa Ríos $$$$

9 miles (14 km) S of Puerto Jiménez ***Tel*** *735-5130*

A soaring *palenque* restaurant and an eclectic gourmet menu are signatures of this acclaimed ecolodge *(see p216)*. The chefs are locals trained to exacting standards. Pineapple honey ginger salad, coconut crusted fish, and delicious coffee cake are typical of the rotating menu. Spiral stairs lead to a lookout with spectacular views.

CIUDAD NEILY Hotel Andrea $$$

23 miles (37 km) E of Golfito ***Tel*** *783-4682*

Set within a Colonial-style hotel *(see p217)* in the heart of town, this clean and well-run restaurant, open to the tropical breezes, offers the best dining for miles. Breakfast is excellent, with *huevos rancheros*, pancakes with honey, and more. The lunch and dinner menu offers international favorites, from onion soup to filet mignon.

DOMINICAL Roca Verde $$$

0.5 mile (1 km) S of Dominical ***Tel*** *787-0036*

This cavernous bar-restaurant at the beachfront Hotel Roca Verde *(see p217)* is popular with the surf crowd. The filling breakfasts include granola with fruit and yoghurt, and *gallo pinto (see p222)*. Lunchtime *casados* (set meals) and light snacks are also served. It has a pool table, TV, and eccentric decor, and the music can sometimes be loud.

DOMINICAL San Clemente Bar and Grill $$$

S of the soccer field ***Tel*** *787-0055*

This informal bar and grill serves American and Tex-Mex favorites, as well as seafood such as mahimahi with honey and orange sauce. Owner Mike McGinnis makes his own searingly hot sauces. The lively bar is festooned with surf boards, and has a pool table and sports TV. The place also runs a hostel a short walk away *(see p217)*.

GOLFITO Bilge Bar and Grill $$$

Banana Bay Marina, S of the plaza ***Tel*** *775-0838*

This bar has a casual waterfront setting at Banana Bay Marina *(see p217)*. The menu specializes in Western favorites, such as the restaurant's trademark Bilge Burger, as well as seafood, including a spicy gumbo, and meat dishes such as pork loin with mushrooms. The decor plays on the sportfishing theme.

GOLFITO Le Coquillage $$$

Hotel Centro Turístico Samoa, N of Pueblo Civil ***Tel*** *775-0233*

This airy restaurant at the Centro Turístico Samoa *(see p217)* encircles a bar in the shape of a ship's prow. It offers international favorites and a wide selection of seafood, including *corvina al ajillo* (garlic sea bass). Bar games include pool, table soccer, and darts.

OJOCHAL Hotel Posada Restaurant $$$

Hotel Posada Playa Tortuga, 0.5 mile (1 km) W of Ojochal ***Tel*** *384-5489*

This open-air restaurant within a peaceful and secluded beachfront hotel offers superb views. On the menu are several Italian seafood dishes and pizzas with real Italian Gorgonzola. A specialty of the restaurant is pumpernickel bread.

OJOCHAL Villas Gaia $$$

Playa Tortuga, 0.5 mile (1 km) W of Ojochal ***Tel*** *244-0316*

Attached to the small Villas Gaia *(see p218)*, this open-air roadside restaurant has colorful, casual decor, and a vast international menu with a selection of soups, salads, and light snacks, as well as exotic cooked dishes, such as macadamia-crusted fish fillet. The eatery features an extensive children's menu, and also prepares boxed lunches.

OJOCHAL Restaurant Exótica $$$$

Ojochal village ***Tel*** *369-9261*

This small and intimate restaurant is acclaimed for its creative tropical nouvelle cuisine that draws upon the best of Continental influences – fish filet with banana curry sauce, for example. The outdoor candlelit dining offers tremendous romantic appeal, and the wine list is extensive. Closed Sunday.

PUERTO JIMÉNEZ Restaurante Carolina $

SE of the soccer field ***Tel*** *735-5185*

Located on the main street and popular with the backpacking crowd, this budget restaurant is adorned with murals of jungle scenes. It offers well-prepared and filling *típico* (typical) dishes, including variations on *gallo pinto*, and seafood served alfresco. International influences are present in the likes of chicken cordon bleu.

PUERTO JIMÉNEZ Juanita's Mexican Bar and Grill $$

SE of the soccer field ***Tel*** *735-5056*

Filling Tex-Mex fare and a genuine Mexican ambience in an atmospheric *cantina (see p220)* that is the liveliest place in town. Choose from expected staples such as taco salads, burritos, and *chimichangas* (deep-fried burritos). Entertainment includes hula hoop contests and live crab races, the fun being assisted by giant margaritas.

PUERTO JIMÉNEZ Monochingo Bar & Grill $$

Playa Platanares, 2 miles (3 km) E of Puerto Jiménez ***Tel*** *735-5205*

Monochingo is a colorful beachfront restaurant with hammocks and a delightful button-down, barefoot ambience. Dishes include Caesar salad, *empañadas* (stuffed turnovers), and grilled chicken club sandwiches. It has pasta night on Fridays. The hardwood bar serves fresh fruit smoothies and exotic tropical cocktails.

SAN ISIDRO DE EL GENERAL Taquería México Lindo $

Calle Central and Ave 2 ***Tel*** *771-8222*

Situated on the northwest side of the plaza, this Mexican restaurant offers a full menu of regional fare at exceptional prices. The chef hails from Mexico, and the burritos, enchiladas, and vanilla flans are as authentic as anywhere in Costa Rica. The place is festooned with *piñatas* (papier-mâché vessels) and other colorful Mexican decor.

SAN ISIDRO DE EL GENERAL Café Trapiche $$

Rancho La Botija, 4 miles (6 km) NE of San Isidro ***Tel*** *770-2146*

This rustic farmstead at Rancho La Botija *(see p219)* has endearing country decor, such as antique farm implements. The simple menu of *típico* and international dishes includes pastas, garlic sea bass, and steaks. It is open only for breakfast and lunch.

SAN VITO Pizzería Liliana $

NW of the plaza ***Tel*** *773-3080*

Splendid pizzas and other Italian staples attest to the heritage of the owners at this simple restaurant located in the center of town. The cooking is homely rather than gourmet, and great value for money. Diners can eat alfresco on a small patio.

UVITA Balcón de Uvita $$$

0.5 mile (1 km) NE of Uvita ***Tel*** *743-8034*

Spectacular coastal vistas are one of the highlights of this small timber restaurant located within the Balcón de Uvita hotel in the mountains *(see p219)*. A professional chef creates Indonesian- and Thai-inspired dishes that include a *rijsttaffel* (rice table). Reservations are required. Closed Monday–Wednesday.

ZANCUDO Cabinas Sol y Mar $$$$

Roy's Zancudo Lodge, 1 mile (1.6 km) S of Zancudo village ***Tel*** *776-0014*

Attached to a simple hotel *(see p219)*, this open-air beachfront bar and restaurant specializing in California nouvelle cuisine attracts the local expatriates. American breakfasts, including outstanding omelettes and home fries, and snacks are also offered, and the bar, which is extremely relaxed, hosts karaoke and lawn games.

Shopping in Costa Rica

For many visitors, shopping is one of the thrills of a trip to Costa Rica. The range of quality *artesanías* (crafts) has grown rapidly in recent years, and most hotels have stores selling coffee, beautiful earthenware pottery in pre-Columbian style, handwoven hammocks, and souvenirs such as bowls and animal figures made of exotic hardwoods. San José has several art galleries, craft stores that stock a range of products including *molas* (reverse-appliqué cloth) from Bahía Drake and Sarchí leather rockers, and city malls that offer a vast choice of boutiques and jewelry stores. Across the country, bustling *mercados* (markets) are full of trinkets, piles of spices and herbs, *talabarterías* (saddle-makers) and *zapaterías* (shoe-makers), while colorful roadside stalls are piled high with fruits and vegetables. Indigenous crafts are increasingly appearing on the market. Note that it is illegal to buy or export pre-Columbian artifacts.

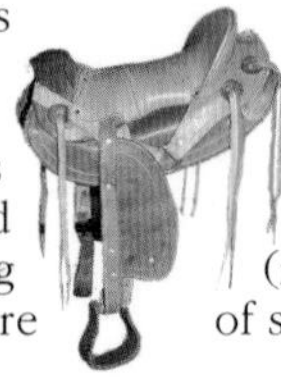

Saddle, Ciudad Quesada

Palm-leaf baskets and hats for sale at a roadside stall

Opening Hours

Shops in San José are usually open from 8am to 6pm, Monday to Saturday. Large US-style malls are open on Sundays, but may close on Mondays. Outside San José, many *tiendas* (shops) close for lunch, typically between noon and 1:30pm. Shops in many tourist resorts remain open all week long, often until 9 or 10pm. Department stores and supermarkets everywhere stay open during lunchtime and often into the evening. Street markets and *mercados* usually open at around 6am and close by 2 or 3pm, although street stalls often stay open late.

Paying and Prices

Cash will be needed to pay for goods bought directly from craftsmen and at street stalls and markets. However, most stores accept VISA, and to a lesser degree, MasterCard and American Express, as well as US dollars. Credit card payments are sometimes subject to a small surcharge. Torn dollar bills are usually refused by shopkeepers. Some shops accept traveler's checks. A 13 percent sales tax will be added to the cost of most consumer goods in shops.

While leather goods are less expensive here than in most other countries, in general prices are relatively high. Items in galleries and hotel gift stores are sold at a fixed price. However, a certain amount of bargaining is expected at craft markets and *mercados*. The local artisans' cooperative markets have the best prices, and being government-regulated, ensure that a large slice of the profit goes directly to the craftsman. In general, larger stores and local export companies will arrange to have purchases shipped to the buyer's home.

Art Galleries

San José has numerous art galleries selling paintings, sculptures, and prints by leading artists. Many of the best are centered around Parque Morazán *(see p66)* and **Centro Comercial El Pueblo**, which has over a dozen galleries. Two good outlets are the **Andrómeda Gallery** and **Kandinsky**. Avant-garde works are sold at **Teorética**, in Barrio Amón, and **Arte 99**, in the upscale western suburb of Rohrmoser.

Many professional artists live in Monteverde. Manco Tulio Brenes sells his lovely paintings and sculptures at **Galería Extasis**, and North American Sarah Dodwell's distinctive works are available at the **Sarah Dodwell Watercolor Gallery**. In the Caribbean lowlands, call in at Patricia Erickson's **Gallery at Home** *(see p164)*, from where the artist sells her vibrant Afro-themed paintings.

Centro Comercial El Pueblo, San José

Shelves of colorful objects in a San José craft store

Craft Stores

The variety of *artesanías* available in Costa Rica is quite large. Quality craft stores sell a range of products, from woodworks, which are created out of exotic hardwoods such as rosewood, ironwood, and purpleheart, to nature-themed books and tapes to Guatemalan weavings and embroideries.

Toad Hall sign, Lake Arenal

The town of Sarchí *(see p86)* in the Central Highlands is the main source of crafts, and produces leather rocking chairs, handmade furniture with bas-relief carvings, and brightly painted miniature *carretas* (oxcarts; *see p87*). Here, the **Fábrica de Carretas Joaquín Chaverrí** has the largest and best selection of crafts. Nearby, the **Plaza de la Artesanía** also has several craft shops.

Many store owners pride themselves on seeking out the finest quality crafts. Two such shops, **Toad Hall** *(see p234)* and **Lucky Bug Gallery** *(see p150)*, are on the north shore of Lake Arenal. A huge array of crafts are displayed at shops along Highway 21, not far from Liberia's Daniel Oduber International Airport.

In San José, the **Boutique Annemarie**, in the Hotel Don Carlos, has a fabulous array of crafts at fair prices, as does **La Casona**, a two-story building with several stores selling a varied range of Central American crafts.

Visitors who like browsing open-air markets should head to the artisans' market on the west side of **Plaza de la Democracía** *(see p70)*. The **Mercado de Artesanías Nacionales** nearby houses a similarly broad range of craft stalls under one roof. The most concentrated crafts shopping, however, is in the northeastern suburb of Moravia, where Calle de la Artesanía is lined with crafts stores. Here, the **Mercado de Artesanía Las Garzas** has several dozen stores. Competition is intense, and bargaining is normal.

Indigenous Crafts

Although Costa Rica does not have as strong an indigenous craft tradition as other Latin American nations, it has many unique handicrafts to offer visitors. The Boruca tribe of **Reserva Indígena Boruca** *(see p184)* make balsa-wood masks and bas-relief wall hangings, available at a discount if bought directly from the artists. When buying directly from the craftsmen, bear in mind that their margin of profit is usually quite low. Many of the finest examples of Boruca art are also available in quality crafts stores in San José, and at **Coco Loco Art Gallery and Café** *(see p234)* in Chachagua near La Fortuna. Coco Loco also sells some fabulous contemporary pottery and marble carvings by leading artists.

Intriguing indigenous pottery comes from **Guaitíl** *(see p143)*, where ocher vases, bowls, plates, and animals emblazoned with traditional Chorotega motifs are sold at the potters' roadside stalls. The women of Agujitas village, near **Bahía Drake** *(see p190)* on the Osa Peninsula, still make and sell colorful hand-stitched *molas* in the style of the San Blas islands of Panama.

The two best commercial outlets for indigenous arts and crafts are **ANDA** and **Galería Namu**, which sells an excellent selection of palm-leaf baskets, Boruca masks, Huetar carvings, and colorful, embroidered Guaymí clothing.

Pottery wares lining a street in Santa Ana, near San José

Woodworks

Popular items sold in stores specializing in woodwork include figurines, kitchen utensils, bowls, and jewelry boxes. Some of the finest wooden bowls and boxes are produced by **Barry Biesanz Woodworks** *(see p75)* – it is possible to buy directly from his Escazú studio. Biesanz's works have been gifted by the government of Costa Rica to many visiting dignitaries.

Gold jewelry on sale, Museo del Oro Precolombino store

Jewelry

Skilled goldsmiths craft exquisite jewelry using both modern designs and pre-Columbian motifs such as frogs and birds, often incorporating semi-precious stones such as lapis lazuli, onyx, and jade. It is best to buy from reputable stores, such as San José's **Esmeraldas y Diseños**. Most deluxe hotels and large malls also have jewelry stores. For good-quality jewelry in 14-carat gold, the Museo del Oro Precolombino store *(see p63)* is worth a visit. Items sold at streetside jewelry stalls are usually gold-washed, not pure gold.

Coffee

Several *beneficios* (coffee-processing factories) are open to visitors and will ship bulk purchases of vacuum-packed coffee. Among these are the Café Britt airport gift stores and the Café Britt *beneficio (see p92)*, which has a well-stocked craft store. Many regional varieties of coffee are sold at **La Esquina del Café**, where traditional Costa Rican coffee-strainers called *chorreadores* are also available. Domestic-quality coffee is sold at shops in San José's **Mercado Central** *(see p58)*, where it is roasted on the spot; ask for *granos puros* (whole beans) rather than *café traditional*, which is coffee ground very fine and mixed with sugar.

Garments

Traditional Guanacasteco (from Guanacaste) dresses and blouses, such as those worn by dancers of Fantasía Folklórico *(see p245)*, are sold at **La Choza Folklórica** in San José. **Angie Theologos** makes colorful jackets with Guatemalan cloth, while Fundación Neotrópica's **Tienda de la Naturaleza**, in the suburb of Curridabat, sells good-quality T-shirts. There are no factory outlets selling discounted designer clothes.

Other Specialty Stores

The suburb of Moravia in San José is known for its leatherwork. Belts and purses are an excellent buy, as are cowboy boots, which range in design from classical to trendy. A wide selection of cowboy boots is sold by *zapaterías* (shoemakers) in Barrio México, northwest of downtown San José. Ciudad Quesada *(see p154)* is the best place to buy ornate saddles – a wide variety is available. Leather costs significantly less than in Europe or North America.

The capital city has several cigar outlets, which stock Cuban cigars. The **Cigar Shoppe** and **Habanos de Costa Rica**, in the city center, and **Casa del Habano** and **Habanos Smoking Club**, both in the San Pedro district, are recommended. Don't buy cigars on the street; the boxed cigars may look genuine but they are almost always cheap fakes. However, US citizens should note that it is illegal for them to bring home Cuban products, even if bought in Costa Rica.

Beautiful orchids in sealed vials are available at several airport gift shops, and in various gardens such as **Jardín Botánico Lankester** *(see p93)* and **Orchid Alley** in La Garita.

Many artists produce stunning *vidriera* (stained glass). Good sources are **Galería de Vitrales y Cerámica**, on Sabana Norte, and Escazú's **Creaciones Santos**.

One of the many specialty leather stores in Costa Rica

Stalls selling fresh produce and other articles at Mercado Central, San José

Markets

Every town has its *mercado central* (central market), selling everything from cowboy hats to medicinal herbs. Good buys at San José's Mercado Central include embroidered *guayabero* shirts (summer shirts for men), and cowboy boots made of exotic leathers. Town markets can be dark warrens, and quite crowded, especially on Saturdays; shoppers should watch out for pickpockets. Not many shopkeepers speak English. Most towns also have *ferias de agricultores* (farmers' markets) on weekends, which sell all kinds of fresh produce. These usually start at dawn and are frequented by locals.

Malls are found only in big towns. **Mall San Pedro** in San José has many boutiques.

Directory

Art Galleries

Andrómeda Gallery
Calle 9 and Ave 9,
Barrio Amón,
San José.
☎ *223-3529.*

Arte 99
Rohrmoser,
San José.
☎ *232-4035.*

Centro Comercial El Pueblo
Barrio Tournon.
☎ *222-5938.*

Galería Extasis
Monteverde.
☎ *645-5548.*

Kandinsky
Centro Comercial,
Calle Real,
San Pedro, San José.
☎ *234-0478.*

Sarah Dodwell Watercolor Gallery
Monteverde.
☎ *645-5047.*

Teorética
Calle 7 and Aves 9/11,
San José.
☎ *233-4881.*

Craft Stores

Boutique Annemarie
Calle 9 & Ave 9, San José.
☎ *221-6707.*

La Casona
Calle Central and Ave Central, San José.
☎ *222-7999.*

Mercado de Artesanía Las Garzas
Calle 8 and Ave 2 bis,
San José.

Mercado de Artesanías Nacionales
Calle 22 and Ave 2 bis,
San José.
☎ *223-0122.*

Plaza de la Artesanía
Sarchí Sur, Sarchí.
☎ *454-3430.*

Indigenous Crafts

ANDA
Calles 5 & Ave 2, San José.
☎ *233-3340.*

Galería Namu
Calles 5/7 and Ave 7,
San José.
☎ *256-3412.*

Jewelry

Esmeraldas y Diseños
Sabana Norte,
San José.
☎ *231-4808.*

Coffee

La Esquina del Café
Guachipelín-Escazú.
☎ *228-9541.*

Garments

Angie Theologos
San Pedro, San José.
☎ *225-6565.*

La Choza Folklórica
Calle 1 and Ave 3,
San José.

Tienda de la Naturaleza
Ave Central, Curridabat.
☎ *253-1230.*

Other Specialty Stores

Casa del Habano
Calle 4 and Ave 1,
San José.
☎ *280-7931.*

Cigar Shoppe
Calle 5 and Ave 3,
San José.
☎ *257-5021.*

Creaciones Santos
Calles 1/3 and Ave 3,
San Miguel de Escazú.
☎ *228-6747.*

Galería de Vitrales y Cerámica
Ave las Américas, San José.
☎ *232-7932.*

Habanos de Costa Rica
Calle 7 and Aves 7/9,
San José.
☎ *383-6835.*

Habanos Smoking Club
Plaza Calle Reál,
San Pedro, San José.
☎ *224-5227.*

Orchid Alley
La Garita.
☎ *487-7086.*

Markets

Mall San Pedro
Ave Central and
Circunvalación,
San José.

What to Buy

Wall hanging

With a wide selection of quality items sold in shops and galleries throughout the country, there is no shortage of mementos to take home. Hand-crafted objects made from tropical hardwoods, such as bowls, boxes, and kitchen articles, as well as aromatic coffee beans and coffee products of various kinds, are must-buys. Ceramics are excellent, as is jewelry, particularly gold necklaces and pendants that replicate pre-Columbian designs. T-shirts with wildlife motifs, and cuddly sloths, curling snakes made of wood, and other such toys, are popular choices.

Forbidden Items

Objects made from various protected species are commonly sold at local markets. It is illegal to buy anything made from turtle shells, furs such as ocelot and jaguar skins, or feathers of quetzals and other endangered bird species. Conservation groups also discourage buying items made of coral, as well as framed butterflies.

Handicrafts

Costa Rica's skilled artisans are concentrated in Sarchí, famous for its miniature oxcarts painted in gaudy patterns and colors, and for homespun rocking chairs of wood and leather. Dozens of artisans' studios produce a dizzying variety of crafts, which find their way into stores throughout the country. Moravia, near San José, is another center of crafts, particularly leather goods.

Leather Goods
Cowboy boots, purses, and attaché cases exude quality and are relatively inexpensive. Those made of caiman and snake skins should be avoided for conservation reasons.

Wooden bowl and spoons

Painted wooden box

Carved box

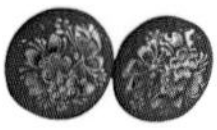
Colorful wooden earrings

Hand-painted miniature oxcart

Wooden Items
Costa Rica's precious hardwoods yield a wealth of objects. They include statuettes, animal figurines, carved boxes, and notably, lathe-turned bowls, some thin enough to be transparent when held up to the light.

Hammocks
Hammocks made of colored hemp rope, in a variety of designs, are sold on the sea shores. Roomy two-person models are also available.

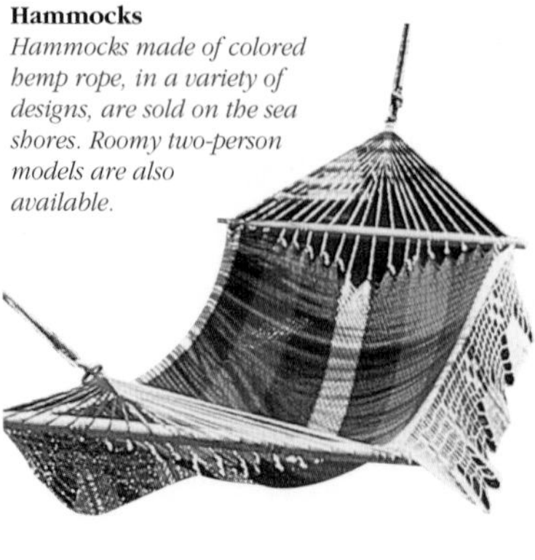

Jewelry
Delicate brooches, necklaces, and earrings in 14-carat gold, often in combination with corals and semi-precious stones, are popular. Street hawkers sell bright necklaces of shells, hardwoods, and seeds.

Brooch

Pearl earrings

Necklace in gold and semi-precious stone

Seed necklace

Indigenous Crafts

Items made by Indian tribes can be bought at quality craft stores and, preferably, in indigenous reserves where income goes directly to the artists. Traditional weavings, carved gourds, painted masks, and musical instruments are often imbued with spiritual symbols.

Carved Gourds
Decorated with wildife motifs, carved gourds are lightweight and can be used as vases.

Painted mask

Ocher Pottery
Pottery adorned with traditional Chorotega motifs are produced in Guaitíl, using traditional firing methods. Pots, plates, and vases of varying shapes and sizes can be bought at roadside stalls and cooperatives throughout Guanacaste.

Boruca mask

"Devil" Masks
Made of balsa wood, these masks made by the Boruca tribe should be bought directly from the carver. Other indigenous wooden goods include wall hangings.

Coffee liqueur

Organic coffee

A regional variety of coffee

Chocolate-coated coffee beans

Coffee

Coffee products range from gourmet roasted whole beans to coffee liqueurs. Be sure to buy export-quality coffee, as coffees sold for the domestic market are often of inferior quality and, if sold pre-ground, adulterated with large amounts of sugar.

Souvenirs

All manner of trinkets, utensils, and miscellaneous artistic creations are for sale at gift stores nationwide, from candles to stained-glass pendants. Typically, they are emblazoned with images of wildlife or rural scenes. The store at San José's international airport has a good selection.

Bright brooch

Candle

Ceramic plate

Painted metal jug

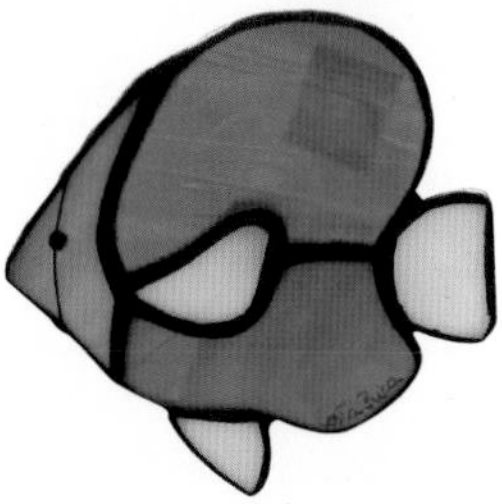

Stained-glass item

ENTERTAINMENT IN COSTA RICA

CULTURAL ACTIVITIES and live entertainment in Costa Rica have traditionally been somewhat restrained by the standards of many other Latin American countries. Nonetheless, Ticos have a tremendous love of music and dance, and recent years have witnessed a blossoming of entertainment venues. Nightlife, especially in San José, is excitingly diverse. Theater and classical concerts are an integral part of San José's social life, and even smaller cities usually have theater spaces and *glorietas* (bandstands) where live musicians perform. Music festivals are staged both indoors and outdoors, and country fairs called *ferías* are in full swing year-round. Every town has numerous discos, and karaoke bars are popular with lower-income Ticos. Entertainment in country towns revolves around *topes* (horsemanship shows) and *retornos* (rodeos) that spill onto the streets with traditional live music and dance.

Guanacaste National Band poster

INFORMATION

A CALENDAR OF major events is carried in Spanish and English on the website of the Instituto Costarricense de Turismo (Costa Rican Tourism Institute, or ICT; *see p256*). The website also has addresses of theaters, nightclubs and similar venues. *Tico Times (see p263)*, which is available in many hotels, also provides listings of artistic events and entertainment, as does the "Viva" section of the *La Nación* daily newspaper. *Info Spectacles* is a free weekly publication that contains information about live concerts, shows, nightclubs and other entertainment venues.

Costa Rican Tourism Institute logo

THEATER

THEATER PRODUCTION in Costa Rica has a long tradition, and Josefinos are passionate theatergoers. San José's many small theaters offer both mainstream and experimental theater, as well as comedy, at affordable prices.

Most productions are in Spanish and are typically restricted to Thursday–Sunday evenings. Mime performances are the attraction at **Teatro Chaplin**, and occasional comedy performances in English are hosted at **Teatro de la Comedia**. The country's oldest theater company, the English- language **Little Theater Group**, performs at the Teatro Eugene O'Neill, inside the **Centro Cultural Costarricense-Norteamericano** (Costa Rican-North American Cultural Center). The center also hosts monthly musical concerts.

The English-speaking community is drawn to the **Teatro Laurence Olivier**, which doubles as a lively cultural center and has a jazz club and movie theater.

CLASSICAL MUSIC, BALLET, DANCE, AND OPERA

COSTA RICA'S middle class are enthusiastic lovers of classical music. The nation's foremost venue for classical and ballet performances is San José's **Teatro Nacional** *(see pp60–61)*. It was inaugurated to great national pride

The opulent interior of the auditorium of Teatro Nacional

A lively traditional dance in progress in Pueblo Antigua, San José

in 1897 with a performance of *El Fausto de Gournod* by the Paris Opera. The theater hosts the **Orquestra Sinfónia Nacional**, founded in 1970, which performs from April to December. It also holds performances by the **Compañía de Lírica Nacional** (National Lyric Opera Company), the country's only opera company, from June to August. The companies feature many of the world's best-known works in their repertoires. International orchestras and singers also perform here. A night at the Teatro Nacional is considered an occasion to dress up for. Prices in the *galeria* (galleries) are generally below $5, depending on the occasion.

Theater production in Costa Rica has a long tradition, boosted in the early 1900s when South American dramatists settled here, and drama was introduced to the high school curriculum. The **Teatro Mélico Salazar** *(see p58)* stages drama, musicals, classical concerts, and folkloric events, including Fantasía Folklórica, a performance of traditional music and dance from Guanacaste, performed each Tuesday night. The theater is also the principal venue of the **Compañía Nacional de Danza** (National Dance Company), a world-class organization founded in 1979, which has a wide repertoire of contemporary and classical works.

It is advisable to book in advance, which you should do directly with the venue or event organizers.

Jazz

Jazz clubs have grown in number in recent years, and jazz trios play in several hotel lobbies and bars. The main venue is San José's **Jazz Café**, a red-brick structure with a classic bohemian ambience. Leading international performers such as Chucho Valdés and Irakere have played here. San José's jazz buffs also frequent the Shakespeare Gallery in the **Sala Garbo**, which hosts live jazz on Monday evenings.

Traditional Music

Rather limited in form and style, the country's popular music is a more restricted version of the *marimba* cultures of Nicaragua and Guatemala. The *marimba* (xylophone), *quijongo* (single-string bow with gourd resonator), and guitar provide the backing for such traditional folk dances as the *punto guanacasteco*, the national dance *(see p247)*. Live *marimba* music is performed at *ferias*, a few tourist venues, and city plazas on weekends. A good place to experience traditional music and dance is **Pueblo Antigua** *(see p75)*. Indigenous communities perform ritual dances accompanied by drums, rattles, and ceramic flutes.

The Teatro Mélico Salazar, one of San José's popular cultural venues

Dancing the night away at a beach resort nightclub

Nightclubs and Discos

San José and key tourist resorts have swanky dance clubs. Many of the best nightclubs are associated with leading hotels, and several larger beach resorts feature discos. Less sophisticated venues are everywhere, catering to the dance-crazy Ticos. The predominant music is Latin: *cumbia*, salsa and, especially, merengue, often interspersed with reggae and world-beat tunes.

In San José, the well-to-do can be found at the various bars and clubs along San Pedro's Avenida Central, and in San Rafael de Escazú. **Planet Mall**, popular with teenagers, claims to be the largest disco in Central America. A more down-to-earth and always crowded option is **El Cuartel de la Boca del Monte**, with an earthy atmosphere, eclectic patrons, and live music by many of Costa Rica's leading bands. Several discos and bars can be found in the warren of alleyways comprising **El Pueblo**, while the Los Yoses and San Pedro districts have many bars and clubs catering to students and well-off young Ticos. Calle de la Amargura (Street of Bitterness), leading to the university, is lined with student bars, and draws few foreigners. Bars in "Gringo Gulch," a red-light area of central San José, mostly cater to an older foreign clientele, including the city's large number of expatriate residents. Take care with whom you interact in this locality, as also on Calle de la Amargura.

Most of the clubs don't begin to liven up until midnight, and many don't close until dawn. Attire is usually quite casual, with jeans permitted; shorts are generally not allowed, except at beach resorts.

Casinos

Costa Rica has dozens of casinos, concentrated in the capital city. They are mostly associated with large, expensive hotels. Several casinos are clustered in the infamous Gringo Gulch. Some casinos are open 24 hours. The most popular games are craps, *tute* (a version of poker), canasta, which resembles roulette, and *veinte un* (21), a variant of blackjack. Visitors should be aware that the odds are far more favorable to the house than they are in the US.

Dance Schools

Many visitors come to Costa Rica to learn to dance. Several reputable *academias de baile* (dance schools) offer residential courses where you can pick up some fancy foot skills in hip-swiveling *cumbia*, merengue, salsa, and whatever the latest dance craze may be. Most classes are typically in Spanish. The well-known **Academia de Baile Kurubandé** and **Merecumbé** each have several schools in San José and major highland cities.

Festivals

The annual calendar is full of festivals, large and small *(see pp34–7)*. Many of them celebrate the country's diverse cultures, such as the Fiesta de los Diablitos *(see p184)* of the Borucas and Puerto Límon's extravagant Caribbean-style Carnaval *(see p165)*. Costa Rica's best known music festivals include the nationwide **International Festival of Music**, and the **Southern Caribbean Music Festival**, held in Cahuita and Puerto Viejo. Many towns of this Catholic country honor their patron saints on specific days

A Caribbean-style performance in a resort in Guanacaste

The Punto Guanacasteco

The national dance is the *punto guanacasteco*, a toe-and-heel dance performed in traditional regional costumes. The women wear white bodices and colorful frilly satin skirts. The men wear white shirts and pants, satin sashes, and cowboy hats. The slow, twirling *baile típico* (typical dance) features the tossing of hats and scarves, as males interrupt the proceedings in turn to shout rhyming verses aimed at winning over a love interest.

Dancers performing the *punto guanacasteco*

of the year, with the most important religious festival being Día del Virgen de los Ángeles, which is celebrated in Cartago's Basilica de Nuestra de los Ángeles *(see pp94–5)* in August. Nicoya's Fiesta de la Yeguïta *(see p142)*, held in December, is one of the nation's most colorful regional festivals.

Cinema

Most cities have cinemas, although those in smaller towns are often ramshackle. San José and other large cities have modern multiplex cinemas up to the standards of North America and Western Europe. **Cines del América** and others show first-run Hollywood and international movies, which are usually subtitled in Spanish. Dubbed films are advertised with the phrase *hablado en español.* International art-house movies are shown at **Sala Garbo**. Costa Rica has no major cinema industry of its own.

Peñas

San José's intellectuals enjoy *peñas* (circles of friends), bohemian get-togethers that evolved from Latin America's Leftist revolutionary movement of the 1970s. Poetry is recited and plaintiff *nueva trova* music is performed at *peñas*, also called *tertulias.* They are leading outlets for experimental music and literature by such avant-garde performers as Esteban Monge and Canto America. Typical venues are private homes and cafés such as **La Peña de Cantares**, where the cultural music group Cantares performs. An active venue is **Teorética**, a hip art gallery.

Directory

Theater and Cultural Centers

Centro Cultural Costarricense-Norteamericano
San Pedro, San José.
Tel *207-7500.*
W www.cccncr.com

Little Theater Group
Tel *289-3910.*

Teatro Chaplin
Calles 11/13 and Ave 12, San José.
Tel *223-2919.*

Teatro de la Comedia
Calles 13/15 and Ave Central, San José.
Tel *223-2170.*

Teatro Laurence Olivier
Calle 28 and Ave 2, San José.
Tel *223-1960.*

Classical Music, Ballet, Dance, and Opera

Compañía de Lírica Nacional
Tel *222-8571.*
W www.mcjdcr.go.cr/musica/compania_lirica.html

Compañía Nacional de Danza
Tel *222-2974.*
@ comdanza@racsa.co.cr
W www.mcjdcr.go.cr/artes_escenicas/cnd.html

Orquestra Sinfónia Nacional
Tel *236-5395.*
@ sinfonic@racsa.co.cr

Jazz

Jazz Café
Calle 7 and Ave Central, San Pedro, San José.
Tel *253-8933.*
@ jaaz.cafe@terra.com

Nightclubs and Discos

El Cuartel de la Boca del Monte
Calles 21/23 and Ave 1, San José.
Tel *221-0327.*

El Pueblo
Ave Central, Barrio Tournón, San José.

Planet Mall
Mall San Pedro, San José.
Tel *280-4693.*

Dance Schools

Academia de Baile Kurubandé
Tel *219-2363.*

Merecumbé
Tel *224-3531.*

Festivals

International Festival of Music
Tel *282-7724.*
W www.costaricamusic.com

Southern Caribbean Music Festival
Tel *750-0062.*
W www.playachiquitalodge.com

Cinema

Cines del América
Mall San Pedro, Ave Central and Circunvalacion, San José.
Tel *222-1034.*

Sala Garbo
Calle 28 and Ave 2, San José.
Tel *222-1034.*

Peñas

La Peña de Cantares
875 yd (800 m) E of Roja Cruz, Santa Ana.
Tel *282-4791.*

Teorética
Calle 7 and Aves 9/11, San José.
Tel *233-4881.*
W www.teoretica.org

Outdoor Activities and Specialty Vacations

The varied terrain, salubrious climate, and diversity of wilderness reserves in Costa Rica combine to afford a wealth of outdoor activities. Some of these, which have been spawned by the tourist boom of the past two decades, are unusual – canopy tours, for example, are a staple of the rain- and cloud forest reserves. Others are more conventional. Ample opportunities for hiking are provided by the trails that lace the superb national parks and reserves. Costa Rica is also well-geared for biking and horseback riding. Both coasts offer fabulous surfing, and windsurfing is world class, with dedicated facilities at Lake Arenal and Bahía Salinas. Whitewater rafting is highly developed, while scuba divers and anglers are in for a treat. Wherever you are in the nation, the great outdoors is close at hand. A handy resource is *Costa Rica Outdoors*, a bimonthly publication available nationwide.

Sign, Playa Flamingo

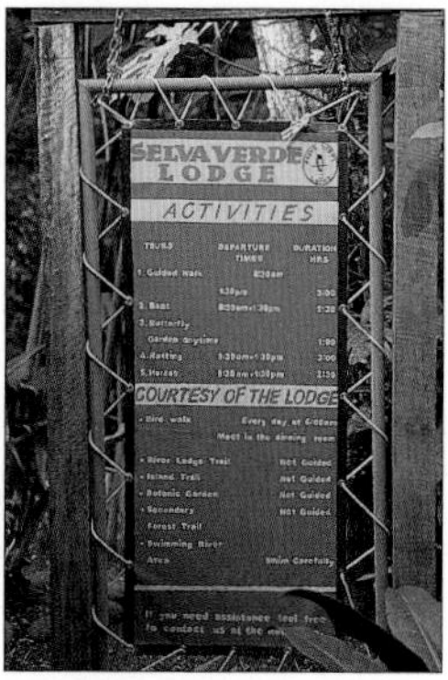

The range of activities offered at Selva Verde Lodge

Organized Tours

A plethora of tour operators in Costa Rica cater to visitors interested in particular activities. Companies offering a range of specialized tours include **Costa Rica Expeditions**, **Costa Rica's Temptations**, and **Costa Rica Sun Tours**. Operators dedicated to a specific activity are listed in the relevant subsection.

National Parks and Wildlife Reserves

Costa Rica has about 190 national parks, wildlife reserves, and related protected areas, with a combined area of almost 6,000 sq miles (15,500 sq km). Dozens of other privately owned reserves protect additional natural habitats. Protected areas continue to be created to link individual parks and reserves with the purpose of creating uninterrupted migratory corridors for wildlife. The national parks and reserves are organized into "conservation areas" administered by the **SINAC** (Sistema de Areas de Conservación/System of Conservation Areas), which is a division of MINAE (Ministerio de Ambiente y Energía/Ministry of Atmosphere and Energy).

La Amistad, covering an area of 675 sq miles (1,750 sq km), is the largest national park *(see p179)*. This is also the most remote and inaccessible one, and hiking can be challenging. The most visited park is Parque Nacional Volcán Poás, which lies within a 2-hour drive of San José and has the most developed facilities *(see p90)*. Also popular is Parque Nacional Manuel Antonio, which offers the advantage of easy access and an assortment of attractions, including beautiful beaches *(see pp118–19)*. Parque Nacional Cahuita, on the Caribbean coast, features similar attractions *(see p170)*. Parque Nacional Chirripó *(see pp180–81)* and Parque Nacional Rincón de la Vieja *(see p132)* offer fabulous mountain hiking – Rincón has the added enticement of fumaroles and boiling mud pools. Guided boat tours make the rainforests and swamps of Parque Nacional Tortuguero accessible *(see p167)*. A more challenging but no less rewarding destination is Parque Nacional Corcovado, perhaps the nation's premier rainforest environment *(see p191)*. Reserva Biológica Bosque Nuboso Monteverde is the top cloud forest reserve *(see p127)*. A useful source of information on various reserves is **Fundación de Parques Nacionales**.

Boat tour in Parque Nacional Tortuguero

Bird-watchers in Parque Nacional Manuel Antonio

Wildlife-Viewing

Viewing animals and birds in the wild is the prime attraction for the majority of visitors to Costa Rica. It's easily done, even without visiting protected reserves, as wildlife is literally everywhere outside city limits. Morpho butterflies, toucans, monkeys, and coatis can be seen from your hotel porch, depending on location. However, most species are well disguised or reclusive, and spotting them often requires a combination of patience and planning. Hiring a naturalist guide is recommended – their trained eyes and knowledge of where and when to look for certain species will greatly increase your success rate. Guides can be hired through Costa Rica Expeditions, which offers nature trips. A good way to view wildlife is to take a natural history cruise aboard a small ship, with daily excursions ashore. Leading companies include **Windstar Cruises** and **Temptress Adventure Cruises**.

On a nature trip, dress in greens and browns to blend in with the surroundings. Silence is imperative. Bring a pair of binoculars. Laminated spotters' charts are available at book- and souvenir stores. The **Birding Club of Costa Rica** offers information on bird-watching.

Hiking

For those who like to experience nature on foot, Costa Rica is a dream come true. Thousands of miles of trails traverse the countryside, offering opportunities to explore the most remote terrain. Many trails are well marked and easy to hike, while others provide a rugged challenge to even the most experienced hikers. **Librería Universal** and the **Instituto Geográfica Nacional** sell detailed topographic maps.

The majority of trails are associated with the national parks and wildlife reserves, where facilities are usually restricted to the ranger stations and/or private lodges near the entrances. Many of the larger parks have only basic huts, sometimes a full day's hike from each other – hikers will need to be self-sufficient in terms of camping equipment and food. Always inquire about the distance to the next hut, and the difficulty of the hike. You will need to get permission to camp anywhere other than at designated campsites. For overnight hikes, always report to a ranger station at the beginning and end of your trip. Permits and local guides are essential for certain hikes, such as those across the remote Talamancas.

Look out for venomous snakes – never leave your tent or cabin door open *(see p259)*. Hikers in Parque Nacional Corcovado and other lowland rainforest reserves may come across bands of aggressive wild pigs called peccaries. If threatened, climb a tree and wait until the animals depart. Otherwise, the best bet is usually to stand still: most charges are bluffs.

Lightweight yet sturdy waterproof hiking shoes are essential, as is a water bottle and a backpack with room for a waterproof jacket with hood. Apart from suncreen and insect repellent, other recommended items are a first aid kit, as well as a flashlight and spare batteries. Pack your gear in a plastic bag before placing it in your backpack to ensure that it remains dry. Clean up the campsite before leaving – only footprints should be left behind.

Canopy Tours

With its soaring trees and deep valleys, it is no surprise that Costa Rica has dozens of canopy tours to whisk you between treetops and across gorges *(see pp24–5)*. Zipline tours provide an adrenalin-packed ride, but don't expect to see much wildlife. The **Original Canopy Tour** has seven locations around the country.

Zipline canopy tour, Arenal Rainforest Reserve

Horseback riding on one of Costa Rica's many beaches

Horseback Riding

With its farming tradition and widespread use of horses, Costa Rica affords numerous opportunities for equestrian pursuits. Tour operators and hotels can make arrangements for rides, usually on the small, mild-tempered local *criollo* horse.

Guanacaste province has several ranches specializing in horse riding. **Hacienda Guachipelín** and **Hacienda Los Inocentes** *(see p132)* are two excellent locations, as is the **Buena Vista Lodge** *(see p211)*. Other good places are **Bella Vista Lodge** in Escaleras *(see p217)*, and **Club Hípico La Caraña**, near Escazú.

Cycling

Touring the country by bicycle is an excellent way to meet local people and to enjoy the spectacular scenery. However, many roads are potholed and cycling in highland areas requires caution due to fog, blind bends, and speeding traffic. Several companies specialize in bicycle tours: **Backroads**, in North America, and **Costa Rica Biking Adventure**, in Costa Rica, are two reputable outfits. Most international airlines will let you bring your own bicycle as checked luggage, if properly packed.

Costa Rica's rugged terrain is particularly suited to mountain biking, and Ticos (Costa Ricans) are enthusiasts of the sport. Several hotels and local tour agencies rent mountain bikes and offer short mountain-biking excursions.

Golf and Tennis

The country has six 18-hole courses, as well as four 9-hole ones. Additional courses are in the offing. In the Nicoya Peninsula, the leading greens are at the **Four Seasons Resort** *(see p208)* and **Paradisus Playa Conchal Beach & Golf Resort** *(see p210)*. The best of the Central Highlands courses are at the **Meliá Cariari** and **Parque Valle del Sol**.

Many hotels and beach resorts have tennis courts available free of charge to guests. Non-guests are usually allowed to play on these courts for a fee.

Whitewater Rafting and Kayaking

Costa Rica's high rainfall and mountain terrain combine to provide ideal conditions for whitewater rafting *(see p102)*. The Reventazón and Pacuare Rivers of the Central Highlands are renowned, but every region has world-class whitewater. Tumbling from the country's highest mountain, Río Chirripó (Class III–IV) creates dozens of explosive rapids. It merges with Río General (Class III–IV), known for its challenging rapids. Río Corobicí (Class I–II) is fed by dam-released waters and flows between tree-lined banks in the heart of Guanacaste. It offers a float perfect for families, as wildlife is plentiful and easily seen. Río Savegre (Class III–V) flows out of the mountains of the Central Pacific. The steep upper section is a demanding thriller; the river slows lower down as it passes through African oil palm plantations.

The rafting industry is well developed and regulated,

The serene Parque Valle del Sol golfing greens

Kayaking in Lake Angostura, near Turrialba

and operators conform to international standards. Life jackets and helmets are mandatory. Trips cost between $70 and $100 per day, including transport, meals, and equipment. Overnight trips involve camping or stays at remote riverside lodges. Numerous companies offer rafting trips, including **Ríos Tropicales**. Take sunscreen and suitable attire. A warm jacket for mountain runs is a good idea. Expect to get wet – pack a set of dry clothes and shoes.

Sea kayaks are an ideal means of exploring the mangrove systems of the coasts. One of the major rafting operators, Ríos Tropicales, also features trips on kayaks. Various other nature tour operators offer kayaking trips, and many resort hotels rent kayaks for exploring sheltered bays. With luck, dolphins may appear alongside. If you plan on kayaking alone, *The Rivers of Costa Rica: A Canoeing, Kayaking and Rafting Guide*, by Michael W. Mayfield and Rafael E. Gallo, is indispensable; it is available from San José's **7th Street Books**.

Surfing and Windsurfing

Thousands of visitors flock to Costa Rica each year to ride the waves that wash ashore along both the Pacific and Caribbean coastlines. Some of the best surfing beaches are in Northern Nicoya *(see p137)*. Most airlines permit you to check a surf board as luggage free of charge. However, there is no shortage of surf shops at key surf spots such as Tamarindo, Jacó, and Puerto Viejo de Talamanca. Dedicated surf camps give their own meaning to the term "bed and board."

Bahía Salinas *(see p130)* and Laguna de Arenal *(see pp150–52)* are marvelous for windsurfing, thanks to consistently high winds. Both have windsurf centers. Playa Zancudo *(see p190)* is another excellent location, but you will need to bring your own equipment.

Sportfishing

The challenge of landing a world-record catch draws hundreds of anglers to Costa Rica's waters every year. Most sportfishing is on a catch-and release basis. The Pacific coast *(see p117)* is fabulous for deep-sea fish, such as sailfish, tuna, dorado, and swordfish. Marlin are the big prize: the fish run off Nicoya in November–March; the central and southern Pacific are best in August–December.

Sportfishing charter sign

On the Caribbean side, anglers use light tackle in rivers, lakes, and lagoons to hook tarpon, snook, and garfish. Caño Negro, as well as the rivermouths of the San Juan and Colorado Rivers, feature some of the world's best tarpon fishing: the best time is December–March. Trout fishing is popular in mountain streams, particularly on the northern slopes of the Talamancas. Laguna de Arenal is renowned for massive rainbow bass; **Rain Goddess** offers fishing trips here *(see p152)*. Permits required for freshwater fishing are organized by the operators. Several sportfishing lodges cater exclusively to anglers. Boat charters offered from sportfishing centers, such as Flamingo, Quepos, Tamarindo, Golfito, and Zancudo, typically cost $250–400 for a half day and $350–650 for a full day. Fishing tackle is sold and rented at **La Casa del Pescador**. Excellent sources of angling information are **Club Amateur de Pesca** and local fishing expert Jerry Ruhlow's weekly column in the *Tico Times*.

Fishing yacht anchored at Bahía Drake

Surfing on the high waves off Playa Jaco

Scuba Diving in Costa Rica

THE WARM WATERS off Costa Rica provide splendid opportunities for divers. The country's prime site is Isla del Coco, which offers some of the world's finest scuba diving for seeing marine animals. Other dive spots include the Murciélagos Islands in Northern Nicoya; the coral reefs of Playa Manuel Antonio, Parque Nacional Ballena Marina, and Isla del Caño on the Pacific side; and Gandoca-Manzanillo and Cahuita on the Caribbean. Marine turtles and moray eels can be spotted everywhere. Other commonly seen large marine creatures include manta rays, grouper, tuna, jewfish, and several types of sharks and whales. However, visibility is less than high at most dive sites, especially during the rainy season when river runoff clouds the oceans.

Scuba diver

Getting ready *for a dive involves careful checking of all equipment, especially the breathing apparatus.*

While underwater, *it is wise to swim in a group so as to assist each other in times of need.*

Starfish can be seen creeping slowly atop the reefs.

Tropical fish of varied hues and shapes inhabit the waters.

Corals, generally poorly developed in Costa Rica, are at their most colorful here.

Several angelfish species, such as king, queen, and French angelfish, are found around Isla del Caño *(see p184)*.

ISLA DEL CAÑO

This island boasts the largest coral formations in Costa Rica, attracting a rainbow of tropical fish. Also seen here are octopus, sea horses, and starfish. Dolphins cavort in near-shore waters. Diving trips are offered from Bahía Drake *(see p190)*.

At Punta Gorda, *off Playa Ocotal, scuba divers are sure to see a vast number of eagle rays flap past. Also seen are golden rays, as well as stone fish and sea horses.*

Isla del Coco (see p193) *is said to be a site of hidden gold, but its real treasure lies underwater, and includes huge schools of hammerhead sharks. Accessed by live-aboard boats, this is only for experienced divers.*

Islas Murciélagos, *the most favored dive site in the northwest, is renowned for white tip sharks, marlin, and other giant pelagics. Several outfitters in Playas del Coco* (see p136) *offer trips.*

Swimming

Most large hotels, and many smaller ones, have swimming pools. Ocean water temperatures typically range between 25 and 30°C (77–87°F). However, extreme caution is required when swimming in the oceans: Costa Rica averages about 200 drownings a year due to riptides. These fast-moving water currents are typically associated with beaches with high volumes of incoming surf and where retreating water funnels into a narrow channel that can drag you out to sea. Many of the most popular beaches have riptides. If you get caught in one, do not struggle against the current or try to swim to shore: this will quickly exhaust you. Swim parallel to the shore to exit the current. Avoid swimming near river estuaries, where crocodiles may lurk, and in ocean waters off beaches where marine turtles nest, as sharks are often present.

Scuba Diving

Almost all beach resorts near prime dive sites have scuba operators. You can rent or buy gear here, and at **Mundo Aquático**, in San José. **El Ocotal Diving Safaris** and **Rich Coast Diving** are two respected dive operators based at Playa Ocotal and Playas del Coco, respectively *(see p136)*. Trips to Isla del Coco, for experienced divers, are offered aboard the **Okeanos Aggressor**, which sails from Puntarenas on 8-, 9-, and 10-day voyages.

Divers about to go underwater off Costa Rica's Pacific coast

Directory

Tour Operators

Costa Rica Expeditions
Calle Central/2 and Ave 3, San José.
257-0766.
www.costaricaexpeditions.com

Costa Rica Sun Tours
Edificio Cerro Chato, La Uruca, San José.
296-7757.
www.crsuntours.com

Costa Rica's Temptations
PO Box 1199-1200, San José.
239-9999.
www.crtinfo.com

National Parks and Wildlife Reserves

Fundación de Parques Nacionales
Barrio Escalante, San José.
257-2239.

SINAC
Calle 25 and Ave 8/10, San José.
283-08004.
www.sinac.go.cr

Wildlife-Viewing

Birding Club of Costa Rica
267-7197.
crbirdingclub@mailcity.com

Temptress Adventure Cruises
c/o Cruise West, 2401 4th Ave, Suite 700, Seattle, WA 98121, USA.
(800) 580-0072.
www.cruisewest.com

Windstar Cruises
300 Elliott Ave W, Seattle, WA 98119, USA.
(800) 258-7245.
www.windstar-cruises.com

Hiking

Instituto Geográfica Nacional
Calles 9/11 and Ave 20, San José.
257-7798, ext 2619.

Librería Universal
Calles Central/1 & Ave Central, San José.
222-2222.

Canopy Tours

Original Canopy Tour
257-5149.
www.canopytour.com

Horseback Riding

Club Hípico La Caraña
282-6106.

Cycling

Backroads
801 Cedar St, Berkeley, CA 94710, USA.
(510) 527-1555.
www.backroads.com

Costa Rica Biking Adventure
Miraflores (Guadalupe), San José.
225-6591.
www.bikingincostarica.com

Golf

Meliá Cariari
670-0321.
www.meliacariari.solmelia.com

Parque Valle del Sol
282-9222.
www.vallesol.com

Whitewater Rafting and Kayaking

Ríos Tropicales
233-6455.
www.riostropicales.com

7th Street Books
Calle 7 and Ave Central/1, San José.
256-8251.
marroca@racsa.co.cr

Sportfishing

Club Amateur de Pesca
232-3430.
clubamateurpesca@racsa.co.cr

La Casa del Pescador
Calle 2 and Ave 16/18, San José.
222-1470

Scuba Diving

El Ocotal Diving Safaris
670-0321.
www.ocotaldiving.com

Mundo Aquático
109 yd (100 m) N of Mas X Menos, San Pedro, San José.
224-9729.

Okeanos Aggressor
222-5307.
www.okeanoscocosisland.com

Rich Coast Diving
670-0176.
www.richcoastdiving.com

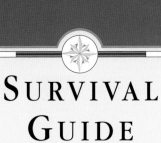

Survival Guide

Practical Information

Costa Rica has a superb tourist infrastructure, especially in the realm of ecotourism and adventure travel. It is possible to visit all but the most remote parts of the country with relative ease by a rented vehicle or public transport. Rarely will visitors be far from tourist facilities. National tourist offices are found only in the capital city; in many of the smaller towns and beach resorts, travel agencies and tour operators double as tourist information bureaus. Most Costa Rican tour operators are extremely professional. However, many aspects of day-to-day life in the country are slow and often bureaucratic. A degree of patience and flexibility is required to help cope with some of the frustrations.

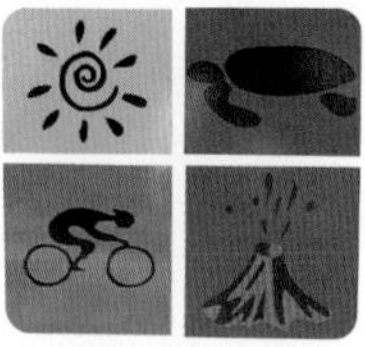

A poster advertising the nation's attractions

When to Go

Weatherwise, Costa Rica is best visited in the dry season between December and April (confusingly called "summer" by Ticos), before the rainy (or "green") season begins. However, regional variations *(see p38)* need to be considered as well – the Caribbean and southwest Pacific can receive torrential rains year-round.

The wet season is also the hottest time of the year, and can be torrid, especially in Guanacaste. Many dirt roads become impassable. However, prices are lower than during the dry high season, when many hotels are also booked solid.

Visas and Passports

Citizens of Australia, Canada, the USA, and western European countries do not need visas to enter Costa Rica. All visitors need a passport valid for six months from the date of travel, a return or onward ticket, and adequate finances for the duration of their stay. You will be issued a tourist card on arrival. Valid for 90 days, it can be extended at a *migración* (immigration office) in any major citiy.

Customs Information

Besides their personal belongings, visitors to Costa Rica are allowed to bring in 500 cigarettes and 6 pints (3 liters) of wine or spirits. You may also bring in a personal computer, two video cameras and/or still cameras, and six rolls of film. (The film restriction is rarely enforced.)

It is illegal to buy or export any archeological artifacts, and harsh penalties are imposed on violaters. Buy only certified reproductions. Items covered under the Convention on International Trade in Endangered Species (CITES) are also prohibited; these include certain bird feathers, objects made of tortoiseshell, furs, and non-farmed crocodile and reptile skins, as well as live animals and birds.

Tour sign in Monteverde

Tourist Information

Brochures and maps are distributed free of charge by the **ICT** (Instituto Costarricense de Turismo) bureaus at the two international airports *(see p264)* and in San José. They can also provide personalized assistance. Outside the capital, visit local tour agencies for information. Backpacker hostels, hotel tour desks, and some websites are other good sources.

Opening Hours

National parks are typically open daily from 8am to 4pm. Museum opening hours vary, with many museums being closed for lunch and on Monday. For opening hours of banks and shops, see pages 260 and 238.

Language

The official language of Costa Rica is Spanish, spoken relatively slowly, without a Castilian lisp. Virtually all Costa Ricans working in the tourist industry speak English, as do most people in

A local tour agency in the surfing hotspot, Jacó

◁ **Stationary motorboats along one of Costa Rica's many forest-backed beaches**

Casually dressed locals at a restaurant in Dominical

banking and other services. However, for anyone traveling off the beaten track, a basic knowledge of Spanish is a distinct advantage.

The Maleku, Bribri, Cabécar, and Guaymí retain their traditional languages, but most of Costa Rica's indigenous peoples also speak Spanish.

SOCIAL CUSTOMS

COURTESY IS greatly valued in Costa Rica. On greeting someone, it is normal to shake hands or kiss on one cheek. Use proper titles such as señor, señora, and señorita. The honorifics "Don" and "Doña" are used for people of social and political importance. Young Ticos generally use first names upon initial introduction. Older people are more formal and may continue to use titles until a friendship develops.

Quedar bien (to appear well) is a Costa Rican form of behavior intended to leave a good impression, but which can involve making false promises and declarations simply to please the listener. It's a good idea to ask more than one person for directions.

Ticos are tolerant of homosexuality, although overt public displays of affection between members of the same sex may provoke strong reactions, especially in rural areas.

WHAT TO WEAR

LIGHT AND CASUAL cotton and synthetic clothes are ideal for Costa Rica's tropical climate. A windproof jacket or sweater is useful for evenings in the highlands, and elsewhere in air-conditioned buildings. Carry an umbrella and waterproof wear year-round.

Evening wear is seldom required except at upscale nightclubs and restaurants. However, business people dress smartly. For formal meetings and church visits, men should not wear shorts or T-shirts and women should avoid revealing clothing.

Costa Rica is a tolerant nation but some conservative attitudes still prevail. Nudism is not allowed, and topless sunbathing is frowned upon.

WOMEN TRAVELERS

IT IS GENERALLY safe for women to travel alone. Some males are apt to offer *piropos* (unsolicited compliments and sexual advances) to women they pass on the street. Saying that you are married will usually put an end to unwanted flirtation.

Women travelers at a stall by the entrance to PN Manuel Antonio

DIRECTORY

CONSULATES

Canada
Oficentro Ejecutivo La Sabana, Edificio 5, Sabana Sur, San José.
242-4400.

UK
Centro Colón, Paseo Colón, Calles 38/40, San José.
258-2025.

USA
Boulevard Rohrmoser, San José.
220-3939.

TOURIST INFORMATION

ICT
E of Juan Pablo II Bridge, Autopista General Cañas, San José.
299-5800.

Websites
www.visitcostarica.com
www.costarica.com

DISABLED TRAVELERS

SOME AIRPORTS and newer hotels *(see p199)* and restaurants have wheelchair ramps and adapted toilets. Few wildlife parks have wheelchair-accessible trails or toilets, although the situation is improving.

TIME

COSTA RICA is 6 hours behind Greenwich Mean Time (GMT) and 1 hour behind New York's Eastern Standard Time (EST), and does not have daylight saving time.

ELECTRICITY

ELECTRICAL CURRENT is 100 volts (60 cycle) – the same as in the US and Canada. However, many hotels in remote areas generate their own power, with a nonstandard voltage. Three-prong, polarized, and European two-pin plugs will need adapters. Power surges are common, and a surge protector for laptops is a wise investment. Power outages occur in some parts: carry a flashlight.

Personal Security and Health

Police Department badge, San José

GENERALLY A SAFE destination, Costa Rica has a reputation for neutrality and stable democracy, which can lull visitors into a sense of security that may occasionally prove to be false. Tourists can be targets for theft, scams, and violent crime, and it is wise to take basic safety precautions. The nation has a relatively advanced health system, and you will rarely be far from medical assistance in times of need. Venomous snakes and other potentially harmful creatures inhabit the wilds, while dangerous riptides and the sun's powerful tropical rays are among the natural hazards that require some precautions.

Police station in Costa Rica's major sportfishing center, Quepos

Police

THE POLICE force has become more professional in recent years, and officers are usually polite and willing to help tourists. The standard police uniform is dark blue. *Tránsitos* (traffic police) patrol the highways and use radar guns to catch speeders. Bicycle police, wearing white shirts and blue shorts, patrol major cities and tourist centers.

Attempts by individual police officers to extract *mordidas* (bribes) are now relatively rare. To make a complaint against any officer, note his or her name and badge number and report to the **Organización de Investigación Judicial (OIJ)**.

General Precautions

VISITORS SHOULD be aware of their surroundings at all times, especially on city streets. Avoid wearing jewelry in public and leaving your belongings unattended. It's best to store valuables in your hotel safe. Make copies of your passport and important documents and keep them in a safe place. Be especially cautious of scams involving your rental car *(see p269)*, and of anyone offering unsolicited assistance of any kind. Women should avoid dark and isolated areas. Never hitchhike. If you are a victim of serious crime, contact the OIJ, or the **OIJ's Victim Assistance Office**.

Lost and Stolen Property

IN THE EVENT of loss or theft of belongings, inform the police within 24 hours – you will need an official report for your insurance. If your passport is lost or stolen, contact your embassy or consulate *(see p257)* immediately. Loss or theft of credit cards should be reported to the relevant company *(see p260)*.

Street Hazards

PEDESTRIANS DO not have the right of way in Costa Rica and extreme care is required when crossing roads. Always look both ways, even on one-way streets, as buses are allowed to travel in both directions on many roads, and the direction of traffic sometimes changes during certain hours. Be careful at junctions too, as many drivers disobey stop signs and red lights. When walking, keep your eyes open for deep holes and uneven sidewalks.

Natural Disasters

COSTA RICA has its share of natural calamities, but they are not a regular occurrence. If there's an earthquake, move away from tall structures and electricity poles. Do not use elevators. If you are

***Tránsito* (traffic police) car parked by a street in San José**

in a building, the safest place to be is usually in a doorway and not under stairways. It's a good idea to keep a flashlight and shoes near your bed at night.

Obey all instructions at volcanic parks, such as Poás and Arenal. Never hike in restricted zones. Arenal is especially volatile and visits to the immediate area – notably Tabacón *(see p148)* – are always risky.

Beware of riptides, which are strong currents that drag swimmers out to sea *(see p253)*. Flash floods are common during heavy rainfall, when waterfalls and rivers are to be avoided.

Vaccinations and Insurance

No specific vaccinations are required to enter Costa Rica. Malaria is prevalent along the southern Caribbean coast, and anti-malarial medication is recommended for this area. It is wise to be immunized against diseases such as typhoid as well as hepatitis A and B, and to make sure your polio and tetanus vaccinations are up to date.

Travel insurance is a good idea, as public health care is not always adequate and treatment in private hospitals and clinics can be expensive.

Medical Treatment

Residents are served by the state-run **Instituto de Seguridad (INS)** hospitals, which also provide a free emergency service to visitors. Most public hospitals are well run, albeit overcrowded, but rural clinics are often poorly equipped. Private hospitals such as **Hospital Clínica Bíblica** in San José conform to North American and European standards. Hotels usually have a list of reliable doctors, as will your embassy.

Farmacias or *boticas* (pharmacies), numerous in cities nationwide, sell medicines over the counter, including many drugs that require a prescription in the US, Canada, and European countries. However, visitors with pre-diagnosed conditions should bring medications. The **Rojo Cruz** (Red Cross) has an ambulance service in major cities and tourist centers. In remote areas, you may find it quicker to take a taxi to the nearest clinic or hospital.

Red Cross logo

Health Hazards

It is easy to underestimate the power of the tropical sun. Sunscreen and hats are recommended for the outdoors. Drink plenty of fluids to guard against dehydration. High humidity and heat may cause heatstroke, with symptoms of thirst, nausea, fever, and dizziness; if this occurs, consult a doctor. Wash and dry clothes often to prevent prickly heat and athlete's foot.

Cover up well and use plenty of insect repellent to avoid diseases such dengue fever – a viral illness spread by mosquitoes that has no vaccination or medication. Symptoms include fever, headaches, and joint pains, usually lasting about 10 days, after which a month-long recovery is normal. Insect repellents and *espirales* (mosquito coils) can be bought locally. Treat minor insect bites with antihistamines. If the bites become infected, seek the advice of a local doctor. Bites by poisonous snakes and other wild animals require immediate medical attention. Do not panic, and avoid too much movement.

Mosquito coil and insect repellent

Shun tap water if possible, and follow basic precautions with food *(see p221)* to avoid diarrhea and parasitic infections such as giardiasis. For diarrhea, drink lots of bottled water, and see a doctor if the condition becomes chronic.

Public Amenities

Public toilets are virtually nonexistent, and the few that are available are generally unclean. However, most ranger stations in national parks have toilets, as do restaurants and hotels elsewhere. Carry toilet paper.

Directory

Emergency Numbers

All Emergencies
911.

OIJ
222-1365.

OIJ's Victim Assistance Office
295-3643.

Police
127.

Rojo Cruz
128.

Hospitals

Hospital Clínica Bíblica
257-5252.

Exterior of a *farmacia* (pharmacy) in Cartago

Banking and Currency

The unit of currency in Costa Rica is the colón, but US dollars are widely accepted throughout the country, and most large hotels, restaurants, and shops take major credit cards. Traveler's checks can also be used at some businesses in major cities and tourist resorts. Foreign currencies, other than the dollar, are generally not accepted, but larger banks will exchange them for colones. Most tourist hotels will also change money, although the exchange rate is usually more favorable at banks. It is wise to have small denomination dollar bills, as many store keepers may not have sufficient change for $50 and $100 bills; others may not accept them, as counterfeit dollar bills are in circulation. There is no limit to the amount of money you may bring in or take out of the country.

Scotiabank's branch in San José

Banks and Changing Money

The largest banks are the state-run **Banco de Costa Rica**, **Banco Nacional**, Banco de San José, Banco del Comercio, and Banco Popular, all of which have branches throughout the country. Several major foreign banks have branches in San José. Banks are usually open only on weekdays: state-run banks are typically open from 9am to 3pm and private banks from 8am to 4pm. Avoid bank visits on Friday, which is payday for many Costa Ricans. In rural areas, you may have to wait in line for a considerable time to transact any business.

Many of the bigger banks have *cajeros automáticos* (ATMs), which accept major bank and credit cards to withdraw colones, usually for a fairly large fee. When drawing cash from ATMs, be aware of your surroundings, and avoid counting your money in public.

Most banks in cities and some tourist centers also have foreign exchange counters, offering more or less the same rates of exchange, which may change daily. The country's two international airports and the major border crossings *(see p265)* have *casas de cambio* (foreign exchange bureaus). All other *casas de cambio* were outlawed several years ago. Avoid money-changers on the street – many tourists are swindled by these touts.

Telegraphic Transfers

Electronic money transfers can be arranged via Moneygram or Western Union to their agents throughout Costa Rica. Money can be made available within minutes of the transaction, but a large commission is charged.

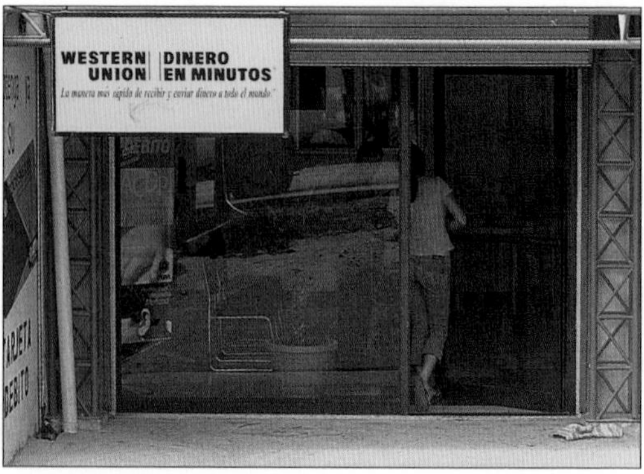

A Western Union agency in Santa Elena

Directory

Banks

Banco de Costa Rica
Calles 4/6 and Ave 2, San José.
Tel: *287-9000.*

Banco Nacional
Calles 2/4 and Ave 1, San José.
Tel: *287-9000.*

Lost Cards and Traveler's Checks

Barclays Bank
W www.barclays.com

MasterCard
Tel: *253-2155.*
W www.mastercard.com

Thomas Cook
W www.thomascook.com

VISA
Tel: *223-2211.*
W www.visa.com

Your home bank can also transfer money to its banking partner in Costa Rica, but this type of transaction usually takes a few days.

Credit Cards and Traveler's Checks

The most widely accepted cards are **VISA** and **MasterCard**, and to a lesser extent, American Express and Diners Card. It is possible to use your VISA card to obtain cash advances at banks, but few accept MasterCard for this purpose. Many hotels will also offer cash advances on your credit card.

Traveler's checks can be purchased from your local bank at home, or via the websites of **Thomas Cook** and **Barclays Bank**. These checks are generally more secure than credit cards: in the event of loss or theft, you can claim a refund on showing the check receipts, which should therefore be kept separate from the checks themselves.

Traveler's checks can be exchanged for cash at banks for a small commission. You will need to show your passport and sometimes a second photo. They can also be used for purchases in some shops. However, there are now fewer places in Costa Rica that are willing to accept traveler's checks because banks here often put a hold of up to a month on these checks while dispersing funds to creditors.

Logo of a credit card company

Currency

The Costa Rican currency is the colón, symbolized by ¢, and often called a peso. Money is sometimes colloquially referred to as *plata* or *pista* by Costa Ricans. Always carry some small denomination coins and bills for tips and minor purchases.

Bank Notes
Bank notes are in denominations of 1,000, 2,000, 5,000, and 10,000 colones, which are nicknamed cinco teja *(five limes),* rojo *(red),* dos rojos *(two reds),* tucán *(toucan), and* jaguar *respectively.*

1,000 colones

2,000 colones

5,000 colones

10,000 colones

Coins
Costa Rican coins come in denominations of 5, 10, 20, 25, 50, 100, and 500 colones. Coins minted earlier are in silver; newer ones are golden in color. Loose change is sometimes called menudo.

5 colones

10 colones

25 colones

50 colones

100 colones

500 colones

Communications

Costa Rican post office logo

TELECOMMUNICATIONS in Costa Rica are highly developed, and the telephone and email are the most widely used means of communication, not least because the postal service is slow and untrustworthy. The state-owned Instituto Costariccense de Electricidad (ICE), which controls all telecommunications, provides a free email account to every citizen. Ticos are large-scale users of mobile telephones, although reception is erratic in many areas. As well as receiving international channels, Costa Rica has 12 local television channels and several radio stations. There are three major Spanish newspapers and a few English-language publications.

Telephone Calls

PUBLIC TELEPHONE kiosks are usually located on main city streets and in plazas in smaller communities nationwide. In remote villages, which rely on public telephones, they are often found at the local *pulpería* (grocery store); sometimes it is necessary for the owners to place your call and charge you by the minute. A few public phones still accept 5, 10, and 20 colone coins, but most require CHIP *tarjeta telefónico* (phonecards), named for the metallic chip each card carries. Available in denominations of 1,000 and 2,000 colones, they can be purchased at supermarkets, stores, and banks. Tarjeta Colibrí 197 cards and Tarjeta Viajero 199 cards can be used with any phones, including cellular, and require you to key in the number 197 or 199, followed by an individual PIN number found on the back of each card. The 197 cards, sold in denominations of 500 and 1,000 colones, are used for domestic calls, while international calls are made using the 199 cards, which are available in denominations of $10, $20 and 3,000 colones.

Logo of Costa Rica's ICE

The ICE's regional offices in towns offer phone services. Most cities and tourist centers have international telephone bureaus, which charge higher rates than public phones but are cheaper than using a hotel phone. If calling from a hotel, it is cheaper to call the operator at international telephone companies such as **AT&T**, **MCI**, **Sprint**, and **Worldcom**, and get the call charged to your credit card.

Generally, visitors from North America can use their mobile phones in Costa Rica. However, phones from Europe cannot usually be used. Mobile phones are useful to have when traveling in wilderness areas, but the coverage is not total due to the rugged terrain.

Using a Public CHIP Telephone

1 Lift the receiver and wait for the dial tone. The display will indicate that you should insert your phonecard.

2 Once the phonecard is inserted, the current value of the card will be indicated on the digital display.

3 Key in the number 1 for instructions in Spanish, or 2 for instructions in English.

4 Key in the number you want to dial. While you are dialing, the number you are calling will appear on the display. Once you are connected, the decreasing value of your card will be displayed.

5 When you finish your call, replace the receiver. Your phonecard will be ejected.

Phonecard used in public telephones

Dialing Codes

- Costa Rican telephone numbers have seven digits; there are no area codes.
- Costa Rica's country code is 506.
- For international calls, dial 00 followed by the country code, then the area code and number. Country codes are: Australia 61; Ireland 353; New Zealand 64; South Africa 27; UK 44; USA and Canada 1.
- To make a collect call, dial 110 (domestic) or 116 (international) for the operator. Dial 113 for information. International operators speak English.

An Internet café in La Fortuna

Fax, Telegram, and Email

Hotels in Costa Rica usually permit you to send faxes for a small fee. International telephone bureaus also offer fax service, as do many post offices. You can send telegrams from major ICE offices, and from **Radiográfica Costarricense** (RACSA), in San José.

Internet cafés are found in every town and even in many small villages. Large hotels usually have business centers, and many modern ones also have rooms with ISDN or broadband connections, enabling you to plug in your laptop computer. RACSA operates a monopoly on local Internet servers, and the service can be slow and erratic.

Mail Service

Most towns and villages have *oficinas de correos* (post offices), which are usually open from 8am to 4pm, Monday to Friday. However, the mail service is slow and inefficient, and subject to theft. Important documents or valuable items should be sent via an international courier service such as **DHL**. You can receive mail poste restante at the main post office in San José *(see p59)*. Postboxes tend to be found at post offices only. Postcards and letters can be left with the front desk of major hotels.

Costa Rican Addresses

Although most towns are organized into numbered *avenidas* and *calles* (streets), few buildings have numbers, scarcely any household or business lists its address, and seldom do people know their own specific street address. Mail deliveries are, therefore, usually made to *apartados* (post office boxes). The government has attempted to introduce a numbered street system, but progress has been slow.

Radio and Television

The majority of the tourist hotels offer in-room TV service, although this is not true for wilderness lodges and budget *cabinas*. Upscale hotels usually have cable or satellite service, with leading US stations such as CNN and MTV and some key European stations, as well as Costa Rica's 12 TV stations, which broadcast in Spanish. Large business hotels also offer pay-per-view films, as well as their own channels, which provide travel and hotel information for guests.

The country has more than 100 radio stations, which mainly broadcast solely in Spanish. Radio Paladin (107.5 FM) features music and news in Spanish and English.

Costa Rican stamp advertising the nation's scenic beauty

Directory

Telephone Companies

AT&T
0800-011-4114.

MCI
162; 0800-012-2222.

Sprint
163; 0800-013-0123.

Worldcom
0800-014-4444.

Telegrams

Radiográfica Costarricense
Calle 1 and Ave 5,
San José.
287-0087.

Courier Services

DHL
Calle 34 and Ave 2/Paseo Colón,
San José.
209-6000.

Newspapers

Casa de las Revistas
Calle 5 and Ave 3/5, San José.
256-5092.

A man reading a newspaper on a park bench in Turrialba

Newspapers

Costa Rica's three big Spanish-language daily newspapers – *La Nación*, *La Prensa*, and *La República* – are sold at streetside stalls, hotel gift stores, and a few newsagents, which are found only in major cities. The *Tico Times* is an English-language weekly covering news, environment, arts and culture, and other facets of Costa Rican life. **Casa de las Revistas** outlets, found in bigger cities, sell international magazines.

Travel Information

Tourist bus laden with luggage

The majority of visitors to Costa Rica arrive at San José's Juan Santamaría International Airport, near Alajuela. The number of international flights landing at Liberia's Daniel Oduber International Airport is increasing, although these are mostly charter flights. Costa Rica is also served by bus companies, and many visitors journey overland from the Americas by car. Cruise ships berth on both the Pacific and Caribbean coasts, bringing passengers on day excursions. Costa Rica has a well-developed transportation system. Small planes serve regional airstrips, and buses of varying quality operate in virtually every part of the country. Rental vehicles are a practical alternative to public transport and grant maximum freedom. Nearly all places in the country are within a day's drive of San José. Road conditions, however, vary from well-paved to muddy dirt tracks. The extensive highway system is dilapidated in parts, and driving can be a challenge in certain areas of the country, especially in the wet season. Costa Rica's train service was discontinued following the 1996 earthquake.

Aircraft at San José's Juan Santamaría International Airport

Arriving by Air

Scheduled flights to Costa Rica are offered by leading US airlines, including **Delta**, **American Airlines**, **United**, and **Continental**. A nonstop service from Phoenix is available with **America West Airlines**, and **Mexicana** flies from Los Angeles. **Grupo Taca**, the regional airline of Central America, has scheduled flights from six cities in the US. Services are either direct, or routed via gateways such as Dallas or Miami, while others make one or more stops en route in El Salvador, Mexico City, or Managua. **Air Canada** offers a service from Canada.

From Europe, **Iberia** operates direct scheduled flights, while **Aeroflot** flies via Miami. **Martinair** and **Condor** have charters from The Netherlands and Germany. Other carriers connect to Miami flights. There are no direct flights from Australia or New Zealand, but passengers can transfer in Los Angeles to a connecting flight.

Timetables are subject to constant change: it is advisable to contact the airline or a travel agent for up-to-date information.

A "welcome" sign at an airlines office

Flight Prices

Ticket prices to and from Costa Rica vary greatly and change frequently. In general, the earlier you buy your ticket, the easier it is to obtain a reduced rate fare. If you make your booking just prior to departure, you may have to pay full price and, in addition, you run the risk that flights may be sold out, especially during the dry season.

Airlines compete very aggressively with one another, and it pays to compare all the companies' fares; also check their websites for special deals and weigh them against fares available at travel websites such as **Expedia**, **Orbitz**, and **Travelocity**.

APEX fares, which have to be bought at least 21 days in advance, are usually much lower than regular fares, but penalties apply for changes, and refunds are rarely given. Round-trip tickets offer substantial savings over one-way fares. Mid-week travel usually costs less than weekend travel, as does a fixed-date return. Charter flights are often cheaper than scheduled flights, although more restrictions apply. Also note that international air tickets are expensive to buy in Costa Rica.

If you are interested in a particular type of vacation, such as a beach holiday, consider air-and-hotel packages offered by charter airlines and many tour operators. These inclusive vacations usually work out cheaper than independent travel.

Arriving by Land

There are three border crossings for vehicles, at Peñas Blancas (between Costa Rica and Nicaragua), and Paso Canoas and Sixaola (between Costa Rica and Panama). In addition, pedestrians can cross to/from Nicaragua at Los Chiles. If you're driving between the US and Costa Rica, allow at least two weeks for the 2,300-mile (3,700-km) journey. Transit permits and insurance can be arranged through **Sanborn's**. Rental cars may not be taken across borders.

Many visitors enter or leave Costa Rica by bus. **Sirca**, **Transnica**, and **Ticabus** offer international bus services between Central American countries. The only company offering bus travel between the US and Costa Rica is **Green Tortoise**, for budget travelers. Another option is to cross the border on foot and catch onward buses on the other side. Take care of your belongings on cross-border bus trips.

Visas are not required to enter either Nicaragua or Panama, which issue temporary tourist visas at the border.

Driving along a deserted road in Costa Rica

Arriving by Sea

Several cruise ships include Puerto Caldera (on the Pacific) and Puerto Limón (Caribbean) on their itineraries, and allow passengers to disembark for day-long excursions. You can also leave the cruise and remain in Costa Rica for a longer stay.

Organized Tours

Several companies in Europe and North America offer organized tours to Costa Rica, often focusing on a particular activity. Nature-oriented trips geared toward bird-watching and other wildlife-viewing are especially popular. Other special-interest vacations include bicycling, whitewater rafting, kayaking, sportfishing, surfing, scuba diving *(see pp248–53)*.

Costa Rica Experts and **Costa Rica Connection** in North America and **Journey Latin America** in the UK feature a range of special-interest vacations, as well as tour arrangements that are customized for individual visitors or groups.

Directory

Airlines

Aeroflot
(44) 020-7355-2233.
www.aeroflot.com

Air Canada
1-888-247-2262.
www.aircanada.com

America West Airlines
800-363-2597.
www.americawest.com

American Airlines
1-800-433-7300.
www.aa.com

Condor
(49) 0180-5-707202.
www.condor.com

Continental
1-800-231-0856.
www.continental.com

Delta
800-241-4141.
www.delta.com

Grupo Taca
1-800-400-8222.
www.taca.com

Iberia
(34) 902-400-500.
www.iberia.com

Martinair
(31) 206-011-767.
www.martinair.com

Mexicana
1-800-531-7921.
www.mexicana.com

United
1-800-538-2929.
www.united.com

Flight Prices

Expedia
www.expedia.com

Orbitz
www.orbitz.com

Travelocity
www.travelocity.com

Arriving by Land

Green Tortoise
(415) 956-7500.
www.greentortoise.com

Sanborn's
800-222-0158.

Sirca
223-1464.

Ticabus
221-8954.

Transnica
256-9072.

Organized Tours

Costa Rica Connection
1124 Nipomo St, Suite C, San Luis Obispo, CA 93401.
805-543-8823.
www.crconnect.com

Costa Rica Experts
12 Heathfield 3166 N, 424 Lincoln Ave, Chicago, IL 60657.
773-935-1009.
www.crexpert.com

Journey Latin America
12 Heathfield Terrace, London W4 4JE.
020-8747-3108.
www.journeylatinamerica.co.uk

Getting Around Costa Rica

Local bus terminal

DESPITE THE country's compact size, land travel can take considerably longer than visitors might imagine. Air travel offers a relatively economical and easy way of reaching remote regions. Internal flights are especially convenient for visitors on a tight schedule and for those who wish to concentrate their sightseeing on two or three attractions spaced far apart. Traveling around by bus is a practical and less costly alternative. Buses can be combined with local jeep-taxi services to visit the more isolated spots. Reaching some sights involves the use of a ferry or boat service. For information on driving, see pages 268–9.

A small airplane ready for takeoff in Tortuguero

Domestic Flights

SCHEDULED domestic flights from San José's international airport are offered by **Sansa**. The company links the capital with 16 domestic airstrips, using 22- and 35-passenger Cessnas. Its published itineraries change frequently and are not 100 percent reliable. A slightly superior service is offered by **Nature Air**, which flies to the same destinations from Tobias Bolaños domestic airport, about 1.2 miles (2 km) west of Parque Sabana in San José.

Airplane tickets can be purchased through travel agents and tour operators, or directly from the airlines. Sansa sells a pass permitting unlimited travel. Nature Air offers children's discounts. Note that the timetables vary between wet and dry seasons *(see pp34–9)*. Reservations should be made as far in advance as possible, especially for travel during the peak Christmas and Easter seasons, and during the December–April dry season.

Private companies offer on-demand charter service to airstrips nationwide using 4- to 8-seater aircraft. You need to charter the entire aircraft, including for the return journey, if no additional passengers sign up.

The baggage allowance is 22 lb (10 kg) for Sansa, and 25 lb (11 kg) for Nature Air. This is considerably less than for international flights, and you should plan your baggage accordingly.

Local Buses and Terminals

MORE THAN a dozen private companies offer local bus service, linking San José to towns and villages nationwide. Bus service between large cities is almost always aboard comfortable air-conditioned buses with reclining seats. Shorter trips between smaller towns and villages are typically on older, more basic second-class buses.

There are two types of intercity travel: *directo* buses offer fast, often nonstop, service, while *corriente*, or normal service, is slower, with more stops en route. The government-regulated fares are rarely more than $10. Advance reservations are recommended for intercity travel. Arrive well ahead of your departure to secure a good seat. Travel with as little baggage as possible, and avoid bus travel on Fridays and Saturdays, when demand peaks. The ICT *(see p256)* publishes a bus schedule. Rural buses can be waved down at *paradas* (bus stops) along their routes.

In most towns, the bus terminal – usually a busy and confusing place – is close to the main plaza. Some towns have several bus terminals. There are two main bus terminals in San José, with additional bus stations dispersed downtown. Buses to the Caribbean leave from Gran Terminal Caribe, and to most other parts of the country from bus stops concentrated in an area called "Coca Cola," which is located west of downtown. The Coca Cola terminal has a

A public bus in the tourist hub of La Fortuna

A *colectivo* (pickup truck) heading for Puerto Jiménez

reputation for pickpockets and muggings: be on your guard in this area.

Buses for Tourists and Organized Tours

Some bus companies cater to the tourist market. Direct bus service linking the most popular tourist destinations is offered by **Interbus** and **Grayline**, which also has shuttles between San José and Juan Santamaría International Airport. Interbus offers door-to-door pick-up and drop-off. Grayline has discounts for children and seniors. Juan Santamaría International Airport is also served by **Tuasa** buses, which operate between Alajuela and San José.

Sightseeing tours on offer give excellent overviews of the nation or specific regions; others specialize in nature-viewing and other activities. Leading operators include Costa Rica Expeditions and Costa Rica's Temptations *(see p253)*.

Taxis and Camiones

Taxis gather around the central plazas in most towns, and can also be summoned by phone. Licensed taxis are red (or orange for airport taxis) and have a white triangle showing the license number on the front door. Fares are regulated for journeys under 9 miles (15 km); the rates for longer journeys are negotiable. Never take a private, unlicensed taxi – many tourists have been robbed by the drivers or their accomplices. Jeep-taxis serve many communities where local roads are mountainous or unpaved. The most remote communities and tourist destinations are also served by *camiones* or *colectivos* – usually open-bed pickup trucks with seats and awnings. They follow fixed routes, and can be flagged down anywhere along the route. *Colectivos* normally charge a flat fee, regardless of distance.

Local taxi

Directory

Airlines

Nature Air
Tel. *220-3054.*
W www.natureair.com

Sansa
Tel. *221-9414.*
W www.flysansa.com

Bus Companies and Terminals

Grayline
Tel. *232-3681.*
W www.graylinecostarica.com

Interbus
Tel. *283-5573.*
W www.interbusonline.com

Tuasa
Gran Terminal Carribe,
Calle Central and Aves 15/17,
San José.
Tel. *221-2596.*

Taxis

Coopetaxi (San José)
Tel. *235-7979.*

Boats and Ferries

Car- and passenger ferries link Puntarenas with Naranjo and Paquera, in Nicoya. Small boats also offer water-taxi service between Puntarenas and Paquera, Jacó and Montezuma, and Sierpe and Bahía Drake, along the Tortuguero Canal, and throughout Golfo Dulce. Visitors can also go on trips on tour- or hired boats along Costa Rica's many rivers, canals, and swamps.

Passengers waiting to board a boat at Isla Tortuga

Traveling by Car

License plate

GETTING AROUND BY car is the most flexible way of exploring Costa Rica, as it grants easy access to some of the country's most remarkable scenery. Roads between towns are usually paved, although even newly laid roads rarely survive a single wet season without developing huge potholes. Many minor roads are dirt and gravel, especially beyond the Central Highlands, and often turn into muddy quagmires during the wet season. A 4WD vehicle is thus essential for exploring beyond the major cities. Drivers need to take precautions, as conditions are frequently hazardous. Do not drive at night. Locally available maps are not reliable: carry a road atlas published by a reputed company.

Street with No Parking sign

Traffic Regulations

COSTA RICANS drive on the right, and the speed limits are 50 mph (80 km/h) on major highways, and 37 mph (60 km/h) on secondary roads. *Tránsitos* (traffic police) patrol the highways in blue cars and use radar guns to catch speeders, but are not permitted to collect money. Occasionally a corrupt police official may try to extract a bribe *(see p258)*. Fines should be paid in a bank, or to the rental car agency.

The use of seat belts is compulsory, but few Costa Ricans use seat belts and laws are rarely enforced. If you're traveling with young children, bring a car seat, as rental car agencies do not supply them.

Road Network and Classification

THE COUNTRY IS covered by 18,650 miles (30,000 km) of highway. However, only 20 percent is paved, with the Central Highlands appropriating a large chunk of the total. The percentage of unpaved roads increases with distance from the capital; however, more and more dirt roads are now being paved. Accurate maps are difficult to come by. The *National Geographic Adventure Map* and the detailed *Costa Rica Nature Atlas* are recommended.

Road Hazards

SINCE MANY roads are severely potholed, drive slowly to avoid bending a wheel. Keep your speed down especially on corrugated and loose gravel roads, where it is easy to lose traction. Watch for pedestrians and animals in the road, especially outside towns, where few roads have sidewalks. Particularly during the wet season, mountain roads are often foggy and subject to landslides, while lowland roads are prone to flooding.

Many river crossings require fording. Use caution in the wet season, when rivers can be too deep or fast-flowing to ford. Ask locals about current conditions. Edge slowly into the river; rushing forward can flood and stall the engine.

Beware drivers running stop signs, overtaking when there is barely enough room to do so, or driving too close behind the vehicle in front (tailgating). Costa Rican drivers often use their left-turn signal to indicate to drivers behind that they are free to overtake. Be careful in such situations: the vehicle may actually be turning left. A pile of sticks and leaves at the roadside often indicates a broken down vehicle or some other hazard ahead.

Avoid parking on a street overnight. Most towns have inexpensive parking lots with security guards. Never leave any items in a parked vehicle.

Fuel Stations

COSTING ABOUT 275 colones per liter, *gasolina* is unleaded, and is called "Super." *Gasolineras* (gas stations) are plentiful in towns, but much scarcer in rural areas, especially in Nicoya. Refill whenever the tank drops to half-full. In remote areas, gasoline is usually available at *pulperías* (grocery stores), where it may cost twice as much as at regular gas stations.

Gas stations are typically open 6am to midnight and are not self-service. Some are open 24 hours, and most will accept credit card payments.

Directions and Road Signs

FEW ROADS IN Costa Rica have directions or mile posts. In towns, street names are rarely signposted and those signs that exist are frequently incorrect. When asking for directions it is best to check where the road goes

Range Rover on a dirt road near Ojochal village, southern Costa Rica

One of the infrequent road signs in Costa Rica

rather than to name your desired destination.

Road signs use international symbols. *Alto* means "stop," *ceda* means "yield," and *mantenga du derecha* means "keep right." *Túmulo* indicates a road bump ahead, while *derrumbe* denotes a landslide or falling rocks.

Accidents and Insurance

If an accident occurs, call **Tránsitos**. Do not abandon your vehicle, and do not let the other party move his or her vehicle. If possible, obtain the *cédulas* (identification) and license number of the other driver. If anyone is injured, call the Red Cross *(see p259)*. Rental cars have a red triangle for emergencies; place this in the road a safe distance from your accident site to warn other vehicles. Otherwise, make a small pile of stones and branches, in the Costa Rican manner. If you own the vehicle, you will need to report the accident to the **Instituto Nacional de Seguridad (INS)**, which handles all insurance claims.

Car and Motorcycle Rental

To rent a car in Costa Rica you must be over 21, and have a valid driver's license. Some agencies require a minimum age of 25 years. Visits of over three months need a domestic drivers' license.

International car rental companies such as **Budget**, **Dollar**, and **Hertz** have local franchises at the international airports, and in San José and a few leading tourist centers; some local agencies also exist. **Discover Costa Rica** offers all-inclusive fly/drive packages. A 4WD vehicle is needed for rural areas, where high ground clearance and extra traction are called for. Companies such as **Europcar** have a wide variety of 4WD vehicles, while Costa Rica's Temptations *(see p253)* offers adventure tours by Land Rover.

Stop sign

Prices are generally lower in the wet season, and unlimited mileage options generally work out the cheapest. When pre-booking, get a written confirmation. Insurance is compulsory and costs extra; check to see if the quotation includes insurance and, if so, get it confirmed in writing.

Many companies, including the chain brands, are not entirely trustworthy. Before signing the contract, ensure that the vehicle is in good condition and keep a note of any scratches or other faults. Companies often require customers to sign a blank credit card slip, which is torn up when the car is returned intact. When returning the car, bring a trusted friend if possible: unscrupulous employees of the agency may tamper with the vehicle if you leave it unattended while clearing your bill. Check the final bill for any questionable charges, which you may dispute.

Bicycles, mopeds, and motorcycles can be rented in San José and major tourist resorts. **María Alexander Tours** rents Harley Davidson motorcycles and has tours for people 25 years or older. Helmets are mandatory.

A line of rental 4WD vehicles awaiting customers

Directory

Accidents

Tránsitos
117; 911; 222-9330.

Insurance

Instituto Nacional de Seguridad (INS)
800-800-80000.

Car Rental Companies

Budget
255-4750.
www.budget.co.cr

Discover Costa Rica
231-5666.
www.allcostaricadestinations.com

Dollar
257-1585.
www.dollarcostarica.com

Europcar
257-1158.
www.europcar.co.cr

Hertz
221-1818.
www.costaricarentacar.net

Motorcycle Hire

María Alexander Tours
289-5552.
www.costaricamotorcycles.com

Getting Around San José

Public bus

MOST PLACES OF INTEREST are centrally located, and within walking distance of one another and downtown hotels and restaurants. The best way to explore central San José is on foot, although you will need to rely on some other form of transport to reach the suburbs and outlying areas. The city's public transportation system is crowded, although an efficient taxi system eases the burden of traveling around by bus. It is not advisable to drive around San José, especially during morning and afternoon rush hour when the roads become extremely congested.

Pedestrians on Avenida Central, San José's busiest pedestrian road

WALKING

THE MOST practical way to explore the heart of San José is by walking, which permits you to enjoy the city at close quarters. Laid out in an easy-to-understand grid pattern, the city center makes for convenient strolling.

However, the sidewalks are narrow and crowded, and pedestrians are often forced to step into the street. Downtown streets are thronged with traffic, and pedestrians should take great care. Do not assume that vehicles will automatically stop at pedestrian crossings, or give way to pedestrians on the road when traffic lights turn to green. Be especially careful of buses, which often drive onto the sidewalks when turning corners.

Beware of pickpockets, especially in crowded places. Avoid wearing jewelry. Carry valuables in a money belt, and hold your camera in front, with the strap over your neck rather than on your shoulder. Keep to busy, well-lit streets at night, when you should avoid the streets northwest of the Mercado Central *(see p58)* and southwest of Parque Central *(see pp56)*, as well as Parque Nacional *(see pp68–9)* and Parque Morazán *(see p66)*.

There is usually a cooling breeze blowing at all times. Remember, however, that the sun's rays are fierce at this altitude and latitude, and you should wear a shade hat and sunscreen. There are usually cafés close at hand, permitting you to escape the heat and noise. Always come prepared for late afternoon showers, especially during wet season, when you will need an umbrella. These can be bought at roadside street stalls.

BUSES

BUSES ARE cheap but overcrowded, and run from 5am to 10pm. There is no central bus terminal for city buses. Routes are identified by destination, shown above the front window, rather than by number. Free route maps are available from the ICT office *(see p257)*. An important bus route is the Sabana-Cementerio one, which links the city center and Parque Sabana, running eastbound along Avenida 10 and westbound along Avenida 3. Public buses to the airport depart from Avenida 2, Calles 12/14. Buses to San José's suburbs fill up fast, and you should board at the original departure point. Watch out for pickpockets while traveling by bus: it's a good idea to wear your money belt inside your clothes.

TAXIS

TAXIS ARE NUMEROUS and can be hailed on the street or via your hotel concierge. However, they are in short supply during rush hour and heavy rains. The main taxi rank in San José is around Parque Central. Licensed taxis are red; a lighted sign on the roof indicates that the taxi is available. Most taxis take four passengers, and the older cabs rarely have seatbelts.

You can pay in dollars or colones. Taxis are good value by US or European standards, and rarely does a fare within the city center cost more than $5. Taxis are required by law to use their *marias* (meters) for journeys of less than 9.5 miles (15 km). Many drivers decline to do so in anticipation of being able to charge you extra. Taxi drivers do not expect tips, although a 10 percent tip is appreciated. Many private drivers offer unlicensed taxi service. They usually charge more than licensed taxis, and have a reputation for being unsafe. Never take an unlicensed taxi, however trustworthy you believe the driver to be.

Sign on local taxis

Bustling street outside the Mercado Central

Driving

Even if you are used to driving in cities, exploring San José by car can be a nerve-racking experience and is best avoided unless you know the city well. Josefinos are aggressive drivers, and often display a marked lack of consideration for other drivers. Many drivers will proceed through red lights if no traffic is coming the other way, especially at night, when extreme care is needed. A green light does not necessarily mean the road is clear. When approaching an amber light, be aware that the driver behind you may not expect you to stop, and may speed up to run the red light.

The speed limit is 18 mph (30 km/h) on urban streets. The city center has one multilevel car park and numerous other parking lots. At most of them, you need to pay an attendant and may be required to leave your ignition keys. Never leave valuables inside the car, even in guarded parking lots. Route 39, the Circunvalación, is a ring road that runs around the west, south, and east of the city. Avenida Central leads east to the University of Costa Rica and the busy suburb of San Pedro *(see p71)*. To the west, Paseo Colón links the city center to Parque Sabana and the Autopista General Cañas, which leads to the airport and Alajuela. Another freeway, the Autopista Prospero Fernández, runs west from Parque Sabana *(see p74)* to Escazú *(see p75)*.

Traffic normally flows in both directions along Paseo Colón, except from 7am to 9am, Monday to Friday, when it is one-way eastbound, and 8am to 5pm on Sunday, when it is closed to traffic.

The one-way system and grid pattern in the city center help lubricate traffic flow, but traffic jams can persist throughout the day on some streets. During rush hour, Avenidas 8 and 9 are usually the best routes to follow when crossing the city from east to west; Avenida 10 is recommended when heading west to east.

Directions and Signs

Within the city center, even-numbered avenidas lie north of Avenida Central and odd-numbered avenidas are to the south; even-numbered calles are west of Calle Central, and odd-numbered calles are to the east as far as the Circunvalación.

Avenida Central is pedestrianized between Calle 6 and Calle 7, as are Calle 2 between Avenidas 2 and 3, and Calle 17 (Bulevar Ricardo Jiménez) between Avenidas 1 and 8. However, streets are poorly signed. Traffic lights, which are normally suspended over the center of junctions, are often difficult to see.

Cautionary sign for seat belts

Traffic along Calle Central, the capital city's main north–south thoroughfare

General Index

Page numbers in **bold type** refer to main entries.

D

E

S

T

Acknowledgments

DORLING KINDERSLEY would like to thank the following people whose contributions and assistance have made the preparation of this book possible:

MAIN CONTRIBUTOR
CHRISTOPHER P. BAKER was born and raised in Yorkshire, England, and received his B.A. with Honours (1976) in Geography from the University of London. While there, his travels included two Sahara research expeditions. Baker holds two Masters' degrees – in Latin American Studies and in Education. He has made his living as a full-time professional travel writer/photographer since 1983.

Baker's numerous books include guides to Cuba, Costa Rica, and Jamaica, and *Mi Moto Fidel: Motorcycling Through Castro's Cuba.* He has also had chapters and articles published in several books and more than 150 newspapers, journals, and magazines worldwide. He has won many prestigious awards for travel writing, addressed prominent entities such as the National Press Club, the National Geographic Society, and the World Affairs Council, and escorted group tours to New Zealand, Hong Kong, Korea, Cuba, and England. Baker's other travel-related activites include teaching travel-writing classes, appearing on radio and TV shows, and lecturing aboard cruise ships.

FACT CHECKER
Ana Voiculescu.

PROOFREADER
Sonia Malik.

INDEXER
Jyoti Dhar.

DORLING KINDERSLEY, LONDON
PUBLISHER
Douglas Amrine.
PUBLISHING MANAGER
Jane Ewart.
SENIOR EDITOR
Christine Stroyan.
SENIOR CARTOGRAPHIC EDITOR
Casper Morris.
SENIOR DTP DESIGNER
Jason Little.

EDITORIAL AND DESIGN ASSISTANCE
Brigitte Arora, Tessa Bindloss, Ellen Root.

DK PICTURE LIBRARY
Hayley Smith, Romaine Werblow.

PRODUCTION CONTROLLER
Wendy Penn.

ADDITIONAL SPECIAL PHOTOGRAPHY
Alan Briere, Jonathan Buckley, Martin Camm, Geoff Dann, Phillip Dowell, Neil Fletcher, Frank Greenaway, Colin Keates, Dave King, Mike Linley, Ray Moller, David Murray, Stephen Oliver, Clive Streeter, Harry Taylor, Mathew Ward, Laura Wickenden, Peter Wilson, Jerry Young.

SPECIAL ASSISTANCE
Many thanks for the invaluable help of the following individuals and establishments: Adolfo Rodríguez Herrera; Mrs. Dora Sequeira, Alejandra Jimenez Solis, and Andrea Bolaños Waters, Museo del Oro Precolombino; Dr. Luis Diego Gómez, Organización para Estudios Tropicales at La Selva; Mauricio P. Aymerich, Small Distinctive Hotels; Michael Snarskis.

PHOTOGRAPHY PERMISSIONS
Dorling Kindersley would like to thank the following for their assistance and kind permission to photograph at their establishments: Café Britt; Centro Costarricense de Ciencias y Cultura, San José; Costa Rica Expeditions; Fábrica de Carretas Joaquín Chaverrí, Sarchí; Museo del Oro Precolombino, San José; Museo Nacional, San José; Teatro Nacional, San José; Zoo Ave Wildlife Conservation Park; and all other cathedrals, churches, museums, hotels, restaurants, shops, galleries, national and state parks, and other sights too numerous to thank individually.

PICTURE CREDITS
Every effort has been made to trace the copyright holders and we apologize in advance for any unintentional ommissions. We would be pleased to insert the appropriate acknowledgments in any subsequent editions of this publication.

Placement Key – t=top; tl=top left; tlc=top left center; tc=top center; trc=top right center; tr=top right; cla=center left above; ca=center above; cra=center right above; cl=center left; c=center; cr=center right; clb=center left below; cb=center below; crb=center right below; b=bottom; bl=bottom left; bc=bottom center; bcl=bottom center left; br=bottom right; d=detail.

The publishers would like to thank the following individuals, companies, and picture libraries for their kind permission to reproduce their photographs:

AKG IMAGES: 42crb; ALAMY IMAGES: 16b; AM COSTA RICA LINK: 34cl, 243tr; JOHN ANDERSON: 18t, 69crb, 70tr, 117cb, 130tr; AXIOM, LONDON: Ian Cumming 37bc, 165br.

BANCO CENTRAL DE COSTA RICA: 261cl, 261clb, 261cr, 261crb(a), 261crb(c), 261bl, 261br; BRUCE COLEMAN PICTURE LIBRARY: Michael Fogden 20crb.

CAFÉ BRITT: 30br; CHRIS BAKER COMPOSITIONS: Christopher P. Baker 26-27c, 26br, 31bc, 31bcr, 34tc, 46bcr, 57tl, 63tl, 63cb, 69tl, 70bl, 70crb, 71tl, 75cl, 85cla, 92cr, 92bc, 93tc, 97cra, 97clb, 97bc, 104cla, 105tl, 114tl, 131cl, 137crb, 137clb, 153bc, 161b, 166clb, 177cr, 185br, 243c(a), 243c(b), 243c(c), 245t, 264cl, 266cl, 268br; CORBIS: 43tr, 44br, 137cra, 171clb, 171crb; Tony Arruza 36b, 117cl; Bettman 7c, 43cb, 44crb, 45clb, 46tr, 46cb, 47clb, 135bc; Gary Braasch 22cl, 22clb, 25br, 28cl, 107b, 186-7; Tom Brakefield 113tc, 113cla; Christie's Images 142bl; Ralph A. Clevenger 193cra; DiMaggio/Kalish 171br; Michael and Patricia Fogden 1c, 20br, 21bca, 26cl, 27tr, 27cb, 27br, 113clb, 125br, 127tc, 129c, 129bc, 157cl, 157crb, 157bl, 164tl; Stephen Frink 134tr, 156bc; Bill Gentile 47bl; Derek Hall/Frank Lane Picture 189tc; Gray Hardel 252c; Jan Butchofsky-Houser 15b, 133ca; Dave G. Houser 31cla, 145b; Hulton-Deutsch Collection 255 (inset); Wolfgang Kaehler 193br; Kit Kittle 247tc; Blue Lantern Studio 195 (inset); Michael Maslan Historic Photograph 45bl; Buddy Mays 26clb; Stephanie Maze 17br; Amos Nachoum 21cra, 174, 193crb, 252bl, 252bc; Jose Fuste Raga 271b; Carmen Redondo 29cra, 141bl; Martin Rogers 18bl, 19cr, 30cra, 51bl, 121b, 163cr, 244tc; Jeffrey L. Rotman 50crb, 252br; Albrecht G. Schaefer 171cl; Kevin Schafer 8br, 12cl, 20clb, 23br, 28tr, 29tl, 88-9, 113cra, 123t, 138-9, 141br, 158tl, 171cra, 177cra, 180cla, 181cr, 193cla; Paul A. Souders 154tl; Roger Tidman 27cr; Brian A. Vikander 21cr, 91tr; Stuart Westmorland 194-5; CORBIS SYGMA: C. Rouvieres 141cla, 141bl; COSTA RICA PHOTO ALBUM: © Rodrigo Fernandez and Millard Farmer 4crb, 9tr, 15ca, 16tl, 17tr, 17c, 19tc, 19br, 35tl, 37tl, 51tl, 96bc, 102cla, 147tl, 149tl, 150tl, 151tl, 151crb, 153tc, 153clb, 153bl, 153br, 181ca, 239br, 249br, 250tl, 250br, 251br.

EL SANO BANANO HOTEL: 199tl, 221tl, 246tl.

RODRIGO FERNANDEZ: 36tc, 94br, 222cla, 223tl, 242tl, 242c, 242cb, 242crb(a), 242crb(b), 243cb, 243crb, 243bl, 243bc, 243br, 246br, 261crb(b), 261bcl, 261bcr, 262bc; FOREST LIGHT: Alan Watson 96t; FOUR SEASONS: 196cla.

PHILIP GREENSPUN: 35br.

LONELY PLANET IMAGES: Chris Barton 30clb, 265tr; Tom Boyden 134cla, Charlotte Hindle 269tl; Ralph Lee Hopkins 2-3; Luke Hunter 27tl, 134bl, 175b, 188bl; Eric L. Wheater 14.

MASTERFILE: Alberto Biscaro 48-9, 64-5, 120, 238cla, 240br, 254-5; Peter Christopher 106; MARY EVANS PICTURE LIBRARY: 44tc, 49 (inset); Explore/Courau 40; JEAN MERCIER: 23cb, 90cr, 90br, 158bl; MUSEO DE CULTURA INDÍGENAS: 5c, 32tr, 32-33c, 33tc, 33cb, 33clb, 33bl, 33br, 34br, 155clb, 173bc, 173br, 184bc, 242bc, 243tc, 243cra; MUSEO DEL ORO PRECOLOMBINO: 62ca, 240cla, 242br; Alejandro Astorga 33cra.

Courtesy THE NATURAL HISTORY MUSEUM LONDON: 167br. Courtesy THE NATIONAL BIRDS OF PREY CENTRE, GLOUCESTERSHIRE: 180tl.

REUTERS: Juan Carlos Ulate 31cra;

SKY PHOTOS: 23crb, 24cl, 25tl, 25cr, 50clb, 124tr, 124cl, 124clb, 149br, 157cra; SMALL DISTINCTIVE HOTELS: 20cr, 150tl, 196bc, 220cl, 251tl.

UNICORN MULTIMEDIA, INC.: Jan Csernoch 10t, 141cra, 143br, 180bl, 181tl, 181bc.

FRONT ENDPAPER:
CORBIS: Amos Nachoum bc; MASTERFILE: Alberto Biscaro tl; Peter Christopher cl.

JACKET:
Front – ALAMY IMAGES: Kevin Schafer main; DK IMAGES: Cyril Laubscher c; Jon Spaull bl; Linda Whitwam br.
Back – DK IMAGES: Linda Whitwam tl and br.
Spine – ALAMY IMAGES: Kevin Schafer.

All other images © Dorling Kindersley. For more information see **www.dkimages.com**

Phrase Book

Costa Rican Spanish is essentially the same as the Castilian spoken in Spain, although there are some differences in vocabulary and pronunciation. The most noticeable is the pronunciation of the soft "c" and the letter "z" as "s" rather than "th."

Costa Ricans tend to be formal, and often use *usted* (rather than *tú*) for "you," even if they know the person well. Common courtesies of respect are expected. Always say *buenos dias* or *buenas tardes* when boarding a taxi, and address taxi drivers and waiters as *señor*. Many colloquialisms exist, such as *¡upe!*, which is used to announce your presence outside someone's home when the door is open. *Buena suerte* ("good luck") is often used to wish someone well on parting.

The most common term throughout the country is *pura vida* ("pure life"), used as a common reply to questions about your wellbeing and as an expression that everything is great. *Tuanis*, popular with youth, is another phrase meaning things are positive. If you hear a Costa Rican referring to *chepe*, he or she is speaking about San José. If you wish to decline goods from street vendors, a polite shake of the head and a *muchas gracias* will usually suffice. Adding *muy amable* ("very kind") will help to take the edge off the refusal.

In an Emergency

Help!	**¡Socorro!**	soh-**koh**-roh
Stop!	**¡Pare!**	**pah**-reh
Call a doctor!	**¡Llame a un médico!**	**yah**-meh ah **oon meh**-dee-koh
Fire!	**¡Fuego!**	foo-**eh**-goh
Could you help me?	**¿Me podría ayudar?**	meh poh-**dree**-yah ah-yoo-**dahr**
policeman	**policía**	poh-lee-**see**-ah

Communication Essentials

Yes	**Sí**	see
No	**No**	noh
Please	**Por favor**	pohr fah-**vohr**
Thank you	**Gracias**	**grah**-see-ahs
Excuse me	**Perdone**	pehr-**doh**-neh
Hello	**Hola**	**oh**-lah
Good morning	**Buenos días**	**bweh**-nohs **dee**-ahs
Good afternoon	**Buenas tardes**	**bweh**-nahs **tahr**-dehs
Good night	**Buenas noches**	**bweh**-nahs **noh**-chehs
Bye (casual)	**Chao**	**cha**-oh
Goodbye	**Adiós**	ah-dee-**ohs**
See you later	**Hasta luego**	ah-**stah** loo-**weh**-goh
Morning	**La mañana**	lah mah-**nyah**-nah
Afternoon	**La tarde**	lah **tahr**-deh
Night	**La noche**	lah **noh**-cheh
Yesterday	**Ayer**	ah-**yehr**
Today	**Hoy**	oy
Tomorrow	**Mañana**	mah-**nyah**-nah
Here	**Aquí**	ah-**kee**
There	**Allá**	ah-**yah**
What?	**¿Qué?**	**keh**
When?	**¿Cuándo?**	**kwahn**-doh
Why?	**¿Por qué?**	pohr-**keh**
Where?	**¿Dónde?**	**dohn**-deh
How are you?	**¿Cómo está usted?**	**koh**-moh ehs-**tah** oos-**tehd**
Very well, thank you	**Muy bien, gracias**	mwee bee-**ehn grah**-see-ahs
Pleased to meet you	**Mucho gusto**	**moo**-choh **goo**-stoh
I'm sorry	**Lo siento**	loh see-**ehn**-toh

Useful Phrases

That's fine	**Está bien**	ehs-**tah** bee-**ehn**
Great/fantastic!	**¡Qué bien!**	**keh** bee-**ehn**
Where does this road go?	**¿Adónde va esta calle?**	ah-**dohn**-deh bah **ehs**-tah **kah**-yeh
Do you speak English?	**¿Habla inglés?**	**ah**-blah een-**glehs**
I don't understand	**No comprendo**	noh kohm-**prehn-doh**
I want	**Quiero**	kee-**yehr**-oh

Useful Words

big	**grande**	**grahn**-deh
small	**pequeño/a**	peh-**keh**-nyoh/nyah
hot	**caliente**	kah-lee-**ehn**-teh
cold	**frío/a**	**free**-oh/ah
good	**bueno/a**	**bweh**-noh/nah
bad	**malo/a**	**mah**-loh/lah
open	**abierto/a**	ah-bee-**ehr**-toh/tah
closed	**cerrado/a**	sehr-**rah**-doh/dah
left	**izquierda**	ees-key-**ehr**-dah
right	**derecha**	deh-**reh**-chah
near	**cerca**	**sehr**-kah
far	**lejos**	**leh**-hohs
up	**arriba**	ah-**ree**-bah
down	**abajo**	ah-**bah**-hoh
early	**temprano**	tehm-**prah**-noh
late	**tarde**	**tahr**-deh
now/very soon	**ahora/ahorita**	ah-**ohr**-ah/ah-ohr-**ee**-tah
more	**más**	**mahs**
less	**menos**	**meh**-nohs
very	**muy**	**mwee**
a little	**(un) poco**	**oon poh**-koh
opposite	**frente a**	**frehn**-teh ah
below/above	**abajo/arriba**	ah-**bah**-hoh/
entrance	**entrada**	ehn-**trah**-dah
exit	**salida**	sah-**lee**-dah
stairs	**escaleras**	ehs-kah-**leh**-rahs
elevator	**el ascensor**	**ehl** ah-sehn-**sohr**
toilets	**baños/servicios sanitarios**	**bah**-nyohs/sehr-**vee**-see-yohs sah-nee-**tah**-ree-ohs
women's	**de damas**	deh **dah**-mahs
men's	**de caballeros**	deh kah-bah-**yeh**-rohs
sanitary napkins	**toallas sanitarias**	toh-**ah**-yahs sah-nee-**tah**-ree-yahs
tampons	**tampones**	tahm-**poh**-nehs
condoms	**condones**	kohn-**doh**-nehs
toilet paper	**papel higiénico**	pah-**pehl** hee-**hyen**-ee-koh
(non-)smoking area	**área de (no) fumar**	**ah**-ree-ah deh (**noh**) foo-**mahr**
camera	**la cámara**	lah **kah**-mah-rah
(a roll of) film	**(un rollo de) película**	(**oon roh**-yoh deh) peh-**lee**-koo-lah
batteries	**las pilas**	lahs **pee**-lahs
passport	**pasaporte**	pah-sah-**pohr**-teh
visa	**visa**	**vee**-sah

Post Offices and Banks

post office	**oficina de correos**	oh-fee-**see**-nah deh kohr-**reh**-ohs
stamps	**estampillas**	ehs-tahm-**pee**-yahs
postcard	**una postal**	**oo**-nah pohs-**tahl**
postbox	**apartado**	ah-pahr-**tah**-doh

cashier	**cajero**	kah-**heh**-roh
ATM	**cajero automático**	kah-**heh**-roh ahw-toh-**mah**-tee-koh
bank	**banco**	**bahn**-koh
What is the dollar rate?	**¿A cómo está el dolar?**	ah **koh**-moh ehs-**tah** ehl doh-**lahr**

Shopping

How much does .. this cost?	**¿Cuánto cuesta esto?**	**kwahn** toh**kwehs**-tah **ehs**-toh
Do you have?	**¿Tienen?**	tee-**yeh**-nehn
Do you take credit cards/ traveler's checks?	**¿Aceptan tarjetas de crédito/ cheques de viajero?**	ahk-**sehp**-tahn tahr-**heh**-tahs deh **kreh**-dee-toh/**cheh**-kehs deh vee-ah-**heh**-roh
discount	**un descuento**	**oon** dehs-koo-**ehn**-toh
expensive	**caro**	**kahr**-oh
cheap	**barato**	bah-**rah**-toh
clothes	**la ropa**	lah **roh**-pah
size, clothes	**talla**	**tah**-yah
size, shoes	**número**	**noo**-mehr-oh
bakery	**panadería**	pah-nah-deh **ree**-ah
bookstore	**librería**	lee-breh-**ree**-ah
grocer's	**pulpería**	pool-peh-**ree**-ah
market	**mercado**	mehr-**kah**-doh
shoe store	**la zapatería**	lah sah-pah-teh-**ree**-ah
supermarket	**el supermercado**	ehl soo-pehr-mehr-**kah**-doh
travel agency	**la agencia de viajes**	lah ah-**hehn**-see-ah deh vee-**ah**-hehs

Sightseeing

bay	**bahía**	bah-**ee**-ah
beach	**playa**	**plah**-yah
building	**edificio**	eh-dee-**fee**-see-oh
cathedral	**catedral**	kah-teh-**drahl**
church	**iglesia**	ee-**gleh**-see-ah
farm	**finca**	**feehn**-kah
forest	**bosque/selva**	**bohs**-keh/**sehl**-bah
garden	**jardín**	hahr-**deen**
lake	**lago**	**lah**-goh
mangrove	**manglar**	mahn-**glahr**
mountain peak	**cerro**	**seh**-roh
mountain range	**cordillera**	kohr-dee-**yeh**-rah
museum	**museo**	moo-**seh**-oh
neighborhood	**barrio**	**bah**-ree-oh
port	**puerto**	poo-**her**-toh
ranger station	**puesto de guardia**	**poo**-ehs-toh deh goo-**ahr**-dee-ah
river	**río**	**ree**-oh
trail	**sendero**	sehn-**deh**-roh
theater	**teatro**	teh-**ah**-troh
tourist information office	**oficina de turismo**	oh-fee-**see**-nah deh too-**rees**-moh
viewpoint	**mirador**	mee-rah-**dohr**
ticket	**el boleto/ la entrada**	ehl boh-**leh**-toh lah ehn-**trah**-dah
guide (person)	**el/la guía**	ehl/lah **gee**-ah
guide (book)	**la guía**	lah **gee**-ah
guided tour	**una visita guiada**	**oo**-nah vee-**see**-tah gee-**ah**-dah
map	**el mapa**	ehl **mah**-pah

Health

I feel ill	**Me siento mal**	meh seh-**ehn**-toh **mahl**
We need a doctor	**Necesitamos un médico**	neh-seh-see-**tah**-mohs **oon meh**-dee-koh
drug store	**farmacia**	fahr-**mah**-see-ah
medicine	**medicina**	meh-dee-**see**-nah
ambulance	**ambulancia**	ahm-boo-**lahn**-see-ah
mosquito coils	**espirales**	ehs-pee-**rah**-lehs

Transportation

When does the... leave?	**¿A qué hora sale el. . .?**	ah **keh oh**-rah **sah**-leh ehl
Is there a bus to...?	**¿Hay un bus a. . .?**	eye oon **boohs** ah...
bus station	**la estación de autobuses**	lah ehs-tah-see-**ohn** deh aw-toh-**boo**-sehs
ticket office	**la boletería**	lah boh-leh-teh-**ree**-ah
airport	**aeropuerto**	ah-ehr-oh-poo-**ehr**-toh
customs	**la aduana**	lah ah-doo-**ah**-nah
taxi stand/rank	**la parada de taxis**	lah pah-**rah**-dah deh **tahk**-sees
car rental	**rent a car**	**rehn**-tah cahr-
motorcycle	**la moto(cicleta)**	lah moh-toh(see-**kleh**-tah)
bicycle	**la bicicleta**	lah bee-see-**kleh**-tah
4WD	**doble tracción**	**doh**-bleh trahk-**siohn**
water-taxi	**una panga/ un bote**	oo-nah **pahn**-gah/ oon **boh**-teh
aerial tram	**teleférico**	teh-leh-**feh**-ree-koh
insurance	**los seguros**	lohs seh-**goo**-rohs
gas station	**gasolinera**	gah-soh-leen **ehr**-ah
garage	**taller de mecánica**	tah-**yehr** deh meh-**kahn**-ee-kah
I have a flat tire	**Se me ponchó la llanta**	seh meh pohn-**shoh** lah **yahn**-tah

Staying in a Hotel

I have a reservation	**Tengo una reservación**	tehn-goh **oo**-nah reh-sehr-vah-see-**ohn**
Do you have a vacant room?	**¿Tienen una habitación libre?**	tee-**eh**-nehn **oo**-nah ah-bee-tah-see-**ohnlee**-breh
double room	**habitación doble**	ah-bee-tah-see-**ohn doh**-bleh
single room	**habitación sencilla**	ah-bee-tah-see-**ohn** sehn-**see**-yah
room with a bath	**habitación con baño**	ah-bee-tah-see-**ohn** kohn **bah**-nyoh
shower	**la ducha**	lah **doo**-chah
The . . . is not working	**No funciona el/la. . .**	**noh** foon-see-**oh**-nah ehl/lah
Where is the dining-room/bar?	**¿Dónde está el restaurante/ el bar?**	**dohn**-deh ehs-**tah** ehl rehs-toh-**rahn**-teh/ehl **bahr**
hot/cold water	**agua caliente/ fría**	**ah**-goo-ah kah-lee-**ehn**-teh/**free**-ah
soap	**el jabón**	ehl hah-**bohn**
towel	**la toalla**	lah toh-**ah**-yah
key	**la llave**	lah **yah**-veh

Eating Out

Have you got a table for . . .	**¿Tienen mesa para . . .?**	tee-**eh**-nehn meh-sah pah-**rah**
I want to reserve a table	**Quiero reservar una mesa**	kee-eh-roh reh-sehr-**vahr oo**-nah **meh**-sah
The bill, please	**La cuenta, por favor**	lah **kwehn**-tah pohr fah-**vohr**
I am a vegetarian	**Soy vegetariano/a**	soy veh-heh-tah-ree-**ah**-no/na
waiter/waitress	**mesero/a**	meh-**seh**-roh/rah
menu	**la carta**	lah **kahr**-tah
fixed-price menu	**menú del día**	meh-**noo** dehl **dee**-ah
wine list	**la carta de vinos**	lah **kahr**-tah deh **vee**-nohs

glass	**un vaso**	**oon vah**-soh
bottle	**una botella**	**oo**-nah boh-**teh**-yah
knife	**un cuchillo**	**oon** koo-**chee**-yoh
fork	**un tenedor**	**oon** teh-neh-**dohr**
spoon	**una cuchara**	**oo**-nah koo-**chah**-rah
breakfast	**el desayuno**	ehl deh-sah-**yoo**-noh
lunch	**almuerzo**	ahl-moo-**ehr**-soh
dinner	**la cena**	lah **seh**-nah
main course	**el plato fuerte**	ehl **plah**-toh foo-**ehr**-teh
starters	**las entradas**	lahs ehn-**trah**-das
dish of the day	**el plato del día**	ehl **plat**-toh dehl **dee**-ah
rare	**término rojo**	**tehr**-mee-noh **roh**-hoh
medium	**término medio**	**tehr**-mee-noh **meh**-dee-oh
well done	**bien cocido**	bee-**ehn** koh-**see**-doh
chair	**la silla**	lah **see**-yah
napkin	**la servilleta**	lah sehr-vee-**yeh**-tah
Is service included?	**¿El servicio está incluido?**	ehl sehr-**vee**-see-oh ehs-**tah** een-kloo-**ee**-doh
ashtray	**cenicero**	seh-nee-**seh**-roh
cigarettes	**los cigarros**	lohs see-**gah**-rohs
food stall	**una soda**	**oo**-nah **soh**-dah
neighborhood bar	**una cantina/ un bar**	oo-nah kahn-tee-nah/oon bahr

Menu Decoder *(see also pp222-3)*

el aceite	ah-**see-eh**-teh	oil
las aceitunas	ah-seh-**toon**-ahs	olives
el agua mineral	**ah**-gwa mee-neh-**rahl**	mineral water
el arroz	ahr-**rohs**	rice
el azúcar	ah-**soo**-kahr	sugar
una bebida	beh-**bee**-dah	drink
boca	**boh**-kah	a type of snack
el café	kah-**feh**	coffee
la carne	**kahr**-neh	meat
el cerdo	**sehr**-doh	pork
la cerveza	sehr-**veh**-sah	beer
el chocolate	choh-koh-**lah**-teh	chocolate
la ensalada	ehn-sah-**lah**-dah	salad
la fruta	**froo**-tah	fruit
el helado	eh-**lah**-doh	ice cream
el huevo	oo-**eh**-voh	egg
el jugo	ehl **hoo**-goh	juice
la leche	**leh**-cheh	milk
la mantequilla	mahn-teh-**kee**-yah	butter
la manzana	mahn-**sah**-nah	apple
los mariscos	mah-**rees**-kohs	seafood
el pan	**pahn**	bread
las papas	**pah**-pahs	potatoes
las papas a la francesa	**pah**-pahs ah lah frahn-**seh**-sah	French fries
las papas fritas	**pah**-pahs **free**-tahs	potato chips
el pastel	pahs-**tehl**	cake
el pescado	pehs-**kah**-doh	fish
picante	pee-**kahn**-teh	spicy
la pimienta	pee-mee-**yehn**-tah	pepper
el pollo	**poh**-yoh	chicken
el postre	**pohs**-treh	dessert
el queso	**keh**-soh	cheese
el refresco	reh-**frehs**-koh	soft drink/soda
la sal	**sahl**	salt
la sopa	**soh**-pah	soup
el sánguche	**sahn**-goo-she	sandwich
el té negro	**teh neh**-groh	tea
la torta	**tohr**-tah	burger
las tostadas	tohs-**tah**-dahs	toast
el vino blanco	**vee**-noh **blahn**-koh	white wine
el vino tinto	**vee**-noh **teen**-toh	red wine

Culture and Society

campesino	cahm-peh-**see**-noh	peasant
canton	cahn-**tohn**	county
carreta	cah-**reh**-tah	oxcart
cumbia	**coom**-bee-ah	Columbian music
Josefino	hoh-seh-**fee**-noh	resident of San José
marimba	mah-**reem**-bah	kind of xylophone
merengue	meh-**rehn**-geh	fast-paced Dominican music
sabanero	sah-bah-**neh**-roh	cowboy
salsa	**sahl**-sah	Cuban dance music
Tico/ costarricense	**tee**-coh/cohs-tah-ree-**sehn**-seh	Costa Rican

Numbers

0	**cero**	**seh**-roh
1	**uno**	**oo**-noh
2	**dos**	dohs
3	**tres**	trehs
4	**cuatro**	**kwa**-troh
5	**cinco**	**seen**-koh
6	**seis**	says
7	**siete**	**see**-eh-teh
8	**ocho**	**oh**-choh
9	**nueve**	**nweh**-veh
10	**diez**	dee-**ehs**
11	**once**	**ohn**-seh
12	**doce**	**doh**-seh
13	**trece**	**treh**-seh
14	**catorce**	kah-**tohr**-seh
15	**quince**	**keen**-seh
16	**dieciséis**	dee-eh-see-**seh-ees**
17	**diecisiete**	dee-eh-see-see-**eh**-teh
18	**dieciocho**	dee-eh-see-**oh**-choh
19	**diecinueve**	dee-eh-see-**nweh**-veh
20	**veinte**	**veh**-een-teh
30	**treinta**	**treh**-een-tah
40	**cuarenta**	kwah-**rehn**-tah
50	**cincuenta**	seen-**kwehn**-tah
60	**sesenta**	seh-**sehn**-tah
70	**setenta**	seh-**tehn**-tah
80	**ochenta**	oh-**chehn**-tah
90	**noventa**	noh-**vehn**-tah
100	**cien**	see-**ehn**
500	**quinientos**	khee-nee-**ehn**-tohs
1,000	**mil**	meel
1,001	**mil uno**	**meel oo**-noh
5,000	**cinco mil**	**seen**-koh meel

Time

one minute	**un minuto**	**oon** mee-**noo**-toh
one hour	**una hora**	**oo**-nah **oh**-rah
Monday	**lunes**	**loo**-nehs
Tuesday	**martes**	**mahr**-tehs
Wednesday	**miércoles**	mee-**ehr**-koh-lehs
Thursday	**jueves**	hoo-**weh**-vehs
Friday	**viernes**	vee-**ehr**-nehs
Saturday	**sábado**	**sah**-bah-doh
Sunday	**domingo**	doh-**meen**-goh
January	**enero**	eh-**neh**-roh
February	**febrero**	feh-**breh**-roh
March	**marzo**	**mahr**-soh
April	**abril**	ah-**breel**
May	**mayo**	**mah**-yoh
June	**junio**	**hoo**-nee-oh
July	**julio**	**hoo**-lee-oh
August	**agosto**	ah-**gohs**-toh
September	**setiembre**	seh-tee-**ehm**-breh
October	**octubre**	ohk-**too**-breh
November	**noviembre**	noh-vee-**ehm**-breh
December	**diciembre**	dee-see-**ehm**-breh

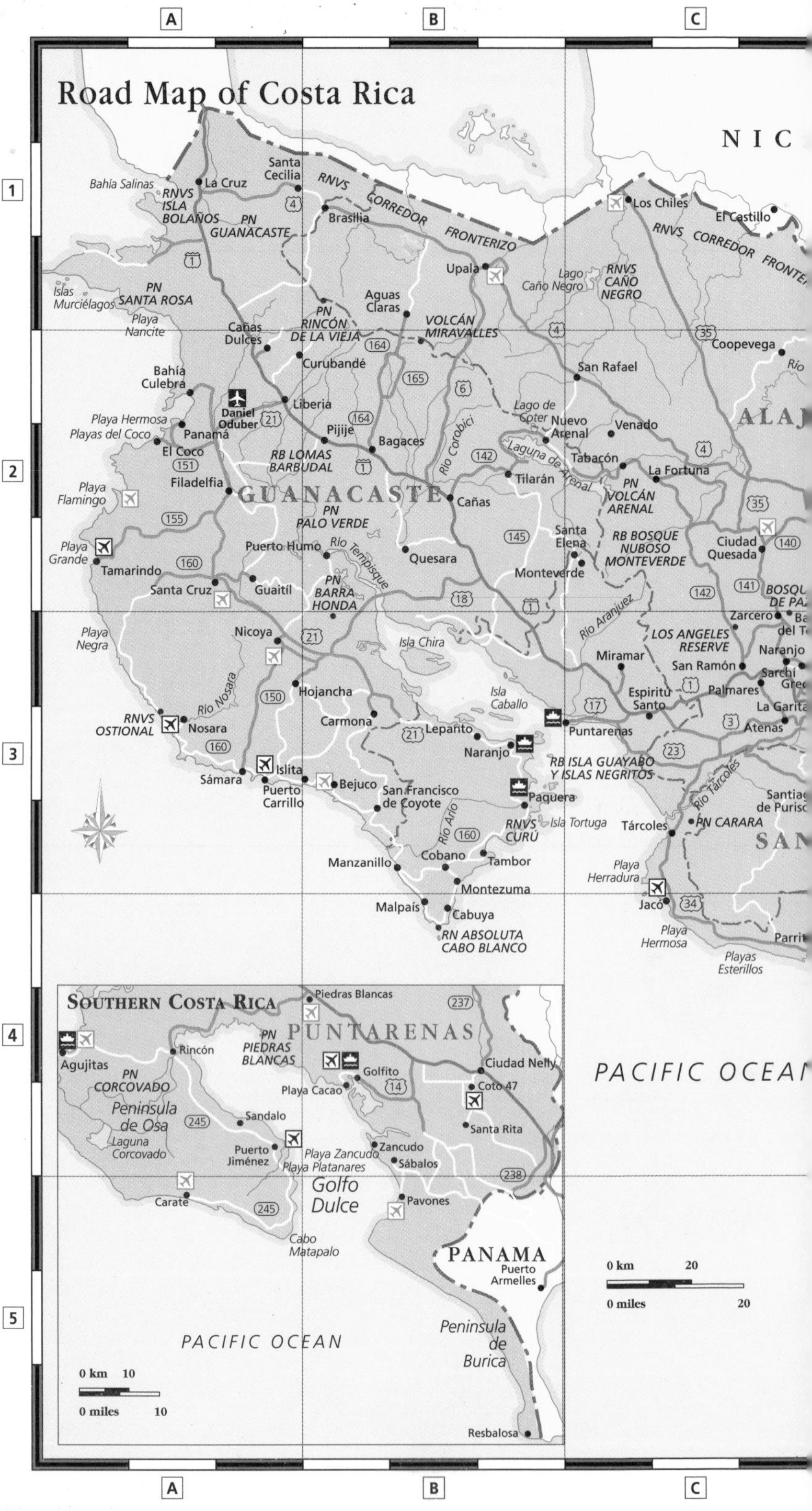
Road Map of Costa Rica
A
B
C
1
2
3
4
5
NIC
Bahía Salinas
La Cruz
Santa Cecilia
RNVS ISLA BOLAÑOS
PN GUANACASTE
RNVS CORREDOR FRONTERIZO
Brasilia
Upala
Los Chiles
El Castillo
RNVS CORREDOR FRONTERIZO
Lago Caño Negro
RNVS CAÑO NEGRO
Islas Murciélagos
PN SANTA ROSA
Playa Nancite
Aguas Claras
Cañas Dulces
PN RINCÓN DE LA VIEJA
VOLCÁN MIRAVALLES
Coopevega
Río
Curubandé
San Rafael
Bahía Culebra
Daniel Oduber
Liberia
Lago de Coter
Nuevo Arenal
Venado
ALAJ
Playa Hermosa
Playas del Coco
Panamá
Pijije
Bagaces
Río Corobicí
Laguna de Arenal
El Coco
RB LOMAS BARBUDAL
Tabacón
La Fortuna
Filadelfia
Tilarán
PN VOLCÁN ARENAL
Playa Flamingo
GUANACASTE
Cañas
PN PALO VERDE
Playa Grande
Puerto Humo
Río Tempisque
Quesara
Santa Elena
RB BOSQUE NUBOSO MONTEVERDE
Ciudad Quesada
Tamarindo
Monteverde
Santa Cruz
Guaitíl
PN BARRA HONDA
BOSQU DE PA
Zarcero
Río Aranjuez
Playa Negra
Nicoya
Isla Chira
LOS ANGELES RESERVE
Naranjo
Miramar
San Ramón
Sarchí
Río Nosara
Hojancha
Isla Caballo
Espiritu Santo
Palmares
RNVS OSTIONAL
Nosara
Carmona
Lepanto
Puntarenas
La Garita
Atenas
Naranjo
RB ISLA GUAYABO Y ISLAS NEGRITOS
Sámara
Islita
Puerto Carrillo
Bejuco
San Francisco de Coyote
Paquera
Río Tárcoles
Santiag de Purisc
Río Ario
RNVS CURÚ
Isla Tortuga
Tárcoles
PN CARARA
SAN
Manzanillo
Cobano
Tambor
Playa Herradura
Montezuma
Malpaís
Cabuya
Jacó
RN ABSOLUTA CABO BLANCO
Playa Hermosa
Parrit
Playas Esterillos
SOUTHERN COSTA RICA
Piedras Blancas
PUNTARENAS
PN PIEDRAS BLANCAS
Agujitas
Rincón
Golfito
Ciudad Nelly
Coto 47
PN CORCOVADO
Playa Cacao
Peninsula de Osa
Sandalo
Santa Rita
Laguna Corcovado
Puerto Jiménez
Zancudo
Playa Zancudo
Sábalos
Playa Platanares
Golfo Dulce
Carate
Pavones
Cabo Matapalo
PANAMA
Puerto Armelles
PACIFIC OCEAN
Peninsula de Burica
Resbalosa
0 km 10
0 miles 10
PACIFIC OCEAN
0 km 20
0 miles 20